last activity 11/6/07

Cultural Diversity

and Social Skills Instruction

Instruction

Understanding

Ethnic and Gender

Differences

"DISCARDED"

"Magale Library
Southern Arkansas University
Magnolia, Arkansas 71753

Gwendolyn Cartledge

with contributions by
JoAnne Fellows Milburn

Research Press ◖ 2612 North Mattis Avenue ◖ Champaign Illinois 61822
www.researchpress.com

Copyright © 1996 by Gwendolyn Cartledge and JoAnne Fellows Milburn

6 5 4 3   02 03 04

All rights reserved. Printed in the United States of America.

Excerpts may be printed in connection with published reviews in periodicals without express permission. No other part of this book may be reproduced by any means without the written permission of the publisher.

Copies of this book may be ordered from the publisher at the address given on the title page.

Cover design by Linda Brown
Printed by McNaughton & Gunn, Inc.

ISBN 0–87822–355–X

Library of Congress Catalog Number 96–69184

Contents

CHAPTER 7

CAROLYN TALBERT JOHNSON, GWENDOLYN CARTLEDGE,
AND JOANNE FELLOWS MILBURN

Tables

Introduction

This book grew out of several years of research and writing about children's social skills, particularly within the context of classroom teachers' and other practitioners' efforts to help children and adolescents develop more adaptive behaviors. As this work evolved, it became apparent not only that young people and adults often value different behaviors but that the differences grow as the gap between the backgrounds of the teacher and the learner widens. Moreover, we increasingly became aware of the special social development conditions that confront youth from racially and ethnically different backgrounds.

This panoply of differences has important implications for the teaching of social skills. To be effective, social skill trainers need to understand learners' motivations and social goals, the ways in which the learners have been socialized in other environments such as the family or the community, and the interference of this alternative socialization with the trainers' goals and the culture of the school and the mainstream society. Equally important, social skill trainers must differentiate between social skill deficits that need to be changed and cultural differences that either need to be respected in their current form or simply need to be switched according to specific social conditions. For example, some students may need to learn the assertive behaviors necessary to become recognized by teachers and peers at school, behaviors that are not acceptable in the home. Likewise, other students may need to learn to make finer discriminations of parental teachings relative to being assertive and protecting themselves.

As our society's diversity increases and our schools become proportionately more minority, it becomes more important to understand and teach social skills from a perspective of cultural diversity. Frequently cited statistics reveal that, within the next 30 or 40 years, at least 40 percent of our public school population will comprise ethnic or racial minorities (i.e., African American, Native American,

Hispanic American, and Asian American). Many of these students, especially from the latter two groups, will be first- or second-generation Americans, frequently speaking English as a second language and subjected to relatively poor socioeconomic conditions. At the same time, fewer minority students are pursuing higher education and teacher education (King, 1993); as a result, the teaching force in U.S. society is increasingly White or European American female, thoroughly entrenched in middle-class American culture. This dichotomy is compounded by the facts that many teacher preparation programs fail to provide coursework or direct experience with special or culturally diverse populations (Kearney & Durand, 1992) and that most graduating students indicate a preference for teaching in suburban settings, where they are least likely to encounter students from ethnic or racial minority backgrounds (Moultry, 1988; Wayson, 1988).

These conditions set the occasion for cultural discontinuities that can undermine students' learning and frustrate teachers. An example is the case of Nicole, a European American female in her first year of teaching. A product of an upper-middle-class family, Nicole was reared in a predominantly white middle-class suburban community in a large metropolitan area. Although Nicole attended public schools, the few classmates from racially or ethnically different backgrounds were of her own socioeconomic status. According to Nicole, her high school graduating class of 700 included no more than 3 African American students. Nicole graduated from a large university with a degree in English education. Again, during her college years she had limited contact with (and coursework on) culturally diverse populations. The suburban school system where she completed her practicum was similar, in racial and cultural terms, to the one where she had grown up. Nicole's teacher preparation program included one 2-hour lecture concerning demographics of the emerging diversity in our society.

Nicole's first teaching assignment contrasted dramatically with her background and preparatory experiences. She found herself in an urban school district, in a school with a majority African American, inner-city population. One day, after beginning her teaching duties, Nicole observed outside her classroom two African American male adolescents engaging in verbal repartee that appeared aggressive and contentious. Being a dutiful and responsible teacher, she immediately marched them to the principal's office to be reprimanded. Much to her surprise and dismay, the principal, an African American woman, criticized Nicole rather than the students, complaining that Nicole had misread the situation and treated the boys prejudicially and unfairly.

What Nicole did not know and—with her limited experience and training—had no way of knowing was that she was observing a unique communication style of African American youth, particularly males. Nicole encountered what Irvine (1990) refers to as "verbal sparring," also called "ribbing," "capping," "woofing," and so forth. Essentially, these interactions are verbal battles characterized by Irvine as black male rituals that are valued and generally conducted in an atmosphere of sport. As in Nicole's case, Irvine points out that "the verbal communication style of black students baffles school personnel, especially white teachers, who fail to understand black students' expressive language" (p. 27). This was a painful and embarrassing lesson for Nicole, but what are the implications for her, the students, and the principal?

Fortunately, Nicole was not discouraged by this sequence of events; she insisted that she really liked working with the students in this setting and looked forward to returning to her teaching assignment. However, she could have been totally derailed by the experience, blaming both the students and the principal for her humiliation and either leaving school if she had other options or remaining and treading water until more lucrative opportunities emerged. In fact, Nicole did have other teaching opportunities in suburban, upper-middle-class settings, but she chose to remain in the city. Following her initial, abrupt confrontation with cultural difference, Nicole greatly valued coursework and discussions on cultural and racial variables that gave her greater insights into her students. Although she is still willing to teach African American students in inner-city settings, she continues to have reservations about the principal.

Cultural misunderstandings can have negative impact on students as well as on teachers. Irvine (1990) notes the occurrence of vicious cycles: Students find that their playful acts are misinterpreted; they become angry and intensify the roughness of their activities; the result is greater fear on the part of whites. Students may feel empowered and rewarded by the effects of their actions on whites, particularly females. This false sense of power may lead them to escalate those behaviors, possibly at the expense of more productive behaviors that relate to school success.

Although well-intended, the principal's reactions are not predictive of the best possible outcomes for students or staff. By validating the students, the principal may have interrupted or slowed the vicious cycle, but she risked undercutting the students' respect for the teacher as well as alienating the teacher. The principal was right to advocate for the students, but she failed to realize that she herself was guilty of the same actions of which she accused the teacher. Just as the male students should not have been punished for engaging in culturally specific, playful behaviors (unless, of course, they were occurring at the wrong time and place), neither should the teacher have been reprimanded for acting in a way consistent with her culture—that is, viewing negative verbal statements as fighting. The situation could have been used as a vehicle for valuable learning and growth for all parties. For instance, rather than confronting Nicole with her shortcomings, the principal might have praised her active interest in the students' overall development and then informed her about this facet of black male interaction. This conference could have been followed with suggestions for readings on this topic, such as the book *Ribbin', Jivin', and Playin' the Dozens* (Foster, 1974) or *Black Students and School Failure* (Irvine, 1990). An especially positive response might have been to ask Nicole to review some of these readings with colleagues for discussion during faculty meetings. Even more important (and consistent with the theme of this book) would be for Nicole to capitalize on her students' communication style as part of her classroom English instruction. Selections from African American literature (see chapter 4 of this book) could be analyzed for examples of these verbal battles. Students could be challenged in classroom contests to be verbally creative in describing fellow students, relatives, love objects, or themselves in *positive* terms. In the context of language learning, these descriptions might be assigned to reinforce grammar objectives and skills being taught (e.g., complete sentences of at least eight words, or three novel adjectives to describe the subject). As long as the results were positive and socially appropriate, students could be encouraged to be as unique and as entertaining as possible. These verbal activities could naturally evolve into creative writing of poetry, essays, and short stories.

Young people are poorly served when their social behaviors are misperceived or excessively punished. Noteworthy in Nicole's scenario, for example, is the fact that her immediate reaction when she thought the boys were being verbally aggressive was to seek out some punishing consequence. Research indicates that female teachers are more likely than male teachers to pursue punishment for adolescent males (Ritter, 1989) and that minority youngsters, particularly African American males, are most vulnerable to punitive actions (Executive Committee, Council for Children with Behavior Disorders, 1989). Punishment for some minority youth seems to be overemphasized.

We do not mean to suggest that youngsters be permitted to misbehave with impunity. However, even if inappropriate social behaviors are accurately perceived, punishment alone rarely is effective in fostering appropriate social development. Youngsters who find themselves caught in a punishment cycle often become more angry, defiant, and intractable. In addition to being confronted with their misdeeds, students sorely need constructive intervention that engages them in productive, socially approved alternatives to previous actions. Let's assume that Nicole's students are actually fighting and that she takes them to the office for justly deserved punishment. What are the lessons learned? Following the punishment, are students helped to learn alternatives to aggression? How might this instruction be conducted so that it is both culturally relevant and effective? In the absence of constructive follow-up, punishment may be not only ineffective but counterproductive. Students may simply learn not to get caught, or they may consider the punishment too mild to warrant a change in behavior. Even if they recognize the importance of acting differently in the future, they may not be able to chart an appropriate course of action on their own. They may not have learned how to manage their behavior in ways that serve their own and others' best interests. Thus, the focus needs to be beyond consequences, on ways to help students grow socially and academically.

At the other extreme from Nicole's students are young people who fail to receive attention because of overly quiet and compliant behaviors. When teachers equate "quiet" with "good," students who internalize excessively tend to be overlooked, frequently experiencing school failure and other social problems as a result. Again, these students are likely to be from particular cultural backgrounds (e.g., Asian Americans). Students struggling to live up to behavioral stereotypes of academic and social superiority may be just as disenfranchised as those who bear the burden of prejudicial inferiority and strive daily to establish their competence and worth, often through self-destructive means.

Borrowing from Ladson-Billings' (1995) "culturally relevant pedagogy," we argue for culturally relevant social skill instruction that will help students learn critical social behaviors that lead to school success and adult competence. Social skill instruction for diverse populations is not an attempt to homogenize the population and mold all young people to some white middle-class standard. To the contrary, we endorse the position of Ladson-Billings and others (e.g., Banks, 1991; Nieto, 1995) that young people need to develop and maintain cultural competence and that their culture should serve as a vehicle for learning. Accordingly, we contend that the student's culture should be the basis for understanding social behavior as well as for teaching social skills. We firmly believe that teachers must attend to the social development needs of all children, but—as Nicole's experience suggests—misinterpretation of social behaviors increases when cultural diversity enters the equation.

Further, we recognize that culturally and linguistically different students are disproportionately represented among the impoverished segments of the population and that they more greatly experience the accompanying stressors. Within each major group considered in our book, there is a subgroup of youth for whom conditions of hardship limit positive models and options, reduce coping strategies, and cloud perceptions relative to long-term survival and success. With a keen sensitivity to their differences, these youngsters are likely to carve out for themselves patterns of behavior that not only are oppositional but are incompatible with school success and often are self-destructive. This tendency can be aggravated by intragroup tension and peer pressure—for example, the "acting white" syndrome, where youth disparage the behavior of more successful group members, often effectively pressuring them to capitulate for less noble ventures. For these and other reasons, students from subpopulations of cultural groups need more help with decision-making strategies and social skills.

An important step in becoming socially competent is developing the sense of self-worth and dignity that results from a strong identity (Nieto, 1995). The schools can play a major role in this process. Nieto provides case studies of "subjugated and economically depressed" adolescents who, through the study of their own cultures, not only were inspired and motivated to learn more but also became more adaptive in their behavior, remained in school, and began to think in terms of postsecondary education and professional careers. Nieto speaks of the transformative power of culturally specific curriculum and pedagogy in reactivating academic interest and success. We believe that such learning can have residual effects on students' social behaviors and, moreover, that direct social skill teaching in a culturally relevant context can be more effective for minority populations than traditional approaches.

We also subscribe to the concept of "equity pedagogy" as advanced by McGee Banks and Banks (1995). In equity pedagogy, teachers' aim in helping students achieve academically is not merely to let them fit into the existing society but to enable them to become active in forging a more just society. Similarly, the goal of culturally relevant social skill instruction is to help students become thoughtful and active participants in the larger society, contributing to the well-being of all.

The basic premise of this book is that the behaviors of young people from culturally diverse populations need to be viewed from a cultural perspective and that instruction should affirm students and empower them to achieve maximally as well as to benefit others. Certain themes are present in each chapter. First, we advocate direct instruction, which involves telling and showing the learner how to perform the desired behavior, then providing opportunities for practice and conditions for maintenance. As we will note later, direct instruction is preferred by certain cultural groups, and the direct approach is considered more beneficial than open-ended discussion, particularly for populations with the disadvantage of low socioeconomic status or language difference. This is especially true with initial social skill teaching.

Because all of the populations we are considering have roots in collectivistic societies, cooperative approaches offer special advantages for both academic and social learning. Students who learn to work cooperatively can perfect their interpersonal skills with members of their own groups as well as with people from different backgrounds. Therefore, we specify cooperative learning activities for each group. We also discuss literature-based instruction for each group: Both nonfiction and fiction are primary means for transmitting cultural themes and making learning culturally relevant. Presenting models and concepts through literature is an established and recognized way to facilitate social learning. Students are more likely to be receptive to the teachings if they can identify with the model. This identification is enhanced by literature portraying characters who reflect the students' culture.

The first chapter in our book emphasizes the relationship between culture and social behavior and highlights the importance of ethnic identity relative to psychological adjustment and adaptive behavior. Culture is not something that we inherit; rather, we are socialized to behave according to traditions established over generations. The culture of the school may or may not be in harmony with the culture each student brings to school. The school greatly influences the way young people see themselves and therefore needs to understand and validate their backgrounds. Schools can be instrumental in the formation of healthy ethnic or racial identities. Also discussed in this chapter are the implications for the comparative social skill assessments of racially and culturally different students.

Chapter 2 outlines generic, empirically validated methods for social skill instruction, consisting of skill training (i.e., direct instruction) and cooperative learning procedures. Cognitive and affective dimensions also are addressed. Because we consider these approaches to be the basic building blocks for all social learning, we have incorporated them into strategies recommended for the specific populations discussed in subsequent chapters. For more detailed information on these approaches, readers might consult *Teaching Social Skills to Children and Youth* (Cartledge & Milburn, 1995) for social skill instruction and *Learning Together and Alone: Cooperative, Competitive, and Individualistic Learning* (Johnson & Johnson, 1987) for cooperative learning.

Consideration of specific cultural groups begins with chapter 3, on Asian Americans. Viewed by some as the most rapidly growing minority group, Asian Americans are perhaps the most diverse. For purposes of our book, this category includes people from East Asia (e.g., Chinese, Japanese, and Koreans), Southeast Asians (e.g., Vietnamese, Laotians, and Cambodians), Asian Indians, and Pacific Islanders (e.g., Filipinos and Samoans). Although these populations share some common features, they differ noticeably in terms of both cultural roots and the issues they present in this society. The most obvious differences concern language and time of immigration to the United States. Asian Americans are unique among minorities in this society in that, despite their prevailing image as superachievers, a sizable minority of their youth do not fit this perception. The discrepancy potentially contributes further to poor academic and social progress. Effective intervention is predicated on accurate behavioral assessments analyzed in the context of cultural knowledge.

African Americans are the subject of chapter 4. With nearly half of its youth growing up in poverty, this group is plagued by the conditions that accompany economic disadvantage and the perceptions typically associated with the poor. This chapter emphasizes the need for professionals to distinguish differences from deficits and to intervene constructively, helping young people to evaluate their options and choose alternatives that will be productive for themselves and others.

Chapter 5 concerns Native Americans, the smallest distinct group discussed in this book. The oldest segment of the U.S. population, Native Americans are distinguished by a culture that emphasizes community and the importance of living in harmony with nature and humankind. Poorly equipped to compete in the larger society, young people from this group are easy prey for social ills such as substance abuse and school failure. Direct instructional approaches that capitalize on their culture appear promising.

Hispanic Americans, the focus of chapter 6, also are diverse in terms of race and country of origin, but they are united by a common language. Although Hispanics in the United States come from many different countries, in this book we consider the three major subgroups: Mexican Americans, Puerto Ricans, and Cuban Americans. We recognize and respect the term *Latino;* however, as noted by Nieto (1992), *Hispanic* is more widely used and is therefore the term primarily used in this book. Although economics and race enter into the equation, language difference may be the most important issue for Hispanics in the United States, and language is the principal point of intervention for addressing social behaviors. While maintaining pride in their cultural background, young people in this group need guidance to acquire skill and ease within the dominant culture so they may participate maximally in the larger society.

The book concludes with a consideration of gender differences. Chapter 7 highlights some points of the ongoing debate concerning the nature and origin of gender differences, identifies some of the most agreed-on differences in social behavior, and discusses some teaching implications.

This book is an effort to define some of the issues surrounding cultural differences and social learning in the United States. Our intention is not to stress differences too much, for we firmly believe that all young people are more alike than different. But as we attempt, along with the rest of society, to grapple with the complexities of increasing diversity (particularly for what appears to be a permanently marginalized segment of each group), we believe that schools and related professionals are a component of an orchestrated effort toward the goal of "success for all." Within that framework, we subscribe to achievement over survival, prevention over intervention, development over containment, and proactive approaches over reaction.

References

Banks, J.A. (1991). *Teaching strategies for ethnic studies* (5th ed.). Needham, MA: Allyn & Bacon.

Cartledge, G., & Milburn, J.F. (1995). *Teaching social skills to children and youth: Innovative approaches* (3rd ed.). Boston: Allyn & Bacon.

Executive Committee, Council for Children with Behavioral Disorders. (1989). Best assessment practices for students with behavioral disorders: Accommodation to cultural diversity and individual differences. *Behavioral Disorders, 14,* 263–278.

Foster, H.L. (1974). *Ribbin', jivin', and playin' the dozens: The unrecognized dilemma of inner city schools.* Cambridge, MA: Ballinger.

Irvine, J.J. (1990). *Black students and school failure: Policies, practices, and prescriptions.* New York: Greenwood.

Johnson, D.W., & Johnson, R.T. (1987). *Learning together and alone: Cooperative, competitive, and individualistic learning.* Englewood Cliffs, NJ: Prentice-Hall.

Kearney, C.A., & Durand, V. (1992). How prepared are our teachers for mainstreamed classroom settings? A survey of postsecondary schools of education in New York State. *Exceptional Children, 59,* 6–11.

King, S.H. (1993). The limited presence of African-American teachers. *Review of Educational Research, 63*(2), 115–149.

Ladson-Billings, G. (1995). But that's just good teaching! The case for culturally relevant pedagogy. *Theory into Practice, 34,* 159–165.

McGee Banks, C.A., & Banks, J.A. (1995). Equity pedagogy, cultural diversity, and school reform. *Theory into Practice, 34,* 152–158.

Moultry, M. (1988). Senior education students' attitudes toward multicultural education. In C.A. Heid (Ed.), *Multicultural education: Knowledge and perceptions.* Bloomington, IN: Center for Urban and Multicultural Education.

Nieto, S. (1992). *Affirming diversity: The sociopolitical context of multicultural education.* New York: Longman.

Nieto, S. (1995, April). *On the brink between triumph and disaster: Exploring tensions between traditional secondary schools and academically unsuccessful students through two case studies.* Paper presented at the annual meeting of the American Educational Research Association, San Francisco.

Ritter, D.R. (1989). Teachers' perceptions of problem behavior in general and special education. *Exceptional Children, 55,* 559–564.

Wayson, W. (1988). Multicultural education in the college of education: Are future teachers prepared? In C.A. Heid (Ed.), *Multicultural education: Knowledge and perceptions.* Bloomington, IN: Center for Urban and Multicultural Education.

CHAPTER 1

The Relationship of Culture and Social Behavior

GWENDOLYN CARTLEDGE AND HUA FENG

A group's culture is based on shared experiences that result in typical ways of perceiving, interpreting, and behaving. Because behavior is greatly influenced by culture, it should be studied within a cultural context. As this society increases in diversity, cultural background grows in importance as a means for interpreting and addressing behavioral differences. The purpose of this chapter is to consider social behavior from a cultural perspective, noting ways in which a society's two major social institutions—family and school—transmit its culture and socialize its young. The issue of ethnic or racial identity is addressed as it relates to self-perception and the potential consequences for social behavior, particularly in children and youth. The chapter's final section details a multimethod social skill assessment of fifth-grade students from racially (and presumably culturally) diverse backgrounds. The study is discussed in terms of its cultural implications and indications for intervention.

Culture Defined

Anthropologists define *culture* as the way of life of a particular group of people, including such dimensions as their traditions, language, religion, marital and family life, values, and organization of the economic system. Culture involves both mental and behavioral phenomena. That is, a cultural group will share values and ways of thinking about events as well as ways of acting (Peoples & Bailey, 1991). The following summarizes Peoples and Bailey's more detailed view of culture:

1. Culture is not genetically determined but socially learned, passed on from generation to generation. This learning is continuous and ongoing. The process of learning one's culture is called *enculturation*. Culture is transmitted first informally, through the family; the school serves as a secondary but formal, structured environment for acquiring culture.

2. Culture does not belong to the individual but is shared. Therefore, we cannot simply observe one person's behavior and conclude that it is based on culture. Rather, we should be aware that it is shared information, such as values, attitudes, and ideas, that provides guidelines for behaviors within a specific group.

3. Culture is integrated. It is like a webbed system, in which various aspects of life are interconnected. The various components of culture are not discrete but interactive. Kinship, economic, and religious subsystems, for example, all affect one another and cannot be understood in isolation.

4. Culture is dynamic and changing, as people constantly change. Although shared ideas and values are usually quite stable within a society, they are not immutable. *Dynamic* implies the capability of undergoing change and of producing change. Because culture is an integrated system, change in one subsystem will undoubtedly affect other subsystems as well.

5. Culture subsumes values, knowledge, and beliefs that affect behaviors. Members of the same culture share basic beliefs about reality, take certain "facts" for granted, accept common standards of behavior, and cherish similar values. The transmitters of culture intend for individuals to share enough of the common elements to be capable of behaving in ways that are acceptable and meaningful to others. Cultural knowledge

provides constraints that shape individuals' decisions and actions around certain events. However, the relationship between culture and behavior is rather complex and does not provide simple explanations. Culture influences rather than dictates behavior. Knowing that one's culture imposes sanctions against teenage dating, for example, may not prevent a pair of teenagers from engaging in a relationship, but it most likely will affect the strategies they employ and the way they interact.

In his review of the related literature, Schneider (1993) notes that a principal means for classifying cultures is according to *individualistic* or *collectivistic* orientation. In a collectivistic culture, group goals supersede those of individuals. The focus is on working toward the common good, with less emphasis on individual goals or aspirations. In collectivistic societies, members assume greater responsibility for one another's welfare, including "shared concern for each other's children, and, very often, collective child-rearing arrangements" (p. 121). Individualistic orientations, by contrast, stress individual effort and self-sufficiency. Members of individualistic societies are more competitive, stressing the goals of individuals over those of the group.

According to Schneider (1993), the most individualistic societies are those of English-speaking countries: the United States, Great Britain, Canada, and Australia. Eastern and developing countries tend to be more collectivistic in orientation. Urban communities also tend to be more individualistic than those in rural areas. Within a culturally diverse society such as the U.S., group membership gains in importance, particularly for members of a minority culture. People moving from a collectivistic culture to an individualistic one may wish to socialize their children to honor the traditional group, but they also may want their children to develop the competencies they will need to compete successfully in the more individualistic society.

In the United States, members of the four principal minority groups—African, Asian, Hispanic, and Native American—have their cultural roots in collectivistic societies. Schneider (1993) reviews a study by Philips (1972) comparing the peer relations among Native American and non–Native American children in rural Oregon. Philips described how, during recess, Native American children would organize themselves and persist in peer-directed activities without incident for much longer periods than non–Native American children. Under structure supplied by the teachers, Native American children would not volunteer to be leaders in these activities. In contrast, under the same conditions, non–Native American children would plead for leadership opportunities.

Children reared with a collectivistic orientation may, for example, have had to assume significant child care responsibilities at home, and this may lead them to exhibit more caretaking or authoritarian behaviors in school. Despite differences attributable to cultural background, it is important to recognize commonalties among children as well as to view behaviors within a developmental context. Across cultures, for example, children are observed to value athletic prowess as a correlate for peer acceptance, and young children are inclined to explain behavior according to specific events that have occurred in the immediate environment (Schneider, 1993). Cultural knowledge not only helps us understand human behavior but also enables teachers to maximize the effectiveness of their instruction. As we study young people's behavior from a cultural perspective, we should note Adler's (1974) basic pluralist principles, as cited by Janzen (1994):

> Every culture has its own internal coherence, integrity, and logic;
>
> No culture is inherently better or worse than another; and
>
> All persons are to some extent culturally bound. (p. 10)

Culture and Child Development

Most of the available research literature on child development is based on information from white middle-class Western children. Authorities in the field recognize that much of this information is not applicable to children from other cultures. As Wagner and Stevenson (1982) point out, "We cannot consider child development in its broad context unless we know how children grow and develop in environments and cultures different from those in which much of our research has already been conducted" (p. vii). As the field of child development gains international perspective, researchers realize that behaviors they have taken for granted as a result of restricting their study to a single culture are not necessarily universal (Bornstein, 1991; Super & Harkness, 1982).

Culture is integral to every aspect of being, influencing to varying degrees one's ways of thinking, acting, and ultimately developing. Without cultural understanding, it is not possible to interpret accurately an individual's development and the forces that have shaped his or her behavior. Culturally diverse groups are poorly served when white middle-class Western perspectives are superimposed upon the interpretation of their behaviors. These altered perspectives not only result in distorted views of those behaviors but also negatively affect cross-cultural interactions as well as the way minority groups see themselves. From his study of the work of Gudykunst and Ting-Toomey (1988), Schneider (1993) makes the same point:

> Since culture influences interpersonal relations . . . the results of virtually any study of children's social competence cannot be readily generalized outside of the culture in which they are obtained. However, this does not mean that psychologists must now begin replicating all studies of children's development one by one, culture by culture. . . . Research which considers culture systematically as an independent variable holds much more promise, as this would enable a more informed understanding of the reasons for cultural influences and the mechanisms by which they operate. (p. 120)

Culture and Socialization

The Family

Socialization is the process whereby children acquire the culture of their society. Parents are expected to be socialized adults, equipped with a stock of knowledge regarding social relationships and the behaviors that are expected and accepted in their society. Accordingly, parents are expected to be first-line facilitators of children's learning about the social environment. Parenting practices vary, however, and as Bornstein (1991) notes, "Parents in different cultures adopt some similar, as well as some different, approaches to childrearing, and . . . parenting is a principal reason why individuals in different cultures are who they are, and are often so different from one another" (p. 3). Little wonder that many psychological theories—for example, psychoanalysis, neopsychoanalysis, social learning theory, and socialization theories—strongly emphasize early childhood experience and its great influence on later adaptation.

In a review of cross-cultural studies on parenting practices and culture, Bornstein (1991) observes the universality of some practices regardless of the country and the background of the parents. Papousek and Papousek (1991) found comparable parent-infant levels of language interaction for Chinese, White American, and German mothers and attributed these similarities to "intuitive parenting." That is, parenting is considered to occur naturally and unconsciously, indicating commonality of parental behaviors across cultures. Similarly, Bornstein, Tal, and Tanis-LeMonda (1991) found that mothers in urban centers in the United States, France, and Japan responded more to their infants' vocalizing than to the infants' looking. But these researchers also noted differences among the mothers: For instance, of the three groups, U.S. mothers tended to have the highest overall rates of interaction with their infants. Nevertheless, a review of these studies and other empirical literature on mother-child interactions across cultures yields no simple conclusions concerning the impact of culture on parenting of infants (Kessen, 1991).

Despite the equivocal nature of the research on culture-specific patterns of mother-infant interaction, there is evidence of more clear-cut patterns where older children are concerned. In some cultures, for example, parents stress independence and growing autonomy, whereas in others the emphasis is on greater dependence and involvement with one's family. The values held by different cultures greatly influence the ways in which parents attempt to socialize their children. These and other culture-specific differences are discussed in some detail in subsequent chapters.

In addition to child-rearing practices, certain other family dynamics potentially influence the socialization process. These include sibling interaction (Schneider, 1993), birth order (Ewen, 1988; Schneider, 1993), and family stress or change (Patterson, 1982). According to Schneider, sibling interactions in the home serve as a point of learning about peer relations that help to shape nonkinship peer relations outside the home. Older siblings often play an important role in passing on to younger brothers and sisters information from parents or from the school that will guide them in interacting with others and responding to novel situations.

Ewen (1988) discusses Adler's birth order theory, which is based on the premise that children from the same family are not shaped in the same environment. According to this theory, personality development and behavior are greatly influenced by one's position in the family constellation (e.g., born first, second, etc.) Adler proposed, for example, that the oldest child may receive the most attention from the parents, an empowering experience that may contribute to a tendency later to dominate peers for power or authority. Middle children may be more inclined to share but also may lean toward competitive or even revolutionary behavior. The greater pampering often accorded the youngest child may foster more dependent behaviors. Schneider (1993) also stresses the importance of birth order in shaping social behaviors and contends that Adler's positions are validated to some extent in the research literature.

Another critical aspect of family life that influences social development pertains to family stressors and modes of interaction. Patterson (1982, 1986) and other researchers (e.g., Baum, 1989; Whalen, 1989) point out that stressors such as poverty, marital conflict, parental psychiatric disorders, and drug abuse—in combination with a biological dysfunction within the child, such as an attention disorder—frequently lead to poor family management practices, and consequently to antisocial behavior in the child. Within such a family system, parents and children often resort to coercive exchanges where children and parents control each other's behaviors through negative reinforcement or pain. Under these conditions an individual acts principally to terminate some aversive event (e.g., the child's or the parent's screaming) or to avoid some punisher (e.g., being grounded for missing a curfew). Typically, positive behaviors are not learned; rather, the undesired behaviors recur as soon as the aversive or punishing event is removed. More important, the child learns to control the behavior of others through these negative means, and dysfunctional behaviors learned in the family quickly generalize to other settings with other persons.

In sum, the family is the first cultural environment every child experiences. The most significant family-based variables contributing to the development of children's social behaviors appear to be child-rearing practices, sibling interactions, birth order, and family stress and interaction systems.

The School

Next to the family, the school is probably the most important socializing agent in our society and is viewed as having considerable influence on the development of the self (Schneider, 1993; Valsiner, 1989). According to Valsiner, formal education in any society performs two major, interdependent functions: (a) It provides students with basic knowledge and skills that cannot be fully gained through informal education; and (b) It promotes the development of personal identification with ideological systems that encompass those of the local community and the child's own family. Formal education provides for the standardization and homogenization of children's socialization processes. Both the physical and the symbolic organization of the school environment play a major role in this process. Schneider elaborates on this concept by pointing out that the school's effect is based on (a) the physical ecology of the school (building, furniture, maintenance, lighting, equipment, utilization of space, etc.) and (b) the school as a social system (implicit or explicit patterns or rules of social interaction in the school).

The physical arrangement of a school influences the nature and extent of the social interaction within it. Features of physical ecology include the size of the school population, the seating arrangements, the playground, and the structure of the building. From his review of several investigations in this area, Schneider (1993) reports evidence that the school's physical ecology can significantly affect children's social interaction. Schneider cites a study by Hallinan (1976), for example, showing fewer social isolates in "open-space" or open-arrangement primary-school classrooms where walls and barriers were minimized. Another study (Weinstein & Pinciotti, 1988) indicates that providing playground equipment increased active play but reduced interactive play; this finding suggests a need to design playground equipment to increase cooperative play. Along these same lines, Sapon-Shevin (1980) relates Kessen's (1976) observations of Chinese nurseries, which intentionally reduced the amount of play equipment in order to promote sharing and cooperation. Another example was the outfitting of children with jackets that buttoned in back, requiring the children to ask for and give mutual help. It appears that the school's ecology can be structured to promote social development, but as Schneider points out, additional research is needed to clarify the interactive effects of the classroom setting, the teacher's leadership style, and the specific characteristics of the children.

In our society, the physical environment of the schools can also affect the psychological development of children. Children of color being disproportionately represented among low-income groups are more likely to live in poorly funded districts and attend schools where structures and materials are inadequate or dilapidated. Income-based school funding results in gross inequities across and within school districts. In his book *Savage Inequalities*, Kozol (1991) reports that state allocations to school districts in New York ranged from 90¢ per pupil for the poorest districts to $14 per pupil for the richest districts. Grossman (1995) reports other disparities, such as that in Texas, where per capita expenditures ranged from $3,000 in the poorest districts to $7,000 in the richest.

Kozol (1991) contrasts schools within the New York City system. He visited one school in the South Bronx that was a converted skating rink with few windows, overcrowded classrooms, a shortage of books and other instructional materials, and a general lack of physical comfort. The school population was 90 percent African and Hispanic American. In contrast, Riverdale School, in an affluent city neighborhood, had only about 12 percent African and Hispanic American students; most of them were poor and placed in the 12 special education classes for students with mental retardation. Riverdale School not only had windows, but the building was nicely decorated with appropriate class sizes and adequate equipment and instructional materials. The Riverdale School library had 8,000 books for 835 students, compared to only 700 library books for 1,300 students in the South Bronx school. To one of the teachers in the South Bronx school Kozol posed a rather poignant question regarding the obvious discrepancies in school conditions: He asked if the students understood these discrepancies as a racial message.

Ladson-Billings (1994), drawing similar contrasts between affluent, attractive schools and poor schools attended by minority children, attempts to answer that question for both groups. She suggests that as these groups of children view each other's situations, White students will probably come to equate African and Hispanic Americans with poverty, perhaps consider them undeserving, and regard the inequities as normal. Likewise, minority children may associate material advantages with Whites. Such thought patterns are unhealthy for either group, but they are likely to be most destructive for children of color. This kind of input contributes to the formation of ethnic or racial identity and, as discussed later in this chapter, may be processed in ways that lead to maladaptive patterns of behavior.

The school's social system is a reflection of the larger society, and as such it is instrumental in transmitting cultural values. The classroom teacher is one of the most important components of that system as far as young people's social development is concerned. Schneider (1993) specifies several teacher characteristics that are important in this respect. They include personal contact with students, feedback, empathy, classroom climate, leadership style, and involvement in students' social relations. In his review of related research, Schneider noted some limited evidence of the impact of teacher behaviors on children's social development. For instance, empathy on the part of teachers was found to have a positive effect on students' self-concepts, but the relationship of teacher empathy to children's social competence was not well defined.

Compassion and flexibility may be particularly important for teachers working with students from culturally and racially diverse backgrounds. The teaching force in this society is predominantly white, while children of color are increasingly numerous in the student population. Current trends suggest that this situation will persist for the foreseeable future (King, 1993). Although race has not been found to be a factor in student achievement (Ladson-Billings, 1994), it is conceivable that students interpret feedback and attitudes differently according to the race of the teacher. Grossman (1995) reports data indicating that African American teachers tend to be less biased toward African American students, evidencing such positive effects as less punishment and higher high school graduation rates.

Grossman (1995) contends that the U.S. schools are inappropriate for culturally diverse populations. He holds that their European American middle-class orientation is manifested in biased expectations, biased evaluations, and biased treatment of culturally diverse students, particularly if those students also are poor. Grossman presents findings indicating, for example, that teachers are inclined to interact more with European American than with African American students and to judge the same transgressions more severely for African American students than for European American students. Grossman points out, however, that not all teachers are biased against different-race students. Some studies have found that teachers treat different-race students better than same-race students, and there is speculation that some of the observed bias is unconscious. Grossman concludes that, for the most part, teacher biases affect non–European American students in detrimental ways. Teachers and other education professionals need preparation to work with culturally and racially different students. A teacher who believes, for example, that the school difficulties of minority students reside solely within the students and who communicates that belief to the students does a great disservice to the students and to the larger society.

Although research directly demonstrating the effects of teacher characteristics on students' social competence is limited and equivocal, teachers are without question powerful forces in children's social development. There is little dispute that a hidden curriculum operates in the classroom, where teachers communicate their likes and dislikes, preferences, and social rules (Cartledge & Milburn, 1995). From a constructivist perspective, this process is illustrated to an extent by Winegar (1988) in a discussion of the co-construction of children's social behavior. According to Winegar, "social others" such as parents and teachers use various strategies to place constraints on children's behaviors and to guide them "toward socially appropriate understandings of their cultural environment" (p. 9). Winegar argues that these understandings are not simplistic scripts but are "co-constructed," both in the child's ability to derive meaning from environmental information paired with previous experiences and in interactions with other individuals, interactions in which knowledge is expressed in words and behavior is used to "co-construct" social knowledge. Winegar points out that "individuals' actions do not have meaning in isolation; actions acquire meaning in their relation to complementary actions of others" (p. 8).

A study of preschool children and their teachers at lunchtime was used by Winegar (1988) as an example. Over a 4-week period, the researchers observed that teachers' directive statements (direct requests for specific behaviors, e.g., "Sit down in your chair") declined in frequency, with corresponding increases in nondirective statements (supportive of children's behavior but with no direct requests to change (e.g., "Who remembers what we do after we finish our snack?"). Teachers' efforts gradually moved away from giving rules and directions to praising actions and asking children to state the rules. According to Winegar, children and teachers co-constructed their lunchtime behavior. The teachers used "explicit instruction, modeling and praise" (p. 24). As children became more self-regulated, teachers adjusted their behavior so that they instructed less, provided corrections when needed, and spent more time socializing with the children.

Whereas the lunchtime study illustrates the co-constructing of desired social behavior, it is also possible to foster undesired behaviors and attitudes inadvertently. Much is made of teachers' tendencies to reinforce academic behavior more strongly for males and affluent youth than for females and students from low-income backgrounds, perhaps leading the latter two groups to shy away from academic endeavors. As noted later in this book, when cultural or racial and socioeconomic differences exist, unfortunately the messages often are interpreted negatively, and the results can be damaging.

School atmosphere—the existence of ability groupings, for example—can have a significant effect on the social and cognitive development of children. Schneider's (1993) research results show that when students are grouped on the basis of academic ability, social boundaries form between high- and low-achieving children, and these boundaries rarely break. Another example can be seen in the contrast between cooperative and competitive environments. Competitive environments have been shown to exacerbate the alienation of disadvantaged students, who tend to leave school as a means of escape. According to Schneider, the promotion of cooperative learning probably has been the most vigorous and widely accepted effort to restructure the social ecology of the school.

Other school-based strategies noted by Schneider (1993) as potentially enhancing students' social competence include active student participation in learning and school governance, peer tutoring, and formal social skill instruction. Of these interventions, direct instruction appears to hold the most promise. On the basis of an extensive literature review, Schneider (1993) concludes that social skill instruction had a significant influence on children's behavior. Small to moderate effects were found for problem-solving techniques, but coaching, modeling, and combined methods appeared more successful. There also is some evidence that social skill instruction is more effective with withdrawn than with aggressive children, but Schneider questions the related instructional and research methods: "There are many reasons to suspect that existing studies underestimate the potential contribution of school-based social competence promotion" (p. 112).

Culture and Language

Through social interaction an infant begins to acquire language— that is, the association of sound and meaning—and the acquisition of culture begins the moment a child starts to use language (Blount, 1982). Peoples and Bailey (1991) note that, although language around the world varies greatly, it is universal that all languages are rule governed, are systematic, and convey meaning. Peoples and Bailey also assert that children learn language intuitively through listening to adults, not according to language rules. Furthermore, regardless of the complexity of the language, children around the world are observed to learn their languages in relatively short periods of time.

Language and culture are intertwined. Language is the principal means for transmitting culture, and language, or one's social communication pattern, is shaped by one's culture (Blount, 1982; Peoples & Bailey, 1991; Robinson, 1988). Discussing the relationship between language and culture, Peoples and Bailey state that language "mirrors" or reflects an individual's or group's lifestyle and that language is used to construct the group's system. Various groups develop specialized languages that are specific to their particular interests—for example, lawyers use "legalese," and bureaucrats use "bureaucratese." According to Peoples and Bailey, "In a diverse society, groups often develop specialized speech to facilitate communication among themselves, to mark themselves off from the rest of us, to help achieve their private goals, and so on" (p. 56). The same phenomenon can be seen in the development of slang among adolescents, particularly youth from minority groups or those participating in a gang culture. Some of these specialized communication systems can become so complex that the typical English speaker may require a special lexicon to decipher the language and make meaningful associations.

Peoples and Bailey (1991) maintain that language is used to construct sociocultural systems. A culture uses words to describe events in certain ways and thereby influences its members' perceptions of the world. An example, based on theories of anthropological linguists, concerns the differences between the ways in which English speakers and Hopi speakers describe time and the ways in which these descriptions influence the perception of time. The English language quantifies time (e.g., in days and weeks) and permits the user to speak of past, present, and future events. The Hopi language, on the other hand, does not include comparable terms, so events are spoken of as continuously unfolding rather than occurring in specific units.

Cultural knowledge influences our manner of speaking to others. Robinson (1988) holds that culture and social communication patterns cannot be separated. Along the same lines, Blount (1982) points out that members of a society use culture as a means to regulate and interpret their own behaviors and make them meaningful in interaction with others. He further notes that people must acquire cultural knowledge to make communication meaningful and acceptable. Speech acts may occur outside of culture, and the statements may communicate, but they might not be acceptable. Robinson offers the following example of the difficulty of effecting meaningful interaction in the absence of shared knowledge:

> [As an American tourist leaves a guesthouse, he greets a villager who is seated near the entrance]
>
> American: Hi, how are you?
>
> Nepali: [to himself: How rude! Prying into my intimate thoughts and emotions! But I will not be discourteous. I will speak with him.] Where are you going?
>
> American: [to himself: Why didn't he answer me? I don't know him. Why is he interested in where I'm going? What is he after? Perhaps he wants to know how long I will be away so that he can rob my room.] (pp. 144–145)

Another example of the importance of cultural knowledge is seen in daily rituals such as greetings. According to Blount (1982), within any particular culture individuals understand when greetings are used and have a set of greetings to be used as needed. Greetings may need to be formal (when one encounters an authority figure), brief (when one is in a hurry to make an appointment), or prolonged (when one has not seen a friend or acquaintance for a long time; Wiig, 1982). Of course, greetings reflect cultural differences—for example, traditional greetings in Japan, which include bowing, and typical U.S. greetings, which involve handshakes. Subcultural differences exist as well. In southern or rural areas of the United States, greetings to strangers or casual acquaintances are much more common than in northern or urban areas. Irvine (1990) points out how differences in cultural knowledge affect meaningful social communication between blacks and whites. She notes, for instance, that blacks believe that a person does not have the right to refuse a communication, whereas to whites this is acceptable. She observes that blacks view a fight mainly as a physical altercation, whereas whites label both verbal arguments and physical confrontations as fights.

Obviously, language learning entails more than acquiring a system of words based on a prescribed set of sounds and grammatical rules. The individual must learn to use this system in the context of the culture so that speech acts will be meaningful and accepted. If the cultural context is misunderstood, social discord can result. Lack of cultural knowledge can also hamper an individual's ability to develop and use socially adaptive behavior. In culturally diverse but segregated societies such as the United States, culturally specific communication patterns are likely to persist, providing ample opportunity for dissonance in cross-group social communication.

Ethnic Identity

As this society becomes more diverse, interest in ethnicity or ethnic identity increases correspondingly. In the past decade, discussions on this topic have multiplied dramatically in the literature, and they permeate nearly all academic disciplines (Trimble, in press). This increased interest is not immune from skepticism and criticism, however. According to Trimble, critics argue that ethnic study is potentially divisive, that it promotes living in the past, that ethnicity tends to disappear after a few generations, and that ethnicity is over-emphasized or contrived, often attributed to practices or social order where it doesn't actually exist. Nevertheless, several proponents underscore the importance of ethnic identity because of its apparent relevance to self-concept and psychological functioning. Development of ethnic identity is considered an essential human need, providing a sense of belonging and historical continuity (Smith, 1991). Trimble likewise points out that it is part of the human experience, dictating the basis for interpersonal interaction in this society. According to Phinney (1990), the issues surrounding ethnic identity become particularly salient for minority groups living under conditions where they are disparaged or disenfranchised.

The term *ethnic identity* generally refers to one's group identification (Phinney, 1990). Proponents of ethnic identity formation theory argue that psychological well-being and subsequent adaptive behavior are greatly determined by individuals' perceptions of their own and others' ethnic groups. Phinney points out, for example, that identity with a low-status group may breed self-hatred, which an individual may attempt to address by "passing," by developing group pride, or by redefining characteristics typically viewed as inferior. Smith (1991) contends that children from low-status groups are affected by their ethnicity at an earlier age than are majority-group children and tend to attribute less favorable characteristics to their racial groups throughout their developing years. The result may be identity conflicts, possibly leading to maladaptive behaviors when individuals attempt to reject descriptions aimed at them by others.

Also noted in the literature is the importance of distinguishing the terms *ethnic identity, racial identity,* and *acculturation* (Kohatsu, 1994; Phinney, 1990). Ethnic identity refers largely to national origin (e.g., Japanese American), whereas racial identity pertains to racial group (e.g., Asian American). Kohatsu found that attitudes toward racial identity influenced cultural adaptation among Asian American college students, but there were differences according to ethnic background. Japanese Americans, for example, evidenced "significantly higher levels of acculturation to White culture than Vietnamese and Korean Americans" (p. 7). However, for African Americans, the overwhelming majority of whom are products of the

West African slave trade and whose ethnicity is obscured, ethnic and racial distinctions are nearly impossible to draw and are somewhat meaningless. The issue is further compounded for Hispanic Americans, who represent distinct racial and biracial groups as well as nationalities. A common unifying feature for this latter group in the United States is language. We use the term *ethnic identity* while recognizing the differences within and among the major ethnic or racial groups.

Ethnic identity and *acculturation* should not be used interchangeably. Phinney (1990) states that acculturation refers to changes in attitudes, behaviors, and values resulting from contact between two cultures. Though several models of acculturation exist, the most common are linear and bipolar. According to the linear model, an individual has a strong relationship with one group and a weak relationship with the other. According to the bipolar model, relationships with the ethnic and the dominant culture may be independent of each other: Strong identity with one group does not preclude a weak relationship or lack of identity with another group. The individual may have a strong identity with both groups (Phinney, 1990; Trimble, in press). Strong identity with both groups, or biculturalism, is often considered a preferred state of acculturation. Other less healthy states include *marginality,* identification with neither group; *assimilation,* exclusive identification with the dominant group; and *separation,* identification solely with one's own ethnic group.

Developmental models often are used to explain the process of ethnic identity formation. Phinney (1990), for example, presents a three-stage model to describe what may be an evolutionary process. The first or unexamined stage occurs before the individual is exposed to ethnic identity issues; at this stage the individual shows a preference for the dominant culture. During the second, or exploration, stage an "awakening" takes place as the individual begins to study and become involved in the ethnic culture. Ethnic identity is achieved at the third stage, when a deeper understanding and appreciation of the ethnic culture causes it to be internalized. According to Phinney, achievement of self-identity, or the third stage, is evident when the individual chooses to label him- or herself with that group's name (e.g., Irish American or Hispanic American), displays a positive attitude toward the group, and engages in the group's social and cultural activities.

The importance of ethnic identity achievement is revealed in empirical investigations showing a positive relationship between the identity process and self-concept. Psychological adjustment appears to be poorest for those at the unexamined stage and best for those having achieved complete ethnic identity formation (Phinney, 1990; Smith, 1991). Although some argue that issues of ethnic identity disappear after a few generations (Trimble, in press), Phinney notes that this is the case mainly for Americans of European extraction. Some groups such as Asian and African Americans do not have the option of ignoring their racial or ethnic backgrounds rather than choosing to label themselves. According to Phinney, research conducted with Japanese and Chinese Americans showed that in subsequent generations there were some changes in behavior or ethnic knowledge but not in importance or positive valuation of ethnicity.

Although much of the research on ethnic identity has been conducted with college students, it is a significant issue for younger people as well. In school-age populations, particularly adolescents, ethnic identity formation has been associated with various adaptive and maladaptive behaviors. Researchers point out that young people from disparaged racial or ethnic minorities may react to others' perceptions in maladaptive ways. Youths most alienated from the dominant culture may engage in "cultural inversion" or oppositional social identity, indicating that they view the behaviors of the dominant group as inappropriate for members of their own ethnic group (Bernal, Saenz, & Knight, 1991). An example of this phenomenon would be African or Hispanic American adolescents' labeling the academically appropriate behavior of their ethnic peers as "acting white." Matute-Bianchi (1986) classified the ethnic identities of California high school students of Mexican descent and observed that youths associating themselves with Chicano or Cholo groups tended to be the most alienated from the school culture and to disparage academic and other values espoused by the dominant society. In contrast, students who were Mexican-oriented or who labeled themselves Mexican-American tended to experience more school success and to subscribe to the academic and social values of the school and larger society. Fordham (1988) observed a similar pattern for African American high school students.

A depressing portrait of destructive ethnic identity is presented by Elrich (1994), a teacher of low-socioeconomic Hispanic and African American elementary students on the outskirts of Washington, D.C. In discussing self-esteem with his sixth-grade class, Elrich discovered that the students held the following extremely negative stereotypes about their own race: (a) Black people are bad because "being bad is the way we are" (p. 12); (b) Blacks are poor because they are dumb and don't work hard; (c) Whites and Asians have money because they are smart; (d) Black boys expect to die young and from unnatural causes; and (e) Hispanics are more like Blacks than like Whites. Most disturbing is the fact that Elrich's students disparaged "wannabees," students who do "their work and behave because they want to be White" (p. 13). The youngsters took pride in being what they perceived their image should be—"being bad." According to Elrich, many of them excelled in this mission, "and the badder they were, the greater their social status" (p. 14). Any thoughts of exercising self-control or pursuing academic success were suppressed in the interest of maintaining the "bad" image.

As Elrich (1994) points out, the perceptions of his students run counter to those held by youth growing up in the same area 30 years earlier. The sixties were a period of hope; certainly most black males did not spend their youth pondering their early demise, nor did they believe that most of life's rewards would be inaccessible through legitimate means. In the interim, however, increasingly segregated environments, crippling conditions of poverty, and negative media attention undoubtedly have transmitted damaging antisocial messages that today's youths have internalized. Development of racial or ethnic identity certainly precedes adolescence (Reese & Vera, 1994), but one questions whether low-income minority youths (like Elrich's students) even accumulate the kind and quantity of beneficial experiences that contribute to healthy identity formation as described by the stage theorists.

Identity issues can likewise be problematic for immigrant minorities. As they try to find a balance between the demands of school and their new society, and family needs and values that are rooted in the country of origin, young people often face identity conflicts. A statement from a Chinese American high school student illustrates this point:

I don't know who I am. Am I the good Chinese daughter? Am I an American teenager? I always feel I am letting my parents down when I am with my friends because I act so American, but I also feel that I will never really be an American. I never feel really comfortable with myself anymore. (Grossman, 1995, p. 144)

Although discussions on the topic are more theoretical than empirically based (Phinney, 1990), ethnic identity formation appears to be significant in the psychological and behavioral adjustment of ethnic or racial minority youth. Most theorists tend to advocate for bicultural identity, where the individual identifies strongly with both cultures. Unhealthy states are those in which the individual identifies exclusively with one culture, denigrating the other or refusing to identify with either. These and related notions—for example, cultural mismatch theory (Ogbu, 1988) and social identity theory (Bernal et al., 1991)—are used to explain oppositional and dysfunctional school and social behavior observed among subsets of youth within ethnic or racial minority groups. This perspective suggests approaches for fostering more constructive behaviors for extremely vulnerable subgroups. Bernal et al. (1991), for example, argue that ethnic identity formation may produce positive, adaptive outcomes if the desired behavior is embedded in that identity. Thus, for instance, a support network comprising enough representatives of the esteemed "in-group" may define academic achievement as part of that group's identity. Vulnerable students might need in-group endorsement and development of adaptive social behaviors (such as their own specialized and unique strategies for negotiating conflict) in order to become receptive to socially approved patterns of behavior.

Social Skill Research on Students from Racial or Ethnic Minorities

Overview

The literature includes few comparative empirical investigations on the social behaviors of racial or ethnic minorities in the schools. Some studies show that teachers tend to give African American children poorer behavioral ratings than their majority group peers receive

(Keller, 1988), and others indicate that students tend to exhibit peer preferences along racial lines (Davey & Mullin, 1982). What we need are comprehensive, multimethod studies that involve a variety of respondents and assessment procedures. This variety is especially important for assessments of racial and ethnic minority students. Teacher assessments through social skill ratings are considered valid measures of children's social development (Cartledge & Milburn, 1995); however, the issue of bias is important, and few if any studies have attempted to correlate teacher ratings with actual social behaviors. The positive or negative evaluations typically given by teachers to students from certain racial or ethnic groups need to be corroborated through direct observation of these students in the schools. Further, assessments by significant others as well as student self-assessments would help provide more accurate profiles of the social patterns for specific groups.

In addition to teacher ratings, social status in the peer group is seen as a measure of social competence. Popular, well-liked children are assumed to be more socially skilled than those who are rejected or disliked. Sociometric measures, using either peer nominations (children select their most liked and most disliked peers) or roster-rating instruments (children indicate the degree of likability on a Likert scale for each classmate) are considered viable methods for assessing peer acceptance. Although positive nominations may be based on features other than social skills (e.g., race, gender, physical attractiveness), sociometrics do provide a useful measure of children's ability to get along with their peers.

It is worth noting, however, that the social skills children value in their peers often differ somewhat from those valued by teachers. Cartledge, Frew, and Zaharias (1985), for example, found that children selected friends on the basis of play and social communication skills. Specifically, the children indicated that they liked other children who had a sense of humor and particularly other children who had good play skills. Teachers, on the other hand, placed more importance on academic-related behaviors such as staying on task. Where teachers and students stress different sets of behaviors, their assessments would not invalidate each other, but they do underscore the need for a multimethod assessment to provide a complete picture of an individual's or a group's social skills. Youngsters with good peer-based skills but who tend not to have good task-related skills, for example, probably would receive poor social skill ratings from teachers.

Self-assessment may be a measure of social self-efficacy or the degree of confidence children feel in certain social situations. This confidence (or lack thereof) may be based on previous successes or failures experienced under the same conditions or on specific or general feedback children receive on their behavior. Social confidence enhances overall social competence, assuring one of the ability to engage in a variety of social situations, including novel ones. Self-assessment may be quite valuable for instructional purposes as well. For example, children who are convinced their task-related skills are adequate when there is much evidence to the contrary may need their misperceptions corrected. The research literature includes much discussion on racial or ethnic self-perceptions relative to self-esteem or self-concept, but little is said about children's evaluations of their own social skills.

A Multimethod Study

Feng and Cartledge (1996) conducted a multimethod social skills assessment of children from three different racial groups: Asian, African, and European American. The methods included teacher, peer, and self-assessment, as well as direct observation by trained observers. The main purpose of the study was to determine how each of these groups was perceived according to respondent or assessment methodology. A second purpose was to determine whether a particular profile emerged for any of the racial minority groups and if that profile evidenced behavioral deficits or simply differences.

The study population included 122 fifth-grade students from low socioeconomic levels: Thirty Asian Americans (20 boys, 10 girls), 42 African Americans (23 boys, 19 girls), and 50 European Americans (22 boys, 28 girls). The Asian American students were all first-generation Americans; their countries of origin included Cambodia, China, Hong Kong, Japan, Laos, Taiwan, Thailand, and Vietnam. Seven fifth-grade teachers completed social skill ratings on the fifth-grade students. Six teachers (five females and one male) were European American, and one teacher was an African American female.

The multimethod assessment was composed of teacher social skill ratings, student self-ratings of social skills, peer sociometric ratings, direct observation of students' social communications, and student interviews. Teachers and students used the Social Skills Rating System (SSRS; Gresham & Elliott, 1990) for social skill ratings. The teacher assessments focused on (a) social skills (e.g., "Invites others to join in activities"), divided into the categories of cooperation, assertion, and self-control, and (b) problem behaviors (e.g., "Argues with others"). The students rated themselves on this instrument according to four areas: cooperation, assertion, empathy, and self-control. Following are sample items:

Assertion: "I make friends easily."

Cooperation: "I do my homework on time."

Empathy: "I listen to adults when they are talking with me."

Self-control: "I ignore other children when they tease or call me names."

Both teachers and students rated behaviors on a 3-point scale (from 0 to 2), with ratings ranging from "never" to frequent performance of the skill.

Students completed sociometric ratings of their classmates, using a roster-rating format. The names of all students were listed according to a 5-point Likert scale. Students rated their peers from 5 ("I like this person a lot") to 1 ("I don't like this person at all").

Observation of students' social communications took place during informal periods such as lunchtime or recess. Researchers observed four sets of three to five students from each racial group for 2 weeks before switching to another set for the next 2 weeks. Targeted and coded behaviors pertaining to initiating and responding to conversations were categorized as positive (e.g., "Thanks for your help"), neutral (intended mainly to give or obtain information; e.g., "I don't like chili"), negative (e.g., "Stop doing that"), and aggressive (e.g., "Shut your big mouth"). The observers designated ethnic group interaction by noting the race of respondent and recipient of the response.

The researchers used semistructured interviews to assess the attitudes of the students toward various social situations. Interview questions pertained to (a) students' beliefs about ways to handle conflict (e.g., "What do you do when another student teases you?"),

(b) students' reported ways of expressing feelings (e.g., "Do you tell others how you are feeling when something bad happens to you?"), and (c) students' beliefs about expressing feelings to others (e.g., "Do you think it is a good idea to tell others how you feel?").

Teachers rated the social skills of the Asian American students within the average range and those of the African and European American students within the low-average range, according to the test norms. Teachers felt Asian American students exhibited significantly more self-control and cooperation than African American students and more cooperation than European American students. Although the differences between African and European American students were insignificant, teachers did rate the latter group slightly higher. Consistent with the social skill ratings, teachers perceived African American students to have significantly more problem behaviors (hyperactivity and externalizing) than Asian American students and to be more externalizing than European American students. European American students differed significantly from their Asian American peers in the category of hyperactivity.

On self-assessment of social skills, although the groups did not differ significantly, European American students gave themselves the highest ratings, and African American students rated themselves lowest in self-control and highest in empathy. Students in all three groups rated themselves lowest in self-control and highest in empathy. A review of responses by group showed Asian American students saw themselves as cooperative and compliant and least likely to negotiate problem situations with others, whereas African American students profiled themselves as people oriented and least skilled in resolving conflict. No discernible pattern emerged for European American students.

On sociometric ratings, the Asian American students received the highest mean scores, followed by the African American and then by the European American students. Significant differences resulted only between the ratings of Asian American (highest) and European American students (lowest). Another finding was that African American students gave significantly higher ratings to their classmates than either of the other two groups.

Social communications among the students occurred mainly along racial lines, but in terms of cross-race interactions, European American students conversed more frequently with African American students than with Asian American students. African and Asian Americans were observed to interact with each other more than either group interacted with European Americans. Asian American students received the lowest rates of social communication and directed proportionately more speech acts outside their group than did their peers. Most of the speech fell within the neutral range, with relatively few positive, negative, or aggressive statements. European Americans emitted the most positives and negatives, followed by African Americans for negatives, then Asian Americans for positives and negatives.

The interviews showed that students differed most on items dealing with receiving unfair treatment and expressing feelings. Unlike their cross-race peers, Asian American students were more likely to say they didn't know what they would do if treated unfairly or that they would not tell a person that he or she had been unfair. African and European American students, on the other hand, tended to respond more assertively or aggressively to the prospect of being treated unfairly, and they interacted with their peers at considerably higher rates.

Cultural Issues in Social Skill Development

The findings from the Feng and Cartledge (1996) study highlight some important cultural features for these minority students. Teacher ratings and student responses for first-generation Asian American students revealed that they were least likely to question unfair rules or to say nice things about themselves. These tendencies underscore principles of deference to authority and self-modesty that are prominent features of their socialization. The Asian culture strongly encourages conformity (Sue, 1981) and dictates that in an ambiguous situation one should keep silent or obey rules, especially when facing authority (Chin, 1983; Ma, 1985) or relating to strangers (Sue, Hu, & Kwon, 1991).

Ironically, the cultural features that apparently contribute to more positive teacher and peer reviews may also cause significant problems to go undetected in this group. Noting the high dropout rate for Asian American students (e.g., Asian Americans represent over 25 percent of all dropouts in New York City) and the increasing criminality in this population, a 1991 report from the Los Angeles

Schools points out that the stereotypical view of the hard-working, high-achieving Asian American student may cause teachers to see these students as self-sufficient and thereby overlook many of their problems.

In the same vein, teachers associated African American students with people-oriented social skills, as well as with the problem behaviors of being argumentative and likely to interrupt others' conversations. Irvine (1990) notes that African Americans tend to employ a direct style, entering heated arguments without following the turn-taking rule. The energetic, fast-paced, confrontational manner to which many of these youngsters are socialized may be misunderstood and may conflict with the classroom culture.

In addition to the socializing experiences of African American students, poverty places them at increased risk of behavior problems (Kauffman, 1989; McLoyd, 1990). Teacher ratings and student review responses indicated a tendency toward employing aggressive options in conflict situations. Aggressive responses to conflict are typical among low-income people, particularly those from violence-prone urban areas. In these areas, children often are encouraged to counter-aggress, ostensibly as a means of survival. Such children are taught not to seek assistance from adults or to negotiate but to respond in kind with verbal or physical aggression.

Culturally different behaviors are not equivalent to social skill deficits or behavior disorders. Standardized or European American–based social skill assessments may not adequately reflect the social competence of culturally different students. Minority students are vulnerable to misperceptions and inappropriate programming. In some ways, the findings of the Feng and Cartledge (1996) study parallel those of Wells, Morrison, Gillmore, Catalano, Iritani, and Hawkins (1992), who found that teachers identified problem behaviors most predictive of drug use among European American youth. For Asian and African American students, teacher perceptions were likely to underidentify and overidentify, respectively. Minority youth are poorly served under these conditions. Not only do punitive interventions fail to help them grow, such actions can exacerbate their problems. School personnel need to improve their cultural understanding so they can accurately perceive and respond to the needs of their students. Interventions need to be positive, constructive, and timely, focused on helping students derive maximum benefit from their schooling and interact successfully with peers and others while maintaining their own unique cultural identities. Behavioral differences are not necessarily pathological; however, if they interfere with school success or normal peer interactions, positive interventions such as social skill instruction are warranted.

Some final observations about the Feng and Cartledge (1996) study are in order. First, teacher ratings and portions of the sociometric, interview, and direct observation assessments showed significant differences among the students from the three racial groups. Second, the teachers perceived these students in rather stereotypical ways, with other assessment procedures yielding some supporting and some contradictory findings. Finally, despite statistically significant differences found in the teacher social skill assessments, sociometric ratings, and direct observations among the three groups, there was no evidence that the peer relationships of the Asian and African American students were impaired. The impact of these culturally specific behaviors and perceptions is not entirely clear from this study. It appears, at least, that a two-pronged approach is warranted: Teachers need better cultural understanding about their students, and this understanding should be the basis for social learning to enhance all students' success in school and adulthood.

Summary

Because all behavior is culture based, social behaviors need to be defined and interpreted in a cultural context. Culture is not inherited but learned, passed on over generations and transmitted largely through the institutions of family and school. Parenting practices and family dynamics greatly influence a child's beliefs, values, social attitudes, and eventual behavioral patterns reflective of these teachings. Parenting styles, for example, may dictate whether a youth grows into adulthood becoming more dependent on or independent of the birth family. Schools provide many types of formal learning that also strongly color people's perceptions of themselves and others. These perceptions contribute to personal belief systems and ultimately affect the way people behave and interact with others. The hidden curriculum in our schools affects the way students view themselves, relate to peers, and deal with academic learning. Positive, affirming school environments paired with opportunities for scholastic success are especially critical for students from racially or ethnically diverse backgrounds.

Language is the principal vehicle for transmitting culture, and cultural knowledge is prerequisite to meaningful communication. As children develop, they learn not only how to speak but also the social conditions and rules for using that speech. This knowledge is the foundation of socially adaptive behavior. Within a given society subgroups emerge, often creating specialized sublanguages that may be obscure to people outside the groups. Intentional as well as unintentional language differences are typical among racially and ethnically different youth.

Ethnic or racial identity issues have drawn attention and gained in importance in recent years. Experts posit a connection between ethnic identity formation and psychological and behavioral adjustment. Young people who fail to form healthy or constructive identities are likely to reject their own or other groups, developing destructive attitudes and behaviors that are potentially injurious to themselves as well as to others. An obvious goal for these youth is to develop behaviors and subscribe to messages that can validate them and enable them to move effectively between cultures while maintaining their own ethnic identity and integrity.

Assessment of children's social behaviors needs to be conducted within a cultural context. Differences observed among racially and ethnically different groups of children may be more indicative of racial or ethnic differences than of deficits. The multimethod assessment study reviewed in this chapter revealed some behavioral patterns among Asian and African American students that suggest these groups differ from their majority peers and from each other in activity levels and in preferred ways of dealing with conflict. These behavioral patterns are rooted in the ways in which different groups are socialized. The issue with culturally different students, as with all students, is not to view these differences as pathological but to assess the degree to which they tend to support or interfere with success in later life. Common practices in which culturally different behavior is stereotyped, and then overlooked or punished, are counterproductive.

References

Adler, P. (1974). Beyond cultural identity: Reflections on cultural and multicultural man. *Topics in Culture and Learning, 2,* 23–40.

Baum, C.G. (1989). Conduct disorders. In T.H. Ollendick & M. Hersen (Eds.), *Handbook of child psychology* (2nd ed.). New York: Plenum.

Bernal, M.E., Saenz, D.S., & Knight, G.P. (1991). Ethnic identity and adaptation of Mexican American youths in school settings. *Hispanic Journal of Behavioral Sciences, 13,* 135–154.

Blount, B.G. (1982). Culture and the language of socialization: Parental speech. In D.A. Wagner & H.W. Stevenson (Eds.), *Cultural perspectives on child development.* San Francisco: Freeman.

Bornstein, M.H. (1991). Approach to parenting in culture. In M.H. Bornstein (Ed.), *Cultural approaches to parenting.* Hillsdale, NJ: Erlbaum.

Bornstein, M.H., Tal, J., & Tanis-LeMonda, S. (1991). Parenting in cross-cultural perspective: The United States, France, and Japan. In M.H. Bornstein (Ed.), *Cultural approaches to parenting.* Hillsdale, NJ: Erlbaum.

Cartledge, G., Frew, T.W., & Zaharias, J. (1985). Social skill needs of mainstreamed students: Peer and teacher perceptions. *Learning Disability Quarterly, 8,* 132–140.

Cartledge, G., & Milburn, J.F. (1995). *Teaching social skills to children and youth: Innovative approaches* (3rd ed.). Boston: Allyn & Bacon.

Chin, J.L. (1983). Diagnostic considerations in working with Asian Americans. *American Journal of Orthopsychiatry, 53*(1), 100–109.

Davey, A.G., & Mullin, P.N. (1982). Inter-ethnic friendship in British primary schools. *Educational Research, 24,* 83–92.

Elrich, M. (1994). The stereotype within. *Educational Leadership, 51,* 12–15.

Ewen, R.B. (1988). *An introduction to theories of personality.* Hillsdale, NJ: Erlbaum.

Feng, H., & Cartledge, G. (1996). Social skills assessment of inner city Asian, African, and European American students. *School Psychology Review, 25,* 227–238.

Fordham, S. (1988). Racelessness as a factor in black students' school success: Pragmatic strategy or pyrrhic victory? *Harvard Educational Review, 58,* 54–84.

Gresham, F.M., & Elliott, S.N. (1990). *Social skill rating scale.* Circle Pines, MN: American Guidance Service.

Grossman, H. (1995). *Special education in a diverse society.* Boston: Allyn & Bacon.

Gudykunst, W.B., & Ting-Toomey, S. (1988). *Culture and interpersonal communication.* Newbury Park, CA: Sage.

Hallinan, M.T. (1976). Friendship patterns in open and traditional classrooms. *Sociology of Friendship, 49,* 254–264.

Irvine, J.J. (1990). *Black students and school failure:Policies, practices, and prescriptions.* New York: Greenwood.

Janzen, R. (1994). Melting pot or mosaic? *Educational Leadership, 51,* 9–11.

Kauffman, J.M. (1989). *Characteristics of behavior disorders of children and youth* (5th ed.). Columbus, OH: Merrill.

Keller, H.R. (1988). Children's adaptive behaviors: Measure and source generalizability. *Journal of Psychoeducational Assessment, 6,* 371–389.

Kessen, W. (1976). *Childhood in China.* New Haven, CT: Yale University Press.

Kessen, W. (1991) Commentary: Dynamics of enculturation. In M.H. Bornstein (Ed.), *Cultural approaches to parenting.* Hillsdale, NJ: Erlbaum.

King, S.H. (1993). The limited presence of African-American teachers. *Review of Educational Research, 63*(2), 115–149.

Kohatsu, E.L. (1994, August). *Racial identity attitudes: Implications and applications for Asian Americans.* Paper presented at the annual convention of the American Psychological Association, Los Angeles.

Kozol, J. (1991). *Savage inequalities.* New York: Crown.

Ladson-Billings, G. (1994). What we can learn from multicultural education research. *Educational Leadership, 51,* 22–26.

Los Angeles Unified School District. (1991). *Issues facing the Asian immigrant learner.* Los Angeles: Author.

Ma, H. (1985). Cross-cultural study of the development of law-abiding orientation. *Psychological Reports, 57,* 967–974.

Matute-Bianchi, M.E. (1986). Ethnic identities and patterns of school success and failure among Mexican-descent and Japanese-American students in a California high school: An ethnographic analysis. *American Journal of Education , 95,* 233–255.

McLoyd, V.C. (1990). The impact of economic hardship on black families and children: Psychological distress, parenting, and socioemotional development. *Child Development, 61,* 311–346.

Ogbu, J. (1988). Cultural diversity and human development. In D.T. Slaughter (Ed.), *Black children and poverty: A developmental perspective.* San Francisco: Jossey-Bass.

Papousek, H., & Papousek, M. (1991). Innate and cultural guidance of infants' integrative competencies: China, the United States, and Germany. In M.H. Bornstein (Ed.), *Cultural approaches to parenting.* Hillsdale, NJ: Erlbaum.

Patterson, G.R. (1982). *A social learning approach to family intervention: Vol. 3. Coercive family process.* Eugene, OR: Castalia.

Patterson, G.R. (1986). Performance models for antisocial boys. *American Psychologist, 41,* 432–444.

Peoples, J., & Bailey, G. (1991). *Humanity: An introduction to cultural anthropology* (2nd ed.). St. Paul, MN: West.

Philips, S.V. (1972). Participant structures and communicative competence: Warm Springs children in community and classroom. In C.B. Cazden, V.P. John, & D. Hymes (Eds.), *Functions of language in the classroom.* New York: Teachers College Press.

Phinney, J.S. (1990). Ethnic identity in adolescents and adults: Review of research. *Psychological Bulletin, 108,* 499–514.

Reese, L.E., & Vera, E.M. (1994, August). *Ethnic identity development in urban African American preadolescents.* Paper presented at the annual convention of the American Psychological Association, Los Angeles.

Robinson, J.A. (1988). "What we've got here is a failure to communicate": The cultural context of meaning. In J. Valsiner (Ed.), *Child development within culturally structured environments.* Norwood, NJ: Ablex.

Sapon-Shevin, M. (1980). Teaching cooperation in early childhood settings. In G. Cartledge & J.F. Milburn (Eds.), *Teaching social skills to children: Innovative approaches* (3rd ed.). Elmsford, NY: Pergamon.

Schneider, B.H. (1993). *Children's social competence in context: The contributions of family, school, and culture.* Oxford, England: Pergamon.

Smith, E.J. (1991). Ethnic identity development: Toward the development of a theory within the context of majority/minority status. *Journal of Counseling and Development, 70,* 181–188.

Sue, D.W. (1981). *Counseling the culturally different: Theory and practice.* New York: Wiley.

Sue, D.W., Hu, L., & Kwon, J.H. (1991). Asian-American assertion: A social learning analysis of cultural differences. *Journal of Counseling Psychology, 38,* 63–79.

Super, C.M., & Harkness, S. (1982). The development of affect in infancy and early childhood. In D.A. Wagner & H.W. Stevenson (Eds.), *Cultural perspectives on child development.* San Francisco: Freeman.

Trimble, J.E. (in press). Toward an understanding of ethnicity, ethnic identity and their relationship with drug use research. In G.J. Botvin, S. Schinke, & M. Orlandi (Eds.), *Drug abuse prevention with multi-ethnic youth.* Newbury Park, CA: Sage.

Valsiner, J. (1989). *Human development and culture: The social nature of personality and its study.* Lexington, MA: Lexington Books.

Wagner, D.A., & Stevenson, H.W. (1982). Preface. In D.A. Wagner & H.W. Stevenson (Eds.), *Cultural perspectives on child development.* San Francisco: Freeman.

Weinstein, C.S., & Pinciotti, P. (1988). Changing a schoolyard: Intentions, design decisions, and behavioral outcomes. *Environment and Behavior, 20,* 345–371.

Wells, E.A., Morrison, D.M., Gillmore, M.R., Catalano, R.F., Iritani, B., & Hawkins, J.D. (1992). Race differences in antisocial behaviors and attitudes and early initiation of substance use. *Journal of Drug Education, 22,* 115–130.

Whalen, C.K. (1989). Attention deficit and hyperactivity disorders. In T.H. Ollendick & M. Hersen (Eds.), *Handbook of child psychopathology* (2nd ed.). New York: Plenum.

Wiig, E. (1982). *Let's talk: Developing prosocial communications skills.* Columbus, OH: Merrill.

Winegar, L.T. (1988). Children's emerging understanding of social events: Co-construction and social process. In J. Valsiner (Ed.), *Child development within culturally structured environments: Social co-construction and environmental guidance in development* (Vol. 2). Norwood, NJ: Ablex.

CHAPTER 2

A Model for Teaching Social Skills

GWENDOLYN CARTLEDGE
AND JOANNE FELLOWS MILBURN

Instruction in social skills is very similar to instruction in academic or other nonacademic behaviors. The learner needs to know what the skill is, how to perform and practice it, and how to apply it continuously, as needed, in other settings and at other times. Assessment of needs and evaluation of skill acquisition are also integral parts of good instructional programs. Effective and viable strategies for social skill teaching have been developed. For the most part, these strategies have been validated empirically and show promise for application in schools and other settings. The purpose of this chapter is to present established procedures for selecting, assessing, teaching, and maintaining social skills in children and youth. The instructional models are drawn from the literature on social modeling, behavioral technology, and cognitive behavior modification. We also include a section on cooperative learning approaches, which, with their potential for creating more inclusive environments, are particularly well suited to culturally diverse populations. This chapter presents instructional approaches in generic form. Applications of the approaches to specific populations are discussed in subsequent chapters.

Definition and Selection of Skills

Before we can teach social skills, we need to define the desired behaviors and choose which ones we will teach. Although definitions of social skills vary, several elements are present in most definitions. These include (a) social skills seen as acceptable, learned behaviors that enable one to interact with others in ways that elicit positive responses and minimize negative responses from others; (b) social skills as instrumental, goal-directed behaviors; (c) social skills as situation specific and varying with social context; and (d) social skills as involving both specific, observable behaviors and nonobservable cognitive and affective elements. The complexities of the definitions reflect the great variability in social conditions and corresponding behavioral demands. The various "audiences" with whom a child relates (e.g., parents, peers, teachers, relatives, neighbors) may all have differing norms and expectations concerning social behaviors. Social skills identified as necessary or desirable for children vary according to age and developmental level, social situation, and cultural milieu (Cartledge & Milburn, 1995).

Developmental considerations are important because children reach certain personal-social milestones in fairly prescribed stages. In moral development, for instance, children typically move first through largely egocentric, authority-governed phases to levels where they are able to engage in role taking and decision making on the basis of others' interests as well as their own desires. At the lower developmental levels, social skill instruction might appropriately focus on rule-governed play skills; for youngsters at higher developmental levels, play-based instruction might build upon the lower-level skills (e.g., playing by the rules) but also emphasize higher-level cognitive and affective dimensions (e.g., fairness and mutually beneficial cooperative structures).

Related to developmental stages are age expectations. Social skills indicative of competence are not always the same for children and for adults. Markers of assertion in adults (e.g., eye contact and duration of speech) may have different counterparts in children (e.g., smiles and lively speech; Weist & Ollendick, 1991). Certain adult behaviors would not be functional for children.

Another important consideration in targeting behaviors for instruction is to choose behaviors that will be valued and reinforced by the child's peers. Peer relationships are among the most important in a child's life, and they contribute significantly to social learning. Unpopular children are likely to be shunned by peers, with the result that they lose opportunities to learn from social experiences. Popular children tend to be distinguished by altruism, participation in play activities, humor, social communication skills, and academic capability. The strongest correlate to peer rejection appears to be aggression; however, not all aggressive children are rejected, and absence of problem behaviors does not emerge as a salient guiding principle in children's selection of friends (Cartledge, Frew, & Zaharias, 1985; Foster, Delawyer, Guevremont, 1986).

Peer-valued behaviors are not easily identified. Behaviors accepted in popular children, for example, are less well received when displayed by unpopular children (Hymel, Wagner, & Butler, 1990). This finding points to the durability of negative or initial perceptions, which persist even after the offending or maladaptive behaviors have been remedied. An obvious implication is the need to structure more receptive peer environments by attempting to identify a different and more compassionate cohort for peer interactions, targeting the group for interventions on peer acceptance, including the peer group in social skill instruction that involves giving mutual rewards for positive interactions, and creating cooperative classroom environments where positive interactions are taught and maintained by peers. LaGreca and Santogrossi (1980) have identified a set of behaviors that relate to peer acceptance and that lend themselves to social skill instruction. These behaviors include smiling, greeting others, joining ongoing peer activities, extending invitations to others, conversing, sharing and cooperating, complimenting others, maintaining physical appearance and grooming, and using play skills.

Situation specificity is an important concept in skill selection because actions appropriate in one setting may be inappropriate in another. The competent child is able to analyze the social situation and select responses according to situational demands. Thus, a child learning to make assertive statements in response to conflict must learn to identify appropriate times to make such statements and to differentiate between assertion with peers and with authority figures. These considerations, which relate to social perception, should be incorporated into the selection and teaching of all social skills. Also relevant is the extent to which learners or their significant others subscribe to or accept the desired behaviors. For instance, a learner who refuses to believe in alternatives to aggression, such as assertive statements, is unlikely to employ them under real-life conditions and will persist in unproductive responses to conflict. Likewise, if the significant people in the child's life (e.g., peers, parents, teachers) continue to prefer aggressive over assertive options, they are unlikely to reinforce the newly taught behaviors. Reinforcement also is unlikely if others in the community value the newly taught behaviors but judge the child's performance as inadequate. Such issues pertain to social validity. They imply a need to teach behaviors that will be valued and validated by the direct consumer (learner) and indirect consumers (significant others) as well as a need to develop skills to an acceptable level of competence. In some cases it may be necessary to alter destructive belief systems held by learners and their close associates.

As stated as the thesis of this book, cultural differences are extremely important factors in the targeting of social skills for assessment and instruction. Kauffman (1993) asserts that there is no culture-free behavior. Cross-cultural studies repeatedly have shown differences in children's social behaviors, particularly between children from Eastern and Western or from collectivistic and individualistic societies (Schneider, 1993). Consider, for instance, body language: People from different cultures stand at different distances when engaged in conversation. Different U.S. subcultures regard expressions of aggression or tender emotions differently. Gender-related differences in expression of feeling are the subject of much discussion. According to certain studies, for example, boys respond to conflict in more physically aggressive ways (Fabes & Eisenberg, 1992), and girls tend to place more emphasis on interpersonal relationships (Crombie, 1988). Gender differences are affected by factors such as cultural norms and socioeconomic status as well as by the continually evolving roles of males and females in the larger society.

With the aforementioned considerations in mind, educators can draw on various social skill inventories and curricula in targeting skills for assessment and instruction. Stephens (1992) has developed a social skills inventory and curriculum on which an assessment instrument is also built (Stephens & Arnold, 1992). Behaviors are grouped into four major categories (environmental, interpersonal, self-related, and task-related), which are further analyzed into 30 subcategories and 136 specific skills. Walker, McConnell, Holmes, Todis, Walker, and Golden (1983) provide a list of skills and a curriculum for elementary children with mild to moderate disabilities. They categorize 28 social skills into classroom skills, basic interaction, getting along, making friends, and coping skills. A skills listing and curriculum for secondary learners developed by Goldstein, Sprafkin, Gershaw, and Klein (1980) includes 49 behaviors in the categories of beginning social skills, advanced social skills, skills for dealing with feelings, skill alternatives to aggression, skills for dealing with stress, and planning skills. Goldstein (1988) has since expanded this instructional program into the Prepare Curriculum.

Although inventories and taxonomies of social skills can provide a useful point of departure, children are often identified as needing social skills instruction because of specific deficits in positive social behaviors or excesses in problem behaviors. For that reason it is important to be able to individualize social skill instruction and target behaviors that are specific to a particular child's needs. Individualized instruction involves identifying positive behaviors that are opposite to or incompatible with problem behaviors and stating the positive behaviors as behavioral objectives, as in Table 1.

Social behaviors are often stated in global terms such as "be polite" or "be respectful." To be instructionally relevant, these concepts need to be analyzed into observable behaviors and communicated clearly to the learner and to others. For example, when being respectful is the object, the teacher may intend for the youngster to make eye contact, listen without arguing, maintain pleasant affect, speak with appropriate voice tone, use courteous words, and so forth. Most social behaviors are actually complex sets of subskills that vary according to social context and other factors discussed previously.

Assessment of Skills

Though time-consuming, social skill assessment is important for several reasons. First, assessment provides a basis for measuring the impact of social skill teaching on behavior. Second, assessment gives direction for choosing methods of intervention. A problem behavior may exist because the desired behavior is not known, because there is insufficient reinforcement to encourage the desired behavior, or because the environment provides reinforcement for the undesired behavior (Mager & Pipe, 1970). Thus, the teacher or clinician must determine whether the problem is one of skill deficit or motivation and therefore whether intervention involves mainly teaching the

Table 1
Problems and Related Social Skills

Problems	Social Skills
The child calls others by uncomplimentary names.	The child makes positive remarks to others.
The child frequently interrupts the conversation of others.	The child waits for pauses in the conversation before speaking.
The child makes negative statements about his or her ability.	The child identifies something he or she does well.
The child cheats when playing a game with peers.	The child plays games according to rules.
The child throws tantrums when teased by peers.	The child responds to teasing by ignoring or some other appropriate responses.
The child laughs at or ignores individuals in need of help.	The child assists individuals in need of help.

Note. From *Teaching social skills to children and youth: Innovative approaches* (3rd ed., p. 30) by G. Cartledge & J. F. Milburn, 1995, Boston: Allyn & Bacon. Copyright 1995 by Allyn & Bacon. Reprinted by permission.

skill or restructuring the environment to create incentives for the desired behaviors.

For culturally diverse populations, assessment considerations are complicated by the issue of differences versus deficits. A child socialized in culturally specific ways may be socially competent in the home environment but may evidence differences when measured against the behavioral standards and norms of another culture. Depending on the nature of the child's behaviors, the differences may be overlooked, the child may need to learn to switch behaviors according to cultural and situational demands, or—if the behavior is dysfunctional or self-destructive—the child may need instruction in replacing inappropriate actions with more productive and self-enhancing ones.

Several problems are associated with social skill assessment. First, because social behaviors are situation specific, a child may display a given behavior in one situation and not in another, and with some people and not with others. A behavior considered a social skill in one situation may not be so regarded in another. Also, when behaviors are rated, reliability among different respondents may be problematic. Achenbach, McConaughy, and Howell (1987) note little agreement between researchers and parents, between parents and teachers, and between adults and children in their ratings of subjects on social behavior. Different people may arrive at different evaluations, making it difficult to determine when a behavior needs to be taught or when a taught behavior has been mastered. The child's developmental level needs to be considered during assessment. An adolescent's conversation skills, for example, are expected to be more extensive and complex than those of a primary-aged child. The presence of a disability also may affect skill expectations.

The primary methods of social skill assessment include direct observation, analogue situations using role-playing scenarios, and a variety of paper-and-pencil measures such as questionnaires or rating scales, self-report measures, and sociometric procedures. For people working with children in applied settings such as schools, the extensive and complicated procedures that researchers use to obtain reliable and valid data may not be necessary or even feasible. Some practical assessment methods are outlined in this chapter. Cartledge and Milburn (1995) offer a more detailed discussion of social skill assessment procedures in *Teaching Social Skills to Children and Youth.*

Checklists and Rating Scales

Behavior checklists offer certain advantages: They are simple to administer and analyze, and they can be used for comparison of assessments by several informants. To be most useful, a rating scale should have items that are clearly defined and thus have the same meaning for all raters, should be descriptive rather than inferential, should be relatively simple and quick to complete, should have established reliability and validity, and should take age and sex differences into account (Rie & Friedman, 1978). Many checklists and rating scales exist. Some are informal instruments designed to accompany curriculum programs; an example is the Social Behavior Assessment (SBA; Stephens & Arnold, 1992), which relates to Social Skills in the Classroom (Stephens, 1992). Most are formal or standardized measures such as the Matson Evaluation of Social Skills with Youngsters (MESSY; Matson, Rotatori, & Helsel, 1983) or the Social Skills Rating System (SSRS; Gresham & Elliott, 1990). The SSRS assesses social skills and problem behaviors from preschool through high school, provides for cross-informant (teacher, parent, self—above third grade) comparisons, and includes normative data according to age, gender, and disability.

As adults closely associated with the target child, teachers and parents often are called upon to complete behavioral checklists or rating scales. Teachers have the opportunity to make comparative evaluations, and their assessments have been found to compare favorably with other measures of social behavior (Walker, Severson, Stiller, Williams, Haring, Shinn, & Todis, 1988). Parent reports tend not to correlate highly with other assessments, perhaps because of situation specificity, but their perceptions provide information useful for instructional programming and allow for comparisons across respondents.

Results of research with parents and teachers point to racial or cultural differences in the use of checklists for social skill assessments. Keller (1988), for example, found that parents' and teachers' social skill ratings of 7-year-old children correlated more closely for White children than for Hispanic or African American children. Other studies (Elliott, Barnard, & Gresham, 1989; Powless & Elliott, 1993) revealed low correlation between teacher and parent ratings of culturally different populations. In the Powless and Elliott study, greater agreement was obtained between parents and teachers of Native American children where five out of six teachers were Native American than for European American Head Start children where all teachers were European American. Elliott et al. observed Black parents of preschool children to rate their children lower in social skills than did White parents. The role of socioeconomics in these findings is not clear, but some racial or cultural factors affecting the perception of social behaviors are indicated.

Self-assessment may be a measure of social self-efficacy, indicating the degree of confidence children feel in certain social situations.

This confidence may be based on actual or perceived previous successes or failures experienced under these conditions or on specific or general feedback children receive on their behavior. Social confidence bolsters overall social competence, assuring one of the ability to engage in a variety of social situations, including novel ones. Self-assessment may be quite valuable for instructional purposes as well. For example, children convinced their task-related skills are adequate when there is much evidence to the contrary may need to have their misperceptions corrected. Much attention is given in the research literature to racial or ethnic self-perceptions relative to self-esteem or self-concept, but little is said about children's evaluations of their own social skills.

Sociometrics

Assessment measures to be used by peers, usually in the form of sociometric techniques, are another source of data on social skills. Peer assessments have proven valuable for identifying and predicting social maladjustment as well as for measuring changes in peer acceptance that result from social skill training. Sociometric assessments generally require young people to rate their peers on acceptance or nonacceptance, responding by such means as completing paper-and-pencil questionnaires, participating in interviews, pointing to pictures, or attaching sad, neutral, or happy faces to pictures of peers. The most common assessment procedures include nominations and ratings. The nomination technique requires youngsters to select peers whom they like the most or the least. Nominations are useful for determining peer relationships and identifying youngsters with the greatest positive or negative impact on their peers.

Rating scales are easier to administer. A typical scale is a class roster on which each name is followed by a 5-point Likert scale. Each youngster rates every other youngster on this scale, according to the degree of likability. The roster technique makes it more probable that each child will be evaluated—in contrast to nominations, in which children can be left out—and makes the child's status with each group member more evident. Sociometric procedures are useful in classifying students (e.g., as popular, neglected, or rejected) but they fail to identify individual assets or deficits that should be targeted for intervention.

The social skills children value in their peers often differ some-what from those valued by teachers. Cartledge et al. (1985), for example, found that children selected friends on the basis of play and social communication skills. Specifically, these youngsters indicated that they liked other children who had a sense of humor; they partic-ularly selected other children who had good play skills. Teachers, on the other hand, placed more importance on academic-related behav-iors such as staying on task. Because teachers and students stress dif-ferent sets of behaviors, their assessments would not invalidate each other, but the differences do point to the need for a multimethod assessment to get a balanced picture of an individual's or a group's social skills. Youngsters who have good peer-based skills but tend not to have good task-related skills, for example, would probably receive poor social skill ratings from teachers; the reverse might also be true.

Interviews

Interviews with parents and other knowledgeable informants can provide information about skill deficits and about situations in which particular behaviors are displayed or are lacking. Such interviews can be most productive, and the resulting data most accurate, if they are somewhat standardized and oriented toward gathering specific information. Gresham and Davis (1988), for example, present a three-phase, multistep behavioral model for conducting interviews with parents and teachers to determine children's social skill needs. The phases entail gathering information, devising an intervention plan, and evaluating treatment effects.

Interviews can be conducted with children old enough and ver-bal enough to provide self-reports about their own social behavior and their own strengths and deficits in dealing with others. An inter-viewer may obtain useful information by observing how the child attends and communicates his or her feelings. Structured interviews with instruments such as the Diagnostic Interview Schedule for Children (DISC; Costello, Edelbrock, & Costello, 1985) are con-sidered a more reliable source of interview information (Witt, Cavell, Heffer, Carey, & Martens, 1988). Although the interview is perhaps one of the most easily available and convenient places to start gathering assessment information, it needs to be combined with other assessment procedures.

Direct Observation

Observation in the natural environment can yield information about children's social skills and can be helpful in the evaluation of interventions. Additionally, observational data can confirm or call into question assessment profiles derived from other informants and by other methods. Because social behaviors are situation specific, behavior should be observed under more than one condition and, ideally, by more than one observer. The observation process may have a "reactive" effect and produce changes in the child's behavior; this effect is minimized if observation can continue over a period of time.

Observational data can vary from anecdotal narrative recording to systematic counts of specific occurrences of pinpointed behaviors. Narrative reporting has the value of providing information about events preceding and following a behavior and can thus contribute to hypotheses about conditions that impede or facilitate social behaviors. More systematic observational techniques can include recording each occurrence of the specified behavior (frequency or event recording), recording how long a behavior lasts (duration recording), and recording occurrences of a behavior during specific time intervals (time sampling). Counting events is most useful with discrete social behaviors like making positive remarks or complying with requests. Duration recording is useful with behaviors that extend over time—for example, engaging in play with peers.

For research purposes, observation requires interobserver reliability and training of observers to produce a high degree of agreement. Compiling observed behaviors into a checklist or a set of observation codes is a method frequently used to enhance agreement among observers as well as to condense the vast amount of observational data that is available in any social situation. In applied settings, however, the data being sought through observation may not require this degree of reliability; rather, the practitioner needs to use simple and efficient recording systems. To record the inappropriate verbalizations of one student, for example, a teacher may simply transfer paper clips from one pocket to another each time the undesired behavior occurs.

Observation is limited as an assessment technique in that it may not readily reveal behaviors that occur only infrequently. Because the natural environment does not always provide opportunities to observe specific behaviors of interest, Stephens (1992) suggests arranging an event that would facilitate the occurrence of targeted behaviors. For example, to observe a child's sharing behavior in a play situation with other children, one might provide a minimum of play materials, thus forcing sharing to occur; one might observe how a child handles winning or losing by setting up a competitive game. An example of an instrument developed to assess classroom social skills is the Contrived Test of Social Skills (CTSS; Shapiro, Gilbert, Friedman, & Steiner, 1985).

Analogue Measures

Other means of assessing low-frequency or more complex social behaviors use situations analogous to real-world situations, usually in the form of role-play scenarios. Role-play assessments usually involve scripts with open-ended sections where young people can respond to audio- or videotaped situations that require responses. Following is an example of a scripted scenario (Edelson & Rose, 1978):

> Your friend got a B on a book report. You got a lower grade. Your friend comes up to you and says, "I got a B on my book report. The teacher said I did a good job."
>
> Now I'll play your friend who says this to you and you act towards me just like you would towards a friend who said this to you, Okay? I'll read the situation once more, then I'll act like your friend. Ready? (Reread situation once.)

Another analogue instrument is the Children's Interpersonal Behavior Test (CIBT; Van Hasselt, Hersen, & Bellack, 1981). Role-play measures have been used extensively in research on social skills, and Hughes, Boodoo, Alcala, Maggio, Moore, and Villapando (1989) suggest that their correspondence with real-life situations can be enhanced considerably if peers are used to deliver prompts and criterion measures are based on ratings from socially competent peers.

Assessment is an important component of social skill instruction. Few if any of the methods described here should be considered sufficient by themselves to give a complete and accurate picture of a child's social behavior; this is particularly true if issues like cultural diversity or class placement are involved.

Skill Instruction

Though social skill teaching may take various forms, two major approaches are common: (a) skills training, characterized by direct instruction, modeling, rehearsal, and behavior generalization, and (b) a cognitive/affective approach where the primary goal is to teach individuals to think through and resolve interpersonal conflicts (Shure, 1992; Spivack & Shure, 1974). A related approach involves cooperative learning activities that might be incorporated into a total social skill program. The following sections describe these approaches for teaching social skills.

Skill Training

The first step in skill training is to present the skill and help the learner understand its purpose and inherent value. Youngsters with skill deficits often persist in destructive or ineffective behaviors because they have limited behavioral repertoires or they are unaware of the benefits of alternative behaviors. The trainer can develop a rationale for learning the skill by various means, such as discussing previous situations where the learner needed the skill or presenting the experiences of others through scripts, books, simple stories, films, and so forth. Visual presentations are especially advantageous because they can be quite relevant, but their use avoids the potentially embarrassing highlighting of personal situations. Cartledge and Kleefeld (1991, 1994), for example, in their curriculum for primary- and intermediate-aged children, employ simple stories, puppet plays, and folktales to set the stage for social skill instruction. One story in the primary curriculum uses personified animal characters to demonstrate the advantages of systematic ignoring over counteraggression in eliminating taunting from others. Along the same lines, Hammond (1991) presents videotaped scenes for adolescents.

The next step, and a major focus of social skill instruction, is modeling, showing the learner how a behavior is performed. The learner's receptivity to and understanding of the modeling depend on several factors. First is the vehicle for modeling. This can be as varied as adults, peers, puppets, and books, all of which may be effective with different target populations. Puppets are particularly useful in maintaining the attention of young children. Models need to be socially competent people to whom the learners can relate. Peer models are especially useful for intermediate-aged children and adolescents. Live and media models have distinct advantages and disadvantages. Media models (videotapes, for example) allow for a variety of models under varying conditions with reinforcing consequences for the modeled behavior. These vehicles permit repeated viewings accompanied by discussions of the situation and the modeled behaviors. Live models, on the other hand, offer more versatility in the modeling situation, enabling learners to observe more varied, more extensive, and perhaps more realistic enactments.

The trainer must ensure that the learner attends to and understands the main aspects of the modeling. Discussing the modeled behavior and connecting specific acts with related consequences is one way to address this issue. The learner may be asked to demonstrate understanding by describing and explaining the steps of the modeling. Initially, it is important to model positive examples where the actors are rewarded for their socially appropriate actions. Because socially unskilled youngsters are inclined to endorse antisocial responses to problem situations or to overgeneralize, negative examples—which may be useful in making finer discriminations about desired behavior—should be delayed until the learner has demonstrated a working knowledge of the skill through a few guided practice and role-playing exercises.

Once the target behavior has been modeled, the next step is to provide practice through role-playing. The trainer prepares the learner by specifying the components of the desired behavior and giving guidelines for the desired response. For example, the following list details components of the skill of ignoring taunting behavior:

1. Don't look at the person.
2. Don't talk to the person.
3. Walk away if possible.
4. Think about the good things that will happen
   to you if you avoid arguing with this person.

In various scenarios, the learner practices with a partner or partners the skills to be learned. The effectiveness of role-playing practice depends on how closely the situations approximate real-life conditions and resemble those typically encountered by the learner. Ideally, the role-play partners should be varied and representative of people in the learner's actual environment.

Feedback, the next step in the training sequence, means giving learners information in positive, nonpunitive ways, telling them exactly what they are doing correctly or incorrectly and how to improve their performance. Whether positive or corrective, feedback should be direct and specific—for example, "You did a good job of ignoring Johnny's teasing by walking away without calling him a name or crying" or "That probably is not a good way to get Johnny to stop calling you names. It might be easier if you simply walked away."

Reinforcement is an important feature of feedback and social skill instruction. Once the skills have been taught, reinforcing contingencies can be applied for the purpose of refining or increasing the desired behaviors. Reinforcement may take the form of praise or of more tangible rewards, such as tokens to be exchanged for backup rewards, depending on the learner's developmental level and reinforcement needs. For children with behavior disorders such as defiance or withdrawal, it may be necessary to implement dual reward systems, with one type of reward for simple participation and other rewards for accurate responses.

An important aspect of feedback is self-evaluation, in which learners rate their own performance and make suggestions for improvement. The use of audio- or videotapes allows learners to perceive themselves somewhat more objectively; this technique may be especially effective with the child who has difficulty accepting feedback from other sources. Because children may lose sight of the intended goals of role-playing, the trainer may need to guide their thinking through a series of questions, helping them determine whether the desired solutions were obtained and identify reasons for the observed outcomes. As part of the self-evaluation process, Broome and White (1995) recommend placing a video recorder at a wide angle and taping throughout the school day. Students could thus analyze the antecedents and consequences of their behaviors, self-monitor by tallying adaptive and maladaptive responses, and analyze the nature and effects of their affective and nonverbal behaviors. Broome and White also suggest having peers evaluate videotaped role-plays according to clearly established guidelines.

The final step in the skill training sequence is application, or instruction for behavioral generalization. Throughout training, particularly when some mastery is demonstrated, the learner is asked to apply the behavior in real-life situations. This request can take the form of assigned homework, with specific instructions and directions to report back to the trainer. An important consideration in applying newly acquired skills in real-world settings is knowing when and with whom to apply them. Discussions that accompany role-playing should help the learner make discriminations related to the appropriateness of specific behaviors in certain settings and with certain people. It would not be desirable, for example, for a child to try out newly learned conversational skills during study time in the library or to apply the same friendship-making skills with both adults and peers. Problems associated with real-life applications can be forestalled if the trainer takes the following steps: (a) Make sure that practice will result in rewarding consequences; (b) When possible, determine the assignment in conjunction with the learner; (c) Define goals clearly and check that the learner understands them; and (d) Design assignments that closely match behaviors taught in training. Training for generalization will receive more attention later in this chapter. Some examples of curriculum programs using this model are Cartledge and Kleefeld (1991, 1994), McGinnis and Goldstein (1984), and Stephens (1992) for elementary students and Goldstein (1988) for adolescents. An annotated listing of additional programs and related materials is provided by Cartledge and Milburn (1995) in the appendix of their text *Teaching Social Skills to Children and Youth*.

Affective and Cognitive Interventions

Cognitive and affective approaches are closely related because cognition and emotion are not easily separated, and most interventions are geared toward helping young people make connections between thoughts, feelings, and behaviors.

Affective Methods

Affective methods approach social skill development primarily through feelings. Emphasis is on identifying and exploring feelings within oneself and in others. Learners are encouraged to think positively about themselves and others and to behave accordingly. Initial instruction with very young children usually centers on the basic emotions of happiness, sadness, anger, and fear. Children are taught to read and label facial expressions and gestures in others and to identify similar feelings and responses in themselves. As the child develops, the emotions to be taught and the affective understandings to be acquired increase in sophistication and complexity. A common approach is to present visual stimuli such as pictures, films, tapes, and real-life enactments to develop the ability to discriminate among emotions. Children also are expected to relate various feelings to themselves and to accept these feelings as normal aspects of the human experience. In addition to reading and identifying emotions, other related skills to be developed include (a) identifying the antecedent events causing the emotions, (b) identifying the behaviors resulting from the emotions, and (c) constructively directing one's behavior while experiencing the emotions.

To be most effective, understandings developed under training conditions needs to be applied to daily, naturally occurring situations. Learners need prompting to identify their own or others' emotional states and the overt behaviors that might be warranted. Following a competitive game, for instance, the teacher might ask, "Roxanne, you and your team won the kickball game. How does that make you feel? How do you think the other members of your team feel? How do you think the other team feels? Why is it a good idea to help them to feel better? Can you think of something you might say to help them to feel better about the game?" Beyond the emotional dimension, affective education is geared toward helping young people to understand and appreciate others, to realize their own personal values, and to establish personal moral codes consistent with the well-being of the larger society. Affective programs tend to be characterized by a rather open structure, with trainers expected to be facilitators, that is, providing stimuli, clarifying, and giving support. Communication and language are stressed. The instructional format usually includes circle groupings wherein each member is expected to contribute, encouraged by the accepting, nonjudgmental atmosphere that has been cultivated. One widely used affective curriculum program is Developing Understanding of Self and Others (DUSO; Dinkmeyer, 1982).

Cognitive Methods

The teaching of problem-solving skills forms the basis for most cognitively oriented social skill instruction. The primary goal is to teach people how to think through and resolve interpersonal conflicts using a four-step process: (a) identifying and defining the problem, (b) generating a variety of solutions, (c) identifying potential consequences, and (c) implementing and evaluating a solution (Shure, 1992; Spivack & Shure, 1974). Problem identification is not always simple, especially for youngsters who tend to misperceive social situations. When disruptive events occur, children often see themselves as victims, focusing mainly on the inappropriate behavior of others rather than becoming aware of their own roles in problem situations. For example, a child may focus on the physical aggression of a peer rather than recognize his or her own verbal aggression and the need to learn more constructive ways to respond to the provocation of others. Through a series of questions and perhaps with the aid of videotapes, the trainer helps the learner to identify and define the problem.

Following problem identification, the next step is to specify behaviors that might be feasible responses to the problem situation. Initially, the learner is encouraged to list as many alternative behaviors as possible, without regard to their adaptive nature. Thus, antisocial as well as socially appropriate alternatives may be listed, with judgment deferred until the next step. In reacting to peer teasing, for example, a child may suggest calling the teaser a name in return, as well as walking away or making a calm but assertive statement. However, caution needs to be exercised in this regard: Some research shows that with aggression-prone populations, aggressive behaviors tend to increase proportionately with the number of antisocial options generated (Olexa & Forman, 1984; Weissberg et al., 1981). It is also recommended that emphasis be on the quality rather than on the quantity of alternatives generated (Amish, Gesten, Smith, Clark, & Stark, 1988; Hopper & Kirschenbaum, 1979; Neel, Jenkins, & Meadows, 1990) and that students acquire strategies for successful verbal mediation of problem social situations (Neel et al.).

In the next step, the learner is helped to match alternative behaviors with possible consequences and to decide on the best course of action. For example, if the trainer points out that responding to teasing with additional name-calling is likely to escalate verbal aggression, the learner may choose walking away or some other more constructive response. Several viable alternatives might be identified and ranked from most through least preferable. Selected behaviors are then modeled by the trainer and practiced by the learner so that the learner knows how the desired skill is to be performed. The learner also is directed to apply the skill under real-life conditions.

After the learner has tried out the behavior in an actual situation, learner and trainer can engage in the final step of evaluation to determine the utility and successful application of the newly acquired behavior. As part of the evaluation process, it is important to differentiate between the appropriateness of the behavior for the problem situation and the learner's skill in performing the desired behavior. A peer-taunting situation, for example, may warrant an assertive response, but the child's delivery of assertive statements may be so inadequate that it fails to have the desired effect. Evaluation not only ascertains success or failure of the application but may reveal a need to identify additional alternatives or simply to improve the child's skill in implementing those previously identified.

Because social problem solving relies heavily on thinking and language skills, young people with language, cognitive, and attentional deficits may require extensive, systematic instruction before cognitive mediation procedures can be taught. In teaching problem-solving skills to preschool children, for example, Spivack and Shure (1974) found that they first needed to teach some basic language skills such as words for consequential thinking *(why, because)* and labels for basic emotions. Other researchers note the importance of teaching children to persist in their problem solving, trying a variety of prosocial solutions to any problem situation (Weissberg, Gesten, Liebenstein, Doherty-Schmid, & Hutton, 1980). Another point of emphasis is the quantity of instruction. Social problem solving is designed to be taught over an extended period, ideally on a daily basis.

Self-instructional training is a related cognitive intervention designed to teach youngsters to restructure their thoughts along more productive and positive lines, with a focus on controlling impulsive or aggressive behaviors. Learners are taught to recognize approaching problem situations, then to stop and problem solve ways to proceed.

Some programs use large colored signs (e.g., Camp & Bash, 1981) to make children stop and think about their plans before dealing with problem situations. Harris (1984), for example, used a large red stop sign in the first step of his instructional sequence. Etscheidt (1991) included physical cues: Before children engaged in verbal aggression, they were to make the self-statement "Don't say it," then to put their fists over their mouths and tuck their hands under their arms before making the self-statement "Don't do it."

Another aspect of cognitive intervention involves teaching young people how thoughts control feelings and subsequent actions. Self-talk can be instrumental in helping to reduce anger and increase self-control. Consider, for example, children who are subjected to peer teasing: The one who says to herself that teasing is awful and that she should not take that kind of behavior is more likely to respond aggressively than the child who tells himself that the teaser is just trying to get attention and he will spoil the person's fun by not talking back. Along the same lines, if the recipient of teasing perceives it to be mean spirited rather than good natured, the response is likely to be negative, possibly precipitating conflict and more negative feelings. The situation is exacerbated if the child sees aggression as a legitimate alternative and an effective means for solving interpersonal problems.

Adults responding to children's interpersonal behavior problems often advise them to ignore the inappropriate behavior of their peers, but they seldom give children cognitive coping strategies for mediating these stressful situations. The child who thinks about how he or she is keeping out of trouble while encountering some provocation is likely to be more successful in self-management than the child in the same situation who is simply admonished not to fight. Cognitive interventions are especially geared for aggressive or impulsive individuals, who need such help to gain the self-control, problem-solving skills, and beliefs that foster more adaptive ways of dealing with problem events.

Hughes and Cavell (1995) cite examples of self-talk instructional strategies developed by Lochman (Lochman, Lampron, Gemmer, & Harris, 1987), intended to curb anger and reduce aggressive behaviors. In one activity, children take turns with puppets receiving and responding to verbal taunts for 20 to 30 seconds. The trainer helps the children explore the emotions likely to be engendered by taunts from others and then guides them in using anger-coping self-statements when taunts are repeated. The group then focuses on the difference in feelings when the self-statements are used and are not used.

Hughes (Hughes & Cavell, 1995) has built on the Lochman model consisting of anger control, problem solving, and goal setting to create the STAR Program (Hughes, 1992), which also includes activities designed to counter inappropriate hostile attributions and to foster self-esteem and warm, caring relationships between trainer and students. Hughes and Cavell assert that such positive relationships are critical to social skill learning, particularly for students who exhibit aggressive behaviors. Additionally, Hughes recommends that social-cognitive training programs provide instruction on the full range of cognitions (i.e., coping skills, irrational beliefs, problem solving, and hostile attributions) and include anger-control training, extensive instruction over several months, contingencies for desired and undesired behaviors, and involvement of the classroom teacher and the parents. Other curriculum programs using a cognitive-social problem-solving model include those of Camp and Bash (1981), Shure (1992), and Weissberg et al. (1980).

Cooperative Learning

Cooperative learning merits special attention in this chapter because it is particularly appropriate for the diverse populations addressed in this book. As noted in chapter 1, African, Hispanic, Asian, and Native Americans all have their cultural roots in collectivistic rather than individualistic societies, and they are likely to do best in cooperative rather than competitive environments. General methods for structuring cooperative learning are discussed here. Application with specific cultural and racial groups will be treated in subsequent chapters.

Cooperative learning focuses on the group rather than the individual. Group members work together for their mutual benefit, supporting and encouraging one another, assuming responsibility for their own and one another's learning, employing group-related social skills such as decision making and trust building, and evaluating the group's academic and social progress (Johnson & Johnson, 1989). Cooperative behaviors are important for both work and school settings. Johnson and Johnson (1987) argue that because cooperative learning activities allow each participant an equal chance to move forward, they may be more motivating than competitive activities. Furthermore, because shared responsibility and good interpersonal relationships are essential in most occupations, teaching students only how to compete does not adequately prepare them for the real world.

The empirical literature documents evidence that cooperative activities contribute to positive peer interactions (Berndt, Perry, & Miller, 1988; Slavin, 1990), acceptance of disabling and racial differences (Goldstein, 1988; Slavin, 1990), and academic achievement (Slavin, 1990). On the basis of his research review, Goldstein observed that the beneficial effects of cooperative learning appear to be greater for minority (African American and Mexican American) than for majority (European American) students.

Cooperative learning involves more than just telling students to work together. There are several distinct cooperative learning models, and students often require direct instruction in engaging in cooperative groups. In the *interdependent group* model, group members must depend on one another to acquire all the information required for a particular learning experience. In what Aronson (1978) calls the Jigsaw Method, each group member becomes responsible for a certain segment of the lesson and becomes the "expert" in order to teach this material to the others. All group members are tested on all the material, and they are evaluated as a group. The teacher may divide into segments a block of subject matter—for instance, the life cycle of a plant, the life of a famous personality, or a social skill such as negotiating a conflict situation with a peer. One student is assigned each segment (e.g., the steps for planting a seed for a particular plant) to research and teach. Members from different teams researching the same topic meet as "expert" groups to discuss their material; they then return to their respective groups to teach the material to their teammates.

Another type of cooperative learning group, called *competitive cooperative groups*, are distinguished by their use of competitive teams. One example is Student Teams—Achievement Divisions (STAD; Slavin, 1978). Students are organized into heterogeneous groups, mixed by race, ability, and gender, to tutor one another on course content. Students are motivated by the knowledge that all students' scores are averaged into a team score. Each individual evaluation, however, is based on the individual's improvement over a previous score. Teams-Games-Tournaments (TGT; DeVries & Slavin, 1978), another competitive cooperative approach, differs from STAD in that students are organized into teams that compete to demonstrate knowledge of the subject matter. Group membership is routinely changed so groups are more comparable and the competition more equal. In classrooms where skill levels are too diverse, Team Assisted Individualization (TAI; Slavin, Leavey, & Madden, 1982) might be employed, with students working in self-selected pairs to practice material.

Johnson and Johnson (1987), in *Learning Together and Alone,* describe procedures for *small group learning,* where heterogeneous groups work together and are evaluated on one learning assignment. Group members may be assigned roles to help the group run more smoothly. Many of these roles—for example, reinforcing desired behaviors—are directly related to the social skills we wish to develop in students.

Several of the references just mentioned are good resources for designing cooperative learning environments in schools. Cartledge and Cochran (1993) point out that cooperative learning skills need to be taught directly, and the skill training model presented earlier in this chapter provides an effective means for such instruction. Specific cooperative group skills such as getting started, asking for help, responding to requests, giving help, and making supportive statements need to be identified, modeled, practiced, and programmed for generalization. The authors used these procedures to develop cooperative group behaviors in elementary-aged students with behavior disorders. Prior to instruction, the researchers simply directed the students to work together and help one another on a math assignment. They observed the students to sit at the same table but to work independently. The children tended to build barriers around their work to hide their papers from classmates, to play and talk about nonacademics, and to ask the teacher for help. If approached for help by a peer, students typically responded by admonishing the peer, "Think for yourself. Don't look at my paper." Following this initial observation, students received direct and systematic instruction in cooperative behaviors; the result was an appreciable increase in cooperative interactions. One group, for example, improved from a mean preinstructional level of .54 cooperative and 4.72 noncooperative responses per minute to 6.2 and 2.6 cooperative and noncooperative behaviors, respectively.

During the course of instruction, the researchers needed to take several important factors into consideration. First, it was necessary to modify the instructional task. For some students, especially those with special needs, it may be too difficult to perform academic tasks at the usual level while simultaneously learning a new set of social behaviors. Instead of using newly taught math skills while developing cooperative learning behaviors, the researchers switched to a review of math computations attractively presented on a game board. This gave the youngsters an opportunity for much-needed practice on critical skills but also freed them to concentrate as needed on the new social skill expectations.

Another important consideration in teaching cooperative behaviors is time. Initially, cooperative group activities should be brief and extended gradually until students acquire the basic social skills needed to participate successfully. Beginning periods might last 5 to 10 minutes for elementary-aged students and no more than 20 minutes for junior high and high school students. Especially at the outset, it might be necessary to stagger cooperative groups so that no two are meeting at the same time and so that the teacher may provide the necessary instruction, modeling, prompting, and reinforcement.

Reinforcement is a third key factor in cooperative learning. Students need to receive reinforcement and learn to give it to others. In teaching social skills, it is crucial to develop consequences that will effectively reinforce the desired cooperative behaviors. Reinforcers may range from social recognition, such as praise, to more tangible rewards, such as stickers or periods for listening to favorite recording artists. Cartledge and Cochran (1993) found stickers very effective with elementary-aged students, but the stickers were gradually faded, and students continued to respond at equal or higher levels after the stickers were discontinued. Learning to support and reinforce group members was an important activity of the cooperative groups. In praising students' academic and social behaviors, the teacher modeled this skill for the students; then the teacher began to prompt and reward students for encouraging one another. Eventually, responsibility for reinforcement was turned over to group members.

To facilitate the independent operation of cooperative groups, as described by Johnson and Johnson (1987), the teacher may train students to assume various roles, such as initiator of positive statements, demonstrator of certain tasks, recorder of peer performance, and so forth. In the Cartledge and Cochran (1993) project, students designated to make positive statements were told they were to provide "build-ups" for the other students. Students fairly proficient in this particular skill were selected first so they could serve as models for others. Subsequently all roles were rotated so that students gained a variety of skills; all students were encouraged to use "build-ups" whenever appropriate.

A final factor for consideration is the use of appropriate games. In cooperative games, the purpose is to overcome some obstacle (such as a time limit) rather than to compete against other players. Cartledge and Cochran (1993) used a circular game board; the goal of the game was to make sure that everyone completed the entire circle on the board. If the time limit was near and one student had not completed the circle, everyone worked to help that student complete it. Cartledge and Cochran offer the following suggestions for cooperative games:

1. Structure games so that players are not eliminated for incorrect responses. Less skilled students require more, not less practice.

2. Teach students how to prompt/instruct peers to respond correctly; the game should not proceed until the target player gives the right answer.

3. Base success upon full participation and accurate responses by all group members.

4. Provide opportunities for unpredictable movements (e.g., backward or additional forward spaces). This may result from landing on a particular space on the game board or drawing a card with such specifications. These elements of surprise help to make the game more enjoyable.

5. Initially, use game boards that are circular, not linear, in format. This eliminates specific beginning and ending points that contribute to the win-lose concept.

6. Base rewards during game on cooperative interactions, not on win-lose behaviors.

7. Provide simple, easy-to-explain directions so that excessive time is not consumed with difficult, lengthy explanations, especially with younger or less able children. (pp. 7–8)

Cooperative games have beneficial effects on social learning. In contrast to some of the negative behaviors elicited in competitive games—for instance, taunting or teasing, grabbing, monopolizing, or using physical force—Sapon-Shevin (1986) argues that cooperative games promote positive social interaction through their emphasis on including others, sharing, touching gently, and talking nicely. She gives the following example of a cooperative game and its application in social skill development:

Nonelimination Musical Chairs (Orlick, 1982)—The object is to keep everyone in the game even though chairs are systematically removed. As in the competitive version, music is played, and more and more chairs are removed each time the music stops. In this game, though, more children have to sit together to keep everyone in the game.

Social Behaviors: Gentle physical contact; sharing, inclusion; group problem solving.

In Nonelimination Musical Chairs, rather than the pushing and exclusionary tactics of traditional Musical Chairs, children must find ways to make room for more and more children. The verbal behavior heard during this game is generally of the form "Come sit on/with me" or "Make room for Johnny."

This game represents an ideal starting point for exploring issues of "limited resources" with children; rather than confirming the "each child must have his own material" notion. Teachers can explore ways in which children can find creative alternatives to exclusion. For example, on the playground, if more than two children want to use the seesaw, how could that be done? (For example, two children on each end; two children count, while two see-saw, then switch places, etc.). (pp. 283–284)

Cooperation and related interpersonal skills do not develop automatically. Indeed, they tend to be thwarted in traditional competitive classroom environments. There is often a need to teach cooperative skills directly and reinforce them through the regular use of cooperative learning activities and games. Cooperative environments appear to be particularly beneficial for minority youth in our society because of their cultural backgrounds and special needs for inclusion.

Skill Generalization and Maintenance

Getting young people to understand and perform newly taught social behaviors appears to be far less challenging than getting them to use these behaviors over time in a variety of settings. Increasingly, researchers are acknowledging the importance of teaching for the long-term, extensive application of these behaviors, recognizing that training for skills that will not be practiced or used is of little or no value. Research indicates that behavior transfer and durability are a function of training and the manipulation of reinforcement variables (e.g., Stokes & Baer, 1977; Stokes & Osnes, 1986, 1988, 1989). The most important considerations relate to settings, trainers, mediators, and reinforcement.

Settings

Social skills taught in one setting will not automatically generalize to other settings, such as from school to home (Wahler, 1969) or from one class to another (Berler, Gross, & Drabman, 1982). One recommendation for encouraging such generalization is to teach social skills in a variety of settings, particularly in the setting where a target behavior is to be exhibited. If the goal is to increase prosocial behaviors in the classroom, for example, then at least some instruction needs to occur in that setting. In teaching restaurant skills to clients with mental retardation, Van Den Pol, Iwata, Ivancic, Page, Neef, and Whitley (1981) provided training in both the classroom and the restaurant to facilitate behavior transfer and maintenance.

It is not always possible to train in the natural environment or to use multiple settings. Other suggestions include "equating stimulus

conditions" (Walker & Buckley, 1974), making the instructional setting approximate real-life conditions as closely as possible. Another
successful approach reported in the research literature entails videotaping the mainstreamed environment, featuring modeling displays
of behaviors appropriate to the setting (Knapczyk, 1988). In these and
other such approaches, learners practice the target behaviors as if they
were in the settings where the behaviors should be applied. A related
technique is the use in training of cues or signs that can be employed
to prompt for the desired behavior in the natural environment. In
the training setting a sign with a small icon could be associated with
each skill taught. The icon signs could then be transferred to classrooms and other locations to remind students of the target behaviors.
For example, a sign reading "Walk Away," illustrated with a walking stick figure, could remind students to walk away from trouble.
A smaller version of the figure could be attached to each student's
notebook, self-monitoring card, wallet, or purse to remind him or
her of this skill in environments outside of school.

Trainers

Because social behaviors can be under the control of more than one
trainer as well as more than one setting, more than one trainer is
recommended for behavior generalization to occur. Often a second
trainer is called for during initial training sessions, especially if a
competent peer is not available to assist with modeling and role-
playing. Significant others in the learner's natural environment (e.g.,
classroom teachers, parents, and peers) are valuable backup trainers.
Classroom teachers play a crucial part in social skill development
because of the extensive time they spend with children, the models
they present, and the control they exercise over children's behaviors.
Classroom teachers need to be instructed in the social skills being
taught, how the target skills are displayed, and how to reinforce those
behaviors. The ability of classroom teachers to function as social skill
trainers has been found to be a determining factor in behavior generalization (Smith, Young, West, Morgan, & Rhode, 1988).

Similar considerations also need to be given to parents. As children's first teachers, parents likewise exert powerful influence on
children's social development. Parents may be unaware of the specific skills their children need in school and may inadvertently be

shaping behaviors that are at cross-purposes with the school's goals. Parents who foster great dependency in their children, for example, may not realize that the ability to work independently is crucial to academic success. Although extensive parental instruction in connection with a social skill program is usually not possible, at the very least, parents should be informed of the skills being taught, the importance of these skills to their children's overall development, and the steps they may take to help their children master these skills. Parent "notes" like those provided in various instructional programs may be useful for this purpose (e.g., Cartledge & Kleefeld, 1991, 1994).

Peers are particularly important because they can take part in the training process and generally exercise considerable mutual influence (Stokes & Baer, 1977; Stokes & Osnes, 1986, 1988). Encouraging results for peer-mediated strategies to develop and reinforce social behaviors are reported in the research literature (Mathur & Rutherford, 1991). One strategy involves including competent peers in the training session to serve not only as models during instruction but also as surrogate trainers and prompts in the natural environment. Middleton and Cartledge (1995) observed competent peers frequently prompting target students in the desired behaviors under regular classroom conditions. Three related models presented by Fowler (1988) involve (a) target students with behavior problems being monitored and rewarded by peers for desired behaviors, (b) target students alternating with competent students to monitor and reward the behaviors of others, and (c) target students being trained to monitor and reward the behaviors of more competent students. Group contingencies have also proven useful in behavior generalization. They typically take the form of reinforcement systems where youngsters work together toward some goal and earn rewards according to established performance standards (Lew & Mesch, 1984; Salend, Whittaker, & Reeder, 1992). These conditions appear to foster positive peer attitudes and the development of appropriate social skills.

Mediators

Linguistic and cognitive processes appear to be useful in effecting behavior maintenance and generalization because they are verbal, rather than visual, and can be transported easily from training to generalization settings (Stokes & Baer, 1977). Language for generalization may reflect either what the youngster will do in a certain situation (e.g., "When I enter the classroom, I will look at the teacher and say, 'Good morning'") or what the youngster did (e.g., "When I went to gym, I looked at the teacher and said, 'Hello, Ms. Jones'"). In the first example, the trainer would have the learner demonstrate during the instructional session the self-talk he or she would use before entering the classroom. After the event, the learner would report to the trainer whether or not he or she performed the skill. Truthful reports of behaviors are shown to have a generalizing effect, causing target behaviors to persist over time (Clark, Caldwell, & Christian, 1979). The problem-solving and self-instructional strategies discussed earlier in this chapter also appear promising for generalization purposes. Park and Gaylord-Ross (1989), for example, found the most lasting effects of training in job-related social communication skills among people who had been taught problem-solving strategies.

Another language-related variable is individual expectations. Bandura (1977) suggests that performance is enhanced by the learner's conviction of his or her ability to perform and achieve the desired results. Bandura and Jourden (1991) found that students persisted longer and performed better when receiving feedback that they were successful than when informed that they were unsuccessful, even though their actual performance might have been better than the feedback indicated. Positive messages that emphasize personal competence may enhance the lasting and varied effects of behavior training.

Reinforcers

Another avenue for programming behavior maintenance and generalization is through manipulation of reinforcement. Trainers can vary the reward schedule, alter the nature of the reward, or change the source of the reward. New behaviors are most effectively learned when reinforcement is continuous or frequent; however, once a skill has been acquired, shifting to a reinforcement schedule of less frequent or intermittent rewards will increase the resistance to extinction. Intermittent and delayed reinforcement schedules can be employed for the purpose of "thinning" the reinforcement (Stokes & Baer, 1977). Reinforcement is systematically faded to the point that the learner's behavior no longer is under direct control of the reward contingencies but has stabilized and become part of the behavioral repertoire. Reinforcement thinning can take various forms. The trainer may gradually reduce the magnitude of the reward so that over time the learner receives fewer and fewer rewards for the same number of responses (e.g., Sullivan & O'Leary, 1990). The frequency of reinforcement may be reduced gradually—for example, from four times an hour to twice an hour and eventually to once every 2 days (e.g., Rhode, Morgan, & Young, 1983). The trainer may delay the reward so that a behavior displayed at a certain time is reinforced only later; the learner feels the need to display the desired behavior on an ongoing basis to receive the reward (Fowler & Baer, 1981). A useful device for the management of reinforcement is the contingency contract, an agreement between learner and trainer that reminds the learner of the behavior to be performed and that allows the learner a positive role in negotiating the conditions of rewards. Over time, as the learner increases in skill, the contract can be renegotiated to alter the amount, frequency, and timing of the rewards, which ultimately can be faded.

The range of reinforcers includes primary rewards, such as food or drink; interim rewards, such as tokens to be exchanged for backup reinforcers; social rewards, such as praise or smiles; and intrinsic reinforcement, where the learner finds performance of the target behavior to be inherently rewarding. For behavior generalization it is important to help learners progress from externally administered to less intrusive, more naturally occurring rewards. In the Rhode et al. (1983) study, for example, the reward system evolved from points through verbal self-evaluations to private self-evaluations. Rhode et al. used another procedure recommended for moving to more natural reinforcement: They paired points with overt self-evaluations and then gradually faded the points and related tangible reinforcers. It is recommended that social reinforcers be exaggerated so students will attend to them, while tangible rewards are gradually faded (Gelfand & Hartmann, 1984).

If newly learned behaviors are to be maintained and generalized, the source of reinforcement must be transferred from the trainer to others in the learner's natural environment. Significant others such as parents or adult caretakers, teachers, peers, siblings, and ultimately the child him- or herself must be prepared to support and reward the new behavior(s). The trainer can enlist the aid of parents and teachers by informing them of the skills being taught and requesting that they reward the child when they observe the target behaviors. Toward this end, the child may be given feedback slips, on which adults in various settings can note appropriate behavioral responses. Peers can also provide effective reinforcement. Not only can other youngsters model and prompt desired behaviors, but the reciprocity implicit in social skills suggests that skill development may expose the learner to a community of natural reinforcers. For example, providing a child who is a social isolate with the skills to make friends may open up new opportunities for positive experiences.

Possibly the most important source of reinforcement is the learner him- or herself. Self-management is a multifaceted process that entails goal setting, self-monitoring, self-evaluation, and self-reinforcement. Goal setting can be a powerful tool to motivate a learner to acquire new behaviors, especially if the goals are realistic and the learner is involved in the selection process. There is some evidence that goal setting alone can bring about a change in behavior (Graham, Harris, & Reid, 1992). Self-monitoring involves observing and recording one's behavior according to some established standard. Using rather simple procedures, children are taught to identify a behavior in specific terms, note when it occurs, and record the occurrence. Consider, for example, a student who tends to leave the classroom or other assigned area without permission. The student might be told that "out of area" behavior involves (a) being in a location other than the one assigned, (b) being in another location without permission, or (c) needing a reminder to return to the assigned area. Each time one of these conditions occurred, the student would note "out of area" on a personal recording form. The next step in the self-monitoring sequence is self-evaluation: The student must determine whether each occurrence of the behavior constituted a violation of the rule (i.e., remaining in the area). Self-evaluation continues as the learner determines whether or not an established standard has been met—for example, fewer than two "out of area" notations for the day. Youngsters who have trouble evaluating their own behaviors accurately may be helped by more precise descriptions of the desired behaviors or by videotaping to see themselves engaged in undesired or desired behaviors under natural conditions.

Self-reinforcement naturally evolves from self-evaluation as the learner rewards him- or herself in some way for meeting established criteria. If the personal record shows fewer than two "out of area" notations, for example, the learner may reward him- or herself with a designated number of points to be exchanged later for some tangible reinforcer, such as time at the listening center. The learner is prompted also to make positive self-statements, including self-congratulation for reaching the day's goal. Over time, backup rewards are faded, as the behavior is maintained solely through positive self-statements and eventually becomes internalized as part of the learner's behavioral repertoire. Systematic instruction in self-management is essential. As part of the learning process, Graham et al. (1992) suggest a gradual transition from collaborative evaluation and reinforcement to total reliance on self-evaluation and self-reinforcement.

Summary

The first step in teaching social skills is to define and identify the skills to be taught. Because social behaviors are complex and opinions vary about which behaviors are valuable or essential, this is not always an easy task. Researchers have developed inventories and taxonomies of social skills around which teaching programs can be built. Even with established curriculum programs, the unique needs of schoolchildren and youth, especially those from culturally diverse backgrounds, often require trainers to individualize the selection by reframing nonproductive behaviors as positively stated social skill objectives.

Assessment of social competence is important for making placement decisions, defining teaching objectives, and evaluating the results of teaching or treatment. Although extensive use of formal assessment procedures is not realistic or practical, the practitioner should be sure to use more than one assessment method, particularly when learners are from racially or ethnically diverse backgrounds and decisions affecting placement are involved. Assessment methods most commonly used in school settings include observation, interviews, rating scales and questionnaires, and sociometric procedures.

Social skill instruction may encompass several components, focusing on observable behaviors, cognition, and emotions. The behavioral methodologies based on modeling and role-playing, probably the most commonly employed teaching techniques, involve skill demonstration, imitation and feedback, practice, and application in real-life situations. Cognitive approaches attempt to develop positive behaviors through improved problem-solving strategies and self-instruction, whereas affective models emphasize the role of emotions.

Behavior maintenance and generalization may be facilitated by programming specific techniques. Varying trainers and training settings is advocated, as well as teaching children to employ different linguistic and thinking styles. Manipulating schedules, forms, and sources of reinforcement can be highly productive. Self-reinforcement, a process of setting goals, then monitoring, evaluating, and rewarding one's behavior, also facilitates behavior maintenance and transfer.

Cooperative learning is a promising approach for the direct and indirect development of social skills. Cooperative learning not only reflects the cultural backgrounds of many minority youth in this country but also provides for more inclusive school environments that facilitate interpersonal interactions, promote social skill development, and contribute to school success.

There is a need for more social skill instruction in applied settings such as schools. The research literature provides ample evidence of the value of the procedures or methods outlined in this chapter. Although they are somewhat varied, they are not incompatible; practitioners are advised to take advantage of their combined benefits.

References

Achenbach, T.M., McConaughy, S.H., & Howell, C.T. (1987). Child/adolescent behavioral and emotional problems: Implications of cross-informant correlations for situational specificity. *Psychological Bulletin, 101*, 213–232.

Amish, P.L., Gesten, E.L., Smith, J.K., Clark, H.B., & Stark, C. (1988). Social problem-solving training for severely emotionally and behaviorally disturbed children. *Behavioral Disorders, 13*, 175–186.

Aronson, E. (1978). *The Jigsaw classroom.* Beverly Hills, CA: Sage.

Bandura, A. (1977). Self-efficacy: Toward a unifying theory of behavioral change. *Psychological Review, 84,* 191–215.

Bandura, A., & Jourden, F.J. (1991). Self-regulatory mechanisms governing the impact of social comparison on complex decision making. *Journal of Personality and Social Psychology, 60,* 941–951.

Berler, E.S., Gross, A.M., & Drabman, R.S. (1982). Social skills training with children: Proceed with caution. *Journal of Applied Behavior Analysis, 15,* 41–53.

Berndt, T.J., Perry, T.B., & Miller, K.E. (1988). Friends' and classmates' interactions on academic tasks. *Journal of Educational Psychology, 80,* 506–513.

Broome, S.A., & White, R.B. (1995). The many uses of videotape in classrooms serving youth with behavioral disorders. *Teaching Exceptional Children, 27,* 10–13.

Camp, B.W., & Bash, M.A.S. (1981). *Think Aloud: Increasing social and cognitive skills—A problem-solving program for children.* Champaign, IL: Research Press.

Cartledge, G., & Cochran, L.L. (1993). Developing cooperative learning behaviors in students with behavior disorders. *Preventing School Failure, 37,* 5–10.

Cartledge, G., Frew, T.W., & Zaharias, J. (1985). Social skill needs of mainstreamed students: Peer and teacher perceptions. *Learning Disability Quarterly, 8,* 132–140.

Cartledge, G., & Kleefeld, J. (1991). *Taking part: Introducing social skills to children.* Circle Pines, MN: American Guidance Service.

Cartledge, G., & Kleefeld, J. (1994). *Working together: Building children's social skills through folk literature.* Circle Pines, MN: American Guidance Service.

Cartledge, G., & Milburn, J.F. (1995). *Teaching social skills to children and youth: Innovative approaches* (3rd ed.). Boston: Allyn & Bacon.

Clark, H.B., Caldwell, C.P., & Christian, W.P. (1979). Classroom training of conversational skills and remote programming for the practice of these skills in another setting. *Child Behavior Therapy, 1,* 139–160.

Costello, E.J., Edelbrock, C.S., & Costello, A.J. (1985). Validity of the NIMH diagnostic interview schedule for children: A comparison between psychiatric and pediatric referrals. *Journal of Abnormal and Child Psychology, 13,* 579–595.

Crombie, G. (1988). Gender differences: Implications for social skills assessment and training. *Journal of Clinical Child Psychology, 17,* 116–120.

DeVries, D.L., & Slavin, R.E. (1978). Teams-Games-Tournaments (TGT): Review of ten classroom experiments. *Journal of Research and Development in Education, 12,* 28–38.

Dinkmeyer, D. (1982). *Developing understanding of self and others (DUSO Program).* Circle Pines, MN: American Guidance Service.

Edelson, J.L., & Rose, S.D. (1978, November). *A behavioral roleplay test for assessing children's social skills.* Paper presented at the meeting of the Association for the Advancement of Behavior Therapy, Chicago.

Elliott, S.N., Barnard, J., & Gresham, F.M. (1989). Preschoolers' social behavior: Teachers' and parents' assessments. *Journal of Psychoeducational Assessment, 7,* 223–234.

Etscheidt, S. (1991). Reducing aggressive behavior and improving self-control: A cognitive-behavioral training program for behaviorally disordered adolescents. *Behavioral Disorders, 16,* 107–115.

Fabes, R.A., & Eisenberg, N. (1992). Young children's coping with interpersonal anger. *Child Development, 63,* 116–128.

Foster, S.L., Delawyer, D.D., & Guevremont, D.C. (1986). A critical incidents analysis of liked and disliked peer behaviors and their situational parameters in childhood and adolescence. *Behavioral Assessment, 8,* 115–133.

Fowler, S. (1988). The effects of peer-mediated interventions on establishing, maintaining, and generalizing children's behavior changes. In R. Horner, G. Dunlap, & R. Koegel (Eds.), *Generalization and maintenance.* Baltimore: Brookes.

Fowler, S., & Baer, D.H. (1981). "Do I have to be good all day?" The timing of delayed reinforcement as a factor in generalization. *Journal of Applied Behavior Analysis, 14,* 13–24.

Gelfand, D.M., & Hartmann, D.P. (1984). *Child behavior analysis and therapy* (2nd ed.). New York: Pergamon.

Goldstein, A.P. (1988). *The Prepare Curriculum: Teaching prosocial competencies.* Champaign, IL: Research Press.

Goldstein, A.P., Sprafkin, R.P., Gershaw, N.J., & Klein, P. (1980). *Skillstreaming the adolescent: A structured learning approach to teaching prosocial behavior.* Champaign, IL: Research Press.

Graham, S., Harris, K.R., & Reid, R. (1992). Developing self-regulated learners. *Focus on Exceptional Children, 24,* 1–16.

Gresham, F.M., & Davis, C.J. (1988). Behavioral interviews with teachers and parents. In E.S. Shapiro & T.R. Kratochwill (Eds.), *Behavioral assessment in schools.* New York: Guilford.

Gresham, F.M., & Elliott, S.N. (1990). *Social skills rating system.* Circle Pines, MN: American Guidance Service.

Hammond, W.R. (1991). *Dealing with anger: A violence prevention program for African American youth.* [Videotape Program]. Champaign, IL: Research Press.

Harris, W.J. (1984). The making better choices program. *Pointer, 29,* 16–19.

Hopper, R.B., & Kirschenbaum, D.S. (1979, September). *Social problem-solving skills and social competence in preadolescent children.* Paper presented at the meeting of the American Psychological Association, New York.

Hughes, J.N. (1992). *Students Taking Assertive and Responsible Steps (STARS) manual.* (Available from author, Texas A & M University, Department of Educational Psychology, College Station, TX 77843–4225.)

Hughes, J.N., Boodoo, G., Alcala, J., Maggio, M., Moore, L., & Villapando, R. (1989). Validation of a role-play measure of children's social skills. *Journal of Abnormal Psychology, 17,* 633–646.

Hughes, J.N., & Cavell, T.A. (1995). Cognitive-affective approaches: Enhancing competence in aggressive children. In G. Cartledge & J.F. Milburn (Eds.), *Teaching social skills to children and youth: Innovative approaches* (3rd ed.) Boston: Allyn & Bacon.

Hymel, S., Wagner, E., & Butler, L.J. (1990). Reputational bias: View from the peer group. In S.R. Asher & J.D. Coie (Eds.), *Peer rejection in childhood.* New York: Cambridge University Press.

Johnson, D.W., & Johnson, R.T. (1987). *Learning together and alone: Cooperative, competitive, and individualistic learning.* Englewood Cliffs, NJ: Prentice-Hall.

Johnson, D.W., & Johnson, R.T. (1989). Cooperative learning: What special education teachers need to know. *Pointer, 33,* 5–10.

Kauffman, J.M. (1993). *Characteristics of children's behavior disorders* (5th ed.). New York: Merrill.

Keller, H.R. (1988). Children's adaptive behaviors: Measure and source generalizability. *Journal of Psychoeducational Assessment, 6,* 371–389.

Knapczyk, D. (1988). Reducing aggressive behaviors in special and regular class settings by training alternative social responses. *Behavioral Disorders, 14,* 27–39.

LaGreca, A.M., & Santogrossi, D.A. (1980). Social skills training with elementary school students: A behavioral group approach. *Journal of Consulting and Clinical Psychology, 48*, 220–227.

Lew, M., & Mesch, D. (1984, August). *Isolated students in secondary schools: Cooperative group contingencies and social skills training.* Paper presented at the convention of the American Psychological Association, Toronto.

Lochman, J.E., Lampron, L.B., Gemmer, T.C., & Harris, S.R. (1987). Anger coping intervention with aggressive children: A guide to implementation in school settings. In P. Keller & S. Heyman (Eds.), *Innovations in clinical practice: A source book* (Vol. 6). Sarasota, FL: Professional Resource Exchange.

Mager, R.G., & Pipe, P. (1970). *Analyzing performance problems.* Belmont, CA: Fearon.

Mathur, S.R., & Rutherford, R.B. (1991). Peer-mediated interventions promoting social skills of children and youth with behavioral disorders. *Education and Treatment of Children, 14*, 227–242.

Matson, J.L., Rotatori, A.F., & Helsel, W.J. (1983). Development of a rating scale to measure social skills in children: The Matson Evaluation of Social Skills with Youngsters (MESSY). *Behavior Research and Therapy, 21*, 335–340.

McGinnis, E., & Goldstein, A.P. (1984). *Skillstreaming the elementary school child: A guide for teaching prosocial skills.* Champaign, IL: Research Press.

Middleton, M.B., & Cartledge, G. (1995). The effects of social skills instruction and parental involvement on the aggressive behaviors of African American males. *Behavior Modification, 19*, 192–210.

Neel, R.S., Jenkins, Z.N., & Meadows, N. (1990). Social problem-solving behaviors and aggression in young children: A descriptive observational study. *Behavioral Disorders, 16*, 39–51.

Olexa, D.F., & Forman, S.G. (1984). Effects of social problem-solving training on classroom behavior of urban disadvantaged students. *Journal of School Psychology, 22*, 165–175.

Orlick, T. (1982). *The second cooperative sports and games book.* New York: Pantheon.

Park, H., & Gaylord-Ross, R. (1989). A problem-solving approach to social skills training in employment settings with mentally retarded youth. *Journal of Applied Behavior Analysis, 22*, 373–380.

Powless, D.L., & Elliott, S.N. (1993). Assessment of social skills of Native American preschoolers: Teachers' and parents' ratings. *Journal of School Psychology, 31*, 293–307.

Rhode, G., Morgan, D.P., & Young, K.R. (1983). Generalization and maintenance of treatment gains of behaviorally handicapped students from resource rooms to regular classrooms using self-evaluation procedures. *Journal of Applied Behavior Analysis, 16,* 171–188.

Rie, E.D., & Friedman, D.P. (1978). *A survey of behavior rating scales for children.* Columbus: Division of Mental Health, Ohio Department of Mental Health and Mental Retardation, Office of Program Evaluation and Research.

Salend, S.J., Whittaker, C.R., & Reeder, E. (1992). Group evaluation: A collaborative, peer-mediated behavior management system. *Exceptional Children, 59,* 203–209.

Sapon-Shevin, M. (1986). Teaching cooperation. In G. Cartledge & J.F. Milburn (Eds.), *Teaching social skills to children: Innovative approaches* (3rd ed.). Elmsford, NY: Pergamon.

Schneider, B.H. (1993). *Children's social competence in context: The contributions of family, school, and culture.* Oxford, England: Pergamon.

Shapiro, E.S., Gilbert, D., Friedman, J., & Steiner, S. (1985, November). *Concurrent validity of role-play and contrived tests in assessing social skills in disruptive adolescents.* Paper presented at the annual convention of the Association for the Advancement of Behavior Therapy, Houston.

Shure, M.B. (1992). *I Can Problem Solve: An interpersonal cognitive problem-solving program for children.* Champaign, IL: Research Press.

Slavin, R.E. (1978). Student teams and achievement divisions. *Journal of Research and Development in Education, 12,* 39–49.

Slavin, R.E. (1990). Research on cooperative learning: Consensus and controversy. *Educational Leadership, 47,* 52–54.

Slavin, R.E., Leavey, M., & Madden, N.A. (1982, March). *Effects of student teams and individualized instruction on student mathematics achievement, attitudes, and behaviors.* Paper presented at the annual convention of the American Education Research Association, New York.

Smith, D., Young, K.R., West, R.P., Morgan, D.P., & Rhode, G. (1988). Reducing the disruptive behavior of junior high school students: A classroom self-management procedure. *Behavioral Disorders, 13,* 231–239.

Spivack, G., & Shure, M.B. (1974). *Social adjustment of young children. A cognitive approach to solving real-life problems.* San Francisco: Jossey-Bass.

Stephens, T.M. (1992). *Social skills in the classroom.* Odessa, FL: Psychological Assessment Resources.

Stephens, T.M., & Arnold, K.D. (1992). *Social behavior assessment inventory: Examiner's manual.* Odessa, FL: Psychological Assessment Resources.

Stokes, T., & Baer, D.M. (1977). An implicit technology of generalization. *Journal of Applied Behavior Analysis, 10,* 349–367.

Stokes, T., & Osnes, P. (1986). Generalizing children's social behavior. In P. Strain, M. Guralnick, & H. Walker (Eds.), *Children's social behavior.* Orlando, FL: Academic.

Stokes, T., & Osnes, P. (1988). The developing applied technology of generalization and maintenance. In R. Horner, G. Dunlap, & R. Koegel (Eds.), *Generalization and maintenance.* Baltimore: Brookes.

Stokes, T., & Osnes, P. (1989). An operant pursuit of generalization. *Behavior Therapy, 20,* 337–355.

Sullivan, M.A., & O'Leary, S.G. (1990). Maintenance following reward and cost token programs. *Behavior Therapy, 21,* 139–149.

Van Den Pol, R.A., Iwata, B.A., Ivancic, M.T., Page, T.J., Neef, N.A., & Whitley, F.P. (1981). Teaching the handicapped to eat in public places: Acquisition, generalization, and maintenance of restaurant skills. *Journal of Applied Behavior Analysis, 14,* 61–69.

Van Hasselt, V.B., Hersen, M., & Bellack, A.S. (1981). The validity of role play tests for assessing social skills in children. *Behavior Therapy, 12,* 202–216.

Wahler, R.G. (1969). Setting generality: Some specific and general effects of child behavior therapy. *Journal of Applied Behavior Analysis, 2,* 239–246.

Walker, H.M., & Buckley, N.K. (1974). *Token reinforcement techniques.* Eugene, OR: E-B Press.

Walker, H.M., McConnell, S., Holmes, D., Todis, B., Walker, J., & Golden, N. (1983). *The Walker Social Skills Curriculum.* Austin, TX: PRO-ED.

Walker, H.M., Severson, H., Stiller, B., Williams, G., Haring, N., Shinn, M., & Todis, B. (1988). Systematic screening of pupils in the elementary age range at risk for behavior disorders: Development and trial testing of multiple gating model. *RASE, 9,* 8–14.

Weissberg, R.P., Gesten, E.L., Liebenstein, N.L., Doherty-Schmid, K., & Hutton, H. (1980). *The Rochester Social Problem-Solving (SPS) Program: A training manual for teachers of 2nd–4th grade.* Rochester, NY: University of Rochester.

Weissberg, R.P., Gesten, E.L., Rapkin, B.D., Cowen, E.L., Davidson, E., Flores de Apodaca, R., & McKim, G.J. (1981). Evaluation of a social-problem-solving training program for suburban and inner-city third-grade children. *Journal of Consulting and Clinical Psychology, 49,* 251–261.

Weist, M.D., & Ollendick, T.H. (1991). Toward empirically valid target selection: The case of assertiveness in children. *Behavior Modification, 15,* 213–227.

Witt, J.C., Cavell, T.A., Heffer, R.W., Carey, M.P., & Martens, B.K. (1988). Child self-report: Interviewing techniques and rating scales. In E.S. Shapiro & T.R. Kratochwill (Eds.), *Behavioral assessment in schools.* New York: Guilford.

CHAPTER 3

Asian Americans

GWENDOLYN CARTLEDGE AND HUA FENG

Asian Americans currently make up 3 percent of the U.S. population. According to the U.S. Bureau of the Census (1993), they are the fastest growing minority group in this country. Between 1980 and 1990, their numbers increased from 3,500,000 to 7,274,000—a 107.8 percent increase. This compares to a 6 percent increase for Whites, a 13.2 percent increase for Blacks, and a 53.0 percent increase for Hispanics. Like other groups discussed in this book, Asian Americans are not a monolith but rather a diverse group of people originating in East Asia (China, Japan, and Korea), Southeast Asia (India, Vietnam, Cambodia, Laos), and the Pacific Islands (Samoa, the Philippines, Guam). Although their diversity is recognized, we use the term *Asian American* to refer to all of these populations.

Beginning in the mid-1800s, many Asian Americans, particularly Chinese, were volunteer immigrants, coming to this country to work in such menial occupations as railroad workers, launderers, and cooks. Many others, however, especially in the past two decades, have come for reasons of education, economics, and personal safety. People of Chinese, Filipino, Japanese, or Asian Indian descent make up the greatest portion of Asian Americans, but in recent years, with changes in U.S. trade and immigration policies (Chin, 1990) and in the aftermath of the Southeast Asian wars, increases have occurred mostly among Vietnamese, Koreans, Asian Indians, and Chinese. Until 1970, Japanese Americans were the largest group of Asian Americans in the United States, constituting approximately

27 percent of the population of Hawaii (Nagata, 1989). Currently, they are the most slowly growing segment of Asian Americans, possibly because of the relatively affluent conditions in Japan. It is estimated that from 1992 to 2000 the Asian American population will increase 45 percent to between 4.1 percent and 4.8 percent of the total population. It is speculated that by 2050 the percentage of Asian Americans in the United States could be as high as 11.6 percent (U.S. Bureau of the Census, 1993).

Although Asian Americans live in every region of the country, they tend to be concentrated in the West (California and Hawaii), and the Northeast (in New York). The respective distributions for these areas are 55.7 percent and 18.4 percent. The metropolitan areas with the greatest concentrations are Los Angeles, San Francisco, New York, Honolulu, and Chicago. Fifteen percent of Asian Americans are located in the South, and the lowest percentage (10.6 percent) is in the Midwest.

Asian Americans are a bit younger than the majority White population, with 24 percent of the former population below age 14, compared to only 21.3 percent for Whites. Of Asian Americans, 50.2 percent are in the 14-to-44 age group, compared to 46.0 of Whites. This means that Asian Americans have and will, for the immediate future, continue to have proportionately more members in the school-age population.

U.S. Census Bureau data from 1993 indicate that the educational status of Asian Americans is higher than that of other groups in the United States. As of 1992, 39.4 percent of Asian Americans reported completing 4 or more years of college, compared to 22.1 percent of Whites and 11.9 percent of African Americans. Their financial statistics also exceed national norms: Of Asian American families, 40 percent are reported to have incomes of $50,000 per year or more, compared to 34.1 percent of Whites and 14.9 percent of African Americans. However, 13 percent of Asian American families are below the poverty line; this figure is higher than the 8.8 percent for Whites but considerably lower than the 30.4 percent for African Americans. Despite greater representation in the upper income brackets, Nagata (1989) reports evidence that Japanese Americans, for example, receive lower salaries than their White counterparts of equivalent occupation, status, and educational level. Among Asian

American households, 79 percent include married couples; slightly over 20 percent of Asian American children live in single-parent homes.

Crime records for 1991 show 0.9 percent of all crimes attributed to Asian Americans. This figure includes 1.2 percent of all serious crimes and 0.9 percent of nonserious crimes. Serious crimes for Asian Americans most often involved auto theft (1.4 percent) or larceny (1.4 percent); the most frequently reported nonserious crimes were gambling (8.2 percent), offenses against family and children (2.7 percent), and runaways (2.5 percent; U.S. Bureau of the Census, 1993). Several authors note that although crime and delinquency rates in Asian American communities traditionally are low, they may be misleading (Chin, 1990; Huang & Ying, 1989; Nagata, 1989). Chin points out that because of restrictive immigration laws, before 1965 there were few adolescent Chinese in this country. He proposes that the crime rate has increased substantially as a result of large numbers of legal and illegal immigrants' crowding into communities with inadequate social supports. Another reason for substantially lower crime figures is that Asian Americans tend to exist in closed societies, choosing not to report infractions to the authorities but to handle these matters within the family or even through gangs or criminal societies. Chin further notes that criminality is becoming more visible because the more affluent members of the Asian American community are inclined to report crimes to the authorities and because delinquent acts are no longer confined to this ethnic group but are now affecting the larger society. Drug trafficking and related criminality are of particular concern. Another warning that emerges from civic and law enforcement officials is that immigrant youth are most vulnerable to engaging in antisocial behavior.

With the influx of immigrants to the United States in the seventies, eighties, and nineties, the statistical profile of Asian Americans is somewhat incomplete. The bulk of this group resides in the West (i.e., California and Hawaii) and exhibits a fairly stable picture in terms of family composition, educational achievement, and economic security. Recent changes in the form of large numbers of legal and illegal immigrants, many among them refugees, signal conditions that could potentially destabilize communities and families and thereby undermine the social and emotional development of their members.

Cultural Distinctions

Philosophical Influences

The teachings of great leaders such as Confucius and Buddha have significantly shaped the cultural distinctiveness of many Asian societies. The Confucian paradigm, for example, has played a dominant role in molding Chinese thought and behavior. According to the contemporary philosopher Mou (1963), Chinese philosophy focuses on human life and morality. The core goal is loving people and respecting nature; achievement of this goal leads to the ultimate position of sainthood. To reach this pinnacle, one must be in harmony and balance with people, matter, and nature, a state that results from introspection and self-cultivation. Thus, becoming well cultivated and highly introspective becomes the essence of one's being.

In contrast to the Western focus on individualism, Confucian philosophy emphasizes that the individual is not a separate or isolated entity but a social interactive being (Hsu, 1985). This concept is illustrated in the Chinese character of *REN*, which depicts two men together, and focuses on relationships with others. Traditional Chinese society is considered neither individual based nor society based but rather relation based. A relational being is sensitive to relationships with all beings regardless of their social status (King & Bond, 1985).

Confucian philosophy gives rules for living by which one may achieve harmonious relationships with others. Failure to act according these rules will be viewed as "uncivilized" or "barbaric" and will bring shame to the individual and the family. The individual is required to be introspective and examine his or her actions to determine their appropriateness. As King and Bond (1985) point out, "The individual consists of a self that is an active and reflexive entity. Confucius assigned the individual self the capacity to do right or wrong, and, ultimately, the individual alone is responsible for what he is" (p. 31).

As influenced by *REN*, Chinese society tends to be group oriented, with the emphasis on relationships. Because everything needs to be considered first according to relationships, Chinese people, whenever encountering a new setting or environment, tend to be quiet because they first need to ascertain the relationship and the rules for dealing with others. As a result, they are inclined to be uneasy with strangers and reluctant to discuss personal matters because no relationship has been established. This orientation is likely to interfere with social or psychological interventions such as counseling. One can also see the effects of Confucian philosophy on other Eastern societies such as that of Japan (King & Bond, 1985).

The Family

The family is the basic unit of the society, but it is predicated on the self-disciplined (or cultivated) individual. According to the Confucian philosophy that undergirds this culture, "Only those who can regulate (or cultivate) themselves can rule their family, only those who can rule their family can rule a kingdom, and only those who can rule a kingdom can rule the world." Of the five basic dyads proposed by Confucius, three pertain to rules of relationship within the family (King & Bond, 1985). These three dyads are (a) father and son, (b) husband and wife, and (c) elder and younger brother. According to these rules, each family member is assigned a specific status, and each one has a unique responsibility to the family. These regulations bind the family so tightly that no single person can exist without the family, and every member is representative of the family. These beliefs lead to a father-dominated household with male and elder children having greater value.

Filial piety *(hsiao)* is the basic rule guiding the relationship of father and son. It is strongly endorsed not only by the family but by the whole society. Filial piety is evidenced through great respect and conformity to the "father," a figure of authority, and through fulfillment of the parents' wishes. This principle is considered to provide the foundation for one's relationship with others *(REN)*, so that if there is no filial piety *(hsiao)*, one forfeits relationships with others *(REN)*. Furthermore, success can be a sign of filial piety. In the Chinese view, one's success honors not only oneself but also one's parents, family, and ancestors. In like manner, one's failure can bring dishonor (i.e., loss of face) to the family as well as to oneself. "Gaining face" for the parents or the family becomes the ultimate objective for every child and the means for displaying filial piety.

In the traditional Chinese family structure, eldest children usually are assigned housework and share the responsibility for taking care of the family. When the parent is absent, the eldest sister or brother takes on the parental role and is considered an authority figure. Within traditional families, birth order implies hierarchic loyalty, which means that younger children need to show respect to the elder ones. Appellation or title designation is one way the younger ones show respect to the elder siblings. This practice also applies in nonkinship situations. A person who is as little as 1 year older may be designated as "bigger sister" or "bigger brother," and those more than 15 years older may be called "uncle" or "aunt." It is inappropriate to address such a person by the first name without including a title of respect.

In Chinese tradition, the extended family was the basic family unit. Being male dominated, the wife was usually absorbed into her husband's family. Women were subservient to their husbands and usually did not achieve status until they became mothers-in-law.

Field work and research conducted by Wu (1985) and Ho (1986) provide some useful insights into the socialization process within Chinese families; their work is the basis for the following observations about child-rearing practices. The Chinese use quite different child-rearing strategies before and after the age of 5 or 6. Before that pivotal age, virtually any behavior is acceptable. Parents tend to be highly tolerant of their young children, rationalizing that a child of that age is not yet capable of "understanding things." The mother is the primary caretaker and spends most of her time watching the young child. After the child reaches the age of presumed understanding, the rules become very stringent, and restrictions on behavior are implemented in the interest of family harmony. The parent is the symbol of authority, and more demands, more restrictions, and more punishing contingencies are used to mold behaviors. Child-rearing emphasizes obedience, proper conduct, and moral training, with little attention given to independence, assertion, and creativity.

The parents' lives revolve around the child until he or she reaches age 10. Hence, when the child is born, the parent-child relation-

ship replaces the husband-wife relationship, and the child participates in social activities with the parents. It is unusual for parents to
go out together for recreation or other activities and leave the child
alone or with another caregiver. A lifelong parent-child bond results,
and because the parents have sacrificed for their child, the child is
expected to care for the parents in their old age.

In Asian societies, individuals are generally socialized to gauge
their actions in terms of filial piety and harmonious relationships with
others. Table 2 shows the relative impact of the family on the individual's worldview and behavior in East Asian and American cultures.

Huang and Ying (1989) suggest that in China, with modernization and migration to the United States, many of these traditional
family roles and practices have undergone changes. The extended
family, for example, may still be a source of support in many cases,
but some Westernized families may view it largely as a burden and
an impediment to their autonomy. In her review of mental health
conditions in Asian American immigrant families, Serafica (1990)
reports that the parents mostly adhere to traditional socialization
goals that include "a sense of collectivity and identification with the
family or clan and the ethnic group, dependence on the family, filial piety and obedience, and a sense of responsibility and obligation
to the family" (p. 226). According to Serafica, immigrant parents
attempt to reach these goals by raising their children to be proficient in the native language as well as in English, living in ethnic
neighborhoods, closely supervising their children's friends and outside influences, and encouraging academic achievement that will
bring honor to the family. These parents appear to experience considerable anxiety and ambivalence about the behaviors their children acquire in the new culture. They recognize that assertive
behaviors are needed for adaptation within U.S. society, but they
are concerned about the possible threat to filial piety. Similarly,
interracial dating may signal acceptance and security within the
dominant group, but it also may lead to a weakening of family ties
and sense of obligation to the parents.

The School

In Chinese and Asian societies, the Confucian influence is also apparent in the socialization that takes place in the school. Confucius

Table 2
Family Structure and Dynamics in East Asian and American Cultures

	East Asian Culture	American Culture
Traditional worldview	Ancestors or spirits of the deceased are revered and appeased.	God is seen as the creator and controller of the world.
Social control	Restraint is internalized according to family values; feelings of guilt or shame can be a powerful means of social control.	Restraint comes from external sources; both achievement and failure are attributed to the individual.
Rules of behavior	Harmony is the basic rule guiding interaction with others.	Sincerity is emphasized.
	Behavior should be based on role expectations.	Behavior should be based on openness and the individual's feelings.
	Self-expression or feelings that may cause conflict are not encouraged but are restrained in the interest of harmonious relationships.	Self-expression and feelings are encouraged, with emphasis on the value of the individual.

Family roles	Family members have clearly defined roles, and individuals act in accordance with role expectations.	Family members tend to relate to one another in an intimate fashion without attention to individual roles.
Parent-child relationships	Parent-child relationships are tight and continue throughout life.	Individuals are encouraged to break away from the family and go their own way.
	Individualism is seen as selfish or inconsiderate toward other family members.	An individual-centered society, individualism, independence, and self-sufficiency are stressed.
Parenting strategies	A child's behavior is a reflection on the family's dignity and "face."	Children are taught to take responsibility for their own behaviors.
	Filial piety and deference to elders are stressed; the child's rights are not emphasized.	Children are encouraged to develop in their own ways.
	Children's obligations to the family are emphasized by their parents or elders.	Rearing children is the parents' duty; the child's obligation to the family is not stressed.

represents both a saint and teacher, and thus teachers are accorded the highest status and greatest respect. The teacher is the authority figure who is permitted to mete out the strictest discipline, even employing rather harsh measures whenever deemed necessary. In traditional Chinese schools and teacher colleges, students are expected to show respect by waiting in the classroom for the teacher's arrival. When the teacher enters, they are to become very quiet, stand and bow to the teacher, and then greet the teacher in unison. As a means for inculcating self-discipline and proper conduct, children are assigned daily chores, cleaning the school and school grounds. Children are to perform these tasks willingly and take pride in fulfilling their obligations. Burton (1986), examining education in the Chinese primary school, highlights a picture in a child's textbook of a young girl happily doing her duties with a caption reading, "I am on duty today."

The collectivistic or group-oriented emphasis of Chinese culture is reinforced in the schools. Children are assigned to groups, and the groups are maintained intact for all subjects, including such subjects as music and physical education. Students continue to be taught in groups even through high school. There is no emphasis on or provision for individual needs—no pull-out programs, elective courses, or changing of classes. Individualism is deemphasized. Competitions are not among individuals but rather among classes; this fosters cooperation among students in the same classroom. Questions are not encouraged, interactions between students and teachers are minimal, and students are coached to focus on the academic material and aim for high achievement. In the elementary schools, children receive direct instruction on rules concerning personal interaction, self-regulation, and moral education. In junior high schools, the Confucian paradigms are integrated into language and literature textbooks; in high schools, Confucianism is taught as a formal subject that supplements instruction in Chinese literature.

Moral education is an important part of the curriculum in traditional Chinese schools (Burton, 1986). From early childhood, children receive formal instruction on unselfishness, concern for group welfare, respect for adults, and pride in fulfilling obligations. Children are trained to work harmoniously together and to understand the value of cooperating for the good of all. Schools directly reward unselfish behavior.

The foregoing discussion reflects the values of traditional Chinese and Asian societies, heavily influenced by Confucian principles. As with the family, modernization and industrialization have brought about changes in educational practices, particularly in urban schools. In Taiwan, for example, the growing economy has increased living costs to the point that a teacher's salary is inadequate for a satisfactory lifestyle. Thus, teaching has become largely a female profession, being replaced in status by more lucrative occupations such as medicine, engineering, and business. Because teachers are among the principal purveyors of moral education and Confucian teachings, it is speculated that this decline in status may be accompanied by an erosion of social and moral behaviors valued in the traditional cultures.

Cultural Influences on Children's Values and Social Skills

Social Orientation and Authority

Findings from cross-cultural studies involving East Asian and Western children repeatedly point to differences in attitudes toward social orientation and authority. Domino and Hannah (1987) compared the themes that emerged in story endings provided by children in Peking and Los Angeles. In completing open-ended stories, the children were to tell what happened, suggest what each protagonist would think and do, and provide realistic endings. Social orientation and concern for authority were the factors that most distinguished these two groups. In terms of social orientation, for example, 27 percent of the Chinese children mentioned public shame in their stories, but this concept did not appear in any of the American children's stories.

According to Chu (1973), the major difference between Eastern and Western cultures is that the former emphasizes shame whereas the latter emphasizes guilt. These very different orientations contribute to two very different kinds of personality that emerge during socialization. Whereas Western culture uses guilt to complete the socialization of children, Eastern culture instills the sense of shame: Children's behaviors are thought to reflect on the family's dignity. Behaviors are governed mainly by the fear of losing face according to others' judgment of one's behavior. The net result of this orientation might be children's social behaviors marked by shyness, high anxiety, and an unwillingness to express opinions or feelings in public. For example, in Asian American children, contrary ideas or independent acts would be considered selfish or inconsiderate and would result in feelings of shame (Sue, 1981).

Implicit in the Asian social orientation is the theme that the group is the ultimate standard for approval and rejection of behavior; therefore, one obeys the majority. This notion emerges in Ma's (1988) discussion of Chinese moral behavior as compared to that in Western society. As Table 3 shows, both Chinese and Western cultures emphasize the maintenance, stability, and prosperity of the society; the major difference lies in the Chinese group orientation and emphasis on conformity. The Chinese tend to have greater tolerance and a more compromising attitude toward conflict; they are more inclined to resolve conflict in the privacy of the home than in the public arena of the police station or courtroom.

In conflict resolution, filial piety comes into play, motivating the individual to maintain the father-son relationship and work toward peaceful resolution. It has been facetiously suggested that in a shipwreck, the English will save their children first, Americans will save their spouses first, and Chinese will save their parents first.

Ma (1989), comparing data on moral development for adolescents in Hong Kong, mainland China, and England, determined that the cultural differences in moral judgment can be summed up as follows: (a) Chinese adolescents are more likely to adhere to rigid norms and to abide by the law under any circumstances; and (b) They value filial piety, group solidarity, collectivism, and humanity, values that correlate strongly with the Confucian paradigm.

The importance of authority figures in Asian cultures has been well documented and is particularly reflected in such child-rearing practices as the strong emphasis on conformity and strict discipline (Breiner, 1980) and the expectations of good behavior, cooperation, and obedience (Sedel, 1972). The central role of authority and its impact on youth is evidenced in the Domino and Hannah (1987) study with the disproportional representation of adult figures in the stories completed by Chinese children. Along similar lines, other

Table 3

Chinese Perspective versus Western Perspective

General Structure	Chinese Perspective	Western Perspective
1. Social order and prosperity	(i) To maintain the stability and prosperity of the society.	(i) To maintain the stability and prosperity of the society.
	(ii) A collectivistic and affective perspective.	(ii) An individualistic and rational perspective.
2. Consensus, norm, and propriety	(i) A soft attitude towards resolving conflicts.	(i) A less tolerating and compromising attitude towards resolving conflicts.
	(ii) Involuntary kinship bondage throughout the whole life span.	(ii) Voluntary kinship bondage, particularly after adolescence.
	(iii) Rigid social norms.	(iii) Less rigid and more flexible norms.
3. Law-abiding	(i) Person-oriented government and loose legal system.	(i) Constitutional government and public institutionalized law.
	(ii) Emphasis on Ching (affection) and Li (reasoning); law is but human affection.	(ii) Emphasis on law.

Note. From "The Chinese Perspectives on Moral Judgment Development," by H. Ma, *International Journal of Psychology, 23*(2), p. 210. Reprinted by permission of the International Union of Psychological Science.

cross-cultural studies concluded that children in Taiwan (Chu, 1979) and Japan (Moriya, 1989) tended to be more conforming and socially dependent than American children. Ma's (1985) study of law-abiding behavior also showed that Chinese students were more likely than English students to abide by the law, a finding he attributed to the fact that Chinese parents usually rear their children to respect and obey authority figures. In a study of over 2,000 Chinese kindergarten children and their parents, Xu, Shen, Wan, Li, Mussen, and Cao (1990) concluded that the traditional cultural values exerted the major influence on socialization practices in China:

> Traditionally and currently, all agents of socialization emphasize the norms of obedience to parents and reverence of authority, performing in accordance with cultural expectations, developing and maintaining high moral standards, and willing [sic] to work hard. Furthermore, Chinese young people have relatively little freedom to choose among value alternatives, lifestyles, or vocational goals. Under such circumstance, strong parental control and guidance in the early years may be of paramount importance in inculcating enduring qualities and responses that are adaptive in Chinese society. (p. 251)

Identity and Self-Concept

Cross-cultural and monocultural investigations of identity and self-concept among Asians and Asian Americans consistently find issues of morality, alienation, body image, social relationships, and group identity to dominate (Leong & Chou, 1994; Serafica, 1990; Turner & Mo, 1984). Studies reported by these and other authors show Asian and Asian American youth scoring higher than their Western counterparts on morality scales but lower on measures of social relationships (particularly as related to dating), attitudes toward physical appearance, and group identity.

Recalling the classic Clark and Clark (1947) studies with African American children, Leong and Chou (1994) report research conducted by Fox and Jordan (1973), who found Chinese American children more likely to refer to pictures of White people as good and pictures of Chinese people as bad. The Chinese American children also expressed fewer same-race preferences than either Black or White children. Leong and Chou inferred from these findings that the Chinese American children were "suffering from media stereotypes that propagate the 'White is better' mentality" (p. 158). There is some evidence that this mindset continues through adolescence and becomes more pronounced with acculturation.

Although Gim-Chung (1994) contends that the terms *cultural identity* and *acculturation* are erroneously used interchangeably, they typically are employed to define individuals' attitudes toward their own group (identity) or the degree to which they shed their own cultural traits and accept new ones. Many models of acculturation and ethnic identity exist. Although there are some notable differences among them, Gim-Chung points out that in all models the ideal state is some form of biculturalism, in which the individual is invested in one or more cultures without judging any one as superior.

With the exception of a few studies such as the one by Fox and Jordan (1973), most of the research in this area has been conducted with college students who tend to be highly acculturated (Gim-Chung, 1994) and show evidence of considerable identification with the White majority culture. Mok (1994), for example, studying Asian American undergraduate college students, found a positive relationship between acculturation and preference for interracial dating and found that preferences for interracial dating correlated positively with statements such as "I believe that White people are better than Asian Americans" and negatively with statements such as "I am proud of my Asian American ethnic background." Some studies with college students revealed particularly high acculturation levels among Japanese Americans (Gim-Chung, 1994; Kohatsu, 1994) and Asian American females (Kohatsu, 1994).

Other research with college students has examined the relationship between alienation and self-concept. Asamen and Berry (1987) found a moderate negative correlation among powerlessness, social isolation, and self-concept for Japanese and Chinese American college students. That is, the more alienated the students felt, the lower their evaluations on self-concept measures. In a study conducted in 1966, Sue and Frank (1973) observed Asian American college students to express more feelings of isolation, loneliness, rejection, nervousness, and anxiety than their non–Asian American counterparts. Similar results were obtained by Abe and Zane (1990), who extended their investigation to foreign-born Asian American college students and found this group to be more vulnerable than U.S.–born Asian Americans to mental health problems.

In the empirical literature, body image and physical appearance emerge as especially important issues related to self-concept among Asian Americans (Serafica, 1990). The youngsters studied tended to assign negative evaluations to their physical characteristics, expressing displeasure with short stature, flat noses, and slanted eyes; as one might expect, such sensitivity increased as the young people moved into adolescence. Nagata (1989) points out that shorter, smaller bodies interfere with some athletic prowess and that Asian features are not consistent with the Western standards of beauty. She reports instances of Asian American females applying cellophane tape to simulate Western-looking double eyelids.

The realm of dating and sexuality is another area where Asian American youth typically deviate from Western norms. In many Asian societies, the emphasis during adolescence is on academic studies and self-cultivation rather than on relationships with the opposite sex (Turner & Mo, 1984). Huang and Ying (1989) point out that sexuality continues to be a taboo topic in many Chinese American families. According to Reglin and Adams (1990), Asian American students spend considerably more time doing homework than participating in the social activities that engage most of the leisure time of their mainstream peers. They tend to defer dating until their late teens and take little interest in popular music, television, or athletics. Along with awareness of their physical differences and preferences for interracial relationships, dating issues heighten Asian American adolescents' awareness of belonging to an ethnic minority and increase the potential for family conflict (Huang & Ying, 1989; Nagata, 1989). Interracial dating patterns show females to have more other-race partners than males (Mok, 1994; Serafica, 1990), but among acculturated Asian American young people, the preference for interracial dating appears to be equal for males and females (Mok, 1994).

Although they possess some obvious advantages in terms of academic behavior, family relationships, and self-regulation, Asian American youth appear to perceive themselves less favorably than they do their peers from other racial groups, especially White Americans. Finding themselves somewhat at variance with the typical images of beauty, power, and success in this society, these young people are likely to devalue their physical attributes and their ethnic background in deference to the majority group. Huang (1981) suggests that no matter how many generations they have been in America, many Asian Americans continue to feel like foreigners, a feeling that is an ongoing source of pain. Without question, the identity factor exerts crucial influence on the social behaviors of Asian Americans attempting to integrate into the mainstream culture. Feelings of not belonging may cause one to retreat from social situations or to respond in awkward or antisocial ways.

Peers

The literature on East Asian cultures suggests that children are socialized to be academic, adult, and family oriented. Harmonious relationships with others are important, but peer relationships receive considerably less attention than in Western cultures. Chen and Rubin (Chen & Rubin, 1992; Chen, Rubin, & Sun, 1992) report on a set of studies suggesting cultural differences between peer relationships of East Asian and Western children. According to Chen and Rubin (1992), childhood friendships in the Chinese culture resemble sibling relationships, so that friends are often called "brothers" and "sisters." These relationships often are found in classrooms, where children restrict their interactions to small, select cliques.

In a cross-cultural study of peer acceptance among kindergarten-aged children, Chen and Rubin (1992) found that Chinese children assigned their peers lower sociometric ratings than did their Canadian counterparts. Assessing social problem solving approaches, such as a child's strategy for obtaining a desired toy that is in another child's possession, they found Chinese children to be more agonistic ("Give it to me") or authority oriented ("Tell his mom to make him share") than the Canadian children, who responded more prosocially (e.g., "Please, may I have it?"). A third finding in this study was that, for both populations, peer acceptance correlated positively with prosocial strategies and negatively with agonistic strategies. Social behaviors associated with peer acceptance in both cultures were the focus of the Chen et al. (1992) study. The researchers observed that, in both cultures, children reacted similarly to sociable and aggressive behaviors, accepting and rejecting respectively peers who exhibited such behaviors. In contrast, however, behaviors indicating shyness, sensitivity, and social reticence (behaviors generally associated with social incompetence in Western societies), are praised and encouraged in Chinese children; accordingly, in this study, such behaviors correlated positively with peer acceptance only for the Chinese children.

Schneider and Lee (1990) compared the social interactions of East Asian (Korean, Japanese, and Chinese) American students to those of European American students. They found that the Asian American parents had higher educational expectations and standards for their children and controlled their children's use of time outside of school more than did the European American parents. The Asian American parents scheduled their children's free time for private lessons in such subjects as music, computer science, martial arts, or language. A significant observation was that "East Asian students spent much of their time studying rather than playing with their friends or participating in organized group activities. Consequently, they have less opportunity to develop social skills" (p. 374).

Even though Asian American children tend to be characterized by shy, internalizing behaviors, the few existing studies indicate generally positive relationships with non–Asian American peers. In a study of African American, European American, Asian American, and Latino American children, Howes and Wu (1990) observed that third graders were more likely than kindergartners to enter cross-ethnic interactions, and that Asian American students were most likely (and European Americans least likely) to enter cross-ethnic interactions. Similarly, as in the Feng and Cartledge (1996) study discussed in chapter 1, although Asian American children had lower levels of social communication than their African American or European American peers, they made proportionately more cross-racial statements, particularly to African American students.

Asian American Youth at Risk

According to Ogbu's (1987) theory of involuntary and voluntary minority groups, East Asians (including Chinese, Japanese, and Koreans) represent a voluntary group: They immigrated to the United States by choice, with the anticipation of improving their lives (Schneider & Lee, 1990). Southeast Asians (Laotians, Cambodians, and Vietnamese), by contrast, came to this country in the seventies, eighties, and nineties primarily as refugees; they are considered an involuntary group (Dao, 1991). The critical distinction between these two groups is that people who choose to immigrate are psychologically prepared, but refugees—forced to leave their countries—are psychologically and economically unprepared and face adjustment and survival problems (Dao, 1991). Language insufficiency, barriers of poverty and prejudice, pervasive uncertainty, and the loss of country, family, friends, and social status make survival in the new country difficult (Rumbaut, 1985). In contrast to East Asian parents, Southeast Asian parents tend to be culturally and linguistically unprepared to provide academic assistance to their children.

Morrow (1994) notes that Southeast Asian refugees tend to fall into two groups: those who are educated and urban in background and those who are educationally disadvantaged, possibly coming from rural or jungle areas or from traumatic experiences, such as witnessing the brutal killing of loved ones. People from Vietnam generally make up the former group, whereas Laotians and Cambodians represent the latter population. The Vietnamese, thanks to relatively higher socioeconomic status and lower incidence of war trauma, have experienced better adjustment in the United States than the Cambodians and Laotians. Morrow (1994) reports that, of these ethnic groups, the Vietnamese exhibited the lowest level of mental health needs and the highest level of school achievement, often surpassing other native-born minority groups. Vietnamese people appeared to hold the philosophical and cultural values noted for East Asians.

On the other hand, people from Cambodia and Laos evidenced significant mental health needs, showing rather high levels of post-traumatic stress syndrome, anxiety, and psychosocial dysfunction. Considering these findings, it is not surprising that a growing number of Southeast Asian American children are at risk for dropping out of school and exhibiting maladaptive behaviors (Dao, 1991). Dao stressed that school personnel should be aware of these needs and backgrounds when assessing Southeast Asian American children. Assessment should not only involve basic skills and learning strategies but also take into account the acculturation process, especially when maladaptive behaviors are present. When identifying emotional problems, it is crucial to consider traumatizing experiences as well (Dao, 1991).

Another distinctive at-risk group includes recent immigrants from China, Hong Kong, and Taiwan. Chin (1990) observes that the great increases in their numbers since the seventies tax the resources of already crowded Asian American communities. Parents often send or bring their children to the United States for educational opportunities that are unavailable in the country of origin because so many are competing for so few positions. Often, however, these young people are frustrated in the new country, where they experience language difficulties, are forced to attend classes with younger students, and often perform poorly in school. Furthermore, they are likely to be taunted by youths from other ethnic groups and held in contempt by American-born members of their own. These youngsters' greatest pressures are related to social adjustment, followed by academic matters (Cowart & Cowart, 1993).

Forced to survive in a foreign country without adequate parental supervision and communication skills, many of these youth resort to socializing themselves by withdrawing from school and joining gangs as a means of belonging. Chin (1990) notes, for example, that Chinese gangs initially began in schools where racial tensions were high and subsequently moved to the community, with increasing criminal behavior. Attempting to escape the pressures of an alien society, many of these youngsters indulge in self-destructive behaviors such as violent action and substance abuse. As reported in the media, incidence of juvenile delinquency, gang membership, and drug abuse is increasing within Asian American populations.

For immigrant Asian American youth, alienation from mainstream American society is common (e.g., Chin, 1990; Serafica, 1990). This condition, coupled with certain types and levels of acculturation, makes these youths especially vulnerable to marginalization. Huang and Ying (1989) underscore the combined effects of poverty and acculturation on Chinese youngsters:

> As Chinese American youth become more acculturated, parental authority begins to erode and constraints against aggression become less effective. . . . For adolescents living in Chinatown, which has all the characteristics of an urban ghetto, the unemployment rate among youth is high, and the impoverished conditions and poor housing are glaring. . . . The phenomenon of gangs among Chinese

American youth, which often receives sensational coverage by the news media, is becoming increasingly alarming to the Chinese community. (p. 43)

A case in point appears in an Associated Press news story. A 13-year-old Asian American youth in New York was used by China-town gangsters as a "gangland enforcer," "terrorizing Chinatown street vendors with a box cutter to extort cash for the Flying Dragons gang" ("13-year old," 1994, p. 3A). His specific offenses included attempted robbery, grand larceny, and attempted kidnapping. This youth was the son of immigrants from Hong Kong. His father, a restaurateur, had died 3 years previously; his mother was in poor health and on public assistance. In an effort to provide for his mother and younger sister, the youth had dropped out of school and begun working odd jobs in the community. His baby face, disarming smile, and impoverished conditions made him ripe for gang leaders, who prey on boys "as young as 10 to carry guns, deliver messages, and watch for police" (p. 3A). According to officials, "This case reflects both the struggles of an immigrant family and the alarming recruit-ment practices of Asian street gangs" (p. 3A).

For Japanese American young people, Nagata (1989) also reports a relationship between degree of acculturation and risk for adjustment problems. Although documented delinquency rates are considerably lower for this group than for other segments of the population, Nagata suggests that these reports may be somewhat depressed due to early efforts by parents to correct certain problems within the family with-out the involvement of social services or law-enforcement officials. More "Americanized" or permissive attitudes appear to put Japanese Americans at greater risk for alcohol- and drug-related problems. Nagata also finds that Japanese American youth have less positive self-concepts than their Caucasian peers. Nagata's observations are consistent with those related by researchers for other Asian American youth. As ethnic traditions fade and restrictions are relaxed, and depending on their socioeconomic and academic status, Asian American youth, crippled by feelings of alienation and poor self-concepts, are vulnerable to many of the same social ills that prey on other minority youth in this society. The risk is compounded by academic difficulty and low socioeconomic status. Intervention is needed if these youngsters are to develop socially approved behaviors that will lead to a healthy state of biculturalism.

A Social Skill Profile of Asian Americans

The existing research presents rather consistent information on the influence of Asian culture on the social skills and social behavior of Asian American children. Given the emphasis on relation-based humanity, social norms, authority, conformity, social restrictions, high parental expectations, and self-cultivation, Asian American children tend to develop social behaviors that are social dependent, authority oriented, conformist, self-inhibited or self-controlled, and cooperative. Teachers consistently rate the social skills of Asian American students highly, valuing their tendency toward compliant, task-oriented behaviors. In the Feng and Cartledge (1996) study, for example, teachers considered the Asian American fifth graders more cooperative, self-controlled, and academically inclined than their African and European American peers.

Extremely compliant behaviors coupled with exceptional achievement cause Asian Americans to be viewed as the "model minority" (Chin, 1990). However, as several authorities note, for some Asian American children the social behaviors taken for strengths may mask deep-seated emotional or behavior problems. Leung (1988) ponders whether perhaps their conditioned "compliant, reserved, restrained, modest, and moderate verbal and nonverbal behaviors . . . may have disguised them, preventing them from having their problems discovered and receiving timely intervention" (p. 93). Likewise, Ishii-Jordan and Peterson (1994), considering Asian American youth and behavior disorders, wonder if "pathology (which in majority Anglo culture might be expressed with acting out behaviors) [might] exist and be expressed in other ways in Asian cultural contexts" (p. 112).

In terms of social skills and problem behaviors, teachers in Feng and Cartledge's (1996) study indicated that their greatest concern for Asian American students pertained to low assertiveness (e.g., "Appropriately tells you when he or she thinks you have treated him or her unfairly") or internalizing (e.g., "Has low self-esteem" or "Likes to be alone"). Particularly troubling and confirming were the students' interview responses indicating that they would do nothing if treated unfairly and would be disinclined to share with others when something good happened to them. Internalizing behaviors and excessive modesty may be problematic for some students, setting them up for victimization and minimizing their opportunities to attain personal or social goals.

Social skill programming may need to focus on skills that promote the self-confidence to challenge inequities and achieve fair treatment. Also, training in skills related to making friends, joining activities, initiating conversation with others, and so forth can help reduce nonproductive internalizing problems that result in loneliness and a reluctance to express feelings. Signs of alienation among Asian American students warrant special attention. The myth of model behavior may cloud the perceptions of Westerners. In identifying problem behaviors predictive of substance initiation, for example, classroom teachers tended to underidentify Asian Americans and overidentify African Americans (Wells, Morrison, Gillmore, Catalano, Iritani, & Hawkins, 1992). The unique experiences of Southeast Asian American students need to be understood as well. Although they might have substantially the same social behavior patterns as East Asians, their refugee status, posttraumatic experiences, and emotional unpreparedness may create a very different context for the teaching of social skills.

Instruction in Social Skills

Because of their relatively high levels of task- or academic-related behavior and their low levels of self-disclosure, the social and emotional needs of Asian American youth may be overlooked or underestimated.

The behaviors valued so highly by teachers and other adults may be counterproductive for peer interactions and may mask inadequacies related to self-confidence and social initiation. Asian American youth, particularly recent immigrants, are especially in need of social skill intervention. Leung (1988) argues that

> social skill instruction should be of major concern in
> the education of minority students in general and Asian
> Americans in particular. . . . Because a learner's cognitive,

affective, and physical conditions are inextricably related, minority students who tend to endure stress and anxiety in their growing years are vulnerable socially and emotionally; this vulnerability may impede their other areas of learning and growth. Therefore, concerned educators should provide supportive, preventive, or corrective measures to promote minority students' healthy emotional and social development. (pp. 93–94)

Direct Instruction

Several authorities propose that direct instruction is more effective than indirect procedures such as counseling with Asian American populations (Hartman & Askounis, 1989; Sue, 1981; Sue & Morishima, 1982; Serafica, 1990). Although the importance of social skill or mental health interventions for Asian Americans is often acknowledged in the literature, we have few examples of social skill instruction with Asian American youth. Fukuyama and Coleman (1992) describe a pilot study of assertiveness training for Asian American college students that has culturally relevant implications for the teaching of social skills. Major considerations in this training were cultural norms, a bicultural model, cultural values, group composition, and trainer background.

Cultural norms are a key factor determining the effectiveness of social skill training. Fukuyama and Coleman (1992) identified deference to authority, interpersonal harmony, modesty, and avoidance of public shame as the Asian-Pacific cultural norms most likely to influence degrees of assertiveness. These norms were highlighted and incorporated into the training so that it would be bicultural rather than unicultural. According to Fukuyama and Coleman, "Bicultural means that two modes of social behaviors (from two cultures) may be appropriately used depending on the social situation" (p. 211). In the bicultural model, the social skill (in this case, assertion) is viewed in a situation-specific context, and the learner is encouraged to draw on the value systems of both cultures and act according to the demands of the situation. Bicultural training does not represent one particular value system as superior; rather, it helps learners to analyze cultural values and social situations and to respond judiciously according to their own belief systems and sense of appropriateness.

In culturally relevant instruction, specific skills are targeted according to the learners' needs and the situations they are most likely to experience. Asian-Pacific college students in the Fukuyama and Coleman (1992) project rated the following skills as most important in increasing their assertiveness: making requests and saying no, engaging in conversations, giving and receiving compliments, dating, and dealing with rudeness, prejudice, and authority figures. Many of these skills are at odds with important Asian-Pacific cultural values. Students had difficulty making requests, for example, because of a sense of pride related to a reluctance to impose or incur obligations. During training, students were helped to construct alternative ways to think about traditional responses to various events. For example, difficulty in accepting compliments was related to the traditional Asian value of being humble and modest, but students were helped to restructure their view as perhaps being ungracious and disrespectful to the compliment giver. Similarly, when students addressed the issue of "saving face" for fear of making a mistake and being laughed at, they were advised to select the appropriate levels of risk for themselves and view the withholding of emotional expression as a culturally appropriate sign of strength. Other instruction concerned allowing oneself to feel good about receiving a compliment, learning how to say no, making a date, and dealing with perceived rudeness and prejudice from the majority group.

Fukuyama and Coleman (1992) recommend composing groups according to level of acculturation. On the basis of various models of acculturation, they note that culturally diverse individuals have varying levels of awareness and cultural identity. At opposite, incompatible extremes, for example, are the person who submits totally to the values of the dominant group and the one who is integrated within the ethnic group of origin but is prepared to negotiate culturally diverse systems. Obvious markers of acculturation include language facility, friendship and family associations, length of time in the United States, and personal values. According to Fukuyama and Coleman, cross-ethnic individuals (e.g., Korean and Chinese Americans) who are at the same stage of acculturation may be more compatible in a group than individuals with the same ethnic backgrounds at different acculturation levels (e.g., first- and second-generation Chinese Americans). The authors also recommend that group leaders or trainers be similar to group members in cultural background and gender.

Although Fukuyama and Coleman (1992) conducted training for college students, their findings have many implications for school-age Asian American youth. First, teachers and other trainers need to be keenly aware of the differences between the cultural norms of the dominant culture and those of most Asian Americans, particularly recent immigrants. As Feng and Cartledge (1993) noted, a prime concern for teachers was children's tendency not to state appropriately when they felt unfairly treated by teachers. In a culture that emphasizes deference to authority and holds teachers in the highest esteem, a teacher's judgment is most unlikely to be questioned. Nevertheless, mistakes do occur, and we all occasionally witness unfair treatment that needs to be addressed. Social skill instruction might be designed to help children see what kinds of things are unfair (e.g., a teacher miscalculated a child's score on a math assignment) and learn how to bring them to the teacher's attention. Modeling and role-playing would then center on respectful times for and ways of approaching the teacher and sharing the concern. The trainer would emphasize that these are appropriate and desired "school" behaviors, being careful not to infringe on parents' behavioral expectations for the home.

With children as well as adults, it is crucial to validate cultural background, making sure learners understand that certain situations will call for different responses, not that their ways of doing things are inferior. Leung (1990) notes the pain reported by sensitive minority children, especially during early school experiences, when they became aware of their physical, language, and cultural differences from the dominant group. Because of cultural differences and inadequate social skills, such children may hesitate to participate in school functions and may be excluded from the peer group. According to Leung, these children often are described as overcompliant, timid, indecisive, and generally incompetent. However, if they are in environments where there are few members of their own group, these youngsters may "overacculturate" to overcompensate for identity problems. Teachers need to model acceptance of culturally different children.

The previously noted issues of acculturation emerge with young children as well. Children who are recent immigrants may not be very compatible with second- or third-generation Asian Americans, even if they are from the same ethnic background. Homogeneous grouping may be important if language difficulties are pronounced. English as a second language (ESL) classes may be an ideal setting for teaching basic social skills: Children can be taught the appropriate speech and behaviors for initiating peer activities, for interacting with the teacher, and for making requests of others. Through modeling, role-playing, and feedback, children can be helped to determine the specific behaviors called for in various social situations.

Number of years in the U.S., however, should not be the principal factor in determining group composition. Children across racial, ethnic, and gender groups may be quite compatible, depending on their skill levels and backgrounds. Middleton (1994), for example, working with primary school children, successfully included a first-generation Asian American female as a competent peer in the social skill training of an African American male. Peer social communication in the Feng and Cartledge (1996) study included much cross-racial interaction, with indications of slightly more compatibility between Asian American and African American students. Because one universal goal is to foster positive peer interactions among different racial and ethnic groups, groups should be as diverse as possible. Group composition should be determined primarily by the students' relative abilities in the skills being taught. That is, given comparable levels of acculturation, groups should be mixed, including competent children as well as those exhibiting low levels of the target skill.

The skills taught to Asian American youth, as to all young people, should be based on individual need. The investigations to date often point to a need for skills related to social communication, initiation, and self-confidence (e.g., Feng & Cartledge, 1996). Beyond direct instruction in social skill groups, learners need conditions where they consistently practice the skills and receive reinforcement from others in the environment. Parents and peers typically are important members of the reinforcing environment.

Cooperative Learning

Culturally and linguistically different youth often find their differences magnified by insensitive peers. Leung (1990) asserts that peers who are helped to see the benefits of cultural diversity can serve as role models for the development of social and language skills. Appreciation and respect for various cultures can be developed and fostered through multicultural education programs (see Banks, 1991; Perry & Fraser, 1993).

Cooperative learning experiences can serve to increase respect and positive interactions among culturally diverse peers (Johnson & Johnson, 1987). There is evidence that Asian Americans may be culturally predisposed to cooperative interactions. Cook and Chi (1984), for example, state that Chinese Americans may have less difficulty than American children in being cooperative "because the impact of the Chinese culture is so powerful that it may facilitate feelings of personal satisfaction through an interest in group cooperation and group success" (p. 170). In a study comparing Chinese American grade school boys to "American" boys, Cook and Chi found the Chinese American boys more cooperative and more efficient than their non-Chinese American counterparts. The authors concluded that "the cultural factors played an essential role in influencing cooperative behavior" (p. 176).

Cooperative learning requires learners to work together to reach a common goal or produce a specific product. To make cooperative learning experiences beneficial for Asian American students, teachers need to heed some specific cultural markers. First, when tendencies toward social isolation exist, teachers need to make sure that projects indeed entail cooperation rather than students' working independently in small groups. Activities need to be structured so that each student must contribute and so that completion requires ongoing interaction among the students. For example, an assignment where each child must solve three math problems and provide the answers is much less cooperative and interactive than an assignment where the students work together in very specific roles to solve each problem. Roles might be as follows: One student decides the algorithm to be performed to solve the problem, the second student computes the problem, and the third student checks to make sure the solution is correct. All students may assist with the problem solving, and roles are rotated for the next problem. To help children interact effectively in cooperative activities, teachers need to identify and specifically teach the collaborative skills of (a) beginning and talking about the assignment (on-task behaviors), (b) teaching academic behaviors to peers and soliciting assistance from them, and (c) reinforcing the academic and social behaviors of peers (Cartledge & Cochran, 1993).

A second point concerns group size. Learning groups should be small enough that each child can join in. Cooperative learning might begin in pairs or groups of three. An internalizing child who has not learned to interact effectively in group situations might get lost in larger groups and fail to derive benefits.

A third consideration relates to heterogeneous grouping. Asian American young people—who are inclined to band together, especially if language difference is an issue—may not readily choose to associate with students of different racial or ethnic backgrounds. All students appear to gain from racial heterogeneity (Johnson & Johnson, 1987). If mixing is not appropriately structured and students are not prepared, however, experiences can be aversive rather than enriching. Teachers need to model and reinforce culturally sensitive, affirming behaviors. All children should feel valued regardless of cultural background. Direct, explicit instruction on desired and inappropriate behaviors may be helpful. For example, in cooperative groups students are allowed to provide appropriate corrective feedback, but belittling and ridiculing are strictly prohibited. Appropriate feedback might be modeled by the teacher and practiced by the students.

A final point concerns the nature of the cooperative activity. Initially, cooperative activities might include nonacademic rather than academic tasks for two reasons. First, because students are learning a new behavior (cooperation), they may have trouble mastering academic tasks at the same time they are concentrating on a new set of social skills. Therefore, it would be wise to use either previously learned practice activities or noncognitive tasks to help students begin to learn how to cooperate. Doing so removes the temptations to place Asian American youth in a stereotypical academic role and to believe that interactions with Asian Americans might be limited to the academic context.

Instruction through Literature

Leung (1990) observes that books provide a form of symbolic modeling and that they may be a particularly effective means for promoting the social and personal development of Asian American youth. Although Asian American literature has received limited attention in U.S. schools (Wong, 1993), Chu and Schuler (1992) document substantial improvement in the number and quality of Asian American children's books since the early seventies. They also observe a decline in the racist, sexist, elitist, and misleading aspects of earlier Asian American literature. For example, illustrations in pre-seventies books often portrayed "Fu Manchu mustaches, short straight cereal-bowl haircuts, buck teeth, myopic vision, and clothing that were cruelly and offensively indicative of ancient ways" (p. 94). Other signs of progress, according to these writers, are that many children's books about Asian Americans are now written by Asian Americans and that the books show conscious efforts to enlighten the uninformed. The desire to educate and to address contemporary issues concerning Asian Americans from a variety of ethnic backgrounds makes this literature an excellent resource for enhancing social understanding or teaching social skills.

Chu and Schuler (1992) provide an extremely useful annotated bibliography of books about Asian Americans for young people from preschool through high school. The books, published since 1975, profile youth from various Asian and South Pacific origins at varying levels of acculturation and in diverse social situations. The authors lament, however, the paucity of (a) books on recent immigrants from the Philippines, Vietnam, or Laos; (b) young adult novels featuring Asian Indian or Pakistani protagonists in the United States; (c) stories from an Asian American teen male's perspective; and (d) biographies of famous Asian achievers. The following selections from the Chu and Schuler bibliography appear particularly suited for social learning.

The Happy Funeral (Bunting, 1982), designated for primary-aged children, concerns the experiences of Laura and her Chinese American family related to the death of Laura's grandfather. The events surrounding the funeral are detailed in a way that conveys information on traditional Chinese culture and highlights specific features, such as the jazzed-up hymns that made the funeral Chinese American. Although the book is appropriate for a wide audience, Chu and Schuler (1992) especially recommend it for the "Chinese-American child who experiences the loss of a loved one . . . [and] as a resource for Chinese-American children not living in a Chinese community who seek to know a little of their own civilization" (p. 96).

Another primary-level book with implications for interpersonal social skills is *Angel Child, Dragon Child* (Surat, 1983), the story of an immigrant Vietnamese girl named Ut who is having difficulty adjusting to her new life in America. Ut misses her mother, who is still in Vietnam, and American students tease her because of her strange dress and language. One day she has a fight with Raymond, and the principal puts them in a room together with instructions for Raymond to write Ut's story. The principal felt that Raymond needed to learn to listen and Ut needed to learn to talk. In the room, they both learn. Later, the principal reads Ut's story as written by Raymond; the story moves the school to raise money to send for Ut's mother. As the story progresses, Ut experiences acculturation as she adopts more Americanized dress and learns to use English. The story ends with her mother's arrival.

In the Year of the Boar and Jackie Robinson (Lord, 1984) is a story for intermediate-aged students, set in Brooklyn in 1947. Bandit, whose name is changed to Shirley Temple Wong, is a Chinese American having trouble shedding Chinese customs and making friends with her new classmates. Eventually she is befriended by an athletic girl in the class who introduces her to stickball, the Brooklyn Dodgers, and the team's hero, Jackie Robinson. Chu and Schuler (1992) especially recommend this book to any youngster who must relocate. They say it is an excellent book to read aloud.

My Best Friend Duc Tran: Meeting a Vietnamese American Family (MacMillan & Freeman, 1987), also appropriate for middle-grade students, introduces an American youth to the customs and traditions of a Vietnamese American family. It shows how the Vietnamese family share commonalities with other Americans while maintaining many of their traditions and values, such as the emphasis on family unity.

For junior high and high school youth, three books provide narratives by Asian American immigrant teens. The first book, *Into a Strange Land: Unaccompanied Refugee Youth in America* (Ashabranner & Ashabranner, 1987), details the experiences of Southeast Asian teens coming to the United States alone. It includes firsthand accounts of these young people's difficulties, adjustments, and successes in an alien land. The second book, *New Kids on the Block: Oral Histories of Immigrant Teens* (Bode, 1989), contains narratives by adolescents from 11 different countries, including Afghanistan, China, India, the Philippines, South Korea, and Vietnam. In addition to sharing their experiences, some of the narrators offer advice on meeting the challenges of adjusting to a new land. Chu and Schuler (1992) note that this is one of the few books that portray experiences of immigrant youth from Southern and Central Asia. The third book, *Dark Sky, Dark Land: Stories of the Hmong Boy Scouts of Troop 100* (Moore, 1989), is about 15 teenage Hmong boys from Laos who escaped to refugee camps in Thailand and then came to the United States. Each boy's story is a profile in courage and survival that could provide an excellent supplement for the study of the history of the period.

Children of the River (Crew, 1989) is an adolescent story with a female heroine, Sundara, who fled the Khmer Rouge in Cambodia. The story relates some of the emotional consequences of that experience, the difficulties Sundara encounters in adjusting to a new life in the United States while honoring the rules of her Cambodian aunt and uncle, and the challenges of an interracial romance. Sundara successfully meets and resolves all of these challenges. Chu and Schuler (1992) state that the characters in this award-winning book are "authentically and honestly rendered" (p. 111) and that the book will have universal appeal.

A final example from the bibliography is another story for adolescents entitled *Picture Bride* (Uchida, 1988). The story begins in 1917 in San Francisco. Hana Omiya is a mail order wife or "picture bride" from Japan betrothed to a young man she has never met. The book details her life through marriage, motherhood, friendships, and a period in a Japanese American internment camp during World War II. The bibliographers describe the book as beautiful, sensitive writing that skillfully presents the fullness of Japanese American family life.

Chu and Schuler's (1992) bibliography lists many more attractive books for and about Asian Americans. Readers are encouraged to review this and other sources to identify books most pertinent to the social and emotional issues of specific youngsters. These and other such books can furnish models and be sources of encouragement and pride for Asian American youth struggling with particular social and internal issues. At the same time, such literature can help promote understanding among non–Asian Americans and thus contribute to more positive social interaction. Literature is best used as a supplement to, not a replacement for, direct social skill instruction.

Cartledge and Kleefeld (1994) illustrate the use of culturally relevant literature, in this case folktales, for direct teaching of social skills in their social skill curriculum for intermediate-aged children. One lesson, particularly appropriate for children with inadequate peer interaction skills, uses a Japanese folktale to teach children how to invite others to participate in social activities. In the folktale "Basho and the Rustics," Basho, a renowned poet, is traveling through the countryside one beautiful moonlit night. He encounters a group of young men who mistake Basho for a poor beggar and invite him to join them in making poems about the moon. Although the young men issue the invitation to ridicule Basho, they soon marvel at his wonderful gift as a poet, and they quickly gather the entire village for a feast in his honor.

Students first listen to the audiotaped story. Then the teacher engages them in a discussion of the story to develop the ideas that (a) we should invite others to join us to enjoy our activities, not to ridicule them, and (b) by inviting Basho, the young men were able to enjoy his special talents and had a much better time. An important understanding, particularly in settings where culturally or linguistically different children are in the minority, is that decisions about including or respecting others should not be based merely on physical attributes or commonalities. As the lesson progresses, children realize that including others not only is enjoyable but also is a way to learn more, make friends, help others feel good, and feel good about ourselves. The teacher helps the children specify the following steps for inviting someone to join in play or participate in a social activity:

Tell what you are doing.

Ask the person to join you.

Include the person in your game.
(Cartledge & Kleefeld, 1994, p. 105)

Practice activities provide opportunities for the students to follow these steps. For example, students assemble in groups of three. Two of the students are assigned a simple game to play for approximately a minute and then receive a signal to invite the third person to play; the three play together for a few minutes. The procedure is repeated two more times so that each student experiences being "inviter" and "invitee." In another practice activity, students develop written invitations to peers to participate in various activities; the teacher arranges for students to issue their invitations at specified times.

During lessons and practice activities, the teacher addresses the affective component of the "inviting" skill by asking children to consider how they feel when they are left out of an activity, how they feel and what happens when they invite others, and how they use this skill with others in different settings. To help maintain the skill, students receive a self-monitoring check sheet, "How Am I Doing," which enables them to observe their own behavior. The teacher also watches for opportunities during the regular school day to recognize and praise students for inviting others to participate in social activities. For students especially deficient in this skill, the teacher might want to ensure initial success by prompting other students to be sure to respond positively to their invitations.

If this skill is a top priority for a particular class (i.e., more than one or two students have difficulty inviting others, or students refuse to include those who are "different," the teacher might establish a "joining jar" into which a marble is placed each time the teacher observes a student inviting a peer to join in some activity. To increase social interaction, the teacher might want to incorporate some conditions, such as adding a marble when students invite or play with peers they had previously ignored. Other follow-up or maintenance activities include writing stories or poems, performing skits portraying invitations, and reading related stories such as *The Secret Garden* by Frances Hodgson Burnett (1911).

Another folktale in the Cartledge and Kleefeld (1994) curriculum, "The Woman from Lalo-Hana: The Country under the Sea," is from Hawaii. It is used to teach appropriate movement about the classroom, which may be a concern for Asian-Pacific Americans. The tale seems to be intended as an explanation for a flood in Hawaii, but for children inclined toward self-isolation the teacher might focus on the greater happiness Lalo-Hana experienced once she leaves her solitary home under the sea and joins the king and others on land. This story, along with others in this curriculum, might be used to emphasize the joy of friendship and the kinds of things people can do to make good friends.

For adolescents, books such as Amy Tan's (1990) *The Joy Luck Club* can be useful in discussing various social and cultural issues. Tan's novel may be especially beneficial for Asian American students whose parents immigrated to this country and who are at different stages of acculturation than their children. This story, which concerns the mother-daughter relationship in four Chinese American families, focuses on the mothers' lives in China before coming to the United States and the lives of the daughters growing up in this country. For non–Asian American students, this book might contribute to a greater understanding and appreciation of a fascinating culture; Asian American students, especially first-generation Americans, may gain insights into some of their pressing daily issues. To maximize social understanding, teachers should read such books with their students, pausing frequently for discussion and helping students analyze critical topics from a variety of perspectives. For example, in *The Joy Luck Club,* one daughter, Waverly Jong, resents her mother's unstylish dress and hair style and blames her lack of fashion awareness on a refusal to assimilate to Western ways. But Wong (1993) suggests that the mother's dress is "due less to Chineseness than to a habit of frugality acquired through years of hardship as an impoverished immigrant" (p. 118). Wong discusses several works of Asian American literature, pointing out their integral position in the American experience.

Readers are cautioned to avoid overly simplistic interpretations of works such as those discussed here. Distortions might occur due to our own cultural stereotypes, and even the perceptions of Asian American writers are tempered by the dominant culture. Nonetheless, books by and about Asian Americans can be valuable resources for social learning for both Asian American and non–Asian American youth.

The Role of Parents

To be effective in addressing the personal and social problems of Asian American students, professionals must become skilled in engaging the students' parents in the socialization process. With any cultural group, it is important to understand and display respect for the parents' socialization goals for their children. Asian American parents, for example, tend to want their children to take and maintain pride in their racial and cultural background, to observe filial piety, and to excel academically. Group alliance is particularly important for recent immigrant parents, who attempt to promote ethnic identity in their children by perpetuating their native languages, remaining in ethnic neighborhoods, and restricting early childhood social relationships to relatives and members of their own ethnic groups (Serafica, 1990).

For many Asian American parents the child's family obligations are met primarily through academic achievement in school. Academic achievement is highly valued among Asian Americans and is associated with the potential for financial success. Stevenson (1992) reports that Asian parents are likely to deemphasize the role of innate ability and stress instead the beneficial effects of effort and perseverance on academic performance. As a result of these views, parents tend to set high goals for their children and apply considerable pressure for them to excel in school (Divorsky, 1988; Yao, 1988). According to Serafica (1990), this pressure may cause many children unnecessary anxiety. With greater stress on effort than on basic abilities, handicaps such as mental retardation or learning disabilities tend to be overlooked or denied by Asian American parents, who are less likely to refer children for school intervention, preferring instead to deal with problems at home.

The high academic achievement of Asian American students is well established. There is evidence of a positive relationship between the child's achievement and the mother's investment in the child's schooling and psychological well-being (Divorsky, 1988). Academic achievement is also correlated with traditional values and close cultural ties, but, as Serafica (1990) notes, Asian American students whose mothers expressed strong ethnic identity tended to evidence higher alienation rates than Asian Americans whose mothers were more acculturated. Higher achievement among Asian Americans also may take its toll if teachers assume them to be self-sufficient and overlook them and if their superior performance provokes hostility on the part of other students (Divorsky, 1988).

The conditions encountered by Asian American immigrant parents translate into special socialization and school problems for their children. According to Serafica (1990), a child's entrance into school can become stressful as the parents become aware of the cultural and physical differences that appear to have negative impact on the self-concepts of Asian American children. As mentioned earlier, Asian American children often come to disparage their physical features and their cultural traditions. Serafica notes that the impact of cultural diversity intensifies during adolescence, when the influence of the dominant culture is increased through peer social activities and cross-cultural interactions between the sexes.

These conditions, along with differences between parent and child in rates of acculturation, further stress parents and strain the parent-child relationship. Because children often adapt quite rapidly to a new culture and a language that their parents continue to find intimidating, parents and children may reverse roles, with the children assuming more responsibility for the management of household affairs (Yao, 1988). These differences in acculturation may lead to wider communication gaps (Serafica, 1990) and conflict over issues such as diet (American versus ethnic food), language (English versus the native language; Yao, 1988), and various culturally specific behaviors such as questioning teachers, participating in certain social activities, and dating during the teen years (Divorsky, 1988).

Another critical point, especially with Asian Americans who are recent immigrants, concerns parents' opportunities to interact with their children. Because of their low socioeconomic status and relatively poor work conditions, both parents often find it necessary to work long hours. Moreover, many immigrants are in this country without their birth parents, living with relatives or guardians. These conditions minimize parental contact and supervision, possibly contributing to problems of delinquency, low self-esteem, and undeveloped self-identity (Chua-Eoan, 1990; Serafica, 1990; Yao, 1988).

Although it is important for professionals to improve their understanding of Asian American parents and to avoid stereotypes, Yao (1988) suggests that we may with validity characterize Asian American parents as quiet, submissive, and cooperative with school personnel. She also points out that they tend to be reluctant to acknowledge or seek counseling for problems and that they are likely to differ from majority group parents on issues such as sex education, dating, and obedience to parents.

Asians' great respect for teachers often inhibits parents from challenging teachers' authority or initiating contact with the school. Yao (1988) advises that to do so is considered disrespectful by many Asian American parents. Therefore, school personnel should initiate contact with Asian American parents to involve them in building a partnership with the school, to educate them about the culture of the school and the dominant society, and to collaborate with the parents in encouraging the child's social development. Yao offers several useful suggestions for working with Asian American parents. She recommends actively involving Asian American parents in school governance—for instance, inviting them to serve on advisory boards. She points to examples in California where this has been done with success. Because immigrant parents need to be educated about the schools, Yao suggests holding seminars, using interpreters if needed, to provide information about the school, its policies, and the services and resources available to parents. Ongoing communication can be assured through regular parent-teacher conferences and periodic newsletters translated into the language of the parents. In some cases parents can be a resource in addressing some sensitive social problems. For example, Yao (1988) tells of visiting her daughter's class to educate the girl's classmates about the origin of her daughter's name— a name that previously had elicited teasing from the classmates.

Teachers should refrain from assuming that their views on child-rearing are superior or always in the best interest of the child. Rather, teachers should know how to obtain information from the parents so they can better understand the parents' attitudes toward social or cultural differences and work with the parents to promote the child's social and academic development.

Summary

We use the term *Asian American* to refer to people from East Asia, Southeast Asia, Asian India, and the South Pacific. Although Asian Americans are a diverse group with distinct backgrounds and histories in the United States, there are sufficient commonalities among them to warrant joint grouping for discussion of social skill instruction. Greatly influenced by Eastern philosophers and teachings, Asian Americans generally are relationship-oriented people with strong family allegiance and reverence for authority. Child-rearing practices emphasize compliant behaviors, respect for elders, and academic achievement. Their high academic achievement and unobtrusive behaviors cause Asian Americans to be viewed as an ideal or "model minority" group. Teachers consistently rate these students more highly in social and academic behaviors than their peers from other racial and ethnic groups.

Despite this prevailing view and their obvious record of achievement, many Asian American youth feel alienated and experience problems related to self-concept. This is especially true for Asian Americans who are recent immigrants and live under conditions of poverty or inadequate parental supervision. Many of these young people are at risk for academic and social failure, often manifested in the form of antisocial, gang-related behaviors during adolescence. Other youngsters may resort to extreme internalizing behaviors, often failing to initiate contact with others or to make their concerns known. A cultural tendency to maintain privacy and handle problems within the family or community somewhat hampers recognition of various behavioral or social concerns.

For Asian American youth and their parents, acculturation levels are a critical issue in social skill instruction. Traditional Asian values appear to be a major factor in fostering academic achievement and in promoting compliant and reserved behaviors. On the other hand, low levels of acculturation may interfere with feelings of belonging and the development of healthy peer relationships. Social skill instruction needs to be culturally relevant and situation specific. Trainers need to be aware of learners' cultural backgrounds and to help learners view culturally specific behaviors as differences, not as inferior or superior ways of doing things. Like members of other racial or ethnic minorities, Asian American youth need social skill instruction that fosters biculturalism, helping them acquire social skills needed for success and emotional well-being in the mainstream culture while retaining, valuing, and applying, as appropriate, the behavioral patterns from their cultural heritage.

Direct instruction, cooperative learning, and the use of literature provide promising approaches for social skill instruction with Asian American students. Special attention also needs to be given to working with the parents of these young people.

References

Abe, J.S., & Zane, N.W. (1990). Psychological maladjustment among Asian and White American college students: Controlling for confounds. *Journal of Counseling Psychology, 37*(4), 437–444.

Asamen, J.K., & Berry, G.L. (1987). Self-concept, alienation, and perceived prejudice: Implications for counseling Asian Americans. *Journal of Multicultural Counseling and Development 15*(4), 146–159.

Ashabranner, B., & Ashabranner, M. (1987). *Into a strange land: Unaccompanied refugee youth in America.* New York: Putnam.

Banks, J.A. (1991). *Teaching strategies for ethnic studies* (5th ed.). Boston: Allyn & Bacon.

Bode, J. (1989). *New kids on the block: Oral histories of immigrant teens.* New York: Franklin Watts.

Breiner, S.J. (1980). Early child development in China. *Child Psychiatry and Human Development, 11,* 87–95.

Bunting, E. (1982). *The happy funeral.* Baltimore: HarperCollins.

Burnett, F.H. (1911). *The secret garden.* Philadelphia: Lippincott.

Burton, G.M. (1986). Values education in Chinese primary schools. *Childhood Education, 62,* 250–255.

Cartledge, G., & Cochran, L.L. (1993). Developing cooperative learning behaviors in students with behavior disorders. *Preventing School Failure, 37,* 5–10.

Cartledge, G., & Kleefeld, J. (1994). *Working together: Building children's social skills through folk literature.* Circle Pines, MN: American Guidance Service.

Chen, X., & Rubin, K.H. (1992). Correlates of peer acceptance in a Chinese sample of six-year-olds. *The International Journal of Behavioral Development, 15,* 259–273.

Chen, X., Rubin, K.H., & Sun, Y. (1992). Social reputation and peer relationships in Chinese and Canadian children: A cross-cultural study. *Child Development, 63,* 1336–1343.

Chin, K. (1990). *Chinese subculture and criminality.* New York: Greenwood.

Chu, C.L. (1973). Tsung she hui ko jen yu wen hua ti kuan hsi lun chung-kuo jen hsin ko ti tzu kan chu hsiang. In Y. Li & K. Yang (Eds.), *Symposium on the character of the Chinese: An interdisciplinary approach.* Taipei, Taiwan: Institute of Ethnology Academic Sinica.

Chu, E., & Schuler, C.V. (1992). United States: Asian Americans. In L. Miller-Lachmann (Ed.), *Our family, our friends, our world.* New Providence, NJ: Bowker.

Chu, L. (1979). The sensitivity of Chinese and American children to social influences. *Journal of Social Psychology, 109,* 175–186.

Chua-Eoan, H.G. (1990, April 9). Strangers in paradise. *Time*, pp. 32–35.

Clark, K., & Clark, M. (1947). Racial identification and preference in Negro children. In T.M. Newcomb & E.L. Hartley (Eds.), *Readings in social psychology*. New York: Holt, Rinehart & Winston.

Cook, H., & Chi, C. (1984). Cooperative behavior and locus of control among American and Chinese-American boys. *Journal of Psychology*, *118*, 169–177.

Cowart, M.T., & Cowart, R.E. (1993, December). Southeast Asian refugee youth and the cycle of violence. *NAASP Bulletin*, pp. 40–45.

Crew, L. (1989). *Children of the river*. New York: Delacorte.

Dao, M. (1991). Designing assessment procedures for educationally at-risk Southeast Asian–American students. *Journal of Learning Disabilities*, *24*, 594–601, 629.

Divorsky, D. (1988, November). The model minority goes to school. *Phi Delta Kappan*, 219–222.

Domino, G., & Hannah, M.T. (1987). A comparative analysis of social values of Chinese and American children. *Journal of Cross-Cultural Psychology*, *18*(1), 58–77.

Feng, H., & Cartledge, G. (1996). Social skills assessment of inner city Asian, African, and European American students. *School Psychology Review*, *25*, 227–238.

Fox, D.J., & Jordan, V.B. (1973). Racial preference and identification of Black, American Chinese, and White children. *Genetic Psychology Monographs*, *88*, 229–286.

Fukuyama, M.A., & Coleman, N.C. (1992). A model for bicultural assertion training with Asian-Pacific American college students: A pilot study. *The Journal for Specialists in Group Work*, *17*, 210–217.

Gim-Chung, R.H. (1994, August). *Measurement of acculturation and cultural identity: A comparative analysis*. Paper presented at the annual conference of the American Psychological Association, Los Angeles.

Hartman, J.S., & Askounis, A.C. (1989). Asian-American students: Are they really a "model minority"? *The School Counselor*, *37*, 109–112.

Ho, D.Y.F. (1986). Chinese patterns of socialization: A critical review. In M.H. Bond (Ed.), *The psychology of the Chinese people*. New York: Oxford University Press.

Howes, C., & Wu, F. (1990). Peer interactions and friendships in an ethnically diverse school setting. *Child Development*, *61*, 537–541.

Hsu, J. (1985). The Chinese family: Relations, problems, and therapy. In W.S. Tseng & D.Y.H. Wu (Eds.), *Chinese culture and mental health.* Orlando, FL: Academic.

Huang, L.C. (1981). The Chinese American family. In C.H. Mindel & R.W. Harbestein (Eds.), *Ethnic families in America: Patterns and variations* (2nd ed.) New York: Elsevier.

Huang, L.N., & Ying, Y. (1989). Chinese American children and adolescents. In J.T. Gibbs, L.N. Huang, & Associates (Eds.), *Children of color.* San Francisco: Jossey-Bass.

Ishii-Jordan, S., & Peterson, R.L. (1994). Behavioral disorders in the context of Asian cultures. In S. Ishii-Jordan & R.L. Peterson (Eds.), *Multicultural issues in the education of students with behavioral disorders.* Cambridge, MA: Brookline.

Johnson, D.W., & Johnson, R.T. (1987). *Learning together and alone: Cooperative, competitive, and individualistic learning.* Englewood Cliffs, NJ: Prentice-Hall.

King, A.Y.C., & Bond, M.H. (1985). The Confucian paradigm of man: A sociological view. In W.S. Tseng & D.Y.H. Wu (Eds.), *Chinese culture and mental health.* Orlando, FL: Academic.

Kohatsu, E.L. (1994, August). *Racial identity attitudes: Implications and applications for Asian Americans.* Paper presented at the annual conference of the American Psychological Association, Los Angeles.

Leong, F.T., & Chou, E.L. (1994). The role of ethnic identity and acculturation in the vocational behavior of Asian Americans: An integrative review. *Journal of Vocational Behavior, 44,* 155–172.

Leung, E.K. (1988). Cultural and acculturational commonalities and diversities among Asian Americans: Identification and programming considerations. In A.A. Ortiz & B.A. Ramirez (Eds.), *Schools and the culturally diverse exceptional student: Promising practices and future directions.* Reston, VA: ERIC Clearinghouse on Handicapped and Gifted Children.

Leung, E.K. (1990). Early risks: Transition from culturally/linguistically diverse homes to formal schooling. *The Journal of Educational Issues of Language Minority Students, 7,* 35–51.

Lord, B.B. (1984). *In the year of the boar and Jackie Robinson.* Baltimore: HarperCollins.

Ma, H. (1985). Cross-cultural study of the development of law-abiding orientation. *Psychological Reports, 57,* 967–974.

Ma, H. (1988). The Chinese perspectives on moral judgment development. *International Journal of Psychology, 23*(2), 201–227.

Ma, H. (1989). Moral orientation and moral judgment in adolescents in Hong Kong, Mainland China, and England. *Journal of Cross-Cultural Psychology, 20,* 152–177.

MacMillan, D., & Freeman, D. (1987). *My best friend Duc Tran: Meeting a Vietnamese American family.* Englewood Cliffs, NJ: Julian Messner.

Middleton, M.B. (1994). *The effects of social skills instruction and parent participation on aggressive behaviors, antisocial behaviors, and prosocial skills exhibited by primary-age students.* Unpublished doctoral dissertation, The Ohio State University, Columbus.

Mok, T.A. (1994, August). *Asian American interracial dating, acculturation, and aspects of ethnic identity.* Paper presented at the annual conference of the American Psychological Association, Los Angeles.

Moore, D.L. (1989). *Dark sky, dark land: Stories of the Hmong Boy Scouts of Troop 100.* Eden Prairie, MN: Tessera.

Moriya, K. (1989). A developmental and cross-cultural study of the interpersonal cognition of English and Japanese children. *Japanese Psychological Research, 31,* 108–115.

Morrow, R.D. (1994). Immigration, refugee and generation status as related to behavioral disorders. In R.L. Peterson & S. Ishii-Jordan (Eds.), *Multicultural issues in the education of students with behavioral disorders.* Cambridge, MA: Brookline.

Mou, C. (1963). *Characteristics of Chinese culture.* Hong Kong: Jen Sheng.

Nagata, D. (1989). Japanese American children and adolescents. In J.T. Gibbs, L.N. Huang, & Associates (Eds.), *Children of color.* San Francisco: Jossey-Bass.

Ogbu, J. (1987). Variability in minority school performance: A problem in search of explanation. *Anthropology and Education Quarterly, 18*(4), 312–334.

Perry, T., & Fraser, J.W. (1993). *Freedom's plow: Teaching in the multicultural classroom.* New York: Routledge.

Reglin, G.L., & Adams, D.R. (1990). Why Asian-American high school students have higher grade point averages and SAT scores than other high school students. *High School Journal, 73*(3), 143–149.

Rumbaut, R.G. (1985). Mental health and the refugee experience: A comparative study of Southeast Asian refugees. In T.C. Owan, B. Bliatout, R.M. Lin, W. Liu, T.D. Nguyen, & H.C. Wong (Eds.),

Southeast Asian mental health: Treatment, prevention, services, training, and research. Washington, DC: U.S. Department of Health and Human Services.

Schneider, B., & Lee, Y. (1990). A model for academic success: The school and home environment of East Asian students. *Anthropology & Education Quarterly, 21,* 358–377.

Sedel, R. (1972). *Women and child care in China.* New York: Hill & Wang.

Serafica, F.C. (1990). Counseling Asian-American parents: A cultural-development approach. In F.C. Serafica, A.I. Schwebel, R.K. Russell, P.D. Isaac, & L.B. Myers (Eds.), *Mental health of ethnic minorities.* New York: Praeger.

Stevenson, H.W. (1992, December). Learning from Asian schools. *Scientific American,* pp. 70–76.

Sue, D.W. (1981). *Counseling the culturally different: Theory and practice.* New York: Wiley.

Sue, D.W., & Frank, A.C. (1973). A typological approach to the psychological study of Chinese and Japanese American college males. *Journal of Social Issues, 29,* 129–148.

Sue, S., & Morishima, J.K. (1982). *The mental health of Asian Americans: Contemporary issues in identifying and treating mental problems.* San Francisco: Jossey-Bass.

Surat, M.M. (1983). *Angel child, dragon child.* Milwaukee: Raintree.

Tan, A. (1990). *The Joy Luck Club.* New York: Ballantine.

13-year-old a Chinatown gang enforcer, police say. (1994, November 29). *Columbus Dispatch,* p. 3A.

Turner, S.M., & Mo, L. (1984). Chinese adolescents' self-concept as measured by the Offer Self-Image Questionnaire. *Journal of Youth and Adolescence, 13*(2), 131–143.

U.S. Bureau of the Census. (1993). *Statistical abstract of the United States: 1993* (113th ed.) Washington, DC: Author.

Uchida, Y. (1988). *Picture bride.* Boston: Simon & Schuster.

Wells, E.A., Morrison, D.M., Gillmore, M.R., Catalano, R.F., Iritani, B., & Hawkins, J.D. (1992). Race differences in antisocial behaviors and attitudes and early initiation of substance use. *Journal of Drug Education, 22,* 115–130.

Wong, S.C. (1993). Promises, pitfalls, and principles of text selection in curricular diversification. In T. Perry & J.W. Fraser (Eds.), *Freedom's plow: Teaching in the multicultural classroom.* New York: Routledge.

Wu, D.Y.H. (1985). Child training in Chinese culture. In W.S. Tseng & D.Y.H. Wu (Eds.), *Chinese culture and mental health*. Orlando, FL: Academic.

Xu, Z., Shen, J., Wan, C.W., Li, C., Mussen, P., & Cao, Z. (1990). Family socialization and children's behavior and personality development in China. *Journal of Genetic Psychology, 152*(2), 239–253.

Yao, E.L. (1988, November). Working effectively with Asian immigrant parents. *Phi Delta Kappan,* pp. 223–225.

CHAPTER 4

African Americans

GWENDOLYN CARTLEDGE AND MYRA B. MIDDLETON

African Americans are largely descendants of West Africans who were imported to North America as slave labor beginning in the 1600s. Since the abolition of slavery in 1863, African Americans have been native-born Americans; they currently constitute the largest minority group in the United States. The U.S. Bureau of the Census (1993) records the 1991 African American population at 31,164,000, or 12.4 percent of the U.S. population. This percentage is projected to increase to 12.9 percent by the year 2000 and to 16.2 percent by 2050. During the same period the White American population is expected to go from 83.6 percent to 71.8 percent, and other minorities will grow from 4 percent to 12 percent.

Although slavery located most blacks in the southern part of the United States, during and since the "great migration" (i.e., 1920s to 1940s), thousands of blacks moved from the South to other urban centers. Today most African Americans (approximately 53 percent) continue to reside in the South, but they are represented in every geographic area of the country, with the second largest segment (19.1 percent) in the Midwest, followed by 18.7 percent in the Northeast and 9.4 percent in the West. Metropolitan areas with the greatest concentrations of African Americans are New York, Baltimore–Washington D.C., Chicago, Los Angeles, Philadelphia, and Detroit.

The African American lifestyle in the United States is characterized by some significant differences from the mainstream. One difference concerns education: As of 1992, 67.7 percent of African Americans were reported to have graduated from high school,

133

20.1 percent had some college, and 11.9 percent had 4 years of college or advanced degrees. Comparable data for Whites allowed 81 percent as high school graduates, 22.5 percent with some college, and 22.5 percent having baccalaureate or advanced degrees (U.S. Bureau of the Census, 1993).

Since the 1960s various forces appear to have had significant impact on the African American family structure and other life circumstances. By 1992, the proportion of Black households including married couples had dropped to 47 percent from the 68 percent recorded in 1970, with females heading 46 percent of the family households. The median family income in 1992 was $21,548 (compared to $37,783 for Whites), and at least 30 percent of African American families lived below the poverty line. Approximately 62 percent of African American children under 18 were reported to live in single-parent households, a circumstance that appears largely influenced by education and economics. Children living with two parents begin to outnumber those in single-parent homes once the parents' education reaches the college level and the family income exceeds $25,000 per year.

Poor economic, educational, and racial conditions converge to create the most dismal of all statistics, those pertaining to mortality and crime. Beginning in infancy, African Americans have a much higher mortality rate. In 1989, the U.S. Department of Health and Human Services reported infant mortality rates per 1,000 births to be 18.6 for African Americans compared to 8.1 for Whites (Horton & Smith, 1990). Total life expectancy is lower, as evidenced by the 1989 data, showing average life spans for African American females and males of 73.5 and 64.8 years, respectively, compared to 79.2 and 72.7 years for White females and males. The substantially shorter life spans of African American males are partly accounted for by the data on homicides. For 1990, the U.S. Bureau of the Census (1993) reported 69.2 deaths per 100,000 for African American males and 13.5 deaths per 100,000 for African American females. These figures are compared to 9.0 for White males and 2.8 for White females. For African American males between the ages of 20 and 24, the homicide rates peaked at a level of 140.7 per 100,000. Suicide rates increased as well for African American males, from 8.0 per 100,000 in 1970 to 12.0 in 1990, but dropped slightly for females, from 2.6

to 2.3, during the same period. African American females have the lowest suicide rates for both races and genders.

Slightly more black (26.7 percent) than white (23.2 percent) families reported being affected by crime, with African Americans being arrested for approximately 34 percent of all serious crimes in the United States. Robbery (61 percent), suspicion of various crimes (58.6 percent), and murder (54.8 percent) were the three most frequent reasons for arrest. Although these are figures for arrests, not convictions, and they do not represent the majority of crime in America, it is important to recognize that for a variety of reasons, African Americans are disproportionately represented in the criminal justice system.

Cultural Distinctions

African Americans are a diverse group, represented within every social, economic, and occupational status in U.S. society. The wide range of appearance and skin tone attests to the varied racial mixture of Native Americans and European Americans in this group's heritage. As the economic gap within the group widens, cultural and social diversity among African Americans will become even greater. Nevertheless, there are certain markers that may be considered cultural traditions and expressions that greatly influence African Americans' experience in this society.

Psychosocial Factors

The role of self-concept in the academic and social progress of African American youth is the focus of significant and protracted study and debate. Since the classic Clark and Clark (1947) study where young black children showed a preference for white dolls, much of the evidence has suggested that black children have lower self-esteem and less self-confidence than their white counterparts. Kuykendall (1992), for example, cites research conducted by Silberman (1971) showing that the percentage of African American students holding a positive self-image declined from 80 percent at school entrance to less than 5 percent by the senior year.

These research findings, however, are not universally accepted, and more recent studies show self-esteem assessments for African American youth to be comparable to, if not more favorable than, those of their European American counterparts (Hare, 1985). According to Spencer (1988), earlier reports suggesting that young African American children generally made negative associations with black colors and people was largely a function of caste-related ecosystem experiences (that is, the child's cognitive development and exposure to racially biased imagery) along with the fact that much of this research was conducted and interpreted by nonblack researchers. Spencer further contends that the predominantly Eurocentric cultural orientation can be favorably altered through an infusion of Afrocentric curricula and that the effects of Eurocentric referencing are reduced during adolescence, producing more positive self-evaluations. This position is supported by Widaman, MacMillan, Hemsley, Little, and Balow (1992). These researchers studied self-concept among African American, White, and Hispanic American eighth-grade students as indicated on the Self Description Questionnaire II (Marsh & Barnes, 1982). They grouped students in three academic categories: (a) regular achieving, (b) educationally marginal, and (c) learning handicapped. The latter students had been placed in special education classes and were considered to have mild mental retardation, learning disabilities, or behavior disorders. With the exception of the educationally marginal White students, who scored much lower than the other two groups, students' self-concept scores were consistent with their academic levels—that is, "regular achieving" students had the highest scores, and the "learning handicapped" group had the lowest scores. Academic achievement scores in reading and math were comparable for African American and White students and slightly lower for Hispanic American students. Self-concept scores were highest for the African American students and lowest for the Hispanic American students in regular classes and those with learning disabilities. The authors explained the higher African American self-concept scores with reference to Miller, Turnbull, and McFarland's (1988) theory of "particularistic" rather than "universalistic" comparison. In the latter, people compare themselves to all possible individuals who make up a group (e.g., the universe of eighth graders). On the other hand, in particularistic comparison, evaluations are made relative to those with whom one "feels a shared identity or bond" (p. 399). They postulated that, in contrast to White students, African American students were more likely to compare themselves to members of their own group than to "more stringent" external standards. And because academic expectations tend to be lower for African American students, performing above expected levels might have elevated the African American students' self-concepts. Another plausible but related interpretation of the Widaman et al. (1992) findings is that group identity becomes most salient for minority youth during adolescence, and during this period they are likely to ignore, discredit, or reject the behaviors and values of the dominant culture.

A recent trend in the analysis of the psychosocial development of African American youth is to move away from deficit models based on comparison against mainstream standards of some construct such as self-concept toward a focus on identity or identity formation (Taylor, 1989). Taylor describes identity formation, viewed as perhaps the most critical function of adolescence, as a complex process that involves making choices regarding how one defines oneself. Using a social learning paradigm, he posits that the role models and significant others in a youth's environment are most critical to this developmental experience. Jackson (1976) describes self-identity as the means by which individuals define their environment, their places in the environment, and the way they address problems of living. According to Jackson, individual identity results from various influences, including, in U.S. society, racism. To illuminate identity issues within a context of ethnicity and racism, Ogbu (1988) introduces the concept of voluntary and involuntary minorities. Voluntary minorities are those immigrating to this country by choice in search of a better way of life. For the most part they see cultural differences as barriers to overcome, actively pursuing language learning and other behaviors in order to become successful in mainstream society. In contrast, involuntary minorities are groups who were either conquered (e.g., Native Americans) or brought to this country against their will (e.g., African Americans). These groups became part of a caste in which they were relegated to menial work, discriminated against, and refused full integration into the dominant society. These conditions led to a distrust of the majority culture and the development of an "oppositional cultural frame of reference" (p. 24). Markers of this resistant mentality include use of nonstandard English and academic underachievement.

Jackson (1976) presents a four-stage developmental model to describe the process of identity formation among African Americans. The first stage, labeled "passive acceptance," is characterized by total acquiescence and belief in the superiority of the dominant culture. People at this stage are inclined to deny their own self-worth and to seek acceptance or validation by the white majority. They are likely to reject the notion that racism exists, to suggest that the problems of African Americans are totally self-induced, and to subscribe to white standards of beauty and "ways of acting." As the individual becomes aware that this thinking does not lead to a positive image of oneself, he or she moves into stage two, "active resistance." This stage is the antithesis of the preceding one: The individual proceeds to reject totally everything associated with the white culture. A fierce antiwhite mindset emerges, and the individual believes in employing "whatever means necessary" to secure control, to obtain money, and to establish a segregated black environment. At stage three, "redirection," the individual turns inward, taking the position that "reacting to whites either by embracing or by rejecting is misdirected energy, a waste of time, distracting and irrelevant" (p. 14). At this stage the individual is no longer seeking or rejecting the white culture. For the most part the individual is indifferent to the majority group's actions but rather seeks self-validation through the African American community and its culture. The stage three individual focuses on exploring and strengthening his or her own culture and traditions. After achieving a positive self-identity, the individual can then move to the fourth stage, "internalization." At this point, according to Jackson, the individual verifies his or her own self-worth and can reach out to others, regardless of race, without feeling "compromised or violated" (p. 19). Jackson's four-stage model suggests that blacks view whites in a variety of ways and that interventions need to be structured according to individuals' worldviews. A stage two individual, for example, is likely to reject anything associated with the dominant culture, even if the benefit of specific messages or values to the individual is obvious.

Jackson's stages are incorporated into the Racial Identity Attitude Scale (RIAS; Parham & Helms, 1981), a means for measuring self-identity among African Americans. Ryujin and Abitia (1992) used this instrument with African American college students. They found relatively low incidences of stage one, the phase where individuals devalue their own race in preference for the dominant group. Although the highest mean scores reflected stage four, indicating feelings of inner security and a "decline in strong antiwhite feelings" (p. 5), the authors expressed surprise at the rather high scores on the subscale depicting intense African American pride and a corresponding denigration of European culture and people. They speculated that this latter finding might be a function of heightened racial tensions on college campuses.

Race is also the central theme used by Fordham (1988) in exploring the identity tensions and conflicts experienced by African American adolescents. Fordham presents the concept of "fictive kinship," which pertains to the notion of a "collective social identity" as seen in commonly used terms such as *brother, sister,* and *blood.* Fictive kinship represents a system of peoplehood and evolves in response to mistreatment from whites. According to Fordham, African American children learn about fictive kinship during their developing years, and they attempt to establish their connectedness to their indigenous culture by subscribing to group-specific values and styles such as use of Black English. Full membership in the subculture means rejecting beliefs and patterns of the dominant group, particularly the schooling process that emphasizes individualism and academic achievement. Fordham postulates that students who wish to pursue school success must assume a position of "racelessness," which includes behaviors such as speaking "properly," minimizing allegiance to the African American community, and denying the presence and importance of racism. In an ethnographic study of inner city high school students, Fordham observed the racelessness phenomenon among several high-achieving students. She also noted that female students were more inclined to subscribe to the behaviors and values of the dominant culture than were males. Fordham elaborates on this gender difference:

> Unlike the male students, whose "duality of socialization"
> is clearly evident in both their behaviors and responses,
> the female students appear to be much less victimized
> by the fact that they are required to live in two worlds

concurrently. Indeed, they appear to be more unanimously committed to the ideology and values of the larger society than they are to the norms and values of the existing fictive-kinship system. (p. 67)

Fordham observed high-achieving male students to have much more difficulty assuming a stance of racelessness; she asks whether the resulting conflict leads the race-conscious African American male adolescent "to respond in a negative way to school-sanctioned norms" (p. 77). Fordham suggests that the individualistic, achievement-oriented school culture puts typical African American students at odds with their own collectivistic culture, forcing them to make apparent choices between community allegiance and academic or individual success.

The compromise described by Fordham (1988) may be quite costly for high-achieving African American students. Clark (1991) suggests that the African American adolescent who adopts a raceless persona risks losing social competence through alienation from peers within the indigenous cultural group. Peer support and interaction are extremely important during this period of development. Two other at-risk groups identified by Clark are those with "oppositional social identity" (p. 43) and those with "diffused identity" (p. 44). Adolescents with oppositional social identity are those who respond to racism with anger and rebelliousness. They dislike and distrust members of the dominant group and therefore resist mainstream socialization. Students with diffused identity are alienated from both African American and White societies. They are characterized by self-esteem problems, poor academic performances, and social incompetence. According to Clark, resilience and adequate coping can occur within a state of "biculturalism" (p. 42), in which an individual can move effectively between the dominant and minority cultures. Clark describes biculturalism as "the ability to draw simultaneously on standardized African-American group behavior and on behaviors accepted by the mainstream cultural system" (p. 42). Socialization for biculturalism is a lifelong process that begins at birth with exposure to various cultures and learning experiences that enable one to value cultural diversity and develop critical social and problem-solving skills. Bicultural youngsters manage to maintain strong identification with their own ethnic group while actively participating in the mainstream culture; they are more likely to be academically and socially competent.

A slightly different approach to self-identity is taken by Taylor (1989), who focuses on the importance of role models and socioeconomic status. Taylor compared the identity formation of African American male college students to that of low-income inner city African American adolescents. For the college students he found that role model identification centered largely on family, with the mother serving primarily a moral and emotional function and the father emerging in later adolescence as a source for other aspects of personal identity. In contrast, nearly half of the inner city youth reported no significant role models, rationalizing this state with comments such as "I want to be myself" and characterizing the use of models as "phony," "childish," and "unrealistic" (p. 165). These adolescent males were less inclined to identify with their fathers, displayed a general distrust of the significant others in their environment, and reported common experiences of disappointment in self and others. School proved to be their greatest source of frustration; they reported few experiences of success or encouragement.

Whereas the college students named individuals from the larger society (e.g., politicians, civic leaders) as influential, the peer group emerged as the major source of influence for the inner city youth. The latter also revealed limited knowledge about and unrealistic attitudes toward future occupations. The tendency for these young men to define themselves so narrowly was an indication to Taylor of "identity foreclosure, i.e., a premature crystallization of identity" (p. 167). Despite the emphasis on role models and significant others in this study, race and racism still emerged as an important factor in identity formation. For the low-income males it undoubtedly contributed to perceptions of limited options. College students in the study who continued to be ambivalent about personal identity were believed to be torn between African American and European American value systems. This ambivalence

> tends to generate strong feelings of indignation and rage
> among these youths and frequently delays or interferes
> with the process of consolidating values, selecting
> appropriate role models, and defining career aspirations.

Indeed, for those youth in our sample whose responses yielded evidence of such a dilemma, their role model identifications and general value orientations tended to be more tentative and less definitive than for youth who were less preoccupied with or aware of the dilemma, or who had succeeded in resolving it. (Taylor, 1989, p. 164)

A variety of factors combine to influence the identity formation of African American youth. Some of these variables are negative (e.g., racism and poverty) and have a corrosive effect on psychological development. Young African Americans need to acquire realistic and constructive attitudes and behaviors toward their own and the dominant culture, and teachers and other professionals need to understand potentially interfering forces in order to create environments and design interventions that will help students achieve these goals.

The Family

The family is viewed as an extremely important and resilient cultural tradition in the African American community (Franklin, 1988; Wilson, 1986). Slavery and other poor living conditions forced African Americans to rely largely on the family for support in nearly every aspect of existence. Perhaps the most significant and prevailing feature of the black family is its structure, often viewed as a collective social network emphasizing a sense of community and the survival of its members. Peters (1988) describes the traditional black family as "strong, functional, and flexible" (p. 233). Others point out that the extended African American family may assume various constellations, reaching as far as cousins or community members (Goode, 1979; Wilson, 1989). Harrison, Wilson, Pine, Chan, and Buriel (1990) report that "three times as many African American children under the age of 18 lived with their grandparents than white children" (p. 351), and Tienda and Angel (1982) similarly observed that blacks had a greater tendency than whites to include extended family members in their households.

Although it may be debated whether this extended family phenomenon is more a function of culture or of economics, it is a well-established pattern within African and African American families. Foster (1983) examined the extended family in precolonial Africa and observed that it was an extremely stable unit, even under the rare circumstance of divorce. Families in this culture fulfilled several needs, including economic stability, socialization, social control, and social security. Within the major function of socialization, for example, all members of the extended family, and sometimes individuals outside the compound, were expected to help teach the young how to act in the society. By pooling resources, systematically applying sanctions and rewards, and providing social and emotional support, these communes garnered the economic, regulatory, and psychological resources needed for an orderly, productive society. Foster contends that the extended family network typically observed among contemporary African Americans is a carryover from the precolonial African culture and has served as a stabilizing force in the African American community.

Likewise, Wilson (1986) proposes that the extended black family is a distinct, healthy system providing financial and emotional support that is particularly valuable for single mothers and their children. Wilson (1989) identifies the beneficial functions of the extended family as (a) providing financial support, (b) allowing adolescent parents more opportunities to engage in self-development such as completing school or pursuing vocational training, (c) providing adequate models for child-rearing, and (d) fostering wholesome behaviors and curbing deviant activities. Wilson found grandmothers in these families to be more responsive and less punitive than the adolescent mothers. Grandmothers and other family members frequently serve as baby-sitters for working parents and volunteer the wisdom that comes with their years. Other researchers found perceptions of support from the extended family to be associated with parents' being better "educators" for their children (Slaughter & Epps, 1987) and with lower levels of depression in black males (Dressler, 1985).

Franklin (1988) stresses the traditional strength of the African American family, pointing out that, despite the hardships of slavery, poverty, discrimination, and legal segregation, until 1960 at least 75 percent of black families were two-parent families. In the intervening three decades, the black family has been severely affected by various crippling forces such as urbanization, ghettoization, and "racially hostile governmental and societal practices, policies and attitudes" (Franklin, 1988, p. 25) so that currently over 60 percent of

African American children are being reared in single-parent households (U.S. Bureau of the Census, 1993). Two major factors contributing to this situation may have been the failure in recent years of black males to achieve gainful employment and the willingness of the social service system to establish independent households for unmarried mothers, often removing them from the previously noted advantages of the extended family and relieving young men of basic family responsibilities. Social scientists such as Foster (1983), however, criticize the pathological image typically painted of the black family, arguing that it should be measured by the presence of its extended network system rather than against the nuclear family structure of Western society.

As with other groups, the African American family plays a central role in the socialization of children, equipping them with "adaptive strategies" that will lead to a positive sense of self and attainment of desired social goals (Harrison et al., 1990). Child-rearing practices of African American families are often described as controlling or authoritarian rather than democratic or authoritative. In the controlling orientation, parents tend to stress obedience, respect for elders, neatness, cleanliness, and staying out of trouble. They are more likely to use physical punishment and are sometimes arbitrary in their discipline. According to Maccoby (1980), this style seems to be more damaging to boys than to girls, a view based on research showing boys in authoritarian families to display more dependent, angry, and defiant behaviors. A similar effect on boys appears to result from permissive parenting. In her review of literature largely pertaining to the dominant culture, Maccoby (1992) contends that "power-assertive" socialization techniques are counterproductive for bringing about self-regulated behavior and internalized standards. According to Maccoby, the optimal parenting style appears to be authoritative, a balance between permissive parenting, where there are few restrictions, and authoritarian methods that use maximum parental control.

Despite the prevailing image of the African American authoritarian parent, Peters (1988) argues that the "strict, no-nonsense" style is not harsh, rigid, or egocentrically motivated but rather represents the "functional, appropriate discipline of caring parents" (p. 233). She also notes parenting similarities across racial groups: Middle-income black mothers were found to speak to their children as much as do middle-income white mothers. Other researchers also dispute the applicability of the uniform authoritarian model, even among African American families of low socioeconomic status. Slaughter and Epps (1987), for example, report evidence showing that mothers in the latter group promote academic and social competence in their children by setting clear and firm standards and exhibiting warm and accepting parenting behaviors. Clark (1983) studied home environments of high- and low-achieving black students from low-income backgrounds and found high-achieving students in homes where parents provided (a) structure and close monitoring of children's activities, (b) "literacy-enhancing learning experiences" (p. 7), (c) supportive and wholesome family environments, and (d) academically oriented values and role models.

Although the "strong" African American mother is often blamed for her children's failures, research shows the African American mother to be a major force in the aspirations and achievement of her children (Shade, 1983; Slaughter & Epps, 1987). Shade reports research showing that (a) the African American mother was the person most likely to support and encourage her child's aspirations and goal pursuits, (b) aspirations and drives were higher among African American youth than in other racial groups, and (c) identification with the mother rather than the father was associated with high achievement in black males. The impact of the African American father has not been extensively researched, but there is some evidence of positive paternal influence on achievement (Shade, 1983) and exceptional independence (McAdoo, 1988) of daughters. Additionally, fathers are shown to influence the sex-role orientation of their sons (Shade, 1983), and their absence from the home appears to be a factor in their sons' incarceration (Marcus, Matlach, McGreavy, Rouse, & Flatter, 1992). According to McAdoo (1988), parenting styles of African American fathers parallel those of the dominant group, and fathers' active participation in the socialization of their children increases proportionately with their economic solvency.

The role of racism is an important issue in African American parenting. Parents at all socioeconomic levels report the need to foster high self-esteem and self-confidence in their children so they can overcome the racial barriers in U.S. society (Peters, 1988). The parents also indicate that they try to socialize their children to have friends in the black community and to be accepted and successful in the white community. Peters suggests that the parenting styles of

African American parents are in a state of flux as many attempt to move into the middle-class and, concomitantly, adopt middle-class values and styles.

The African American family has experienced some pronounced changes that likely will produce corresponding changes in parenting practices and children's behaviors. As the economic gap within the black community widens, differences in parenting styles and child behaviors will increase accordingly. A review of the literature indicates that beneficial effects of traditional African American families on their children include (a) higher levels of self-esteem (Hare, 1985), (b) higher levels of independence among females (McAdoo, 1988), (c) higher levels of drive and aspiration (Shade, 1983), and (d) reduced levels of illicit drug and alcohol use among school-aged youth (Allison & Leone, 1994). The impact of unrelenting poverty, premature parenting, family isolation, and chronic joblessness, however, have weakened these potential effects for low-income families.

The School Experience

Schools are a major socializing institution in our society. The potential impact of schools is highlighted when one considers that children spend approximately one-third of all their waking hours in school settings for most of their developing years—that is, from age 6 until mid- to late adolescence. During this period, students' beliefs and behaviors are influenced by the culture of the school and by the attitudes of and interactions with teachers, peers, administrators, and others. This implicit but powerful process is often called the "hidden curriculum." In providing a rationale for teaching social skills in the schools, Cartledge and Milburn (1995) comment on this process:

> It has been suggested that the teaching of social skills
> goes on in the classroom all the time as a "hidden
> curriculum," even when the teacher does not deliberately
> engage in social skills instruction. The instructor, like the
> parent, is a powerful and influential person in the child's
> life and, as such, serves as a model for social behaviors.
> He or she shapes the child's social behaviors, intentionally
> or not, through the process of reinforcement. (p. ix)

Although this informal instruction is universal in our schools, some authorities contend that it is differentiated according to the students' backgrounds, and in the case of African American students of low socioeconomic status, the effects can be particularly damaging. Irvine (1990) defines the hidden curriculum as "the unstated but influential knowledge, attitudes, norms, rules, rituals, values, and beliefs that are transmitted to students through structure, policies, processes, formal content, and social relationships of school" (p. 5). Irvine gives the following examples:

Teachers are more powerful than students; principals are more powerful than teachers.

Some children are called on to perform favors for teachers; others are not.

Teachers call on well-dressed children more often than poorly dressed children.

Teachers praise boys more than girls.

Interruptions and intrusions are frequent and unavoidable.

No matter how hard some children try to gain the favor and attention of the teacher, some will never succeed.

Teachers behave more favorably toward the children whose parents participate in school activities. (pp. 5–6)

Results of research studies cited by Irvine (1990; e.g., Anyon, 1981; Rist, 1970) showed that teachers structured more creative and critical thinking activities for learners from middle-income families, whereas rote, meaningless activities were more common with low-income students. In addition to being influenced by economic status, teachers were described as making decisions about their students' learning potential on the basis of appearance, gender, and language ability (absence of Black English). The effects of these decisions appear to persist over time (Irvine, 1990; Kuykendall, 1992). In the Rist (1970) study cited by Irvine (1990), for example, African American kindergarten children were organized into ability groups during the first 8 days of school. These groups reflected socioeconomic class, grooming, and skin color so that the more affluent, better groomed, lighter-complexioned children were seated closest to the teacher and the children with the fewest of these attributes were seated farthest away. These groupings and seating arrangements were observed to continue with other teachers for the remaining 2 years of the study, which followed the children through the second grade. It is noteworthy that the teachers in this study also were African Americans, a fact that underscores the importance of social status when race is removed.

Perhaps one of the most powerful means for transmitting negative messages to African American students is ability grouping or tracking. Referred to as a "caste system" (Kuykendall, 1992) or "educational ghettos" (Irvine, 1990), these instructional practices are observed to relegate poor black students disproportionately to segregated classes where the teachers are less skilled, experienced, reinforcing, positive, friendly, attentive, informative, and patient (Irvine, 1990). As a result of tracking where African Americans are frequently represented in low-ability or special education settings and much less often in advanced tracks, students begin to see themselves as low achievers and inferior. This perception is aggravated by poor learning conditions, which cause students to devalue school as well as themselves and their African American peers. These conditions undoubtedly contribute to high rates of school dropout, functional illiteracy, poor adjustment in the workplace, and peer-peer aggression among African American youths.

Methods of behavior management also have negative impact on African American students. Demographic studies repeatedly show that African American youth, particularly males, are disproportionately referred for behavior and learning problems compared to their majority counterparts (Executive Committee, Council for Children with Behavioral Disorders, 1989; Hilliard, 1980; Maheady, Algozzine, & Ysseldyke, 1985). Irvine (1990) notes that black students are two to five times more likely to be suspended at a younger age and to receive lengthier suspensions. In one major Ohio city, for example, black males were one-third more likely than white males to be referred for disciplinary actions, and these figures were consistent across socioeconomic levels (Carmen, 1990). In this school system African American males, who constituted 24 percent of the total student body, accounted for 52 percent of the students placed in programs for behavior disorders. Beyond overrepresentation, other related data indicate that, compared to majority populations,

African American youths with behavior problems are likely to be directed to punishment facilities such as juvenile court rather than to treatment, are given more pathological labels than warranted, and are less likely to have appropriate family involvement in their treatment plans (Forness, 1988).

The basis for this phenomenon is not entirely clear; however, one contributing factor undoubtedly is the growing cultural "mismatch between the educators and the children and their communities" (Hilliard, 1980, p. 586). The combination of poverty and race will cause teachers to misperceive and tolerate poorly the behaviors of low-income African American children. Irvine notes that "stereotyping occurs when teachers perceive black students, particularly black males ... to be potential sources of classroom disruptions" (1990, p. 17), and Kuykendall (1992) cites research showing that both "White and Black teachers viewed Black males as most negatively 'different' from the valued characteristics and White females as the most positive" (p. 32). Irvine delineates cultural differences between the behaviors of black children and white children, as shown in Table 4.

The "different" behavioral patterns of African Americans are likely to be viewed negatively by middle-class majority teachers who may not understand, for example, that a child's intense, high-key manner is more indicative of a cultural style than of a behavior disorder. Schools communicate many important, often damaging, messages to African American youth. From the outset of their formal schooling, many of these youngsters learn that school personnel often devalue the way they look, talk, think, share experiences, behave, and live. Failing to be affirmed in the schools, they often turn to other environments to verify their self-worth. Shortsighted as this reaction may be, it is little wonder that psychologically alienated African American youth actively denigrate the schooling process and its stated goals.

Friendships and Peer Relations

Peer social support is seen to contribute to overall psychological well-being. During adolescence, when the importance of peer relationships peaks, African American youth in racially integrated settings may be at a distinct disadvantage as to friendship opportunities and peer support. Several studies of black-white friendships in desegregated

Table 4

Comparison of African Americans and European Americans in Communication Behaviors

	African American	European American
General behavior	High key Animated Interpersonal Confrontational Intense Dynamic Demonstrative	Low-key Dispassionate Impersonal Nonchallenging Emotionally restrained
Arguing style	Distinguish between arguing different opinions and argument to ventilate anger and hostility. Tend to enter the heated discussion whenever possible.	Tend to avoid affect and confrontation when arguing different opinion. Turn-taking is the usual style of any discussion or debate.
Attitude toward communication	Individual has no right to refuse a communication. Tend to involve and engage others in a conversation.	Individual has right to refuse a communication.
Questions about knowledge/ideas	Personal experiences used to question the authority of published knowledge/ideas.	Likely to regard as authoritative anything attested to by experts
Sharing attitude	Tend not to share information about their personal life.	Tend to start conversations with personal information such as one's occupation, place of residence, etc.

	African American	European American
Eye contact	May not maintain eye contact with teacher as often.	Maintains eye contact more often.
Beliefs about leadership	More likely to challenge school personnel due to belief that leadership is derived through attributes of strength, forcefulness, persuasiveness, and generosity.	Less likely to challenge school personnel, hold belief that leadership is related to position, credentials, or experience.

settings indicate less than favorable peer relationships for black students. For example, although members of both groups reported having cross-race friendships, black students reported cross-race friends more often than whites (Asher, Oden, & Gottman, 1977; DuBois & Hirsch, 1990), were found to be friendlier to whites than the reverse (Hallinan & Teixeira, 1987), and were less likely to have their friendship choices reciprocated in these settings (Clark & Ayers, 1988; Clark & Drewry, 1985). Friendship reciprocity in the Clark and Ayers study was associated with physical attractiveness and perceived success, not with personality traits or social behaviors. At least two factors appear to contribute to these outcomes. The first and probably most obvious is the existing racial dichotomy in U.S. society. Studies on race and friendship consistently show that students tend to select friends along racial lines (Hallinan & Williams, 1989). Under integrated conditions where black students are most likely to be in the minority, the greater number of available whites undoubtedly leads to more cross-race (nonreciprocated) friendship selections by blacks. It also means that these students have fewer options for mutual friendship even with same-race peers.

A second contributing factor may be the importance placed by white students on academic competence. Hallinan and Teixeira (1987) found academic performance to be most important to white students in the selection of cross-race friends. In classrooms where academic status was deemphasized (i.e., in noncompetitive conditions such as cooperative learning), whites were more likely to select blacks as best friends. These findings lead the authors to recommend "status-leveling," where schools establish interracial classrooms according to academic ability, thereby minimizing the possibility of academic discrimination and increasing the likelihood of cross-race friendship selections by whites.

The friendship difficulties experienced by black students in deseg-regated settings may explain the finding that black students report more out-of-school friendships than do white students (Clark & Ayers, 1988; DuBois & Hirsch, 1990). In these studies, black students, particularly males, reported more extensive friendship networks outside of school, suggesting that they found limited peer support in integrated school settings and that under these conditions the black community probably takes on even greater significance.

Academic achievement was not found to be a factor for African American students in choosing cross-race friends. It appears to play merely a utilitarian role in friendship selection for low-income black students within segregated conditions. Morris and Jackson (1986), in a study of fourth-, sixth-, and eighth-grade low-income African American students, found that academic achievement was associated only with nominations for workmates and was inversely related to selections for playmates or best friends. One possible interpretation of this finding is simply that these students differentiate peer popularity according to specific situational demands. On the other hand, this outcome may reflect other studies pointing to the unique tendency of low-income African American youth to devalue academic achievement and students who strive for school success (Fordham, 1988).

Another interesting observation in the friendship research is the relatively greater importance of peer relations to African American males. In an analysis of peer support according to race and gender, DuBois and Hirsch (1990) found that black males reported significantly more often than white males that they talked with friends about personal problems and felt that their best friends could be relied upon when needed. The level of peer support related by black males was comparable to that of black females, a picture that contrasted with the sizable and significant differences between white males and females. Nearly half of the white males reported no emotional support from their friends, whereas this was the case for only one-fourth of the black males. White females, on the other hand, indicated the highest level of peer support, followed closely by black females.

Peer relations may be particularly important for low-income black youth from single-parent homes in communities with few resources (Gibbs, 1989; Shade, 1983). For one group of African American males the peer group was found to be more influential than the family, and ages 10 to 11 appear to be most critical for developing this orientation (Shade, 1983). Although reliance on the peer group may appear to contradict the popular image of the African American male as "tough" (Schofield, 1981) or "bad" (Cross & Foley, 1993), it actually may be quite consistent with the African American male's view of masculinity. Hare (1985), for example, found that in contrast to African American females, who related more strongly to academic achievement, African American males were more inclined to base self-image on social ability and peer acceptance. This thinking is illustrated by Nathan McCall (1994) in his popular autobiography, *Makes Me Wanna Holler: A Young Black Man in America:*

> I eventually realized that there were only two types of dudes at Waters: solitary lames like me and those who got into the slick in-crowd. The slickest among these guys were the older dudes, the thugs, who ran the school and hung in the streets. They were the most popular. They got all the attention from the fly girls. They set the standards for hip and cool at Waters, and everybody else followed suit. . . . I was captivated by these guys. They seemed to have all the self-confidence I lacked. I was into honor rolls and spelling bees. They were into sock hops and talent shows. I looked all neat and boring, like my mama dressed me for school. They looked—exciting. . . . After watching the older cats, I knew I *had* to work on getting my act together. Shyness or not, I had to break into the social scene or risk being victimized in some way by it. (pp. 26–27)

In a study conducted by MEE Productions (1992) entitled *Reaching the Hip-Hop Generation,* the observation of this subset of black males was that the "strongest claim to allegiance of this audience is to its own subculture. Messages perceived as being from outside the culture have very little chance of getting in" (p. 5). They observed that messages, to be effective, must be peer based, authentic, entertaining, delivered in the language of the street, and devoid of evidence of mainstream origins. Ogbu (1981) suggests that this attitude among urban black males is rooted in their observation of generations of African Americans who subscribed to the rules and behaviors of mainstream society yet failed to reap commensurate gains.

According to Gibbs (1989), poor African American males from unstable home and community environments are inclined to form intense bonds and to be extremely conforming to their peer group. Lacking typical family and community resources, these young men may turn to one another for emotional, psychological, and social support. This phenomenon is portrayed on a much smaller scale in the psychological literature (Freud & Dann, 1951, as cited by Perry & Bussey, 1984). Six orphaned German-Jewish infants reared in an orphanage during World War II formed such intense bonds that "they refused to separate for even brief periods and became hostile and destructive toward adults who threatened to disturb their group" (p. 307). The children's within-group behavior was characterized as extremely loyal, prosocial, and altruistic, but they resisted intrusions by other adults or by children outside their group. Similarly, African American youth from unstable environments are likely to resort to the peer group for protection and identity. Gibbs (1989) warns, however, that these intense bonds can cause fierce rivalries and conflicts, leading to self-destructive behaviors such as poor school performance, premature sexuality and parenting, and delinquent behavior.

Peer relationships play a major role in the lives of African American youth. Yet, within integrated settings, opportunities for close, reciprocated friendships are limited, and within low-income, segregated environments, youth are inclined to develop tightly knit circles, shutting out mainstream influences and fellow students engaged in adaptive pursuits such as working for academic success. Such circumstances mitigate against positive peer relationships, and, accordingly, seriously threaten the social-emotional development of a significant portion of this population.

The Influence of the Media

Television and other media are extremely important forces in the socialization of African American children and youth (Shade, 1983; Stroman, 1991). It is estimated that African American children of low socioeconomic status spend more than 40 hours per week watching television (Stroman, 1991). Poverty and limited resources cause their families to rely heavily on television as a principal source of entertainment and baby-sitting. Stroman notes that the messages transmitted by television are both positive and negative. Many children's programs (e.g., *Sesame Street*) as well as other programs (e.g., *The Cosby Show*) have contributed positively to cognitive and social development. Most of the attention, however, has focused on the negative impact of television.

Television viewing apparently has a curvilinear effect: The cognitive benefits diminish with more than 10 hours per week, after which viewing ostensibly interferes with other worthwhile pursuits such as reading and schoolwork. Furthermore, much of the programming watched by these children contains explicit sex and excessive violence and is not intended for young people.

Stroman (1991) cites research (e.g., National Institute of Mental Health, 1982) showing violent programs to have the greatest negative effect on males and youths living in violence-prone neighborhoods. An example of the impact of videotaped models on African American males can be seen in a study by Bridgeman and Burbach (1976). Black and white second-grade students viewed videotapes showing either black or white peer models succeeding in an academic task. After viewing the tape, students told the experimenter the score they expected to get and then completed the academic task themselves. Black males were more affected by the models than black females or white students. Results showed that when black males observed the black models, they predicted and achieved significantly higher scores than black males viewing white models. Results of comparisons for black females and for white students were not significant. Mean scores for the black females indicated that they were not affected by models' races.

Considering that nearly 50 percent of African American children are being reared in poverty within communities where violence reigns, antisocial TV messages may have disproportionate impact on African American youth. Violence in the media is often defended via the argument that evil forces are conquered by prosocial ones. That message is often lost, however, especially when a violent law enforcement officer (a role often played by an African American) is the one to capture the violent lawbreaker (Taylor & Dozier, 1983). The actual message communicated in such programs may be that the goals of power, material possession, and social control are best attained through violent means. The beneficial long-term returns of right over might receive little if any attention. Having grown up during the seventies, McCall (1994) describes the impact of popular black movies, such as *Superfly* and *The Mack* and their accompanying sound tracks, on himself and his male companions. The principal characters in these movies portrayed high-living, flamboyantly dressing, fast-talking, aggressive drug dealers and pimps who accumulated substantial sums of money outside of the white mainstream. McCall reflects on the antisocial effects of the movies and the related music:

> The irony of the sound tracks to *Superfly* and *The Mack* is that they both contained songs with strong anti-drug, pro-black messages. I was so caught up in the glitz and glamour of the street-smart stars that those messages went right over my head. Also lost on me was the contradiction in the whole notion of getting over. Drug dealers and pimps operate on familiar turf, preying on their own people. But like so many other guys, I reasoned that the end justified the means—any hustle that kept you out of the system was justifiable. (p. 101)

Beyond antisocial behaviors, Shade (1983) suggests that for African Americans the media also reinforce stereotypical images of intellectual inferiority, academic and occupational failure, and social incompetence.

The Role of Music

Music is an integral part of the black experience, often functioning as a means for communicating with God, a vehicle for courtship, and a source of comfort. In some ways music and its related expressions capture the essence of African American culture, conjuring up images of spirituals, gospels, blues, jazz, soul music, and rap. It is noteworthy that jazz is viewed as the only indigenous American music.

As with other groups and previous generations, the music of adolescence takes on distinctive rebellious and sexual overtones. Although teen music historically has met with disapproval from adults, the rap music of the seventies and eighties, with its explicit sexual, misogynous, and violent messages, has caused considerable alarm within the African American community as well as in the larger society. Many rap artists offer prosocial or innocuous lyrics; however, rap songs promoting violence, sex, and sexual abuse are equally plentiful and arguably more popular. This music is widely enjoyed by African American youth, and its messages are heard. A study by MEE Productions (1992) points out that "ninety-seven percent of urban African-American teens like and listen to rap music. It is the universal element in their experience" (p. 9).

Empirical evidence of the impact of rap music can be seen in a study conducted by Johnson, Jackson, and Gatto (in press) with 46 11- to 16-year-old low-income African American males. The youths were divided into three groups and assigned to view violent rap videos, to view nonviolent rap videos, or to view no rap at all (control group). The youths watched the videos for approximately a half hour, then responded to two scenarios. In the first scene, a young man was physically aggressive toward his girlfriend and another boy to whom his girlfriend had displayed affection (i.e., a big hug and a small kiss). The boyfriend pushed his girlfriend and admonished her never to kiss another boy. He punched the other boy, telling him to leave his girlfriend alone. The youngsters who saw the violent rap videos were significantly more likely than those watching the nonviolent videos or the control subjects to find the young man's physical aggression to be acceptable or to indicate that they would respond in like manner.

In the second scenario, two young African American males were described: one preparing to go to law school and one focused on driving his expensive car and wearing fancy clothes, giving no attention to academics. Youngsters viewing both the violent and nonviolent rap videos were more likely than the controls to report a desire to emulate the latter, high-living youth rather than the academic, career-oriented one. These youngsters also expressed greater doubt that the academic youth would reach his goal of becoming a lawyer. The findings of the Johnson et al. (in press) study support the notion that aspects of popular culture such as rap music may not only contribute to escalated violence in our society but also adversely affect aspirations toward socially approved goals such as education and legitimate occupations. Although the periods of video viewing in this study were brief and the effects potentially short-lived, one should recall that many of these young people, particularly low-income minority youth, spend more hours watching television and listening to music than in any other waking endeavor.

The contribution of the media to escalating violence and unstable relationships in the African American community is a matter of legitimate concern. In addition to curtailing children's media exposure through parental monitoring and institutional pressure, significant adults in children's lives need to provide a value-based standard by which young people may reasonably assess the messages being sent. It is also proposed that the media be used more effectively to transmit prosocial messages to young people (MEE Productions, 1992).

A Social Skill Profile of African Americans

Research systematically analyzing the social skill strengths and needs of African American students is extremely limited. Despite obvious cultural and communication differences, social skill researchers have given little or no attention to this area (Turner, Beidel, Hersen, & Bellack, 1984). In one of the few existing studies, Keller (1988) compared the adjustment scores of White, Black, and Hispanic 7-year-old students and found that Black children consistently received lower teacher ratings than their non-Black peers. Although the races of the teachers were not identified, teacher bias was suspected: Teacher and parent correlations "overlapped" only for the White children, and significant correlations among all teacher ratings and measures of ability and achievement were found only for the White sample. Race emerged as an influential factor as well in other studies designed to assess the social behaviors of African American children (Lethermon, Williamson, Moody, Granberry, Lemanek, & Bodiford, 1984; Lethermon, Williamson, Moody, & Wozniak,

1986; Turner et al., 1984). One investigation showed that gifted African American students received less praise and more criticism than even their nonachieving Black counterparts (Shade, 1979).

In the Feng and Cartledge (1996) study described in chapter 1 of this book, again it was noted that African American students received lower teacher social skill ratings than their Asian American and European American classmates. The teachers perceived the African American students to be particularly strong in people-related skills and least competent in dealing with conflict, both with peers and with adults. The behavioral styles of African American students are easily misunderstood (Irvine, 1990), and misinterpretations can lead to inaccurate labeling of their behaviors; the results can be repeated punitive consequences and eventual psychological alienation from authority figures and the educational process itself. Moyer and Motta (1982) found an inverse relationship between psychological alienation and academic performance for both black and white students, but high alienation scores were associated with school suspensions only for the black students.

Alienation combines with castelike social conditions and poverty to push African American youth into a subculture of disengagement, which Taylor (1988/1989) describes as characterized by violence, substance abuse, homicide, suicide, delinquency, and emphasis on nonacademic pursuits. Aggression and violence are becoming increasingly problematic for African American youth, especially males, who are disproportionately identified for disciplinary actions in schools (Irvine, 1990) and delinquent activities in the community (Prothrow-Stith, 1991).

Aggression may be defined as specific observable actions manifested in poor interpersonal relationships with adults and peers (Rubin, Bream, & Rose-Krasnor, 1991), but Okey (1992) points out that "conferring the label of aggression on human behavior involves some degree of social judgment; no specific behavior can be termed aggressive without knowledge of its social context" (p. 53). These behaviors should be interpreted against culturally based standards and criteria. Nevertheless, there is no denying the dismal statistics that show African American youth subscribing to and employing antisocial means to achieve their goals. Although rates of negative expression were comparable to those of their European peers, it is noteworthy in the Feng and Cartledge (1996) study that African

American students reported more often than the other two groups that they would employ aggressive alternatives when treated unfairly. A tendency to believe in aggressive alternatives, coupled with extremely stressful living conditions, undoubtedly contributes to the higher levels of aggression exhibited by many low-income African American youth.

Existing practices emphasizing containment and punishment have not been successful in curbing aggression in our society. Indeed, the reverse is the case. Homicide is the leading cause of death among teenage African American males, at least four times greater than for any other segment of our society—in spite of the fact that incarceration rates have increased over the last decade (Prothrow-Stith, 1991). Although no single institution or program can address these concerns fully, in terms of school-based interventions and social skill instruction, there is no question that one area of greatest need pertains to constructive peer and adult relations based on conflict management and behavioral alternatives to aggression.

Social Skill Interventions

Nonpunitive, humane interventions that teach African American youth productive alternatives to aggression can be more constructive than most current exclusionary or punitive practices. Some suggested alternatives are direct instruction, various peer-based approaches, and the use of literature as a vehicle for learning. Whatever approach is used, the involvement of concerned adults can help ensure positive outcomes.

Direct Instruction

Direct instruction in social skills has been used successfully with a variety of populations (Cartledge & Milburn, 1995) and appears promising for African American youth as well. Some of its key features are early intervention, parent participation, and culturally specific teaching techniques. Ideally, interventions to teach adaptive behaviors might occur as early as the preschool years in the home and in established programs such as Head Start. Children are extremely impressionable during this period, when important and often antisocial learning is taking place. As authors of the study by MEE Productions (1992) point out, "The decisions about drugs and other forms of behavior are made much earlier than the mainstream culture imagines on these hard streets where childhood can be very, very brief" (p. 2). Barone, Ayers, Weissberg, Voyce, Kasprow, and Schwab-Stone (1993) report data from one urban sample showing that as early as sixth grade 5.5 percent of youth had tried marijuana, 9.5 percent had carried guns within the previous 6 months, and 28 percent had engaged in sexual intercourse.

Middleton and Cartledge (1995) provide an example of successful direct social skill instruction with young African American children. The researchers used a social skill curriculum (Cartledge & Kleefeld, 1991) to reduce aggression among five low-income first- and second-grade African American males. They identified students displaying aggression through social skill assessment instruments (Gresham & Elliott, 1990) completed by the classroom teacher and their own direct observations, which were used to confirm the teachers' perceptions. Students were taught in small groups of two to four peers. Socially competent peers were included in the instructional groups to serve as models during the social skill lessons as well as under regular classroom conditions.

The researchers targeted three specific skills from the curriculum: ignoring aggression, controlling one's temper, and speaking kindly and using courteous words. Short stories, along with puppets, were used to introduce and model each skill. Following modeling by the researchers and competent peers, each child had the opportunity to act out and role-play the desired behavior. For example, in the lesson on ignoring, the children heard a story about how one of the animal puppets learned to stay out of trouble by thinking about the good things that would happen if he managed to refrain from fighting when taunted by a fellow puppet. The children then practiced the skill, making helpful self-statements and exercising self-control when provoked by others. Children who cooperated received stickers at the end of the lesson for their participation. Each lesson contained several related activities, which gave students many varied opportunities to practice the skill. The instruction was conducted over 10 weeks, and the lessons were repeated several times.

In addition to conducting pull-out instructional sessions, the researchers coached the students when observing their behavior within the classroom. That is, if an aggressive or antisocial act occurred, the observer reminded the student of the social skill lesson and asked what should be done instead. Classroom teachers were asked to praise children and distribute stickers for appropriate behaviors in the classroom.

Parent involvement is critical to the success of social skill instruction for African American children. Hammond and Yung (1993) point out that one means for making this instruction culturally relevant is through home-based therapy or education. Parents can be important allies, teaching their children how to assert themselves in socially appropriate ways in order to achieve desired goals without aggressing. Middleton and Cartledge (1995) considered parent involvement to enhance student skill development because they observed more progress with students whose parents participated. Specific procedures for parent participation are described later in this chapter.

In the Middleton and Cartledge (1995) study, a multiple baseline design across students, combined with a withdrawal feature, showed substantial reductions in aggression in four of the five males. The one exception was the youngster whose mother refused to participate in the study. This boy displayed persistent behavior problems, and only slight reductions in aggression occurred. The results of this study demonstrate that social skill instruction can be effective and that parents can be instrumental in the maintenance and generalization of prosocial behaviors for low-income African American students who behave aggressively in public school settings. Also indicated is the potentially valuable role of competent peers. A special significance of this study is that, to assist at-risk youngsters, school and mental health personnel need to seek them out and provide interventions such as in-depth social skill training for both treatment and prevention purposes. Early, prolonged social skill instruction promises to be one critical weapon in an arsenal of interventions needed to remedy escalating self-destructive tendencies and to improve the educational process for a significant segment of our population.

Many instructional programs exist to address social behaviors and prevent aggression and violence in target adolescents (e.g., Goldstein, 1988; Hammond, 1991; Hammond & Yung, 1991; Prothrow-Stith,

1991); however, the impact of their teachings may be undercut by already established behavior patterns and attitudes. Hammond and Yung, for example, initially targeted males in their mid- to late teens, and although some success was noted in terms of skill development, the effects were limited because of chronic truancy. As a result, Hammond and Yung refocused the project on middle-school students. By adolescence, African American youth, particularly low-income males, have developed their own subculture so that self-image is most likely to be based on social ability and peer acceptance (Hare, 1979), and the greatest allegiance tends to be to their own peer group (MEE Productions, 1992).

To make instruction more relevant and more likely to be accepted, Hammond (1991) incorporated several culturally specific markers into social skill strategies used with African American adolescents. Following are some of the most salient illustrations. First, the problem situations and role-play scenarios reflected the life experiences of these youths. For example, low-income African American males tend to place great value on expensive name-brand athletic shoes and other garments, which often inspire antisocial acts among peers. One conflict scene in the videotaped instructional program *Dealing with Anger: A Violence Prevention Program for African American Youth* (Hammond, 1991) depicts a problem where one youth notices that the pump shoes worn by another are the shoes that were stolen from his locker. The youth wearing the shoes states that he bought them from a friend. The social skill to be learned is negotiating or working out a problem without resorting to aggression or violence. Although the importance young people place on such possessions is highly questionable, and the need to eliminate such attachments may be legitimately emphasized, the critical issue is how to resolve conflict regardless of one's value system. The scenarios used in this curriculum incorporate problems and circumstances common to this particular population.

A second feature of Hammond's (1991) approach was the use of models from the learners' cultural group. Thus, because the program targeted African American males, African American males served as models and exclusively made up the instructional groups. One African American male and one African American female taught the group lessons jointly. Some implied or less obvious cultural features included language, group composition, and social sensitivity.

The language of the instructional tapes was informal and in a style familiar to the intended audience. That is, the actors used common African American phrases (e.g., "just acting the fool") and words (e.g., "fussing"); however, they avoided nonstandard English and profanity.

Although the group was homogeneous according to gender, race, age, and socioeconomics, members did appear to vary in social competence. Their videotaped statements suggested that some young people were more socially skilled than others. Including more competent but respected youth as group participants as well as for modeling displays may be especially beneficial for this peer-oriented population. Socially appropriate actions or ideas presented by well-regarded age-mates may be more effective than the best-designed lesson delivered by the best-intentioned adults.

Finally, discussions need to be conducted in the context of the particular psychological and social issues of concern to the target group. For example, respect from others is a prominent need among African American males and frequently is the basis for interpersonal conflict. Numerous acts of violence arise from feelings of being "dissed" (i.e., disrespected) by others (McCall, 1994). A poignant statement made by one peer in the "Takin' It" lesson (Hammond, 1991) reveals how this issue of disrespect and the importance of saving face in front of the peer group contribute to conflict. In recognition of this issue, when role-playing this scene the teacher took steps to prevent embarrassment by telling the student that he wanted to address the problem in private, outside of the room where the infraction took place and away from the peer group. If teachers and peers recognize and understand the culturally specific concerns and thinking styles of the targeted learners, more productive instruction results.

Hammond and Yung (1991) reported using these strategies with 14 African American adolescent males over a 6-month period. "Success dollars" (paper scrip) that could be exchanged for backup rewards of cassette tapes, jewelry, t-shirts, and games were used as reinforcers for participation and appropriate behavior. Observer ratings of videotaped role-plays, teachers' ratings of daily behaviors, and school records of student suspensions and expulsions were more favorable for trained than for untrained students.

Moore, Cartledge, and Heckaman (1995) also used a skill training model to improve social skills during games and sports activities in the classroom and the gym. The six adolescent subjects (five males, one female) were enrolled in a self-contained inner city school for students with emotional and behavioral disorders (EBD). Two of the males were European American, and the remaining four students were African Americans; all were from low socioeconomic backgrounds. The teacher was a European American female with 5 years experience teaching students with EBD. The specific purpose of this project was to develop skills in anger control, losing appropriately, and winning appropriately while playing competitive games.

As part of her instruction, the teacher prepared and presented scripts of scenes considered representative of the students' daily experiences (Moore, 1994). Using the scripts, the teacher and students discussed, modeled, and acted out the desired behaviors. The following are examples of teacher-created skits centering on anger control. The first skit illustrates inappropriate behaviors; the second, appropriate.

Role-Play 1

Situation: Two students are waiting in line for their lunch. Billy does not have enough money to buy his lunch and feels embarrassed. Joe, who is in line behind him, is in a hurry to get his lunch.

Joe: What's the problem, Billy? Can't your mom afford to feed you?

Billy: You shouldn't talk, Joe. Your family can't afford to buy you decent clothes.

Joe: *(Becoming angry)* Your family has less money than mine. And if you don't stop talking mess I'm going to bust you up!

Billy: *(Very angry)* Come on, Joe, let's just see what you are really made of!

Role-Play 2

Situation: Same as above.

Joe: What's the problem, Billy? Can't your mom afford to feed you?

Billy: No, that's not it. I forgot my money this morning because I was in a hurry to catch the bus.

Joe: Yeah, I bet you are just too poor.

Billy: Joe, I don't appreciate the way you talk about me and my family. *(Walks away.)*

The training took place 3 days a week for approximately 30 minutes per lesson. After the first couple of weeks, the teacher made two important observations: First, the students began inserting their own words into the scripts; second, they started showing and expressing boredom with the lessons. When the teacher shared these observations, the teacher's graduate faculty advisor recommended that the students be encouraged to devise their own skits and perhaps videotape their role-plays. She noted that the teacher's language was too formal and in some cases foreign to the students. For example, in one scene the teacher used the word *klutz* to describe a peer's inept behavior. Although the students didn't produce their own videotapes, they did construct their own scripts. The following student-created scripts illustrate inappropriate and appropriate behaviors, respectively.

Role-Play 1

Situation: Six kids are playing 3-on-3 basketball outside. The score is close and Terry misses his "J" (jump shot). John is furious 'cause he was wide open under the basket.

John: Yo' Punk! What's up with not passing the ball to me?

Terry: Man—you know my "J" is better than your lay-up!

John: You ain't all that now. Your "J" is broke (no good).

Terry: I'm phatt (good, awesome) and you can't beat me!

John: I'll kick your butt.

Terry: *(Up in John's face with his hands ready to scrap)* Let's go! Bring it on!

Role-Play 2

Situation: Same as above.

John: Hey, Terry, I was wide open under the basket, man.

Terry: All right—I'll get you. I thought I could hit it.

John: Let's just get the ball back.

(They play hard and get the rebound and score on a lay-up by John.)

The students not only displayed more comfort and motivation with their own scripts, but the teacher noted that the activity evolved into friendly competition, where students tried to "outwrite" one another. They genuinely enjoyed writing and sharing their scripts with the class. The only limitation imposed by the teacher was that the students had to refrain from using vulgar language or situations. Another advantage of the student-developed scripts, according to the teacher, was that it was easier to call students on misbehavior under regular school conditions by referring to strategies or suggestions they had devised.

To enhance the relevance and generalizability of the instruction, the teacher had students monitor their own behavior following each competitive game in the classroom or gym. They completed forms indicating whether, during the competitive activity, they had controlled their temper, lost appropriately, or won appropriately.

Data were collected on three of the six students who had begun training with the greatest deficits in the target skills: two African American males and one European American male. The results showed substantial gains for all three students. In the classroom, for example, the group had mean gains of 12.1 in the desired behaviors and mean decreases of 11.3 in the undesired behaviors. Similar improvements were noted in the gym; this indicated that the new skills had transferred to other settings. Self-monitoring helped the students maintain these gains through the end of the school year, even though direct instruction lasted only 8 weeks.

Another promising instructional method to address aggression emerges from the study of children's attributions or beliefs about aggression. Attribution theory establishes links among thoughts, emotions, and behavior. Findings in this area of research show that aggressive children are more likely to attribute hostile intent to the ambiguous behaviors of others (Dodge, 1993) and believe in the beneficial effects of aggression (Guerra & Slaby, 1990). Erdley and Asher (1993) compared children's beliefs about aggression (e.g., "It's OK to hit someone if he or she does something mean to you") to their attributions and projected actions under provocative situations. For example, in one assessment item, the child is asked to imagine a situation in the lunchroom where another child spills milk on him or her. Then the child is asked to propose why the act occurred, whether or not the other child acted from hostile intent, how he or she would respond (e.g., ignore the spill or say something mean to the other child), and whether or not the other child should be punished for spilling the milk. Peer assessments also were used to measure aggression. The researchers found that aggressive children very often selected aggressive options as responses to provocation and recommended more severe punishment for the sources of provocation.

Research by Graham, Hudley, and Williams (1992) with African Americans similarly found aggressive students reporting tendencies toward biased attributions and hostile reactions to ambiguous provocations. These findings led the authors to advocate teaching aggression-prone youth to view peers' actions more constructively. Accordingly, Hudley and Graham (1993) developed and implemented a curriculum designed to reduce aggressive behaviors by altering perceptions of peer intent relative to ambiguous negative events. The curriculum included three major components, focusing on (a) accurately determining intentionality, (b) making nonhostile attributions when intent is unclear, and (c) responding appropriately to ambiguously caused negative events. After 4 months of instruction, experimental subjects showed more favorable responses on these dimensions than did their control peers. Although posttreatment ratings by teachers indicated reductions in aggression, follow-up assessments showed that the intervention had no effect on the rate of office referrals. These findings are comparable to those reported by Guerra and Slaby (1990), who found that institutionalized adolescents receiving similar interventions showed improvement in attitudes about aggressive alternatives and a reduction in aggressive behaviors but showed no reduction in recidivism following their release. It may be that in addition to addressing cognition, professionals need to attend more to the social contexts within which these young people operate. Goldstein (1989), for example, experienced greater success in reducing recidivism among formerly incarcerated adolescents when parents participated with the youth in social skill instruction than when parents were not involved.

In underscoring the need to analyze the social environments of aggression-prone youth, Hudley and Graham (1993) question whether attribution-altering strategies may inadvertently make these youngsters more vulnerable to the negative elements in their surroundings:

> For some of our young research participants, violence and aggression are part of everyday experience. It is therefore unclear to what extent being quick to assign blame or having a low threshold for retaliatory behavior might operate as genuine survival strategies for coping with the perilous conditions that have become common in racially isolated, economically depressed inner city neighborhoods. Some children by the age of 10 or 12 are already so traumatized by the conditions of their existence that an intervention based on attributional change is likely to have insufficient impact on their lives to change their behavior. (p. 136)

Hudley and Graham further stress the need to apply such strategies differentially according to whether or not a youngster's life conditions render nonretaliatory behaviors appropriate. The often-cited contention that aggression is a survival skill in violence-torn neighborhoods has superficial merit, but a closer analysis reveals that the most aggressive youth are those most likely to be victims of homicide, incarceration, underachievement, and other destructive outcomes.

Violence has escalated to the extent that premature death is commonplace and nearly one-quarter of all African American males are known to the criminal justice system for disciplinary reasons. Counteraggression is not the key to breaking this cycle. Perhaps the critical need is to analyze urban environments to determine nonviolent, constructive, and safe responses to ambiguous negative experiences. Along with learning to avoid attributing hostile intent to others' unclear actions, children must also learn to choose the best course of action to avoid getting hurt or hurting others. Within these highly stressful communities are many socially competent young people who not only manage to survive but survive without using aggression. Little attention is given to competent children and adolescents in these settings, but a study of their behavior patterns and skills might provide clues about productive survival skills to be taught to their less successful peers. Some situations, for example, may demand reactions of physical defense, others may require calm assertiveness, and still others may call for rapidly getting away from the source of conflict. Determining situational demands and competent responses should be an important focus of instruction for aggressive populations.

In sum, young people need to learn how to perceive the events in their environment accurately and constructively. They also need to be equipped with a variety of responses to those events in order to maximize their own and others' well-being. The actions taught should be tailored to specific social environments.

Peer-Based Approaches

Peer Mediation

The combination of conflict-ridden environments and fierce allegiance to the peer group points to the potential benefit of peer mediation for low-income African American youth. Peer mediation gives young people a way to manage their own conflicts. Students trained in conflict resolution skills can help other students embroiled in some dispute to resolve their problem peaceably, preferably with a win-win outcome. The particular attraction of this model for African American youth is that it is managed by peers, who often exert more behavioral influence than do the adults in their lives. Additionally, it forces students to use cognitive problem-solving skills (i.e., brains over brawn) to consider previously unexplored unique and peaceful ways to solve problem situations.

Peer mediation in the schools has gained much attention since the mid-1980s. Lane and McWhirter (1992) cite research reports showing peer mediation to result in greater student cooperation, more prosocial attitudes (e.g., McCormick, 1988), and reduced fighting (e.g., Koch, 1988). Lane and McWhirter point out that training for peer mediation often begins with getting school staff to commit to the program and to participate in approximately 8 hours of training to develop their own mediation skills. Following staff training, the program is introduced to the students through activities that will motivate them to volunteer as mediators. Selected students then participate in five half-day training sessions. Lane and McWhirter describe the four stages of the peer mediation sequence: (a) peer mediators introduce themselves, offer their services, and describe the conditions of the mediation; (b) peer mediators guide the disputing students in communicating their respective sides of the dispute; (c) peer mediators help disputing students state what each wants; and (d) peer mediators help disputing students determine how each can help to resolve the problem. This sequence is detailed in Table 5. After completing the preceding sequence, the disputants are expected to fill out a peer mediation report.

A special attraction of peer mediation is that by permitting students to make decisions about their own lives it can be empowering, bringing about improvements in self-esteem and self-management. Even greater returns are realized if conflict-prone students are effectively trained to be mediators. Lane and McWhirter (1992) cite empirical and anecdotal evidence of attitudinal changes expressed by peer mediators who formerly were conflict makers.

Training and participation in mediation can help build thinking and problem-solving skills. Many young people resort to aggression simply because they have not explored other ways to handle problem situations. Instruction in conflict resolution skills might begin with very young children as an established part of the curriculum, as youngsters are taught to think about conflict in ways that will promote win-win outcomes. If this learning continues through the grades, children will more easily regulate their own behavior and more effectively mediate their own disputes. Adults can use a variety of strategies to teach children ways to manage conflict. In *Creative Conflict Resolution,* Kreidler (1984) suggests many classroom applications to teach elementary-aged children to become "peacemakers." While reading a story, the teacher may stop at the point of conflict to have children generate possible resolutions. If the solution given

Table 5
Peer Mediation Process Checklist

Introduction

1. Introduce yourself. Ask disputants' names.
2. Ask both persons if they want to solve the problem.
3. If yes, move to a different area to talk.
4. State the four rules:
   a. Agree to solve the problem
   b. No name calling or put-downs
   c. Be as honest as you can
   d. Do not interrupt
5. Go back and ask each person if he or she agrees to each rule. Restate rules one at a time and get a yes answer.
6. Explain that whatever is discussed will not be shared with others by the mediators.

Listening

7. Decide who will talk first.
8. Ask person #1 what happened . . . restate. Ask person #1 how he or she feels . . . restate.
9. Ask person #2 what happened . . . restate. Ask person #2 how he or she feels . . . restate.

Wants

10. Ask person #1 what he or she wants . . . repeat it.
11. Ask person #2 what he or she wants . . . repeat it.

Solutions

12. Ask person #1 what he or she can do to solve the problem . . . repeat.
13. Ask person #2 what he or she can do to solve the problem . . . repeat.
14. Evaluate solution for balance and fairness.
15. Ask each person if he or she agrees to the solution. Ask if problem is solved.

16. Ask each person what he or she could do differently.
17. Ask each person to tell friends that the conflict has been solved to prevent rumors.
18. Congratulate students for their hard work.

Note. From "A Peer Mediation Model: Conflict Resolution for Elementary and Middle School Children" by P. S. Lane & J. J. McWhirter, 1992, *Elementary School Guidance & Counseling, 27,* pp. 22–23. Copyright 1992 by *The American School Counselor Association.* Reprinted by permission.

---

in the story is not satisfactory, children might be guided in suggesting a more desirable ending. Kreidler suggests ways to incorporate these skills in various subject areas. In math, for example, children are encouraged to determine a fair way to negotiate sharing 14 cookies among five children; in social studies they may determine how to negotiate sharing newly settled land with Native Americans.

At the secondary level, Prothrow-Stith (1991) describes a "Peacemakers" program for aggressive urban youth in the Brooklyn schools. A component of the communication skills training focuses on helping students substitute assertive statements for aggressive ones—for example, "Don't bother me" instead of "Get your ugly face out of here" (p. 174). Peer mediators are trained to help both sides air their grievances without interruption, determine the nature of the problem, work out a fair settlement, and write out the settlement, which is then signed by both sides. As an incentive to participate, disputants are often given a choice between mediation or a week of in-school suspension; students generally prefer the former. Mediation takes place quickly and privately to avoid the complications of rumors, and students who have a dispute settled by mediation may be asked to become mediators.

Prothrow-Stith (1991) also outlines her own 10-session curriculum on violence prevention. Students are first given information on violence and homicide, which helps them realize that all people, including themselves, are vulnerable to committing such acts, given poor sclf-management skills. Once this understanding is in place, students receive lessons on emotions and recognizing how they typically handle anger. They are then helped to conduct a "cost/benefit analysis" of fighting to determine if the actual returns are worth the fight. In a discussion, students identify the good points (e.g., winning) and the bad points (e.g., killing someone or getting killed) of fighting. A resulting list, where the negative outcomes far outweigh the beneficial effects, is used as the basis for helping students to question the wisdom of fighting and to begin exploring constructive alternatives. Through prompting and guidance from the teacher, students are helped to devise their own strategies for stopping or avoiding fights.

Johnson and Johnson (1991, 1994) also have developed a peer mediation program entitled *Teaching Students to be Peacemakers.* Using a similar format, they teach students how conflict evolves, how to negotiate agreements, and how to mediate their peers' conflicts. Rather than training a small "cadre" of students, Johnson and Johnson (1994) advocate the "total student body approach," where all students are trained in peer mediation procedures with the goal of managing conflict constructively. On the basis of their research, Johnson and Johnson contend that "students are involved in conflicts with each other daily and either refer the conflict to the teacher for arbitration or use destructive strategies that tend to escalate the conflict" (pp. 23–24). They maintain that peer mediation is effective in promoting more disciplined, self-regulated behavior among students and that the total student body approach is more effective than one involving a limited number of students. They also urge that peer mediation training be provided throughout all 12 years of formal schooling.

Cooperative Learning

Cooperative learning environments involve small, structured learning groups in which students work closely together to achieve some common goal. Students are encouraged to do their best in order to contribute to the group's success. The principal anticipated outcomes of cooperative environments are improved academic performance and better social relationships. The cultural background of African American students helps make them uniquely prepared for the conditions of cooperative learning. As noted earlier in this chapter, African Americans typically have extended family systems, where strong bonds are created and members serve one another, providing for psychological and financial support. Haynes and Gebreyesus (1992) speculate that children reared under these conditions are likely to be oriented toward a collectivistic rather than individualistic or competitive worldview. Individuals with this orientation are predisposed toward helping, sharing, collaborating, cooperating, and trusting. The focus is on contributing to others and promoting the group rather than achieving one's own ends, and the expectation is a more prosocial orientation. Because of this perceived meshing of the demands of cooperative learning and the group-oriented structures of the African American home and community, Haynes and Gebreyesus argue that African American students should do well under cooperative classroom conditions. Furthermore, they argue that the individualistic, competitive environment of the typical U.S. classroom may be detrimental to the academic progress of African American youth. They warn,

> When the cultural world of the child is very different
> from the cultural world of the school and classroom, the
> child often is forced either to adapt to the alien culture of
> the school or to withdraw in disgust and frustration. (p. 583)

Much of the pertinent research confirms the beneficial effects of cooperative learning for African American students (Haynes & Gebreyesus, 1992; Johnson, Johnson, Tiffany, & Zaidman, 1983). Zahn, Kagan, and Widaman (1986) found that both Anglo and minority (African American and Mexican American) students preferred cooperative structures to the traditional whole-class format. However, there was a difference between minority and majority students in the type of cooperative groups preferred. Anglo children indicated a much stronger preference for cooperative groups that involved weekly tournaments (Teams-Games-Tournaments; TGT), where individual members of comparable ability from each team competed in front of the class. On the other hand, minority children were more inclined toward Students Teams—Achievement Divisions (STAD), where they took weekly quizzes and earned points for their teams by scoring well. Both cooperative groupings had competitive elements, but the TGT format allowed competition on a individual basis, a feature obviously more attractive to Anglo than to minority children. This finding suggests the potentially debilitating effects of explicit individual and competitive conditions on the academic and social performance of minority students. It also lends indirect support to the contentions of Hallinan and Teixeira (1987), who stress the need to minimize academic competitions in order to facilitate cross-racial social interaction.

More direct confirmation of the facilitating effects of cooperative groups on social interactions is found in a study by Johnson et al. (1983) involving minority and majority youngsters of varying abilities. Students worked together to complete a set of papers, making sure all group members mastered the subject matter. The researchers found that, contrary to commonly held beliefs, low-achieving children from minority groups were not systematically rejected by their higher-achieving majority peers. In addition to cooperative learning groups, cooperative games can be useful in promoting cross-racial interactions. Rogers, Miller, and Hennigan (1981), for example, used cooperative playground games to increase the play interaction between African American and European American females.

The positive effects of cooperative learning on social relationships are documented in the empirical literature (Goldstein, 1988; Slavin, 1990). African American students, especially females, appear to have a special affinity for this classroom style (Johnson & Engelhard, 1992; Zahn et al., 1986). They tend to respond most positively to group conditions that emphasize collaboration rather than competition. Peer relationships are important to and for African American youngsters. Teachers would be wise to use noncompetitive, cooperative activities as a means to foster and reinforce desired academic and social learning.

Peer Tutoring

Peer or cross-age tutoring is another peer-based classroom intervention considered especially attractive for the African American learner, providing benefit in terms of both academic and social interaction. Tutoring experiences may aid peer relationships in that students occupy mutually helping roles and praise and encourage each other's efforts. The emphasis on mutual support, constructive feedback, and positive speech naturally curbs tendencies toward abusive or adversarial interaction. Positive relationships are most likely to evolve if all students serve as tutors as well as tutees. Otherwise, vertical rather than positive peer relationships might result. That is, the student who always serves as the tutor might assume the role and behavior of an authority figure, to the detriment of friendships and good peer interactions.

With cross-age tutoring, positive relationships also are expected to evolve. Under these conditions, where the tutor and tutee roles are held constant, tutees and tutors are likely to emerge making admiring or altruistic statements about each other—for example, "I liked my tutor" and "I liked helping the younger students learn" (Giesecke, Cartledge, & Gardner, 1993). Although many reports of the social benefits of peer or cross-age tutoring are anecdotal (Scruggs & Richter, 1985), there is some limited empirical evidence that these experiences may lead to improved self-concepts (Giesecke et al., 1993) and social interactions (Cochran, Feng, Cartledge, & Hamilton, 1993). An important feature of the Cochran et al. study was the use of fifth-grade low-achieving African American males with behavior disorders to teach reading words to second-grade low-achieving African American males with behavior disorders. The tutoring took place in clinical settings. Direct observation of the interactions showed from the outset much higher rates of positive than of negative statements, and the positives increased systematically as students were reinforced by the researchers for being more positive with each other. Another outcome was that teacher ratings of classroom social behaviors showed greater social skill gains for tutoring students than for their nontutoring matched peers, suggesting that the positive effects of tutoring generalized to other settings with other peers. Although somewhat limited by its sample size (16 students), this study not only supported previous findings of academic gains resulting from cross-age or peer tutoring but also documented its potential impact on social and emotional development.

Peer-based interventions hold considerable promise for African American learners. Children can be effective teachers for fellow students, and at certain stages of development, they are more receptive to lessons from one another than from adult authority figures. Well-designed peer-based interventions can be valuable in helping teachers promote both academic and social development with African American students. However, these interventions will be effective only if the students are adequately prepared. Students need direct instruction in the skills that will enable them to participate in cooperative learning groups (e.g., Cartledge & Cochran, 1993) or tutoring pairs (e.g., Heward & Orlansky, 1992) or to prompt desired social behaviors in their peers (e.g., Odom & Strain, 1984). Once critical social skills are learned, students can participate successfully in these peer approaches. Teachers may well view peer-based interventions as a means of maintaining previously taught social skills as well as—in some cases—enhancing academic performance.

Instruction through Literature

Folktales and other narratives, initially transmitted orally, are a prominent feature of the traditional African American culture, and it is reasoned that this art form can be used to teach a variety of school-based skills, including social behaviors (Cartledge & Kleefeld, 1994; Murrell, 1993). Many of the early folktales traced back to Africa, the West Indies, or the southern United States are intended to promote virtuous and moral behavior. For example, in the Jamaican folktale "Rooster and Roach," as retold by Ramona Bass (Goss & Barnes, 1989), cooperation, friendship, and industry are emphasized. Roach tries to deceive Rooster into doing all the field work by feigning an illness. When Rooster discovers this deception, he devours Roach with a gulp. The reader or listener is admonished with the final three sentences: "Now anytime a Rooster sees a lazy Roach, he takes care of him (gulp)! Which goes to say, 'When you work together, well, things can work out. But when you don't, you'd better watch out' (GULP)" (p. 46).

An important figure in the African oral tradition is the griot, "who is regarded by the community as the possessor of special wisdom and insight and whose role is to provoke introspection and thoughtful reflection through his or her narratives" (Murrell, 1993, p. 247). The narratives delivered by the griot entertained as well as fostered cultural awareness, cognitive development, and social mores. These functions are reflected in the common African theme of the signifying monkey, which appears in various rhymes. The following is a version by Oscar Brown, Jr., that appears in an anthology compiled by Goss and Barnes (1989):

Said the signifyin' monkey to the lion one day:*
"Hey, dere's a great big elephant down th' way
Goin' 'roun' talkin', I'm sorry to say,
About yo' momma in a scandalous way!

"Yea, he's talkin' 'bout yo' momma an' yo' grandma, too;
And he don' show too much respect fo' you.
Now, you weren't there an' I sho' am glad
'Cause what he said about yo' momma made me mad!"

Signifying' monkey, stay up in yo' tree
You are always lyin' and signifyin'
But you better not monkey wit' me.

The lion said, "Yea? Well, I'll fix him;
I'll tear that elephant limb from limb."
Then he shook the jungle with a mighty roar
off like a shot from a forty-four.

He found the elephant where the tall grass grows
And said, "I come to punch you in your long nose."
The elephant looked at the lion in surprise
And said, "Boy, you better go pick on somebody your size."

But the lion wouldn't listen; he made a pass;
The elephant slapped him down in the grass.
The lion roared and sprung from the ground
And that's when that elephant really went to town.

I mean he whupped that lion for the rest of the day
And I still don't see how the lion got away
But he dragged on off, more dead than alive,
And that's when that monkey started his signifyin' jive.

The monkey looked down and said, "Oooh we!
What is this beat-up mess I see?

---

* © 1962—Edward B. Marks Music Company. Copyright renewed and
assigned in the United States to Edward B. Marks Music Company and
Bootblack Publishing. All rights for the world outside the United States
controlled by Edward B. Marks Music Company. Used by permission.
All rights reserved.

Is that you, Lion? Ha, ha! Do tell!
Man, he whupped yo' head to a fare-thee-well!

"Give you a beatin' that was rough enough;
You s'pposed to be king of the jungle, ain't dat some stuff?
You big overgrown pussycat! Don' choo roar
Or I'll hop down there an whip you some more."

The monkey got to laughing and a' jumpin' up an' down,
But his foot missed the limb and he plunged to the ground.
The lion was on him with all four feet
Gonna grind that monkey to hamburger meat.

The monkey looked up with tears in his eyes
And said, "Please, Mr. Lion, I apologize,
I meant no harm, please, let me go
And I'll tell you something you really need to know."

The lion stepped back to hear what he'd say,
And that monkey scampered up the tree and got away.
"What I wanted to tell you," the monkey hollered then,
"Is if you fool with me, I'll sic the elephant on you again!"

The lion just shook his head, and said, "You jive . . .
If you and yo' monkey children wanna stay alive,
Up in them trees is where you better stay"
And that's where they are to this very day.

Signifyin' monkey, stay up in yo' tree
You are always lyin' and signifyin'
But you better not monkey wit' me. (pp. 456–457)

As a fable, this rhyme attempts to explain why monkeys live in trees, but it also invokes guidelines for social behavior, putting the listener on guard against bearers of negative messages intended to cause ill will and harm to others. Verbal sparring in the form of "signifying," "ribbing," "woofing," "capping," or "playing the dozens" is a common cultural form, valued in the African American community, particularly among males (Irvine, 1990). Because such verbal repartee is so commonplace, Murrell (1993) suggests that the principal lesson is not to avoid signifying but to be sufficiently responsible and self-controlled to avoid letting others provoke us into foolish actions.

In dealing with peer interaction or conflict resolution, however, it is necessary to address both the instigating and the responding behavior. Prothrow-Stith (1991), for example, notes that many acts of violence and aggression are escalated by incendiary statements from peers. During these verbal sparring matches, which frequently start off good-naturedly, bystanders are often observed to promote anger and aggression through statements such as "Don't let him talk to you like that!"—comments that lead participants to believe they must take excessive action to save face. Prothrow-Stith recommends the use of slogans such as "Friends for life don't let friends fight" (p. 190), which stress that true friends will act in your best interest, helping you to avoid trouble rather than egging you on into conflict and potentially dangerous situations.

Rhythmic verses such as the narrative about the signifying monkey (see Goss & Barnes, 1989, for other examples and additional references) were the precursors of the contemporary rap music that is so popular with African American youth. The rhythm and amusing lyrics make this literary form a particularly attractive and culturally relevant way to provide rationales for specific social skills. These verses could provide a natural segue into current prosocial commercial rap tunes, which could then be followed by student-constructed raps embodying social skill lessons. Students should be encouraged to incorporate into their rap verses repeated refrains such as "Staying out of fights leads to a longer and better life," which might help them remember the instructions and transfer them to other settings.

Written narratives—stories, novels, biographies, and so forth—can also be effective vehicles in social skill instruction as long as they include characters and situations that students can identify with and that they feel reflect their own experiences. In her historical review, Harris (1993) laments the dearth of literature about African American children without stereotypical or demeaning images. Furthermore, many of the existing well-written, positive books suffer from lack of exposure and fail to reach African American children through either parents or teachers. Although many creditable authors of African American children's literature date back to the late 19th and early 20th centuries (e.g., Paul Lawrence Dunbar, Arna Bontemps, and Claude McKay), it is not uncommon for African

Americans who grew up before the 1970s to relate that the only book about blacks that they read during childhood was *Little Black Sambo,* at best a controversial book considered by many to be pejorative in its depiction.

Since about 1970, however, books for African American children have increased not only in quantity but in what Sims in 1982 labeled "cultural consciousness" (Harris, 1993). That is, these books make a deliberate attempt to reflect the contemporary lives of African American youth. One such book, a picture story for elementary-aged children, is *Amazing Grace,* by Mary Hoffman (1991). Grace is a little girl with a vivid imagination who likes to act out all kinds of stories, fairy tales, and portrayals, ranging from Joan of Arc to the family doctor. Grace loves drama. When she asks to play the role of Peter Pan for her racially diverse class, some classmates tell her it is not a part for a black girl. But encouraged by her mother and her grandmother, who take her to a ballet in which the female lead in *Romeo and Juliet* is played by a black woman, Grace auditions and wins the part of Peter Pan. Her success in the play convinces her of her potential to be whatever she wants to be.

A similar theme in an animal tale for slightly older students is "The Frog Who Wanted to Be a Singer" by Linda Goss (Goss & Barnes, 1989). The frog aspires to sing but is belittled and pummeled off stage by the other animals. When the animals are lulled to sleep by the sweet chirping of the performing birds, the frog, convinced of his talent, returns to the stage and delivers a beat and sound in boogie-woogie form. The other animals are awakened and enjoy the sound so much that soon they are all dancing and proclaiming the frog's genius and talent.

These and other similar stories can provide valuable resources for learning about oneself—that is, positive self-statements, personal goals, personal interests, the importance of perseverance, and so forth. Such content is important for African American students, who are often led to believe that their aspirations should be modest and limited to roles traditionally held by African Americans in this society. In discussions of literature, students can be helped to identify personal experiences in which they were inappropriately discouraged from some worthwhile pursuit. What would have happened to Grace and the frog if they had agreed with their peers?

The teacher can help students note how they felt when discouraged and how they felt if and when they attained personal goals. Special emphasis should be placed on the things students must say to themselves and the steps they might take to accomplish worthwhile goals. For maximum benefit, instruction should help students focus on immediate as well as long-range goals. For example, a student who aspires to become a major political figure might also aim to achieve a high score on weekly social studies quizzes or to complete an essay on the life of Barbara Jordan or Adam Clayton Powell, Jr.

For lessons on setting and achieving goals, Kuykendall (1992) recommends using "The Success Chart," on which students formally state what they hope to achieve by age 25. They also specify the attributes needed for this achievement, possible barriers, and strategies they might use to succeed. Kuykendall recommends the following techniques for motivating students:

> Schedule a monthly "show-and-tell" in which students share with the class non-school-related goals they have set and accomplished.
>
> Conduct weekly reviews of famous Black . . . Americans who have achieved their goals. Continue to remind students that success is very much a part of their culture and experience.
>
> Applaud all efforts students put forth to reach their goals.
>
> Set monthly academic achievement goals with and for each student and share them with parents or guardians.
>
> Assist students in developing sequential strategies for meeting goals.
>
> Help students to see failure as a learning experience by discussing failure as part of the road to success. (pp. 60–61).

Since the 1970s, a relatively large number of writers have emerged whose "works are decidedly African American in tone and range of content [and whose] literary quality . . . equals and in many cases, surpasses the quality of general children's literature" (Harris, 1993, p. 177). Prominent among them are authors such as Virginia Hamilton and Walter Dean Myers. Using the urban setting of Harlem, Myers wrote several award-winning books dealing with the daily real-life challenges of youth. One book, *Hoops* (Myers, 1981), depicts the pressure encountered by a talented 17-year-old basketball player who must decide between obtaining immediate gratification through unethical actions and trying to persevere toward some more fruitful and noble goal. This easy-to-read, engaging story presents many opportunities for discussions of social behavior. In one scene, for example, Lonnie, the central character, depressed about a series of events, goes to the basketball court to shoot some hoops. At the court he has a confrontation with a wino who is sleeping in his way. As the man is walking off the court, Lonnie screams:

> "Get off the court, old man, before I hit you!"
>
> "Why don't you put me off the court, youngblood?"
> he says, still grinning.
>
> I look at him for a minute, and he don't look like much.
> But I'm six three and he's maybe six four, and he's heavier.
> I wasn't scared of the cat, but I figured it wasn't worth
> my while. I could hit him and he'd have a heart attack
> and die and I'd be up for manslaughter or something.
>
> I picked up the ball and shot it. He turned and walked
> off, still singing that stupid song about feet. (pp. 8–9)

The leader might lead students in discussing whether Lonnie was justified in his anger at this wino. What really caused Lonnie's anger? What less contentious strategies could Lonnie have used to get the wino to move? What thoughts kept Lonnie from fighting the wino? Were these thoughts constructive or not? The discussion could move from the story to personal application. The teacher could help students think of times when they had displaced anger and "picked a fight" with someone. What were the precipitating events? How might they avoid such confrontations in the future? Teacher and students could identify some constructive thoughts for use in avoiding or defusing arguments. Other noteworthy books by Myers are *Fast Sam, Cool Clyde, and Stuff* (1975) and *Scorpions* (1988), which portray inner city youth dealing with various stressors, including gangs and guns. In addition to Hamilton and Myers, Harris (1993) lists several other equally prominent authors (e.g., Lucille Clifton, Eloise Greenfield, Rosa Guy, Patricia McKissack, Emily Moore, John Steptoe, Mildred Taylor). For a more comprehensive listing of youth books written from an African American perspective, the reader is referred to a work by Bishop (1994).

A final literary resource for social skill instruction is biography. Harris (1993) describes the explicit purpose of many early biographical writers as "providing literary models for children to emulate" (p. 176). She highlights the efforts of noted writers such as W.E.B. DuBois and E. Haynes, who during the early 1900s wrote and published biographies (e.g., Frederick Douglass, Harriet Tubman, Paul Lawrence Dunbar) in order to inform children and their parents of the achievements of their people, to instill racial pride, and to provide models of behavior. Many such books continue to be published today, featuring not only established historical figures but also contemporary personalities, as well as unsung heroes. For example, Silver Burdett publishes a series of books on leaders from the 1960s civil rights movement, including Ella Baker, Stokely Carmichael, Fannie Lou Hamer, Jesse Jackson, Martin Luther King, Jr., Malcolm X, Thurgood Marshall, Rosa Parks, and A. Phillip Randolph. These easy-to-read narratives can be inspirational and instructive, teaching about the beneficial returns of setting worthwhile goals, persevering against the odds, and using nonviolent, direct, or assertive action.

For maximum effect, portions of these stories might be singled out for very specific points of learning—for example, Fannie Lou Hamer's insistence on registering to vote even though she was the target of threats and most other blacks in her town were afraid to register. Discussions might focus on times when students have the option of doing what is right or pursuing worthwhile goals even when threatened or scorned by peers. Students should be encouraged to raise their own peer-based issues, such as walking away from a fight or endeavoring to excel academically.

A particularly poignant biography and model for dealing with aggression comes from the life of Jackie Robinson. As the first black player in the major leagues, Robinson faced much verbal and some physical abuse during his first year or so as a member of the Brooklyn Dodgers. Before Robinson joined the team, the manager, Branch

Rickey, conducted an intense 2-hour training session where he role-played the kind of abusive behavior his new player would encounter and the way Robinson was expected to respond. Essentially, Robinson was to say nothing and avoid any counteraggressive verbal or physical acts. Although this sort of response was inconsistent with his normal temperament, Robinson complied and managed to make a successful career for himself as well as blazing a trail for many other people of color in professional sports.

Students might be engaged in a discussion of the long-term benefits of avoiding counteraggression, based first on the life of Jackie Robinson, then on events in their own lives. They could be invited to speculate on the possible outcomes if Robinson had tried to respond in kind to every taunt received in his early career. Relevant current examples could come from the sports news of players' fines or ejections for poor conduct or from the section of Arthur Ashe's autobiography (Ashe & Rampersad, 1993, pp. 63–110) in which he describes the damaging psychological, monetary, and performance consequences John McEnroe incurred through some of his abusive on-court behavior. This behavior can be contrasted with Jackie Robinson's course of action. A goal of the discussion would be the listing, in column format, of the good and bad outcomes of both retaliating and ignoring taunts while playing a game. It is hoped that students will see that more good outcomes (e.g., remaining in the game, avoiding fines, earning the respect of others, having more friends) result when they exercise self-control.

The next step might be to help students identify and list constructive reactions to anger and alternatives to aggression. A list elicited from students might include walking away, ignoring the person, listening to music, talking to a friend, making an assertive statement, finding something else to do, and so forth. After making this list, students are to describe a personal experience and then select one of the constructive alternatives to act out in that scenario. The teacher should evaluate the role-play, then prompt students to reenact the scene with various constructive responses and select the ones they are most likely to use under similar real-life conditions.

Autobiographies that portray achievement under particularly trying circumstances may be most useful for social skill instruction. Some examples are *Makes Me Wanna Holler*, by Nathan McCall

(1994), and *Laughing in the Dark,* by Patrice Gaines (1994). Both books graphically depict the difficulties of urban living for a young African American, and both provide fertile text for designing lessons concerning healthy and destructive social behaviors. The authors reveal their thought processes around events, their self-analyses of reasons for actions, and their short- and long-term misgivings over behaviors. For example, thoughts and consequences (immediate and long-term) that follow from Nathan McCall's shooting of another youth dramatize the detrimental effects of using violence as a means to resolve conflict. Particularly instructive are the detailed steps these writers took to overcome circumstances that could have led to their social, if not physical, demise.

It is important to exercise caution in using such literature for social skill instruction. Because some young people are inclined to glamorize the unsavory and overlook the salutary messages, trainers should read these works *with* the students, discussing the essential points and helping students make personal applications for correction of behavior. Another warning pertains to the explicit nature of some of these materials. It may be best in some cases to expose students only to selected excerpts, according to school and parental policies and approval.

Family Involvement

To be most successful in developing social skills, trainers should elicit the support and involvement of the learners' families. Parents, siblings, and other relatives can be instrumental in prompting and reinforcing newly taught skills, helping these behaviors to transfer to other settings and to become well established in the youngster's behavioral repertoire. Because the parents are the child's first teachers, the behaviors they value and encourage will carry much weight. African American parents want their children to lead disciplined and socially appropriate lives, but social conditions may mislead them about the skills most critical to children's success; like teachers, parents often inadvertently reinforce the behaviors they wish to extinguish. Many parents, for example, rely heavily on corporal punishment for behavioral control, but for youngsters predisposed to aggressive actions, this parental response is likely to strengthen rather than reduce tendencies toward physical aggression. Similarly, parents in crime-ridden communities are inclined to encourage aggression in their children as a means for survival, when the reality is that each aggressive response only exacerbates rather than improves current living conditions and further jeopardizes the child's safety and survival.

The typical "uninvolved" parent is profiled to be the minority, low-income parent who has minimal contact with schools or parent organizations (Marion, 1980; Shea & Bauer, 1985). At least two major factors may account for this finding: (a) school personnel tend to be less inclined to correspond with minority parents than with mainstream parents, assuming indifference on the part of the former (Turnbull & Turnbull, 1986), and (b) the disproportionate referrals of their children to special education programs or for disciplinary actions cause many African American parents to view schools with anger, dismay, and suspicion (Marion, 1980). If these attitudinal barriers are to be overcome and cooperative relationships encouraged, initial contacts must be positive ones. Many parents complain that they are contacted by school personnel only when their children misbehave. Often parents become less and less responsive as the behavior problems and calls mount, and the result is a greater chasm between the home and school and worsening behavior problems in the child.

Ideally, parents should be contacted before serious behavior problems emerge so that the school might build an alliance with the parents in the student's best interest. Kuykendall (1992) gives a very brief script for teachers to use in the initial parent contact. It includes an introduction, a statement of delight over having the child in class, two statements about the child's strengths, and a closing statement concerning a future meeting to work together to enhance the child's performance. This initial telephone contact might be followed with written correspondence that also has a positive, upbeat tone. Like telephone calls from the school, the majority of notes sent home tend to bear bad news. Again, this first note should be brief, informing parents of the upcoming social skill instruction and giving examples of specific skills to be taught. Depending on school policy and the purpose of the instruction, it may be necessary to get parental permission for the student to participate.

At this point an individual or group meeting (depending on number of students) with parents might be scheduled to discuss the nature of the social skill instruction program and the parents' role. Middleton (Middleton, 1994; Middleton & Cartledge, 1995) found that parents typically understood that social skills related to their children's behavior but generally were unaware of the specific skills that were expected in school. Parents were asked to complete the parent form of the Social Skills Rating System (SSRS; Gresham & Elliott, 1990) for their children. This process not only yielded information on the parents' views of their children's social skills and problem behaviors relative to the views of classroom teachers, it also gave the parents insight into the kinds of behaviors valued by the school as important for success. During this session, the curriculum and methods for teaching social skills were described, and parents were informed of their important role in reinforcing desired behaviors.

Parental involvement consisted of prompting and reinforcing social skills taught in school. A parent form and weekly follow-up telephone calls were used to facilitate this involvement. The parent form "Gaining Appropriate Behaviors" (or GAB Sheet; see Table 6) was sent home via the students at the beginning of each new lesson. The GAB Sheet listed questions or activities that were to be completed as homework and outlined a process to evaluate the child's performance. The questions or activities listed on the parent form related to the components of the social skill lesson currently being taught. Parents were asked to discuss the questions or activities with their child after the child had done the homework and to praise the child for completing the tasks. When the child responded to the parents with an incorrect answer, the parents were instructed to mark the box indicating an incorrect answer, then to say, "Good try, but the answer is . . . ." The child repeated the correct answer, and the homework session for that day was ended. Homework sessions were scheduled for 3 days a week.

The trainer telephoned the parents on Monday evening to make sure they had received the form and understood the task. For parents without telephones, the note urged them to contact the trainer (by using a neighbor's phone or a pay phone, coming to the school, or sending a note) as soon as possible if they had questions. The student was to return the GAB Sheet to school. Initially students received stickers for taking the notes home and returning them. After the first week, students received only verbal praise at school; parents were encouraged to deliver verbal praise as well.

Table 6
GAB Sheet

Dear Parent:
   This week your child, _____, will
participate in the social skills listed below. Remember to talk with
your child about the activities and practice the skills at least three
times before Friday. If your child completes the skills without
your help, place an X on the "Happy Face." If the child needs
help with a skill, mark an X on the "Star," tell the child the correct
answer, then have the child repeat the correct answer to you.
Please call me at _____ anytime you have
a question. Thanks for helping your child do a good job! Don't
forget to return this letter to your child's teacher on Friday.
Thanks.   *Mrs. M.*

Lesson 1
Monday
What did you learn in the GAB program today?
(*Answer:* Being kind and courteous to others
by saying thank you, please, excuse me, and
I'm sorry; watching your tone of voice.)
Tuesday
What are the steps in speaking kindly or politely?
(*Answer:* Think of what you want to say, think
of a way to say it kindly, and use a nice voice.)
Thursday
Tell me what you would say to someone who
is standing in front of the TV so you can't see
the program you are watching.
(*Answer:* In a nice voice, I would say, please
move, I can't see the TV. After they move,
I say thank you.)

COMMENTS:

Using these procedures, Middleton (1994) was able to obtain ongoing participation from 8 of 10 parents contacted. A particularly effective means for securing and maintaining parental involvement in the first year was to engage the assistance of one mother in the community who was active in the school, knew many of the other parents, and had one son in the project. The first year, 77 percent (14 out of 18) of the parent notes were returned; 52 percent (12 out of 23) were returned the second year. The least social skill improvement was noted in the two students whose parents had failed to participate in the project. All of the participating parents responded positively to the social skill instruction, indicating that they saw improvements in their children's behavior (e.g., requesting more help with homework, asking more questions, and speaking more nicely to siblings). The parents felt that the social skill instruction kept their children out of trouble, that parents should be involved in the social skill instruction, and that it should continue the following year. The parents were apologetic about the times they had failed to follow through, but they expressed genuine pleasure at the opportunity for ongoing participation, indicating that this project was a refreshing change from their past sporadic and typically "disciplinary" school contacts.

Parent notes such as the one illustrated here can also be found in commercial social skill programs (e.g., Cartledge & Kleefeld, 1991, 1994). Notes alone will be of little benefit, however, in the absence of efforts to establish rapport and convey genuine positive interest in the child. It is important to communicate to parents that their child is valued and has the ability to learn. Regular newsletters that contain contributions from the learners (e.g., social skill strategies, verses, drawings) might be a useful vehicle for communication. Additionally, teachers might regularly send home individual positive notes that tell of some good deeds performed by the students. Periodic telephone calls or home visits may be needed for low-literacy parents or those who have been unresponsive to written correspondence.

Mentoring

Mentoring can be performed by a variety of individuals and can take many forms, perhaps the most common and enduring being the Big Brother and Big Sister programs. The importance of same-race male mentors for young, low-income African American males cannot be overstated. Often reared in female-dominated households and taught by female teachers, they are inclined to view values espoused by females as feminine or weak. As Taylor (1989) speculates, the failure of these young people readily to identify possible role models, in contrast to their more affluent counterparts, may be a direct result of the lack of adequate models in their immediate environments. Social skill instruction under mentoring conditions is informal at best, but as noted in the social learning literature, models in our environment greatly influence our social behaviors and our worldviews.

A somewhat novel and attractive mentoring program is described by educators in a self-contained inner city elementary school for students with behavior disorders (Petri, Mungin, & Emerson, 1992). The focus was to provide African American male role models for a student body that was 88 percent male, from families with 89 percent single mothers, in a school with a professional staff that was 86 percent female. The mentors for the first year included an architect, two police officers, two social workers, and two professionals from the private sector. The mentors spent 4 hours per month working with the students in their classes, performing various tutoring and monitoring duties.

Stephens and Mand (1995) also developed a school-based mentoring project in which African American male college students were hired to tutor African American middle school males identified as potentially at risk for antisocial and self-destructive behaviors. The program is conducted after school in four inner city middle schools. The tutors, who meet with the youngsters for 1½ hours at the end of the school day, attempt to establish positive relationships, provide informal instruction in social behaviors, and tutor in various academic skills. Once weekly the college students provide an hour of instruction in math, followed by a half-hour group activity focused on developing group cohesion through trust exercises and math games. Additional components of the project include sponsored outdoor adventure activities and various cultural and social events such as trips to African American cultural centers and bowling outings. Camping activities, which include adventure-filled high ropes courses, are scheduled monthly for each group, along with a 3-day camping experience during the summer. Along with improvement in academic performance, desired outcomes of this project include self-confidence, prosocial peer orientations, and positive mentoring relationships with high-achieving, same-race adult males. Another academically oriented program for inner city delinquents used retired persons as tutors and mentors.

The close mentor-mentee relationship that reportedly emerges in such programs could be the basis for providing and reinforcing valuable social skill lessons. A special advantage of school-based mentoring programs is that contact is more likely to be regular because school attendance is required for the mentee, and the mentor makes the project part of the working day rather than drawing on valuable and possibly limited personal time. Male same-race mentors are particularly important for the social development of minority males.

Summary

African Americans currently make up 12 percent of the U.S. population, and that percentage is expected to increase steadily into the middle of the 21st century. With a history in this country of over 300 years, African Americans are represented in every geographic area at every socioeconomic level. Despite their diversity, they are disproportionately represented within the low socioeconomic stratum, with approximately half of their children being reared in poverty. The accompanying conditions of inadequate schooling, discrimination, and stressed families and communities combine to undermine the social development of African American youth and marginalize their existence in this society.

The African American community has many strengths, the most important of which continues to be the family. Reflecting a collectivistic worldview, the African American family tends to be extended in structure, reaching out to a wide variety of traditional and nontraditional family members and providing financial, emotional, educational, and social support. This system has contributed to the resilience of African Americans, enabling them to withstand tremendous adversity, but recent conditions have had an eroding effect, causing some alarm about the development of a rather fragile segment of its population, youth of low socioeconomic status.

The larger society tends to respond to the problems of low-income African American youth through programs emphasizing punishment and control. Failing to teach prosocial behaviors or to create more constructive attitudes, these efforts are more likely to exacerbate than to eliminate behavior problems. Direct instruction in social skills that takes account of these young people's unique cultural and developmental factors is promising. To be effective, formal instruction needs to begin early in children's lives, incorporating parents and as many members of the children's immediate environments as possible. Psychological orientation is an important aspect of the instruction; trainers assess and program for the learners' values, beliefs, and methods of most effective communication. Valuable messages are best delivered through learner-sanctioned formats and messengers.

Direct instruction may be very useful as a means to provide a foundation for social skill learning and to teach students to instruct and coach their peers in critical behaviors. Peer-mediated learning may be especially beneficial for African American youth, who tend to be particularly peer oriented. Strategies such as peer mediation and cooperative learning deserve special attention in social skill instruction for these youngsters. There also is a need for good adult same-race models who work regularly with young people to build good relationships and reinforce social skill learnings. Finally, formal social skill instruction needs to be viewed as a crucial, ongoing part of the curriculum throughout the school years.

References

Allison, K., & Leone, P.E. (1994). The dual potentials model: Understanding alcohol and other drug use among ethnically and racially diverse adolescents. In R.L. Peterson & S. Ishii-Jordan (Eds.), *Multicultural issues in the education of students with behavioral disorders.* Cambridge, MA: Brookline.

Anyon, J. (1981). Social class and the hidden curriculum of work. In H.A. Giroux, A.N. Penna, & W.F. Pinar (Eds.), *Curriculum and instruction.* Berkeley, CA: McCutchan.

Ashe, A., & Rampersad, A. (1993). *Days of grace.* New York: Ballantine.

Asher, S.R., Oden, S., & Gottman, J. (1977). Children's friendships in school settings. In Katz, L. (Ed.), *Current topics in early childhood education* (Vol. 1). Norwood,NJ: Ablex.

Barone, C., Ayers, T.S., Weissberg, R.P., Voyce, C.K., Kasprow, W.J., & Schwab-Stone, M.E. (1993, August). *Prevalence and co-occurrence of problem behavior involvement among urban adolescents.* Paper presented at the convention of the American Psychological Association, Toronto.

Bishop, R.S. (1994). *Kaleidoscope: A multicultural book list.* Urbana, IL: National Council of Teachers of English.

Bridgeman, B., & Burbach, H.J. (1976). Effects of black vs. white peer models on academic expectations and actual performance of fifth grade students. *Journal of Experimental Education, 45,* 9–12.

Carmen, B. (1990, April 4). More blacks are disciplined. *Columbus Dispatch,* p. 1D.

Cartledge, G., & Cochran, L.L. (1993). Developing cooperative learning behaviors in students with behavior disorders. *Preventing School Failure, 37,* 5–10.

Cartledge, G., & Kleefeld, J. (1991). *Taking part: Introducing social skills to children.* Circle Pines, MN: American Guidance Service.

Cartledge, G., & Kleefeld, J. (1994). *Working together: Building children's social skills through folk literature.* Circle Pines, MN: American Guidance Service.

Cartledge, G., & Milburn, J.F. (1995). *Teaching social skills to children and youth: Innovative approaches* (3rd ed.). Boston: Allyn & Bacon.

Clark, K., & Clark, M. (1947). Racial identification and preference in Negro children. In T.M. Newcomb & E.L. Hartley (Eds.), *Readings in social psychology.* New York: Holt, Rinehart & Winston.

Clark, M. (1991). Social identity, peer relations, and academic competence of African-American adolescents. *Education and Urban Society, 24,* 41–52.

Clark, M., & Drewry, D. (1985). Similarity and reciprocity in the friendships of elementary school children. *Child Study Journal, 15,* 251–264.

Clark, M.L., & Ayers, M. (1988). The role of reciprocity and proximity in junior high school friendships. *Journal of Youth and Adolescence, 17,* 403–411.

Clark, R.M. (1983). *Family life and school achievement: Why poor black children succeed or fail.* University of Chicago Press.

Cochran, L.L., Feng, H., Cartledge, G., & Hamilton, S. (1993). The effects of cross-age tutoring on the academic achievement, social behaviors, and self-perceptions of low-achieving African-American males with behavioral disorders. *Behavioral Disorders, 18,* 292–302.

Cross, M., & Foley, R. (1993). Reclaiming an endangered species: The male responsibility program. *Journal of Emotional and Behavioral Problems, 1*(4), 33–36.

Dodge, K.A. (1993). Social-cognitive mechanisms in the development of conduct disorder and depression. In L.W. Porter & M.R. Rosenzweig (Eds.), *Annual Review of Psychology* (Vol. 44). Palo Alto, CA: Annual Reviews.

Dressler, W.W. (1985). Extended family relationships, social support, and mental health in a Southern black community. *Journal of Health and Social Behavior, 26,* 39–48.

DuBois, D.L., & Hirsch, B.J. (1990). School and neighborhood friendship patterns of blacks and whites in early adolescence. *Child Development, 61,* 524–536.

Erdley, C.A., & Asher, S.R. (1993, August). *Linkages between aggression and children's legitimacy of aggression beliefs.* Paper presented at the conference of the American Psychological Association, Toronto.

Executive Committee, Council for Children with Behavioral Disorders. (1989). Best assessment practices for students with behavioral disorders: Accommodation to cultural diversity and individual differences. *Behavioral Disorders, 14,* 263–278.

Feng, H., & Cartledge, G. (in press). Social skills assessment of inner city Asian, African, and European American students. *School Psychology Review.*

Fordham, S. (1988). Racelessness as a factor in black students' school success: Pragmatic strategy or pyrrhic victory? *Harvard Educational Review, 58,* 54–84.

Forness, S.R. (1988). Planning for the needs of children with serious emotional disturbance: The national special education and mental health coalition. *Behavioral Disorders, 13,* 127–139.

Foster, H.J. (1983). African patterns in the Afro-American family. *Journal of Black Studies, 14,* 201–232.

Franklin, J.H. (1988). A historical note on black families. In H.P. McAdoo (Ed.), *Black families* (2nd ed.). Newbury Park, CA: Sage.

Freud, A., & Dann, S. (1951). An experiment in group upbringing. In C.L. Rothgeb (Ed.), *The psychoanalytic study of the child* (Vol. 6). New York: International Universities Press.

Gaines, P. (1994). *Laughing in the dark: From colored girl to woman of color.* New York: Crown.

Gibbs, J.T. (1989). Black American adolescents. In J.T. Gibbs & L.N. Huang (Eds.), *Children of color: Psychological interventions with minority youth.* San Francisco: Jossey-Bass.

Giesecke, D., Cartledge, G., & Gardner, R. (1993). Low-achieving students as successful cross-age tutors. *Preventing School Failure, 37,* 34–43.

Goldstein, A.P. (1988). *The Prepare Curriculum: Teaching prosocial competencies.* Champaign, IL: Research Press.

Goldstein, A.P. (1989). *Social skill instruction.* Presentation at the Central Ohio Special Education Regional Resource Center, invited conference for Severe Behavior Handicaps, Columbus.

Goode, K.G. (1979). From Africa to the United States. In G. Henderson (Ed.), *Understanding and counseling ethnic minorities.* Springfield, IL: Charles C Thomas.

Goss, L., & Barnes, M.E. (1989). *Talk that talk: An anthology of African-American storytelling.* New York: Simon & Schuster/Touchstone.

Graham, S., Hudley, C., & Williams, E. (1992). Attributional and emotional determinants of aggression among African-American and Latino young adolescents. *Developmental Psychology, 28,* 731–740.

Gresham, F.M., & Elliott, S.N. (1990). *Social skills rating system.* Circle Pines, MN: American Guidance Service.

Guerra, N.G., & Slaby, R.G. (1990). Cognitive mediators of aggression in adolescent offenders: Part 2. Intervention. *Developmental Psychology, 26*(2), 269–277.

Hallinan, M.T., & Teixeira, R.A. (1987). Opportunities and constraints: Black-white differences in the formation of interracial friendships. *Child Development, 58,* 1358–1371.

Hallinan, M.T., & Williams, R.A. (1989). Interracial friendship choices in secondary schools. *American Sociological Review, 54,* 67–78.

Hammond, W.R. (1991). *Dealing with anger: A violence prevention program for African American youth* [Videotape Program]. Champaign, IL: Research Press.

Hammond, W.R., & Yung, B.R. (1991). Preventing violence in at-risk African-American youth. *Journal of Health Care for the Poor and Underserved, 2*(3), 359–373.

Hammond, W.R., & Yung, B.R. (1993). Psychology's role in the public health response to assaultive violence among young African-American men. *American Psychologist, 48,* 142–154.

Hare, B. (1979). *Black girls: A comparative analysis of self perceptions and achievement by race, sex and socioeconomic background.* Baltimore: Johns Hopkins University.

Hare, B. (1985). Reexamining the achievement central tendency: Sex differences within race and race differences within sex. In H.P. McAdoo & J.L. McAdoo (Eds.), *Black children: Social, educational, and parental environments.* Beverly Hills, CA: Sage.

Harris, V. (1993). *African American children's literature: The first one hundred years.* In T. Perry & J.W. Fraser (Eds.), *Freedom's plow: Teaching in the multicultural classroom.* New York: Routledge.

Harrison, A.O., Wilson, M.N., Pine, C.J., Chan, S.Q., & Buriel, R. (1990). Family ecologies of ethnic minority children. *Child Development, 61,* 347–362.

Haynes, N.M., & Gebreyesus, S. (1992). Cooperative learning: A case for African-American students. *School Psychology Review, 21,* 577–585.

Heward, W., & Orlansky, M. (1992). *Exceptional children* (4th ed.). New York: Merrill.

Hilliard, A.G. (1980). Cultural diversity and special education. *Exceptional Children, 46*(8), 584–588.

Hoffman, M. (1991). *Amazing Grace.* New York: Dial.

Horton, C.P., & Smith, J.C. (1990). *Statistical record of black America.* Detroit: Gale Research, Inc.

Hudley, C., & Graham, S. (1993). An attributional intervention to reduce peer-directed aggression among African-American boys. *Child Development, 64,* 124–138.

Irvine, J.J. (1990). *Black students and school failure: Policies, practices, and prescriptions.* New York: Greenwood.

Jackson, B.W. (1976). *Black identity development theory.* Austin, TX: New Perspectives, Inc.

Johnson, C., & Engelhard, G. (1992). Gender, academic achievement, and preferences for cooperative, competitive, and individualistic learning among African-American adolescents. *Journal of Psychology, 126,* 385–392.

Johnson, J., Jackson, L.A., & Gatto, L. (in press). Violent attitudes and deferred academic aspirations: Deleterious effects of exposure to rap music. *Basic and Applied Social Psychology.*

Johnson, D.W., & Johnson, R.T. (1991). *Teaching students to be peacemakers.* Edina, MN: Interaction.

Johnson, D.W., & Johnson, R.T. (1994, April). *Teaching students to be peacemakers: Results of five years of research.* Paper presented at the conference of the American Educational Research Association, San Francisco.

Johnson, D.W., Johnson, R.T., Tiffany, M., & Zaidman, B. (1983). Are low achievers disliked in a cooperative situation? A test of rival theories in a mixed ethnic situation. *Contemporary Educational Psychology, 8,* 189–200.

Keller, H.R. (1988). Children's adaptive behaviors: Measure and source generalizability. *Journal of Psychoeducational Assessment, 6,* 371–389.

Koch, M. (1988). Resolving disputes: Students can do it better. *NASSP Bulletin, 72*(504), 16–18.

Kreidler, W.J. (1984). *Creative conflict resolution.* Glenview, IL: Scott, Foresman.

Kuykendall, C. (1992). *From rage to hope: Strategies for reclaiming Black & Hispanic students.* Bloomington, IN: National Educational Service.

Lane, P.S., & McWhirter, J.J. (1992). A peer mediation model: Conflict resolution for elementary and middle school children. *Elementary School Guidance & Counseling, 27,* 15–23.

Lethermon, V.R., Williamson, D.A., Moody, S.C., Granberry, S.W., Lemanek, K.L., & Bodiford, C. (1984). Factors affecting the social validity of a role-play test of children's social skills. *Journal of Behavioral Assessment, 6,* 231–245.

Lethermon, V.R., Williamson, D.A., Moody, S.C., & Wozniak, P. (1986). Racial bias in behavioral assessment of children's social skills. *Journal of Psychopathology and Behavioral Assessment, 8,* 329–337.

Maccoby, E.E. (1980). *Social development.* New York: Harcourt Brace Jovanovich.

Maccoby, E.E. (1992). The role of parents in the socialization of children: An historical overview. *Developmental Psychology, 28,* 1006–1017.

Maheady, L., Algozzine, B., & Ysseldyke, J.E. (1985). Minorities in special education. *The Education Digest, 51,* 50–53.

Marcus, R.F., Matlach, E., McGreavy, M.M., Rouse, R., & Flatter, C. (1992). *Family correlates and social skills deficits in incarcerated and non-incarcerated adolescents.* Unplublished manuscript. University of Maryland at College Park, Maryland.

Marion, R.L. (1980). Communicating with parents of culturally diverse exceptional children. *Exceptional Children, 46,* 616–623.

Marsh, H.W., & Barnes, J. (1982). *Self Description Questionnaire II.* Sydney, Australia: University of Sydney.

McAdoo, H.P. (Ed.). (1988). *Black families* (2nd ed.). Newbury Park, CA: Sage.

McCall, N. (1994). *Makes me wanna holler: A young black man in America.* New York: Random House.

McCormick, M. (1988). *Mediation in the schools: An evaluation of the Wakefield Pilot Peer Mediation Program in Tucson, Arizona.* Washington, DC: American Bar Association.

MEE Productions, Inc. (1992). *Reaching the hip-hop generation* (Executive summary of a study by MEE Productions, Inc., to The Robert Wood Johnson Foundation). (Available from West Philadelphia Enterprise Center, 4601 Market Street, Philadelphia, PA 19139.)

Middleton, M.B. (1994). *The effects of social skills instruction and parent participation on aggressive behaviors, antisocial behaviors, and prosocial skills exhibited by primary-age students.* Unpublished doctoral dissertation, The Ohio State University, Columbus.

Middleton, M.B., & Cartledge, G. (1995). The effects of social skills instruction and parental involvement on the aggressive behaviors of African American males. *Behavior Modification, 19,* 192–210.

Miller, D.T., Turnbull, W., & McFarland, C. (1988). Particularistic and universalistic evaluation in the social comparison process. *Journal of Personality and Social Psychology, 55,* 908–917.

Moore, R.J. (1994). *The effects of social skill instruction and self-monitoring on anger-control, reactions-to-losing, and reactions-to-winning behaviors of ninth-grade students with severe behavior handicaps.* Unpublished master's thesis, The Ohio State University, Columbus.

Moore, R.J., Cartledge, G., & Heckaman, K. (1995). The effects of social skill instruction and self-monitoring on game-related behaviors of adolescents with emotional or behavioral disorders. *Behavioral Disorders, 20,* 253–266.

Morris, K.T., & Jackson, J. (1986). Academic achievement and popularity in low socioeconomic status black children. *Journal of Psychopathology and Behavioral Assessment, 8,* 39–46.

Moyer, T.R., & Motta, R.W. (1982). Alienation and school adjustment among Black and White adolescents. *Journal of Psychology, 112,* 21–28.

Murrell, P. (1993). Afrocentric immersion: Academic and personal development of African American males in public schools. In T. Perry & J.W. Fraser (Eds.), *Freedom's plow: Teaching in the multicultural classroom.* New York: Routledge.

Myers, W.D. (1975). *Fast Sam, Cool Clyde, and stuff.* New York: Viking.

Myers, W.D. (1981). *Hoops.* New York: Dell.

Myers, W.D. (1988). *Scorpions.* Cambridge, MA: Harper & Row.

National Institute of Mental Health. (1982). *Television and behavior: Ten years of scientific progress and implications for the eighties: Vol. 1. Summary report.* Rockville, MD: Author.

Odom, S.L., & Strain, P.S. (1984). Peer-mediated approaches to promoting children's social interaction: A review. *American Journal of Orthopsychiatry, 54,* 544–557.

Ogbu, J. (1988). Cultural diversity and human development. In D.T. Slaughter (Ed.), *Black children and poverty: A developmental perspective.* San Francisco: Jossey-Bass.

Ogbu, J. (1981). Origins of human competence: A cultural-ecological perspective. *Child Development, 52,* 413–429.

Okey, J.L. (1992). Human aggression: The etiology of individual differences. *Journal of Humanistic Psychology, 32,* 51–64.

Parham, T.A., & Helms, J.E. (1981). The influence of black students' racial identity attitudes on preferences for counselor's race. *Journal of Counseling Psychology, 28,* 250–257.

Perry, D.G., & Bussey, K. (1984). *Social development.* Englewood Cliffs, NJ: Prentice-Hall.

Peters, M.F. (1988). Parenting in black families with young children. A historical perspective. In H.P. McAdoo (Ed.), *Black families* (2nd ed.). Newbury Park, CA: Sage.

Petri, A.E., Mungin, C., & Emerson, B. (1992, April). *More precious than gold: African-American male mentors.* Paper presented at the annual convention of the Council for Exceptional Children, Baltimore.

Prothrow-Stith, D. (1991). *Deadly consequences.* New York: HarperCollins.

Rist, R.C. (1970). Student social class and teacher expectations: The self-fulfilling prophecy and ghetto education. *Harvard Educational Review, 40,* 411–451.

Rogers, M., Miller, N., & Hennigan, K. (1981). Cooperative games as an intervention to promote cross-racial acceptance. *American Educational Research Journal, 18,* 513–516.

Rubin, K.H., Bream, L.A., & Rose-Krasnor, L. (1991). Social problem solving and aggression in childhood. In D.J. Pepler & K.H. Rubin (Eds.), *The development and treatment of childhood aggression.* Hillsdale, NJ: Erlbaum.

Ryujin, D.H., & Abitia, F.B. (1992, August). *Self-esteem and anger among African-American students.* Paper presented at the annual meeting of the American Psychological Association, Washington, DC.

Schofield, J.W. (1981). Complementary and conflicting identities: Images and interaction in an interracial school. In S.R. Asher & J.M. Gottman (Eds.), *The development of children's friendships.* New York: Cambridge University Press.

Scruggs, T.E., & Richter, L.L. (1985). Tutoring learning disabled students: A critical review. *Learning Disability Quarterly, 8,* 286–298.

Shade, B.J. (1979). Social-psychological characteristics of achieving black children. In G. Henderson (Ed.), *Understanding and counseling ethnic minorities.* Springfield, IL: Charles C Thomas.

Shade, B.J. (1983). The social success of black youth: The impact of significant others. *Journal of Black Studies, 14,* 137–150.

Shea, T.M., & Bauer, A.M. (1985). *Parents and teachers of exceptional students.* Boston: Allyn & Bacon.

Silberman, C. (1971). *Crisis in the classroom.* New York: Vintage.

Sims, R. (1982). *Shadow and substance: Afro-American experience in contemporary children's fiction.* Urbana, IL: National Council of Teachers of English.

Slaughter, D.T., & Epps, E.G. (1987). The home environment and academic achievement of Black American children and youth: An overview. *Journal of Negro Education, 56,* 3–20.

Slavin, R.E. (1990). Research on cooperative learning: Consensus and controversy. *Educational Leadership, 47,* 52–54.

Spencer, M.B. (1988). Self-concept development. In D.T. Slaughter (Ed.), *Black children and poverty: A developmental perspective.* San Francisco: Jossey-Bass.

Stephens, T.M., & Mand, C. (1995). *Drug-free middle schools: Adventure-based initiatives.* Washington, DC: U.S. Department of Education.

Stroman, C.A. (1991). Television's role in the socialization of African American children and adolescents. *Journal of Negro Education, 60,* 314–327.

Taylor, H., & Dozier, C. (1983). Television violence, African Americans, and social control. *Journal of Black Studies, 14,* 107–136.

Taylor, R.L. (1988/1989). African-American inner city youth and the subculture of disengagement. *Urban League Review, 12,* 15–24.

Taylor, R.L. (1989). Black youth, role models and the social construction of identity. In R.L. Jones (Ed.), *Black adolescents.* Berkeley, CA: Cobb & Henry.

Tienda, M., & Angel, R. (1982). Headship and household composition among Blacks, Hispanics, and other Whites. *Social Forces, 61,* 508–531.

Turnbull, A.P., & Turnbull, H.R. (1986). *Families, professionals, and exceptionality: A special partnership.* Columbus, OH: Merrill.

Turner, S.M., Beidel, D.C., Hersen, M., & Bellack, A.S. (1984). Effects of race on ratings of social skill. *Journal of Consulting and Clinical Psychology, 52*(3), 474–475.

U.S. Bureau of the Census. (1993). *Statistical abstract of the United States: 1993* (113th ed.). Washington, DC: Author.

Widaman, K.F., MacMillan, D.L., Hemsley, R.E., Little, T.D., & Balow, I.H. (1992). Differences in adolescents' self-concept as a function of academic level, ethnicity, and gender. *American Journal on Mental Retardation, 96,* 387–404.

Wilson, M.N. (1986). The black extended family: An analytical consideration. *Developmental Psychology, 22,* 246–258.

Wilson, M.N. (1989). Child development in the context of the black extended family. *American Psychologist, 44,* 380–385.

Zahn, G.L., Kagan, S., & Widaman, K.F. (1986). Cooperative learning and classroom climate. *Journal of School Psychology, 24,* 351–362.

CHAPTER 5

Native Americans

JEANETTE W. LEE AND GWENDOLYN CARTLEDGE

The historical origins of diversity in our society rest with immigration for all its various cultures—with one exception. American Indians inhabited the continent before the time of Columbus. The population currently consists of over 500 tribes, all having their own customs, codes of behavior, and languages. Although the term *Native American* may call up a stereotypic image, Native American people are not only culturally diverse but vary considerably in appearance. Skin color ranges from light to dark; hair texture, stature, and facial features also vary widely.

As of 1990, over 1,900,000 people (.8 percent of the total U.S. population) identify themselves as Native Americans (U.S. Bureau of the Census, 1993). Although most (67 percent) live in urban areas, much of the literature regarding these people is based on studies of the 33 percent minority who reside on the 304 federal reservations in the United States. States with the highest concentrations of Native Americans are Alaska, New Mexico, Oklahoma, South Dakota, and Montana; the largest tribes are Cherokee, Navajo, Sioux, Chippewa, and Choctaw (Goley, 1992).

Unemployment among Native Americans living on or near reservations ranges from 50 to 75 percent (Kallam, Hoernicke, & Coser, 1994). The average annual income of all Native American families in the United States is $6,000 to $7,000 below that of the general population. Approximately 45 percent of reservation citizens and 28 percent of all Native Americans fall below the poverty line (Kallam et al., 1994).

Compared to the rest of the population, Native Americans have a lower death rate for cardiac diseases (137 per 100,000 versus 183.6 per 100,000), but they have a higher rate of accidental death (81.3 per 100,000 versus 35 per 100,000). Suicide among school-aged Native American children is three times higher than among majority children (LaFromboise, 1988).

Cultural Distinctions

Psychosocial Factors

Native American youth find themselves confronting psychological identity issues similar to those that affect youngsters from other "involuntary" minority groups (Ogbu, 1978). Caught between two somewhat alien and incompatible cultures, many of these young people find themselves struggling against substantial odds to create for themselves a lifestyle that is both satisfying and self-validating. Many of them fail to identify with either the dominant or the traditional Native American culture. Brendtro, Brokenleg, and Van Brockern (1990) note that the child-rearing philosophies of traditional Native American culture emphasized (a) a sense of belongingness, (b) a spirit of mastery, (c) a spirit of independence, and (d) a spirit of generosity. Belonging to the community was an integral feature of traditional Native American society. Child care and instruction were viewed to be not simply the province of the biological parents; rather, these duties were assumed by all members of the society. This situation created a state of kinship among group members as well as fostering "a world view that all belong to one another and should be treated accordingly" (Brendtro et al., p. 37). Children were encouraged to strive for mastery in every aspect of their existence: cognitive, physical, social, and spiritual. Mastery did not mean competition and besting one's peers; instead, youth were directed to use others' superior achievements as models and aim to accomplish their own personal goals.

In guiding children toward independence, traditional Native American culture emphasized instruction through modeling and giving youngsters ample opportunity to accomplish things on their own. For example, Brendtro et al. (1990) describe a situation where adult Blackfoot Indians sat for a half hour while a toddler struggled to open a door by himself. After the child opened the door, the adults praised him for being able to do it himself. The traditional societies focused on building inner discipline. Children were respected, and direct demands and coercion were minimized. Rather than ordering, group influence and gentle prompts such as "Son, some day when you are a man you will do this" were used to mold behavior (Brendtro et al., p. 43). This "circle of courage" was completed by the components of generosity and altruism. A salient feature of traditional culture was the emphasis on giving and on refraining from selfishness. Moral lessons began in early childhood, when parents deliberately involved their children in giving to the needy. Personal acquisitions were not to be held for a show of wealth but rather to be shared with others, and caring for others, particularly children, was often seen as the purpose of life. Brendtro and colleagues contend that fragments of these principles, particularly the emphasis on generosity, continue to be evident in contemporary Native American communities.

Changes in the traditional Native American lifestyle and the influence of other cultures have noticeably altered the circle of courage, leading many of the youth to pursue alien and possibly self-destructive behaviors as a means of establishing their "identity and place in the surrounding world" (Deyhle, 1986, p. 125). Conducting an anthropological study of Ute, Navajo, and Anglo high school students in a high school in Utah, Deyhle found that many of the Native American students used "break dancing" as a vehicle for self-identity and social interaction. Break dancing, a competitive dance form originated by African and Hispanic American youth in other parts of the country, was performed mainly by Native American students in this school and served as a means for social support. Deyhle identified three groups in the school's student population according to social status: (a) highest-status students comprising mostly upper-income Anglos and perhaps some Native American athletes; (b) a middle-status group, composed of a combination of Anglos and Native Americans; and (3) a lowest-status group, made up of Native American "breakers."

The "breakers" defined themselves according to group membership, which to a large extent dictated dress, social communication, entertainment, and values. They dressed in red and black, their outfits typically including black nylon zippered pants, long single earrings, and short-crowned, narrow-brimmed hats. They used nonverbal communication and performance to establish identity and solidarity with other "breakers." For example, Deyhle (1986) observed these students using constant "undulating rippled arm movements" as they passed fellow students or sat in classrooms. "Breakers" enjoyed watching break dancing movies, which depicted happy endings with the "breaking youth winning status, friends, recognition, and sometimes money . . . [reinforcing] fantasies of beauty, grace, and success" (p. 122), qualities rarely reflected in the lives of the "breakers."

Finding themselves juxtaposed between two cultures and occupying marginal positions in both, young people like these tend to reject both cultural systems, risking ethnic identity problems and the accompanying behavioral maladjustment, as discussed in chapter 1. Deyhle (1986) observed that "breakers" denied the importance of schooling, accentuated their oppressed state, and sought self-validation in their peer group through break dancing. The portrayal of Native American "breakers" is consistent with the profiles drawn by other researchers for segments of African American (e.g., Fordham, 1988) and Hispanic American (e.g., Bernal, Saenz, & Knight, 1991) youth.

Given this alternate route toward affirmation, teachers and other key adults need to recognize the forces driving these behaviors and try to capitalize on those forces to move young people toward more socially approved goals. The activities and competitive efforts of the "breakers" were disparaged and trivialized by all segments of the school population outside their immediate peer group. As Deyhle (1986) notes, "An irony exists in that the school refused to recognize break dancing as evidence of a desire of the motivation for success and dismissed it as irrelevant to their purpose of educating youth" (p. 126).

The Family

Traditionally, Native American families have been extended families, with a strong network of relationships with others in the community. At a very early age, children assume responsibility in their communities. Non-community members are considered outsiders. Consultations of a personal or professional nature are made only with trusted members of the community. Harmony with others is valued and reinforced. Family is considered the first priority. Locust (1988) explains the conditions underlying these values:

> It was the unity of the tribe, clan, or even family that enabled its members to survive. This survival instinct is still present in Indian communities, and it dictates behaviors that are frequently misunderstood by non-Indians. . . . All members work together and contribute to the group, supporting each other in times of stress, for they know that they will find the same network of support for themselves should they require it.

> Another aspect of the group membership concept often conflicts with educational systems: that of justifying membership in the group through one's contribution and loyalty. Junior high girls will stay home to baby-sit younger siblings while their parents work, enabling the family to have two incomes without the cost of child care. Young boys, pressed to go to work to help buy food and unable to find employment because of their age, may turn to stealing in order to contribute to the group. So strong is the membership bonding that students go hungry rather than ask their parents for lunch money, for in asking they would be putting their needs in front of the group's needs. (p. 328)

Elders receive much respect in the community. Children listen without interrupting elders and are encouraged to seek their counsel. Likewise, children are treated with respect. Adults assume minimal authoritative posture, being more likely to respond to misbehavior with a disapproving look rather than with verbalized displeasure, chastisement, or other consequences. Brendtro et al. (1990) point out that, in traditional Native American parenting, "The main strategy of behavior control was kindly lecturing which began as soon as the child was able to communicate" (p. 42). The authors also share a quote by Blue Whirlwind, who states, "We never struck our children for we loved them. Rather we talked to them gently, but never harshly. If they were doing something wrong, we asked them to stop" (p. 42).

The traditional teachers in Native American communities are the grandparents. They, rather than the parents, provide instruction on responsibility, loyalty, and behavioral expectations. Children are assigned chores, but autonomy is encouraged as caretakers leave the children to perform often difficult tasks with little adult supervision. When assistance is needed, children often turn to peers or siblings.

Peer Relations

Gender Dynamics

Although children play freely across genders between the ages of 2 and 7, distinct lines are drawn when they reach 8 years of age. From that time on and through young adulthood, same-gender dyads and triads are seen interacting (Vogt, Jordan, & Tharp, 1987). This phenomenon has been noted for Navajo, Hopi, and Sioux tribes. Specific roles for each gender are learned through precept and example. Another feature noted by Cartledge, Lee, and Feng (1995) is that within many groups, young boys begin to separate themselves from the younger children at age 10. At this point they begin to move into the roles of men, avoiding physically combative one-on-one activities and other play behaviors characteristic of younger children.

Relationships

In many traditional Native American societies, best friends and close peer relationships often evolve from family relationships rather than from classroom interactions (Schneider, 1993). Alexander (1991), for example, describes her best friend as a cousin who was like a sister but lived 20 miles away. Their weekly meetings were special times. These Native American groups emphasize knowing and respecting one's larger family. As noted in the Deyhle (1986) study, peer relationships may gain in importance, especially for marginal youth feeling alienated from both the majority and the Native American culture. Achieving social identity and support through their peer group, these youngsters are inclined to adhere to a peer-based value system and related behaviors.

Schooling and Learning Styles

Older Native Americans have experienced the trauma of being separated from their families and communities to be sent to boarding schools. As a result of an inferior education that prepared them poorly for assimilation in the majority culture and also isolated them from their native one, many family heads of households are fearful or skeptical of European American schools (Pitton, Warring, Frank, & Hunter, 1993). It is likely that such fears have been communicated to their children and grandchildren—students in our current school systems.

Traditionally, young Native Americans have learned tasks by silently observing others. Current literature indicates that many contemporary Native American children learn more efficiently in the visual mode, being culturally oriented toward visual style perspectives (Cazden & John, 1971; Guilmet, 1976). Without interacting verbally or physically, children and youth were expected to watch carefully and later attempt the observed activities in private. Only after attaining a degree of mastery in private would a youngster demonstrate knowledge or skills in the presence of others, including peers.

Learning by this method requires strong visual attention skills as well as visual perception and memory. This method may be at odds with learning situations in many mainstream classrooms, where the emphasis is on auditory attention skills. Much instruction emphasizes listening, and when demonstrations are given in mainstream classrooms, they are usually accompanied by verbal instructions directed at the naive student. The student is usually interacting with the teacher, who often checks for understanding by asking questions and requiring several demonstrations from students as they practice the skill.

Following an extended period of observation in silence, Native Americans historically practiced in private, then participated in an activity in the presence of a superior. This stage of learning might be compared to the guided practice typically used in direct instruction and viewed as an effective teaching technique. Whereas the usual sequence of instruction in mainstream classrooms includes the stages of introduction, demonstration, guided practice, independent practice, and review, for Native Americans the sequence has included demonstration, independent practice (trials in private), and then guided practice.

Another issue related to Native American learning styles or preferences stems from a basic cultural value of cooperation and harmony: Competition between individuals is avoided. Classroom teachers note that Native American students will often pace themselves to keep from outshining slower students. Rather than being singled out for praise or criticism, Native American students keep a low profile in class to blend in with the group (Brown & McGrew-Zoubi, 1995). Because bragging is inappropriate in Native American cultures, many will even deny or disavow their own accomplishments in conversations with others. Team competition is accepted to a greater degree than individual competition.

Although they may be reluctant to participate when called on individually, Native American students demonstrate willingness to participate in small-group work and in student-initiated activities. They appear to pay more attention to peers than to the teacher.

In processing information, elementary-aged Native Americans are considered to attend to global issues and the context of reading material (setting, situation, and outcomes of events) more than they attend to details such as names of characters, time elements, and specific characteristics. As for other youngsters in early childhood, thinking is on the concrete level of development. Reasoning is logical and based on the manipulation of objects in the real world.

Verbal Communication

With Native Americans, conversation is largely purposeful. They will usually give careful consideration before verbalizing an idea. Pitton et al. (1993) note that "rambling thoughts or aimless conversations are not usually found in the Native American culture. The traditional teachings of quiet observation promote thoughtful responses given in conversation" (p. 17).

Children from various Native American groups are often reported by teachers to be shy or unresponsive in the classroom, even if it is clear that they know the answers. In teacher ratings of the social skills of Native American and Anglo preschool children, Powless and Elliott (1993) found the two groups to differ most on verbal initiating behaviors, which were exhibited more frequently by Anglo children. The authors explained that Native Americans often use nonverbal gestures or eye contact for social communication and that talking is not always valued.

Spirituality

Although there are differences from tribe to tribe and also from clan to clan within tribes, most Native American religious systems share a common set of beliefs. According to Locust (1988), some of these commonalities include the following:

1. An omnipotent Supreme Creator exists.

2. Humans are made up of spirit, mind, and body, and the spirit exists prior to the emergence of the physical body and continues following the body's demise.

3. Wellness results from harmony in the spirit, mind, and body; individuals are responsible for their own wellness.

4. The spiritual world includes plants and animals as well as humans.

A Social Skill Profile of Native Americans

Researchers have posited characteristics of Native American students that distinguish them from other groups in terms of social skills. Keeping in mind that Native American culture is not monolithic, but rather is represented by hundreds of distinct groups (tribes), we can consider some common attributes that have been noted through experience in multicultural classrooms and work with different ethnic groups (Rosando, 1994; Saracho & Gerstl, 1992). Whenever possible, characteristics noted will be associated with particular tribes. The descriptions are followed by implications and applications for classroom teachers.

Nonverbal Behaviors and Symbols

Understanding culturally specific nonverbal communication gives educators a concrete tool that can lead to significant changes in their attitudes and behaviors. Use of this knowledge assists in the attainment of some of society's goals, such as reducing prejudice and discrimination and assuring social justice.

Eye Contact

Hall (1969) notes that with many Native American youth, direct, open-faced eye contact is avoided. For instance, he observed that when spoken to directly Navajos "froze up." Even when shaking hands, Navajos looked at the other person through peripheral vision. Medicine (1985) made a similar observation among Lakota (Sioux) children. The Lakota culture disapproves of direct eye contact. Pitton et al. (1993) generalize that most Native American cultures teach that eye contact is intrusive. As a sign of respect, therefore, children and adults often avoid looking at the people speaking to them, especially if the people are authority figures, such as teachers.

Facial Expression

Custom dictates that it is undesirable or abnormal to show emotions. Therefore, the young person learns to maintain an expressionless face. Feelings of pleasure, pain, joy, and surprise are not exposed or reflected by the countenance. A smile in response to a passing stranger's greeting would not be expected. Others should not interpret the lack of facial response negatively but rather as part of a culture that nurtures restraint as a sign of respect. According to Pitton et al. (1993), this manner of greeting strangers is similar to practices observed in Israeli culture.

Touch

In keeping with the importance of the inexpressive countenance, public displays of affection are rare among those past middle childhood. Young students and small children do receive gentle touches and hugs for encouragement. Handshakes involve a very gentle clasping of hands; a more intense clasp is considered disrespectful. Gentleness is a sign of deep respect that permeates the Native American culture.

Gestures

Gestures are used sparingly. In the oral tradition, gestures are used to reinforce the main idea of a conversation. They are not used to convey emotions.

Personal Space

In conversation, Native Americans prefer to stand 2 to 3 feet from one another; This is comparable to the European preference of 20 to 36 inches. Rather than standing face to face, however, persons frequently converse side by side. A Native American wishing to speak to someone will stand just out of the line of vision and catch the person's eye, then wait to be recognized.

Symbols

For some tribes, jewelry and clothing are important markers of one's cultural heritage. In other tribes, however, such symbols may be considered vulgar displays of wealth. Hair often has spiritual meaning. Some tribes believe that hair length is related to health and knowledge and is a sign of a person's adherence to traditions.

Time

Time perception is different from that in the mainstream culture. Because they regard time on a continuum, as having no real beginning or end, Native Americans are not clock watchers. Lives outside of school are not regimented by strict schedules. The present is much more significant than the future.

Speech

Pitton et al. (1993) explain that silence is viewed as a strength, so words are very carefully chosen. In the oral tradition of Native American cultures a few select words are used to represent feelings. The language used in conversations may be allegorical because, to the Native American, the message or content is more important than a person's emotional reaction.

When authority figures are present, the voices of Native Americans will often be quiet and flat in affect. Not comfortable expressing their emotions to strangers, Native Americans typically speak in low tones and soft voices, with moderate vocal variety. Polgar (1960) adds that Native American children equate loudness of the teacher's voice with meanness or anger.

Engaging Behaviors

Interruptions are considered rude in Native American cultures. In the presence of adults, youngsters learn to listen respectfully. Listening with the eyes closed is a sign of very careful attention. Children usually don't initiate conversations in mixed-aged groups, and they learn early the importance of formal turn taking. Because observational learning is important, many will watch and reflect before trying something new. Before speaking, the individual will pause to think of an appropriate response.

Although taught to respect and seek the counsel of elders, young Native Americans are often unaccustomed to viewing adults as authorities who place extensive external controls on them. Rather, many are reared to have an internal locus of control. Children are encouraged to be independent, to make their own decisions and abide by them. They are treated with the same respect as adults. To outsiders, Native American child-rearing seems permissive, but as Brendtro et al. (1990) point out, parents in this culture have traditionally stressed self-discipline and personal responsibility. If children failed to meet their responsibilities, they were thoroughly lectured on their wrongdoings and the negative impact of their actions on others. Little Soldier (1989) notes that a child entering school for the first time may respond with confusion and passivity to a teacher whose role is traditionally that of active commander.

Property is considered community owned. What one has and is not using is deemed available to another in need. Teachers have mistakenly accused Native American children of stealing when they lifted pencils or other needed items without asking. Frequently coming from extended families, Native Americans tend to be group centered rather than self-centered. Personal property is not a universal concept.

Formal Assessment Findings

Although the unique features of their socialization and related behaviors are documented in the literature, there have been few systematic investigations of the social skills of Native American youth relative to those of their majority peers. One such study, conducted by Powless and Elliott (1993) with Native American and

Anglo Head Start children, showed that parents and teachers gave Anglo children higher ratings on social skill frequencies than they gave Native American children. The greatest differences between the groups were in assertive behaviors: That is, the Native American preschoolers were perceived to emit fewer verbal initiations than their mainstream counterparts. The researchers found no differences between the two groups in terms of problem behaviors. The two groups of children were in different settings. Five of the six teachers rating the Native American children were Native American, and the sixth was Anglo American. All of the teachers of the Anglo children were Anglo American. There was greater agreement on social skill ratings between the teachers and parents of the Native American children than between the teachers and parents of the Anglo children. Agreements between teachers of the two groups also were low, with the teachers of the Anglo children placing greater importance on items related to classroom control such as complying with the teacher's directions, attending to the teacher's instructions, and making transitions in the classroom. In contrast, the teachers of the Native American children expressed more concern with peer-based skills such as getting along with peers and managing peer conflict.

The authors explain these results largely in terms of cultural factors. Unlike the teachers of the Anglo preschoolers, the Native American teachers lived in their students' communities and were part of the culture of those communities. As noted previously, Native American child-rearing practices tend to be less concerned with external control, rather emphasizing more self-discipline and independence. Furthermore, the assertive behaviors, characterized largely by verbal initiations, may be somewhat misleading and inappropriate for children reared in a culture that places more value on actions and nonverbal expressions than on speech. This study provides further evidence of the cultural dimensions of social skills and the need to assess those skills within a cultural context.

Risk Factors

Despite this country's affluence and the fact that Native Americans were its original residents, their living conditions have not substantially improved. Indeed, risk factors for Native American youth appear to be worsening, particularly as regards education, substance abuse, and suicide (LaFromboise & Low, 1989).

Inadequate Education

With high school dropout estimates as high as 85 or 90 percent (LaFromboise & Low, 1989; Ogbu, 1978) and one-third of the population classified as illiterate (LaFromboise & Low, 1989), Native Americans are considered one of the most poorly formally educated groups in the United States. School performance is often hampered by specific disabilities, health disorders, and poor social conditions, with students' achievement stalled at levels one to four grades below those of normally achieving age-mates (Deyhle, 1986; LaFromboise & Low, 1989). Academic underachievement, poor attitudes toward schooling, and poverty combine to limit greatly the numbers of college-educated Native Americans (LaFromboise & Low, 1989; Little Soldier, 1989). This limitation, in turn, reduces the number of Native American professionals with the cultural knowledge to address the social and mental health concerns of this population most effectively.

Substance Use

An alarming 50 percent of Native American youth are at some risk because of drug and alcohol use (Beauvais, Oetting, & Edwards, 1985). Compared to 5 percent regular users among non–Native American participants, more than 33 percent of Native American youth (grades 7 through 12) were found to use marijuana and alcohol regularly (Oetting, Beauvais, Edwards, Waters, Velarde, & Goldstein, 1983). The overall rate of alcoholism is two to three times the national rate, with patterns of abuse varying among tribes and regions and within tribes (Trotter, Rolf, Baldwin, & Quintero, 1992). In the Trotter et al. study, nearly one-fourth of Navajo youth responded that they had used alcohol at school events, 9.8 percent had used it on the way to school, 8.6 percent had been drinking during school hours, 22.1 percent had been drinking during school hours but off campus, and 22.7 percent reported drinking while driving.

A number of research studies have investigated the possibility of biological differences that make Native Americans more susceptible to alcoholism, but there is little evidence to support such theories (Beauvais et al., 1985; Bennion & Li, 1976). When questioned, youngsters report that drinking is often a family affair. Many got started because of their parents' drinking, because of peer pressure, or because of pressure from other family members.

Suicide

Grossman, Milligan, and Deyo (1991) state that from 1950 to 1986, suicide rates for all adolescents tripled in the United States, increasing from 4.5 per 100,000 to 13.1 per 100,000, but that Native American adolescents had the highest rates, with reports of 26.8 per 100,000 in 1987. In examining conditions associated with suicide, Grossman et al. found the two strongest risk factors to be (a) a history of mental, behavioral, or emotional problems requiring professional help and (b) extreme alienation from one's family and community. Other risk factors noted were exposure to suicide attempts or completions by family and friends, alcohol consumption, self-perception of poor general health, and past physical and sexual abuse. Females were more likely than males to attempt suicide.

These negative conditions are not discrete but closely interrelated and predictive of one another. Offspring of a family- and relationship-oriented people, Native American children are disproportionately removed from their close family networks to attend schools in somewhat foreign cultures; their circumstances intensify feelings of alienation and isolation. LaFromboise and Low (1989) point out the sense of anonymity these children have upon entering school and state, "Many of them speak an entirely different first language, practice an entirely different religion, and hold different cultural values than the dominant culture, and yet they are expected to perform successfully according to conventional Anglo educational criteria" (p. 119). These conditions undoubtedly contribute to depression, substance abuse, and other self-destructive behaviors. Substance abuse, for example, "is a widely modeled means of coping with depression" (LaFromboise & Low, 1989, p. 119) and relates directly to the morbidity and mortality rates of Native Americans, which are four times higher than the national average (Okwumabua, Okwumabua, & Duryea, 1989).

Social Skill Intervention

The challenge for teachers who have students of Native American origin is multidimensional. The first dimension requires an adjustment of attitude from the teacher. It calls for, as Garcia (1994) says, a "responsive teacher," a person who understands the roots of diversity and who delivers instruction and creates climates that are responsive to diverse students' needs. Garcia asserts that teachers who are truly effective learn to adjust their teaching strategies in response to the learning styles of individual students. Any such adjustment would follow an attitude of genuine concern for each child's welfare and a respect for the child's own identity. Additionally, it would follow a belief that different perspectives can enrich learning opportunities for all. An attitude that all of us together are smarter than any of us separately would prevail.

The Classroom Climate

When different ethnic groups exchange cultural elements, acculturation is occurring. Although many exchanges are made in both directions within American society, Banks (1991) asserts that "we hear too little about the cultural traits that dominant groups have acquired from ethnic minorities" (p. 70). Teachers and others are therefore encouraged to highlight such traits and their origins. Contributions from Native Americans have included the harvesting and use of various crops, methods of irrigation, dress styles, the selection of sites for many cities, and much more. Focusing only on tangible cultural products, however, reinforces popular yet stereotypical images of groups. A caveat from Banks suggests that the "essence of a culture can be understood only by studying its central values" (p. 77). Thus, teachers can emphasize Native American values related to preserving the earth and respecting all plant and animal life. The preparation of food, the use of natural products in artworks, and the purposes of dances, for instance, become meaningful in relation to the central theme that conveys the other culture's perspective on people and nature. In the American tradition, the basing of decisions on group consensus reflects the respect of Native Americans for the rights and dignity of the individual. It should be pointed out that our representative government imitated the process of tribal councils and incorporated its concepts into constitutional documents. A responsive classroom climate must directly convey to its student-citizens that the American culture is multiethnic, and it must make salient the products and values of all its members. It must teach about the different ways of living and convey the message that "different" means neither inferior nor superior.

Garcia (1994) cites a list provided by Sullivan (1992) of 11 "Sheltered English Techniques in the Mainstream Class," which may be a helpful resource for responsive teachers whose classes include Native Americans. For a more detailed discussion, the reader is referred to Garcia (1994; pp. 170–271). To summarize some of these points, teachers are advised to (a) give students enough time to think and process information before requiring them to respond; (b) respond to the content of the students' statements, not their grammar; (c) facilitate comprehension through simplified language, rephrasing, use of concrete/modified materials, and multisensory approaches; (d) create cooperative learning environments, pairing students with native speakers; (e) learn about the child's culture and the child; and (f) bring the child's home language and culture into the classroom.

The Teacher's Response

The concepts just discussed relate directly to teacher-led activities and teacher attitudes that would help create a responsive classroom climate. Diversity in the student body also calls teaching techniques into question. The teacher cannot now assume that all students will respond to a lesson in similar and familiar ways. Thus, the second dimension of challenge involves teaching strategies. What are some strategies for empowering children to integrate socially in mainstream classrooms when their home culture advocates passive behavior, in contrast to the active, assertive behaviors encouraged in mainstream contexts? The concern is how to teach Native Americans in ways that are compatible with their culture. The values of many Native American tribes (cooperation over competitiveness and reticence over self-assertiveness, for example) may be at odds with the value system of the teaching environment. When that is the case, the intervention program must be examined with care. If the aim is to convert the child to majority-culture ways, then respect for the child's identity is not being demonstrated and the intervention would take on a "them versus us" tone. A genuinely responsive approach requires an open-minded teacher who considers the need for reciprocal adjustments. In short, we must question our society's assumptions and leave room for modification in our emphasis. We must learn about traditional Native American family life and child-rearing practices to create or recreate a school environment that is compatible with the home environment.

Our response must go beyond the concept of assimilation, which has traditionally been recognized as the solution to the "problem" of ethnicity. Indeed, classrooms across the nation have changed somewhat in emphasis, with more cooperative learning groups, hands-on instruction, and so forth. Still, successful individual effort and self-assertion in private and public continue to be applauded and promoted. How much assimilation should be made? On whose part?

Brown and McGrew-Zoubi (1995) summarize the literature from those who have studied culture and learning styles, noting some points of agreement:

Learning styles are a function of both nature and nurture.

Within a group, the variations among individuals are as great as their commonalties.

Cultural conflict exists between some students and the typical learning experiences in schools.

High- versus Low-Context Cultures

Successful teaching in culturally diverse classrooms, Brown and McGrew-Zoubi (1995) assert, requires that instructors understand basic cultural distinctions. Some cultures are said to be high-context cultures, while others are classified as low-context cultures. In high-context cultures, members derive meaning from communications by attending to the setting and the situation of an encounter. They consider previous conversations, the status of the person speaking, and the context of the conversation. Furthermore, individuals in high-context cultures rely on a strong network of others to develop their identities. They prefer to be "with their own people." Native Americans exhibit such attributes, as do Arabs, southern Europeans, Mexicans, and people in the rural United States.

Brown and McGrew-Zoubi (1995) explain that in low-context cultures, individuals derive meaning largely from the literal significance of the language. Little consideration is given to the history behind the statement or the history of the speaker. Contrary to the practice in high-context cultures, analysis of conversation is based on the immediate or current message. Low-context cultures nurture people who base their identities on individual efforts rather than on a network of others. Urban and suburban dwellers in the United States, Scandinavians, and Germans exhibit such attributes.

The school systems of the United States reflect the low-context style. They stress individual achievement, independence, and personal responsibility, and they operate according to strict schedules. They deemphasize nonverbal communication, interdependence, and interpersonal relationships. Some students learn well under these conditions, but others from culturally diverse backgrounds do not. "Consideration of the impact of culture on learning style . . . as well as attention to specific cultural attributes, can allow teachers to provide instructional experiences that accommodate different learning needs so that each child may have the experiences necessary to develop more fully" (Brown & McGrew-Zoubi, 1995, p. 8).

Instructional Approaches

Multisensory Presentations

Strong kinesthetic learners with visual, auditory attending, and tactile skills, Native Americans students benefit from learning opportunities that incorporate observation, touch, and movement as well as other learning modalities. Additionally, they understand new material better when the information is presented globally. The individual parts of the scheme should be related to the "whole picture." Teachers are encouraged to accompany oral presentations with a variety of visual aids. Pictures and models should represent all groups of people and include an array of items. As Little Soldier (1989) explains, education must have personal meaning for students; educators must begin where students are, with material that is relevant to their culture.

Storytelling and Books

Real experiences—with manipulations and simulations, map development, and face-to-face interviews—tend to be more instructive than abstractions. One tool that does have potential for conveying abstract concepts is storytelling. With a strong storytelling tradition of their own, Native American students listen attentively to narratives that recreate reality and involve real-life dilemmas and complex concepts. A story can precede instruction in any subject, from mathematics and science to language arts and health. Accompanying stories give the teacher an opportunity to present the rationale for specific skill exercises—an important first step in any lesson presentation.

Storytelling and written narratives that focus on the lives of Native Americans can be especially beneficial for the social and emotional development of these students as well as for non–Native American youth. Critical to the social development of children from any cultural group is a realistic, honest, yet largely optimistic, portrait of its history, culture, contributions, and importance to contemporary society. With Native Americans there is a need to avoid and counter previous traditional and often dishonest portrayals— for example, that of the bloodthirsty savage, which was the prevailing image for anyone growing up in this country before the sixties. Historical books about Native Americans, in addition to presenting a balanced and accurate picture of their conflicts with the settlers, should point out the overall gentleness of their cultures as well as the Native American emphases on harmony with others and with nature. However, the books chosen should provide accurate information about the real lives and emotions of Native Americans, unlike the superficial, guilt-ridden books written by whites during the sixties (Goley, 1992).

Goley (1992) presents an annotated bibliography of authentic books about Native Americans, intended to lead the reader on "a continuing journey in search of cultural understanding and appreciation" (p. 159). The books listed are appropriate for preschoolers through adolescents, and those most directly related to social skills will be noted here. Many of the stories by and about Native Americans, particularly stories for young children, are renditions of myths and legends. This is particularly true of stories for young children. One story designated for preschoolers is *Baby Rattlesnake by Te Ata* (Moroney, 1989), a 92-year-old Chickasaw storyteller. It centers on an impetuous baby rattler who gets into trouble by attempting to use a skill for which he has not sufficiently matured. Despite this infraction, the loving family is forgiving and nurturing to the baby rattlesnake. This story points to the importance of inner control and self-discipline, important themes in Native American culture. Another book appropriate for this age group is *Hawk, I'm Your Brother* (Baylor, 1976), which addresses love of and harmony with nature. In this story a boy establishes his kinship with nature through his relationship with a hawk.

Arrow to the Sun: A Pueblo Indian Tale (McDermott, 1974), also a story for primary-aged children, likewise depicts the Native American's close relationship with nature. This narrative relates the myth of how the spirit of the sun was brought to earth. According to Goley (1992), "This book remains one of the most beautiful and important books in the renaissance of Native American folklore published since the early 1970s" (p. 161). A story for young children based on Alaskan Inuit life and customs is *Mama, Do You Love Me?* (Joosse, 1991). This story addresses a young girl's desire to be assured of her mother's unconditional love, a universal need of all young children. The book is presented in the style of a Native American folktale, is vibrantly illustrated, and provides information about life in the Arctic. A final example of literature for this age group is *The People Shall Continue* (Ortiz, 1988). This 24-page book stresses the cultural principle that one is responsible for all life and is designed to familiarize young children with the history of Native Americans. Goley (1992) describes it as "a teaching story, a role played by many Native American myths, and it has an authentic feel of tribal storytelling" (p. 162).

A historical book for intermediate-aged children (grades 4 through 6) is *Sequoia* (Cwiklik, 1989). Sequoia is a revered figure from the Cherokee Nation who attempts to preserve the culture of his people by developing an alphabet to capture the Cherokee language in written form. The book details the "forced march" and the severe conditions imposed on the Cherokee by the settlers. It is a realistic and compassionate tale told from the perspective of Native

American peoples and gives the reader an understanding of their philosophies and cultures. Perennial and contemporary Native American issues of land use and environmental concerns are presented in *Buffalo Hunt* (Freedman, 1988). This book, which describes the importance of the buffalo to the lives of American Indians and the needless destruction of the buffalo by the settlers, is considered unusually accurate and well illustrated. Another book by this author, *Indian Chiefs* (Freedman, 1987), is a Newbery Award winner that provides similarly authentic accounts of the lives of the chiefs of six western tribes. *Racing the Sun* (Pitts, 1988) deals with the conflicts and complexities of assimilation that confront many minority youth. The central character, 12-year-old Brandon, has a college professor father and is reared in middle-class conditions off the reservation. Brandon takes little note of or pride in his Native American heritage until his grandfather comes from the reservation to live with the family and gradually teaches Brandon to appreciate and embrace aspects of his Navajo roots. This book has the potential to boost self-esteem in all children regardless of cultural background.

The theme of assimilation and the potential for enhancing one's self-esteem is addressed for older youngsters (grades 7 through 9) in *Julie of the Wolves* (George, 1972). A restless 13-year-old Eskimo girl attempts to run away to San Francisco but gets lost and is forced to call upon the wisdom of Native American ways to survive in the wilderness. In the process she gains a greater appreciation for her heritage and culture. The same theme, but in a story appropriate for high school males, is present in *The Shadow Brothers* (Cannon, 1990), which is set in Utah. In addition to revealing the struggles involved in traversing two cultures, the author shows the cultural differences between different Native American tribes. The problem of being caught between two cultures is depicted as well in *Ceremony of the Panther* (Wallin, 1987). This book has particular appeal because it deals with a teenage male's potentially destructive behavior, such as excessive drinking. The young man is sent to live with his great-grandmother on the reservation, where he gradually becomes attached to his family, learns to respect his heritage, and recognizes the benefits of mature, socially responsible behavior. A slightly different treatment is given the problems of a troubled teen, Cloyd, in *Bearstone* (Hobbs, 1989). Cloyd is sent from the reservation to a group home in an effort to deal with his poor conduct at home and at school. Cloyd is a loner who eventually establishes a relationship with his white employer and learns to appreciate his own identity and heritage. Ashabranner (1984) addresses the issues of assimilation directly through the personal narratives of contemporary individuals who share their stresses and successes in *To Live in Two Worlds: American Indian Youth Today.*

An account of the near decimation of the Native American peoples and their culture is given for the junior high age group in *Wounded Knee: An Indian History of the American West* (Brown, 1975). This story is an adaptation of Brown's classic and compelling narration, *Bury My Heart at Wounded Knee.* An important aspect of both Native and African American heritage is these groups' extensive intermarriage. A nonfiction account of this history is recorded in *Black Indians: A Hidden Heritage* (Katz, 1986). This book tells how the Seminoles of Florida accepted and adopted many runaway slaves as full members of their tribe. Similar privileges were extended to whites, a fact that highlights the generous, nonprejudicial ways of these Native Americans. Dorris (1987) gives a contemporary fictional account of the problems and strength of a 15-year-old African and Native American female in the book *A Yellow Raft in Blue Water.* The story depicts some of the special problems of Native Americans, including alcoholism, loss of traditions, and biculturalism.

One book recommended for high school students (grades 10 through 12) is *The Mythology of North America* (Bierhorst, 1985). Goley (1992) describes Bierhorst as "the foremost scholar of Native American mythology and folklore" (p. 182). The stories collected in this volume were ones handed down through the oral tradition over generations. The collection conveys an understanding of both the traditions and values of North American Indians. Fetal alcohol syndrome, a byproduct of alcoholism and a pervasive problem among Native Americans, is the focus of *The Broken Cord: A Family's Ongoing Struggle with Fetal Alcohol Syndrome* (Dorris, 1989). Dorris gives a personal and vivid account of the pain and struggle experienced with his adopted son, who was diagnosed with this syndrome and with developmental delay as a result of having an alcoholic birth mother. This provocative book can deliver powerful messages to teens about responsibility and consequences of behavior. The resilience and inner strength of Native American women are profiled in *Tracks* (Erdrich, 1989), one of a trilogy of intergenerational books portraying life on the reservation and in the city. A particular appeal of this book is that the author is an Ojibwa Indian who grew up in North Dakota.

The use of literature by and about Native Americans is fruitful for all students, not only for those of Native American background. Young people need to be aware of and take pride in their own history and traditions, and youngsters from all backgrounds need to respect and appreciate the culture of others. These understandings can foster a positive sense of oneself and others. As noted previously, maladaptive behaviors often evolve from young people's misguided attempts at affirmation and self-validation. Nearly all of the books noted in this section were written since about 1975; many of them deal with contemporary problems experienced by children and adolescents, some of which are specific to Native Americans. The books invite readers to identify with the principal characters, to analyze characters' problems and self-management styles, and to explore possible strategies for addressing their own personal situations. Many times it is helpful to young people simply to know that their own external and internal conflicts are not unique. Teachers and other professionals should read and discuss these books with students, stopping short of using literature as an opportunity to sermonize but making sure students understand what they have read and do not misconstrue important messages.

Cooperative Learning

One approach that has obvious benefits for heterogeneous classrooms and that has gained acceptance since the 1980s is cooperative learning. This approach is based on teaching students to work together to develop the knowledge and skills they need to succeed. Cooperative learning is highly appropriate in a society where most adults work in teams, units, and departments rather than in isolation. With their efforts orchestrated by the teachers, students in the classroom can and do learn such basic principles as the benefits of collective efforts of individual team members for the whole group, the importance of each member, the joy of shared experiences, and the pride that accompanies success. A significant product of carefully planned cooperative group activities is peer interaction. While working together, students learn about their peers' skills and ideas. Rather than being threatened by others' achievements, they learn how they benefit from the associations. Students gain mutual respect as they work together on projects, coaching one another and holding all accountable for the outcome. Although external distinctions separate people into categories, our country and our school-worlds are one nation. Mixed-group activities strengthen the ties that bind. We are, after all, on the same team, and teammates are allies.

Cooperative learning involves groups, but it entails much more than simply placing students in groups. Lest one mistakenly assume that cooperative learning is synonymous with traditional group work, Hirst and Slavik (1989) outline differences:

1. In typical groups, one leader is chosen by the teacher; in a cooperative group, leadership is shared so that all students are responsible for completion of the task and all group members are included.

2. In typical groups members are homogeneous in nature; in cooperative groups . . . members are selected . . . so that the groups are as heterogeneous as possible.

3. In typical groups, members create their own product, have their own materials and have rewards based on individual accomplishment. In a cooperative group, the group creates one product and/or shares materials, and/or has a group reward based on the success as a group.

4. In typical groups, students are told to "cooperate" with no attempt to teach social skills. In a cooperative group, social skills are defined, discussed, observed and processed.

5. In typical groups, the teacher interrupts group work to solve problems, warn students and remind them. In a cooperative group, the teacher encourages group problem solving. S/he is an interacter rather than an intervener.

6. In a typical group, the top priority is to accomplish the task—get the job done. In a cooperative group, the top priority is to accomplish the task and to include every member through each person's use of social skills. (p. 137)

Higher levels of self-esteem, more positive attitudes toward the subject matter, more positive attitudes toward the teacher, greater achievement motivation, and greater persistence in completing tasks are benefits of cooperative (versus competitive and individualistic) learning experiences (Johnson & Johnson, 1983; Little Soldier, 1989). Slavin (1985) and Slavin and Oickle (1981) found cooperative learning useful in increasing academic achievement and promoting interracial friendships in urban classrooms. Their study suggests that cooperative learning would be especially suitable for Native American students. The approach is compatible with traditional Native American values. Furthermore, the role of the teacher (as resource, guide, and catalyst rather than director) more closely matches the student-elder interaction in the Native American community.

Because many Native American students respond adversely to individual attention and direct confrontation, calling on these students by name (for answers or content questions, for personal information, for rewards, or for redirection) is to be avoided. Schaffer (1988) explains that calling on an individual student puts the student in an adversarial relationship with the teacher. In front of peers, the student is singled out, expected to respond instantly and on demand. This situation contradicts Native American cultural upbringing, which allows much time for contemplation and privacy during practice stages and which does not advocate self-promotion.

It is suggested that, in classrooms that include students of Native American heritage, teachers refrain from randomly calling on students individually for answers and even from singling out individuals for compliments. Instead, attention should be given to the efforts and accomplishments of the group.

These suggestions contrast with teaching strategies promoted as a result of effective schools research (with studies based on majority-group classrooms). Such research advocates, for instance, that teachers direct students to keep hands down and call on students randomly to allow equitable opportunities for practice (Brophy & Good, 1986). Specific compliments are encouraged for individuals as well as for groups.

The Role of Altruism

Brendtro et al. (1990) argue that a principal means for countering the apparent escalation of selfish and irresponsible behaviors among contemporary youth is to place greater emphasis on the development of truly caring and altruistic behaviors. They distinguish genuine altruism from "pseudo-altruism" with a citation from Batson (1987):

> Genuine altruism is evoked by empathy with another person. Persons with empathy can understand the perspective of another. Empathy motivates helping behavior aimed at meeting the other person's needs. Of course it is possible that genuine altruism will also lead to some social or self-rewards. However, these are not the goal of helping, simply the incidental consequences. (p. 90)

Brendtro et al. (1990) advocate the deliberate use of what they call "service learning" programs as part of young people's regular school experience. These are activities in which students learn to contribute to others in their immediate or larger communities and experience the beneficial effects of genuine altruism. The authors recommend that, to be most successful, service learning projects should (a) involve direct people-to-people contact rather than indirect service, (b) be challenging and appeal to the student's strengths, and (c) include the student in the planning, implementation, and evaluation of the project. Rather than demanding or cajoling students to participate in such projects, they advise attracting young people by appealing to what they have to offer and assuring them that they are needed. Brendtro et al. (1990) give examples of service learning projects from their "Hooked on Helping" program:

> Youth from an alternative school for delinquents assisted in the Special Olympics and went on camping trips with students who were blind.

> Elementary children bought groceries for needy families using money accumulated as a result of no vandalism in their school over an extended period.

> Youngsters prepared a home for a refugee family, planting flowers and bringing toys to welcome the children.

> Teenagers chopped firewood for the disabled, visited senior citizens and organized a clown show for a day care center. (p. 93).

Cartledge et al. (1995) describe the National Indian Youth Leadership Project (Hall, 1993), which draws on Native American traditions to prepare young people to become "servant leaders." During their early teens, youngsters attend leadership camp to acquire skills that will enable them to assume leadership roles in various altruistic endeavors. Upon returning to their communities, they might pursue projects such as tutoring younger children or helping seniors. These activities are considered to strengthen the teens' self-esteem as well as to help problem-solving and conflict resolution skills.

Direct Instruction

Do any programs directly address the social skill needs of Native American young people? Symptoms of their poor adjustment in mainstream schools may be measured by the alarming rates of substance abuse, the high dropout rate, and the figures on truancy and suicide. Specific social skill enhancement programs have shown promise among majority culture adolescents. However, research on the application of models for Native American youngsters is sparse. Descriptions of three such models follows.

Model 1. One noteworthy "culturally tailored" program for Native Americans was designed by Gilchrist, Schinke, Trimble, and Cvetkovich (1987). Their research was conducted over a 2-year period with 102 Native American youth in three intervention sites and in four control sites. The children were in reservation and nonreservation settings in the Pacific Northwest; they participated in pre- and posttests, with a 10-session program between the tests. The mean age of participants was 11; 49 percent were female. At each site, a two-person team delivered the intervention. One team member was an Indian research staff member, and the other was a community leader (a Native American teacher, a school counselor, or a drug treatment staff member known and respected by the students). Leaders had received 10 hours of training before delivering the curriculum. Sessions took place in school classrooms and in tribal center rooms that were familiar and easily accessible to the youngsters. The content of the sessions is summarized in Table 7.

The program yielded some positive outcomes. Among students in the treatment groups, there were better interpersonal skills for the work reported by LaFromboise and Rowe used adult participants and scenarios, their instructional procedures are equally appropriate for adolescents, as established in chapter 2 of this book and in numerous other professional resources (e.g., Cartledge & Milburn, 1995; Goldstein, 1988; Stephens, 1992). What appears most important for Native Americans is understanding how specific skills might be perceived differently in their own and in the dominant culture, and learning to assess various social situations accurately and apply the needed skills accordingly.

To make these discriminations, the learner needs instruction from a knowledgeable and understanding teacher. The importance of cultural understanding is made vivid in the following excerpts from *An Indian Father's Plea* (Lake, 1990). The plea is intended to enlighten a kindergarten teacher about the cultural discontinuities adversely affecting a son's social and cognitive development. Even though the teacher labels him a slow learner, the youngster has acquired a wealth of information based on his culture. The father describes the child's early years and the many things he has learned through his cultural experiences:

> He has attended the sacred and ancient White Deerskin Dance of his people and is well acquainted with the cultures and languages of other tribes. . . . He learned his basic numbers by helping his father count and sort the rocks to be used in the sweat lodge—seven rocks for a medicine sweat, say, or 13 for the summer solstice ceremony.

> He is not culturally "disadvantaged," but he is culturally "different." If you asked him how many months there are in a year, he will probably tell you 13. He will respond this way not because he doesn't know how to count properly, but because he has been taught by our people that there are 13 full moons in a year according to the native tribal calendar and that there are really 13 planets in our solar system and 13 tail feathers on a perfectly balanced eagle, the most powerful kind of bird to use in ceremony and healing. (p. 21)

managing pressures to use drugs as well as fewer instances of alcohol, marijuana, and inhalant use at a 6-month follow-up compared to those in the control groups. Changes in tobacco use were not found, however, nor were significant changes in self-esteem. Nevertheless, the data are grounds for optimism that a program specially tailored for Native American youth can prevent self-destructive behaviors in early adolescence. Additional feedback from the young people supports the optimism of the participants in the treatment. Seventy-five percent said they would advise their friends to take part in future programs. On an assessment instrument with a 10-point scale (10 meaning very high), students ranked the program 9.0 on sensitivity to American Indian culture, 8.4 on immediate applicability to their lives, and 8.1 on effectiveness for drug abuse prevention.

Model 2. In a similar study, Schinke, Orlandi, Botvin, Gilchrist, Trimble, and Locklear (1988) used cognitive and social learning methods to help Native American adolescents develop skills to avoid substance abuse. Specifically, the youngsters were taught self-instruction and problem-solving procedures to determine situations entailing high risk of substance abuse and to practice positive self-statements for avoiding substances. Appropriate behaviors were modeled and role-played. To make this training culturally relevant, the trainers infused the lessons with biculturally relevant examples—for example, presenting nonoffensive ways to resist inappropriate pressure from Native American and non–Native American peers. Likewise, culturally based examples helped participants learn to identify potential high-risk situations—that is, places and times substance abuse is most likely.

Model 3. LaFromboise and Rowe (1983) advocate a training model to teach bicultural assertiveness skills to Native Americans. The authors contend that such a model is especially appropriate for Native Americans and is less culturally biased because it permits trainers to select target behaviors and their respective outcomes according to individual needs. Additionally, it utilizes small group instruction, which is common in the American Indian experience, and it is applicable to an array of problem situations that may be important to Native American people. LaFromboise and Rowe state

Table 7
Overview of Skills Enhancement Intervention

Session	Topic
1	Introduce program rationale. Discuss myths concerning Indian drinking and drug use. Discuss the impact of stereotypes on behavior. Complete a self-esteem promotion activity.
2	Review health education information on drugs and alcohol through games, films, handouts, and posters.
3	Discuss factors that encourage drug use among Indians. Introduce peer guest speaker to share personal reasons for rejecting drug use.
4	Discuss the role of values in decision making. Complete activities to encourage identification of personal values. Introduce the SODAS problem solving model.
5	Focus on the "S" (Stop) and "O" (Options) of the SODAS model. Teach students to identify precipitants of drug and alcohol use and the need to think like an elder to maintain the Indian Way and avoid drugs. Practice brain-storming techniques and generating multiple ideas for dealing with opportunities to use drugs.
6	Focus on the "D" (Decide). Practice consideration of personal goals, personal values, and drug-alcohol facts during decision making. Use SODAS to think like an elder to resolve situations involving drugs and alcohol.
7	Focus on the "A" (Act/Communication skills) and the "S" (Self-praise). Use cartoons and stick puppets to practice effective responses to overt and covert pressures to use drugs.
8	Generalize use of SODAS to nondrug and alcohol problems. Use puppets to practice skills.
9	Provide skills practice by working with student create a SODAS "commercial" on videotape.
10	Finish videotaping. Review drug-alcohol facts. Introduce adult guest speaker from tribal alcohol treatment program. Outline plans for follow-up.

Note. From "Skills Enhancement to Prevent Substance Abuse among Americ Indian Adolescents" by L. D. Gilchrist, S. P. Schinke, J. E. Trimble, and G. T. Cvetkovich, 1987, *The International Journal of Addictions, 22*(9), p. 874. Reprinted by courtesy of Marcel Dekker, Inc.

that "the American Indian traditions of role modeling, apprenticeship training, and group consensus [parallel] the social skills training intervention principles of instruction, modeling, behavior rehearsal, reinforcement, feedback, skill improvement and generalization to the natural environment" (p. 593). In addressing bicultural assertiveness, the trainers focused on developing skills appropriate to the population being addressed (i.e., Native American or Anglo American) as well as to the social relationship (e.g., employer or friend) and the nature of the interaction (e.g., refusing an unreasonable request from an employer versus refusing unneeded assistance from a friend). In being assertive with Anglo Americans, for example, Native American learners might be encouraged to become more skilled with eye contact, timing, voice volume, and delivery of a direct, succinct message. On the other hand, in interactions with other Native Americans, the emphasis would be on assessing the cultural appropriateness of being assertive with another Native American.

Training along these lines is especially important for Native Americans who find themselves positioned between two worlds, often without the requisite skills to cope effectively. LaFromboise and Rowe (1983) advise stressing the situation-specific nature of the training (i.e., these skills are to be applied according to the dictates of the specific culture and the environment) in order to involve Native American participants successfully and eliminate fears that learners "may become habitually competitive or aggressive" (p. 594). Although

The father details various actions on the part of the teacher, the boy's peers, and the larger society that may appear innocuous and are somewhat commonplace but that help to undermine the child's self-esteem and sense of himself:

> On the first day of class, you had difficulty with his name. You wanted to call him Wind, insisting that Wolf somehow must be his middle name. The students in class laughed at him, causing further embarrassment. . . .

> Yesterday, for the third time in two weeks he came home crying and said he wanted to have his hair cut. He said he doesn't have any friends at school because they make fun of his long hair. I tried to explain to him that in our culture, long hair is a sign of masculinity and balance and is a source of power. But he remained adamant in his position.

> So now my young Indian child does not want to go to school anymore (even though we cut his hair). He feels that he does not belong. . . . He asks why the other kids in school are not taught about power, beauty, and essence of nature or provided with an opportunity to experience the world around them firsthand. . . . He asks why one young white girl at school who is his friend always tells him, "I like you, Wind-Wolf, because you are a good Indian." (p. 22)

Finally, the father not only validates his son but points out the potentially damaging effects of these experiences and advises the teacher of a recommended course of action:

> He stems from a long line of hereditary chiefs. . . . He has seven different tribal systems flowing through his blood; he is even part white. I want my child to succeed in school and life. I don't want him to be a dropout or juvenile delinquent or to end up on drugs and alcohol because he is made to feel inferior or because of discrimination. . . .

My son, Wind-Wolf, is not an empty glass coming into your class to be filled. He is a full basket coming into a different environment and society with something special to share. Please let him share his knowledge, heritage, and culture with you and his peers. (p. 23)

It is important to recognize, with respect, the characteristics that distinguish Native Americans and other cultural groups from the mainstream. However, it is critical also to orchestrate the weaving of ties that bind the separate groups into a cohesive unit that considers itself a whole. In spite of our differences, we have more common traits than differences.

Summary

Though Native Americans represent less than 1 percent of the U.S. population, they are a dominant force in the history, culture, and current lifestyle of this country. Traditional cultural markers include emphases on the importance of the group, generosity, and living in harmony with others and nature. Child care is characterized by respect and creation of conditions that foster mastery, independence, and self-discipline. Children are observed to be less verbally assertive than their Anglo age-mates.

Over the years, Native American culture has greatly altered so that contemporary youth often find themselves marginalized, out of touch with their heritage, and alienated from the dominant culture. This state is aggravated by poverty, poor schooling, and academic underachievement. Often unable to cope effectively, Native American youth disproportionately fall victim to substance abuse, school failure, and suicide.

Teachers and other professionals are encouraged to become familiar with the cultural distinctions of Native Americans in order to interpret their behaviors accurately and to develop appropriate, culturally relevant instructional programs. Interventions that capitalize on storytelling, cooperative learning, altruistic experiences, and direct instruction appear to hold much promise. Instruction needs to be concrete, meaningful, and situation specific; instructors managing pressures to use drugs as well as fewer instances of alcohol, marijuana, and inhalant use at a 6-month follow-up compared to those in the control groups. Changes in tobacco use were not found, however, nor were significant changes in self-esteem. Nevertheless, the data are grounds for optimism that a program specially tailored for Native American youth can prevent self-destructive behaviors in early adolescence. Additional feedback from the young people supports the optimism of the participants in the treatment. Seventy-five percent said they would advise their friends to take part in future programs. On an assessment instrument with a 10-point scale (10 meaning very high), students ranked the program 9.0 on sensitivity to American Indian culture, 8.4 on immediate applicability to their lives, and 8.1 on effectiveness for drug abuse prevention.

Model 2. In a similar study, Schinke, Orlandi, Botvin, Gilchrist, Trimble, and Locklear (1988) used cognitive and social learning methods to help Native American adolescents develop skills to avoid substance abuse. Specifically, the youngsters were taught self-instruction and problem-solving procedures to determine situations entailing high risk of substance abuse and to practice positive self-statements for avoiding substances. Appropriate behaviors were modeled and role-played. To make this training culturally relevant, the trainers infused the lessons with biculturally relevant examples—for example, presenting nonoffensive ways to resist inappropriate pressure from Native American and non–Native American peers. Likewise, culturally based examples helped participants learn to identify potential high-risk situations—that is, places and times substance abuse is most likely.

Model 3. LaFromboise and Rowe (1983) advocate a training model to teach bicultural assertiveness skills to Native Americans. The authors contend that such a model is especially appropriate for Native Americans and is less culturally biased because it permits trainers to select target behaviors and their respective outcomes according to individual needs. Additionally, it utilizes small group instruction, which is common in the American Indian experience, and it is applicable to an array of problem situations that may be important to Native American people. LaFromboise and Rowe state

Table 7

Overview of Skills Enhancement Intervention

Session	Topic
1	Introduce program rationale. Discuss myths concerning Indian drinking and drug use. Discuss the impact of stereotypes on behavior. Complete a self-esteem promotion activity.
2	Review health education information on drugs and alcohol through games, films, handouts, and posters.
3	Discuss factors that encourage drug use among Indians. Introduce peer guest speaker to share personal reasons for rejecting drug use.
4	Discuss the role of values in decision making. Complete activities to encourage identification of personal values. Introduce the SODAS problem solving model.
5	Focus on the "S" (Stop) and "O" (Options) of the SODAS model. Teach students to identify precipitants of drug and alcohol use and the need to think like an elder to maintain the Indian Way and avoid drugs. Practice brain-storming techniques and generating multiple ideas for dealing with opportunities to use drugs.
6	Focus on the "D" (Decide). Practice consideration of personal goals, personal values, and drug-alcohol facts during decision making. Use SODAS to think like an elder to resolve situations involving drugs and alcohol.
7	Focus on the "A" (Act/Communication skills) and the "S" (Self-praise). Use cartoons and stick puppets to practice effective responses to overt and covert pressures to use drugs.
8	Generalize use of SODAS to nondrug and alcohol problems. Use puppets to practice skills.

9   Provide skills practice by working with students to create a SODAS "commercial" on videotape.

10   Finish videotaping. Review drug-alcohol facts. Introduce adult guest speaker from tribal alcohol treatment program. Outline plans for follow-up.

Note. From "Skills Enhancement to Prevent Substance Abuse among American Indian Adolescents" by L. D. Gilchrist, S. P. Schinke, J. E. Trimble, and G. T. Cvetkovich, 1987, *The International Journal of Addictions, 22*(9), p. 874. Reprinted by courtesy of Marcel Dekker, Inc.

---

that "the American Indian traditions of role modeling, apprenticeship training, and group consensus [parallel] the social skills training intervention principles of instruction, modeling, behavior rehearsal, reinforcement, feedback, skill improvement and generalization to the natural environment" (p. 593). In addressing bicultural assertiveness, the trainers focused on developing skills appropriate to the population being addressed (i.e., Native American or Anglo American) as well as to the social relationship (e.g., employer or friend) and the nature of the interaction (e.g., refusing an unreasonable request from an employer versus refusing unneeded assistance from a friend). In being assertive with Anglo Americans, for example, Native American learners might be encouraged to become more skilled with eye contact, timing, voice volume, and delivery of a direct, succinct message. On the other hand, in interactions with other Native Americans, the emphasis would be on assessing the cultural appropriateness of being assertive with another Native American.

Training along these lines is especially important for Native Americans who find themselves positioned between two worlds, often without the requisite skills to cope effectively. LaFromboise and Rowe (1983) advise stressing the situation-specific nature of the training (i.e., these skills are to be applied according to the dictates of the specific culture and the environment) in order to involve Native American participants successfully and eliminate fears that learners "may become habitually competitive or aggressive" (p. 594). Although the work reported by LaFromboise and Rowe used adult participants and scenarios, their instructional procedures are equally appropriate for adolescents, as established in chapter 2 of this book and in numerous other professional resources (e.g., Cartledge & Milburn, 1995; Goldstein, 1988; Stephens, 1992). What appears most important for Native Americans is understanding how specific skills might be perceived differently in their own and in the dominant culture, and learning to assess various social situations accurately and apply the needed skills accordingly.

To make these discriminations, the learner needs instruction from a knowledgeable and understanding teacher. The importance of cultural understanding is made vivid in the following excerpts from *An Indian Father's Plea* (Lake, 1990). The plea is intended to enlighten a kindergarten teacher about the cultural discontinuities adversely affecting a son's social and cognitive development. Even though the teacher labels him a slow learner, the youngster has acquired a wealth of information based on his culture. The father describes the child's early years and the many things he has learned through his cultural experiences:

> He has attended the sacred and ancient White Deerskin
> Dance of his people and is well acquainted with the
> cultures and languages of other tribes. . . . He learned his
> basic numbers by helping his father count and sort the
> rocks to be used in the sweat lodge—seven rocks for a
> medicine sweat, say, or 13 for the summer solstice
> ceremony.

> He is not culturally "disadvantaged," but he is culturally
> "different." If you asked him how many months there are
> in a year, he will probably tell you 13. He will respond
> this way not because he doesn't know how to count
> properly, but because he has been taught by our people
> that there are 13 full moons in a year according to the
> native tribal calendar and that there are really 13 planets
> in our solar system and 13 tail feathers on a perfectly
> balanced eagle, the most powerful kind of bird to use
> in ceremony and healing. (p. 21)

The father details various actions on the part of the teacher, the boy's peers, and the larger society that may appear innocuous and are somewhat commonplace but that help to undermine the child's self-esteem and sense of himself:

> On the first day of class, you had difficulty with his name. You wanted to call him Wind, insisting that Wolf somehow must be his middle name. The students in class laughed at him, causing further embarrassment. . . .
>
> Yesterday, for the third time in two weeks he came home crying and said he wanted to have his hair cut. He said he doesn't have any friends at school because they make fun of his long hair. I tried to explain to him that in our culture, long hair is a sign of masculinity and balance and is a source of power. But he remained adamant in his position.
>
> So now my young Indian child does not want to go to school anymore (even though we cut his hair). He feels that he does not belong. . . . He asks why the other kids in school are not taught about power, beauty, and essence of nature or provided with an opportunity to experience the world around them firsthand. . . . He asks why one young white girl at school who is his friend always tells him, "I like you, Wind-Wolf, because you are a good Indian." (p. 22)

Finally, the father not only validates his son but points out the potentially damaging effects of these experiences and advises the teacher of a recommended course of action:

> He stems from a long line of hereditary chiefs. . . . He has seven different tribal systems flowing through his blood; he is even part white. I want my child to succeed in school and life. I don't want him to be a dropout or juvenile delinquent or to end up on drugs and alcohol because he is made to feel inferior or because of discrimination. . . .

My son, Wind-Wolf, is not an empty glass coming into
your class to be filled. He is a full basket coming into a
different environment and society with something special
to share. Please let him share his knowledge, heritage,
and culture with you and his peers. (p. 23)

It is important to recognize, with respect, the characteristics that
distinguish Native Americans and other cultural groups from the
mainstream. However, it is critical also to orchestrate the weaving
of ties that bind the separate groups into a cohesive unit that considers itself a whole. In spite of our differences, we have more common
traits than differences.

Summary

Though Native Americans represent less than 1 percent of the U.S.
population, they are a dominant force in the history, culture, and current lifestyle of this country. Traditional cultural markers include
emphases on the importance of the group, generosity, and living in
harmony with others and nature. Child care is characterized by respect
and creation of conditions that foster mastery, independence, and
self-discipline. Children are observed to be less verbally assertive than
their Anglo age-mates.

Over the years, Native American culture has greatly altered so
that contemporary youth often find themselves marginalized, out
of touch with their heritage, and alienated from the dominant culture. This state is aggravated by poverty, poor schooling, and academic underachievement. Often unable to cope effectively, Native
American youth disproportionately fall victim to substance abuse,
school failure, and suicide.

Teachers and other professionals are encouraged to become
familiar with the cultural distinctions of Native Americans in order
to interpret their behaviors accurately and to develop appropriate,
culturally relevant instructional programs. Interventions that capitalize on storytelling, cooperative learning, altruistic experiences,
and direct instruction appear to hold much promise. Instruction
needs to be concrete, meaningful, and situation specific; instructors

must exercise caution not to violate long-held traditions and beliefs that are part of young people's value systems. More research is needed on effective interventions for countering self-destructive behavior among young Native Americans.

References

Alexander, M. (1991). [Unpublished interview]. The Ohio State University, Columbus.

Ashabranner, B. (1984). *To live in two worlds: American Indian youth today.* New York: Dodd, Mead.

Banks, J. A. (1991). *Teaching strategies for ethnic studies* (5th ed.). Boston: Allyn & Bacon.

Batson, C. (1987). Prosocial motivation: Is it ever truly altruistic? *Advances in Experimental Social Psychology, 20,* 65–122.

Baylor, B. (1976). *Hawk, I'm your brother.* New York: Scribners.

Beauvais, F., Oetting, E.R., & Edwards, R.W. (1985). Trends in the use of inhalants among American Indian adolescents. *White Cloud Journal, 3,* 3–11.

Bennion, L., & Li, T.K. (1976). Alcohol metabolism in American Indians and whites. *New England Journal of Medicine, 294,* 9–13.

Bernal, M.E., Saenz, D.S., & Knight, G.P. (1991). Ethnic identity and adaptation of Mexican American youths in school settings. *Hispanic Journal of Behavioral Sciences, 13,* 135–154.

Bierhorst, J. (1985). *The mythology of North America.* New York: Morrow.

Brendtro, L.K., Brokenleg, M., & Van Brockern, S. (1990). *Reclaiming youth at risk.* Bloomington, IN: National Educational Service.

Brophy, J., & Good, T. (1986). Teacher behavior and student achievement. In M. Wittrock (Ed.), *Handbook of research on teaching* (3rd ed.). New York: Macmillan.

Brown, D. (1975). *Wounded knee: An Indian history of the American West.* New York: Dell.

Brown, G., & McGrew-Zoubi, R. (1995). Successful teaching in culturally diverse classrooms. *The Delta Kappa Gamma Bulletin, 61,* 7–12, 17.

Cannon, A.E. (1990). *The shadow brothers.* New York: Delacorte.

Cartledge, G., Lee, J.W., & Feng, H. (1995). Cultural diversity: Multicultural factors in teaching social skills. In G. Cartledge & J.F. Milburn (Eds.), *Teaching social skills to children and youth: Innovative approaches* (3rd ed.). Boston: Allyn & Bacon.

Cartledge, G., & Milburn, J.F. (1995). *Teaching social skills to children and youth: Innovative approaches* (3rd ed.). Boston: Allyn & Bacon.

Cazden, C.B., & John, V.P. (1971). Learning in American Indian children. In M.L. Wax, S. Diamond, & F.O. Gearing (Eds.), *Anthropological perspectives on education.* New York: Basic.

Cwiklik, R. (1989). *Sequoia.* Englewood Cliffs, NJ: Silver Burdett.

Deyhle, D. (1986). Break dancing and breaking out: Anglos, Utes, and Navajos in a border reservation high school. *Anthropology & Education Quarterly, 17,* 111–127.

Dorris, M. (1987). *A yellow raft in blue water.* New York: Holt.

Dorris, M. (1989). *The broken cord: A family's ongoing struggle with fetal alcohol syndrome.* Baltimore: HarperCollins

Erdrich, L. (1989). *Tracks.* Baltimore: HarperCollins.

Fordham, S. (1988). Racelessness as a factor in black students' school success: Pragmatic strategy or pyrrhic victory? *Harvard Educational Review, 58,* 54–84.

Freedman, R. (1987). *Indian chiefs.* New York: Holiday House.

Freedman, R. (1988). *Buffalo hunt.* New York: Holiday House.

Garcia, E. (1994). *Understanding and meeting the challenge of student cultural diversity.* Boston: Houghton Mifflin.

George, J.C. (1972). *Julie of the wolves.* New York: Harper and Row.

Gilchrist, L.D., Schinke, S.P., Trimble, J.E., & Cvetkovich, G.T. (1987). Skills enhancement to prevent substance abuse among American Indian adolescents. *The International Journal of Addictions, 22*(9), 869–879.

Goldstein, A.P. (1988). *The Prepare Curriculum: Teaching prosocial competencies.* Champaign, IL: Research Press.

Goley, E. (1992). United States: Native Americans. In L. Miller-Lachmann (Ed.), *Our family, our friends, our world.* New Providence, NJ: Bowker.

Grossman, D.C., Milligan, C., & Deyo, R.A. (1991). Risk factors for suicide attempts among Navajo adolescents. *American Journal of Public Health, 81,* 870–874.

Guilmet, G.M. (1976). *The non-verbal American Indian child in the classroom: A survey.* Tacoma, WA: University of Puget Sound.

Hall, E.T. (1969). Listening behavior: Some cultural differences. *Phi Delta Kappan, 50,* 379–380.

Hall, M. (1993). In our own language: Youth as servant leaders. *Journal of Emotional and Behavioral Problems, 1,* 27–29.

Hirst, L.A., & Slavik, C. (1989). Cooperative approaches to language learning. In J. Reyhner (Ed.), *Effective language education practices and native language survival: Proceedings of the Ninth Annual International Native American Language Issues (NALI) Institute.* Billings, MT: NALI Board of Executors and Jon Reyhner.

Hobbs, W. (1989). *Bearstone.* New York: Atheneum.

Johnson, D.W., & Johnson, R.T. (1983). The socialization and achievement crisis: Are cooperative learning experiences the solution? In L. Bickman (Ed.), *Applied social psychology: Annual 4.* Beverly Hills, CA: Sage.

Joosse, B.M. (1991). *Mama, do you love me?* San Francisco: Chronicle.

Kallam, M., Hoernicke, P.A., & Coser, P.G. (1994). Native Americans and behavioral disorders. In R.L. Peterson & S. Ishii-Jordan (Eds.), *Multicultural issues in the education of students with behavioral disorders.* Cambridge, MA: Brookline.

Katz, W.L. (1986). *Black Indians: A hidden heritage.* New York: Atheneum.

LaFromboise, T.D. (1988). American Indian mental health policy. *American Psychologist, 43,* 388–397.

LaFromboise, T.D., & Low, K.G. (1989). American Indian children and adolescents. In J.T. Gibbs, L.N. Huang, & Associates (Eds.), *Children of color.* San Francisco: Jossey-Bass.

LaFromboise, T.D., & Rowe, W. (1983). Skills training for bicultural competence: Rationale and application. *Journal of Counseling Psychology, 30,* 589–595.

Lake, R. (1990). An Indian father's plea. *The Education Digest, 55,* 20–23.

Little Soldier, L. (1989). Cooperative learning and the Native American student. *Phi Delta Kappan, 71*(2), 161–163.

Locust, C. (1988). Wounding the spirit: Discrimination and traditional American Indian belief systems. *Harvard Educational Review, 58*(3), 315–330.

McDermott, G. (1974). *Arrow to the sun: A Pueblo Indian tale.* New York: Viking.

Medicine, B. (1985). Child socialization among Native Americans: The Lakota (Sioux) in cultural context. *Wicazo Saturday Review, 1*(2), 23–28.

Moroney, L. (1989). *Baby rattlesnake by Te Ata.* San Francisco: Children's Book Press.

Oetting, E. R., Beauvais, F., Edwards, R., Waters, M. R., Velarde, J., & Goldstein, G. (1983). *Drug use among Native American youth: Summary of findings (1975–1981).* Fort Collins: Colorado State University.

Ogbu, J. (1978). *Minority education and caste.* New York: Academic.

Okwumabua, J. O., Okwumabua, T.M., & Duryea, E. J. (1989). An investigation of health decision-making skills among American Indian adolescents. *American Indian and Alaska Native Mental Health Research, 3,* 42–52.

Ortiz, S. (1988). *The people shall continue.* San Francisco: Children's Book Press.

Pitton, D., Warring, D., Frank, K., & Hunter, S. (1993). *Multicultural messages: Nonverbal communication in the classroom.* (ERIC Document Reproduction Service No. ED 362 519)

Pitts, P. (1988). *Racing the sun.* New York: Avon.

Polgar, S. (1960). Biculturation of Mesquakie teenage boys. *American Anthropologist, 62,* 217–235.

Powless, D.L., & Elliott, S. N. (1993). Assessment of social skills of Native American preschoolers: Teachers' and parents' ratings. *Journal of School Psychology, 31,* 293–307.

Rosando, L. (1994, March). *Promoting effective cross cultural communication.* Presentation at the Texas Education Agency, Center for Professional Development, Multicultural Institute, Dallas.

Saracho, O. N., & Gerstl, C. (1992). Learning differences among at risk minority students. In H. Waxman, J. de Selix, J. Anderson, & H.P. Baptiste (Eds.), *Students at risk in at risk schools: Improving environments for learning.* Newbury Park, CA: Corwin.

Schaffer, R. (1988). English as a second language for the Indian student. In J. Reyhner (Ed.), *Teaching the Indian child: A bilingual/multicultural approach* (2nd ed.). Billings: Eastern Montana College.

Schinke, S.P., Orlandi, M. A., Botvin, G.J., Gilchrist, L. D., Trimble, J.E., & Locklear, V. S. (1988). Preventing substance abuse among American-Indian adolescents: A bicultural competence skills approach. *Journal of Counseling Psychology, 35,* 87–90.

Schneider, B.H. (1993). *Children's social competence in context: The contributions of family, school, and culture.* Oxford, England: Pergamon.

Slavin, R.E. (1985). Cooperative learning: Applying contact theory in desegregated schools. *Journal of Social Issues, 41,* 45–62.

Slavin, R.E., & Oickle, E. (1981). Effects of cooperative learning teams on student achievement and race relations: Treatment by race interactions. *Sociology of Education, 5,* 174–180.

Stephens, T. M. (1992). *Social skills in the classroom.* Odessa, FL: Psychological Assessment Resources.

Sullivan, P. (1992). *ESL in context.* Newbury Park, CA: Corwin.

Trotter, R. T., Rolf, J. E., Baldwin, J. A., & Quintero, G.A. (1992). *Tough issues for Navajo youth and Navajo schools.* Washington, DC: U.S. Department of Education, Office of Research and Improvement.

U.S. Bureau of the Census. (1993). *Statistical abstract of the United States: 1993.* (113th ed.). Washington, DC: Author.

Vogt, L.A., Jordan, C., & Tharp, R.G. (1987). Explaining school failure, producing school success: Two cases. *Anthropology and Education Quarterly, 18*(4), 276–286.

Wallin, L. (1987). *Ceremony of the panther.* New York: Bradbury.

CHAPTER 6

Hispanic Americans

LESSIE L. COCHRAN AND GWENDOLYN CARTLEDGE

Hispanic Americans are now the second largest minority group (22 million people) in the United States (Castex, 1994; Delgado-Gaitan & Trueba, 1991). With a fertility rate about 60 percent higher than the non-Hispanic average and with continuing immigration from Cuba, Central and South America, and Puerto Rico, Hispanic Americans are one of the fastest-growing minority groups in this country. Soon they will numerically surpass African Americans as the nation's largest minority group. Identified within the Hispanic American population are several subgroups: Cubans, Chicanos or Mexican Americans, Central Americans, and Puerto Ricans (Castex, 1994). Although Hispanic Americans are thought to share language backgrounds and confront similar social issues within the United States, we must consider several historical, racial, and cultural differences when formulating guidelines for instruction. Demographic data for these subgroups may vary with the source, as some references record only legal immigrants (Banks, 1991; Castex, 1994; Delgado-Gaitan & Trueba, 1991).

According to the Office of Management and Budget, a Hispanic is "a person of Mexican, Puerto Rican, Cuban, Central or South American or other Spanish culture or origin, regardless of race" (Castex, 1994, p. 289). This definition is based only on country of origin and assumes that all individuals originating from one country are the same. This has not been shown to be true. Approximately 26 nations account for the origins noted in this definition. If language were to be used to define the Hispanic culture, what language would it be? Five different languages (Spanish, Portuguese, French, Dutch, and English) are native languages for people considered Hispanic. Racial characteristics cannot be used to define these people because these characteristics reflect a wide range of skin color, hair texture, and class status. Even religion cannot be used. Although most Hispanics are Roman Catholic, many within and outside the United States are Protestant. Self-identification allows individuals to indicate how they view themselves. Do they identify themselves according to governmental or nongovernmental terminology? To recognize the real difficulty of applying a label like *Hispanic,* one must look at these people's historical origins (Castex, 1994).

Although found throughout the United States, Hispanic Americans tend to be concentrated in certain sections of the country. The majority are found in western states—Arizona, California, Colorado, New Mexico, and Texas—with substantial numbers also located in New York, New Jersey, Illinois, and Florida. The unique history of each subgroup reveals its role in the formation of Hispanic American culture (Banks, 1991; Castex, 1994).

Mexican Americans are the largest subgroup of the Hispanic American population. The history of the Mexican American people has been one of assimilation, beginning in the 1500s with the initial conquest by the Spaniards of the Native Indians living in the Mexican region. Spanish conquistadors mated with female natives, and later African Moors were added to the mix. The result was a unique blend: not a combination of separate parts but rather a new and different Mexican culture. With the introduction of the westward-moving Anglos, these new people were subjugated and reduced in status. After Texas's independence (1845) and the Mexican-American War (1848), several states heavily populated with Mexicans and Anglo Americans experienced difficulties when the two major cultures were unable to live in harmony. Anglos legally and financially outmaneuvered the Mexicans, who were unfamiliar with the Anglo laws and customs. The result was the loss of property and status for the now native Mexican Americans. While cheap labor was needed for agribusiness, Mexican American migrants were readily accepted within U.S. boundaries. Then, during the Depression in the wake of the 1929 financial crash, Mexican Americans were viewed as burdens to the welfare system. Attempts were made to deport many natives and stop new arrivals. Upswings in the agricultural and financial arenas transferred the focus from welfare back to the need for cheap labor, and Mexican Americans were again welcomed. The majority of Mexican Americans are concentrated in California and Texas, with Illinois and Arizona having the next largest populations (Banks, 1991). Recognizing the importance of cultural pride and political clout, Mexican Americans currently are placing more emphasis on accepting and propagating their cultural uniqueness, especially for their children (Banks, 1991).

Mexican Americans are not the only Hispanic American group advocating cultural awareness and power: Puerto Ricans also have sought to strengthen cultural identity. Puerto Ricans, the second largest Hispanic American group, are descendants of Spanish con-quistadors, native Indians (Tainos), and former African slaves (Banks, 1991). With the initial conquest, Spanish rule was established on the islands, and for nearly 400 years Spanish governors controlled most aspects of Puerto Ricans' lives. An outcome of the United States' victory in the Spanish-American War (1898) was the gain of the Philippine and Puerto Rican islands as well as American Guam. In 1900, U.S. military governors, appointed by the president, ruled Puerto Rico as a colony. Later, in response to attempts by Puerto Ricans to organize self-governance, the U.S. government granted them citizenship to arrest the struggle. Finally, in 1947, Puerto Ricans were given the opportunity to elect their own governor, who sought to bring the Commonwealth of Puerto Rico into the industrial age.

From the 15th century, during most of the period of colonization, Puerto Rico was controlled by foreign powers who contributed little to the economic growth and political stability of the island. The need for improved economic and social stability led to mass migrations to the mainland, starting in the 1920s and 1930s. Most Puerto Ricans originally settled in New York, but over the years they have settled in other parts of the mainland, including New Jersey, Florida, and California.

Because they were now citizens, Puerto Ricans could migrate back and forth between the island and the mainland in search of better opportunities. The majority of them settled in various states throughout the country, with New York, New Jersey, Illinois, Florida, and California being the top five choices (Banks, 1991). Some Puerto Ricans continue to move back and forth between island and mainland, never establishing permanent roots on the mainland. Others, however, recognize that political, economic, and educational opportunities result from maintaining residence in the States and accumulating power through group unity (Banks, 1991; Suarez-Orozco, 1987).

This search for cultural uniqueness is shared with a third and relatively new Hispanic American group, the Cuban Americans, who began large-scale immigration after the 1959 Castro revolution (Banks, 1991). Seeking greater political, religious, and economic freedom, many middle- and upper-class Cubans left their island for the United States. Later immigrants were predominately lower-class and blue-collar workers along with others considered by the Cuban government to be undesirables. The majority of the Cuban immigrants settled in urban areas in Florida, New Jersey, New York, and California, where isolated groups of Cuban Americans formed support systems. Older Cuban Americans attempted to maintain the family roles that prevailed in Cuba; younger or second-generation Cuban Americans are adopting more liberal ways of thinking and behaving. Cuban Americans have had opportunities to communicate openly with family members still in Cuba, thus strengthening the connection with their Cuban roots. Virtually all Cuban Americans believe this to be positive but for different reasons: The older generation holds to the ideal of a possible return to Cuba when the current government releases its restrictions, and the younger generation seeks reestablishment of cultural identity and strengthening of familial contacts (Banks, 1991). Cuban Americans in the United States are acquiring economic and political power, first within their smaller, separate communities, later expanding their influence to be felt on the state level.

Though their histories are quite different, the three largest groups of Hispanic Americans do share some commonalties. For instance, Spanish is often their native language, family and religious affiliations often guide their decisions, and friendships and peer relations are influential in their lives. These in no way illustrate all of the similarities.

Cultural Distinctions

Language

In a survey by Banks (1991), over 91 percent of Puerto Ricans were found to speak Spanish in the home, compared to 90 percent of Cuban

Americans and 64 percent of Mexican Americans. Most Hispanic Americans who still speak Spanish tend to be older and/or first generation. The younger and second-generation individuals may speak Spanish at home, but they rarely speak it outside the home. As assimilation occurs, language is usually one of the first characteristics to change. To access educational services, immigrants must learn English. Schools offer English as a second language (ESL) courses for students who lack proficiency in English. In some schools, bilingual education is available, with Hispanic American students receiving instruction in both English and Spanish, with the focus on improving their English. Hispanic Americans who are fluent in English find that they have more occupational and political options, but at the same time they may be ostracized from their families and cultural group.

The Family

Hispanic families are characterized by close relationships and extensiveness. That is, as in African American families, family members may include nonrelatives, known as *compadres* (Harrison, Wilson, Pine, Chan, & Buriel, 1990). The family is considered the ecological system that supports the development of its members as well as the primary source of education for children (Martinez, 1988; Suarez-Orozco, 1987). From birth, mothers and fathers are expected to instruct their children in the skills necessary for survival. Ramirez (1989) describes the Mexican American home as typically family centered, with permissive, nurturing childrearing attitudes prevalent during the child's early years. Children are expected to assume more responsibility for their behavior during the latency period, with the father assuming the role of disciplinarian for older children while the mother is largely the protective nurturer. In the typical family structure, the parent/child relationship is emphasized over the marital dyad, and there is a hierarchy of gender in which the father's position is superior to the mother's. When children address their parents, for example, the father is addressed first.

In the Hispanic family, mothers direct the instruction of their children (Martinez, 1988). According to Martinez, maternal teaching in Hispanic households varies in style from authoritative to authoritarian to permissive. An authoritative style of parenting is associated with competitive and individualistic middle-class Anglo

American values, which are considered antagonistic to the communal and cooperative values of many Hispanic people. The authoritarian style, incorporating the use of punishment in interactions with children, is generally associated with low socioeconomic status. Few Hispanic parents employ the permissive style of parenting, which poses no boundaries or limitations. The type of maternal control depends on various factors such as the mother's age, the number of generations the family has been in the United States, the family's religious preference, the mother's and father's educational levels, the father's employment status, the child's gender, and the number of male and female siblings (DeRosier & Kupersmidt, 1991; Graf, 1986; Hidalgo, 1993). Language preference and use and ethnic density of the neighborhood may also be influential. Mothers who are second- and third-generation and beyond, living in middle-class homes in communities with high percentages of non-Hispanics, have been acculturated to the point that they assume many characteristics normally associated with Anglos. For example, they encourage competition and individual achievement in their children. Mothers of lower socioeconomic status are still influenced by "old" values, are more likely to live in Hispanic neighborhoods, to be actively involved in their churches, and to utilize the authoritarian style. Parents set the rules and expect their children to follow, encouraging cooperation and community involvement.

The length of time a family has been in the United States correlates with the level of acculturation. Younger mothers are more likely to have been in this country longer and therefore more likely to be two or more generations removed from their native country. They are more likely to speak fluent English as well as Spanish. They are likely to have completed more schooling, to have white-collar jobs, and to live in predominantly Anglo neighborhoods. The majority of Hispanic American families are of the Catholic faith, with the rest being Protestant. The rigors and restrictions of the Catholic religion are more strongly observed by those families most recently arrived from their home countries.

Older Hispanic American family members believe that their children have opportunities to study and to better themselves, opportunities many of them did not have in their homelands. Problems often arise because Hispanic American parents may not know how to be involved in their children's dreams, and educational institutions may not reach out to involve them (Martinez, 1988).

Often the expectations for a child's future depend on gender. Ramirez (1989) points out that in Mexican American homes females are reared in a protective environment, whereas males have more freedom, often joining informal groups known as *palo millas* where they are socialized into typical male roles. Though males usually are considered more dominant than females, the mother is still head of the household, especially in first- or second-generation homes. As families become more assimilated in this country, other influences— friends and peers—become more important.

Self-Concept and Identity

Much of the existing research on Hispanic American youth focuses on issues of self-esteem and identity, particularly in relation to other ethnic or racial groups. Fu, Hinkle, and Korslund (1983), for example, compared the self-concept ratings of Mexican American, African American, and European American preadolescent girls. They found that the Mexican American girls not only consistently scored lower than the other two groups across age levels (9, 10, and 11 years) but also failed to show significant increases in self-concept scores with age, unlike their peers from the other two groups. Other studies with preadolescents (Fu, 1979) and adolescents (Widaman, MacMillan, Hemsley, Little, & Balow, 1992) also found that Hispanic American youth scored lower on self-concept ratings than did their African and European American counterparts. An explanation for this pattern of lower self-concept scores for Hispanic American children and youth is not readily evident, but Fu et al. (1983) speculate that it may be due to "the restricted sociocultural environment and the less effective conveyance of ethnic pride and identity in their environment" (p. 72).

Ethnic identity, which is a component of self-concept, may contribute to academic success and a heightened sense of self-worth (Bernal, Saenz, & Knight, 1991), but it appears to be somewhat complicated for Hispanic American youth (Malgady, Rogler, & Costantino, 1990). Identifying a group of people by a label tends to diminish the uniqueness of individuals. Under the broad label of

Hispanic exist several other separate labels (i.e., *Mexican, Puerto Rican, Cuban, Central* and *South American*). We have seen that these groups have unique histories; now we need to address the application of labels to those groups and the impact of labeling. According to Rotheram-Borus (1990), labeling is a manifestation of social identity:

> A social identity as a member of an ethnic group evolves slowly with age, as one subjectively identifies with a group, assimilating into one's self-concept ethnic characteristics and feelings of belonging. Labeling oneself as a member of an ethnic group is one of the earliest manifestations of one's social identity, typically acquired by the age of eight. (p. 1075)

The choice of label indicates which group a person sees him- or herself as belonging to and which group others see the person as belonging to. This membership may be based on common ancestry, political beliefs, socioeconomic status, or psychological attributes (Quintana, Villanueva, & Castaneda-English, 1994; Valdez, 1994). According to a study by Quintana and colleagues (1994), Mexican American adolescents whose parents exposed them to their culture developed significant cultural behaviors, attitudes, and values. These children also had a strong sense of belonging and affirmation in their ethnic group. Valdez found that although Mexican American college women were significantly lower in socioeconomic status and acculturation level, they had higher scores on ethnic identification relative to sex roles and attitudes than did their white European American female counterparts.

Mexican Americans, frequently called Chicanos, are distinct from Mexicans (who are not citizens of the United States). *Latino,* another term applied to people coming from Central America, has gained popularity. These terms at one time were used in derogatory fashion by both Hispanic Americans and Anglos. With the increased focus on cultural identity and group membership, labels that in the past caused shame or anger now evoke pride and joy (Rotheram-Borus, 1990; Rotheram-Borus & Phinney, 1990).

If people choose to adopt the label *Chicano* rather than *Hispanic,* they are likely to act, think, and feel differently about their ethnicity. For example, using a label that is unique to Mexican Americans rather than a term that applies to all Spanish-speaking people allows individuals to relate directly to their historical roots. As children age, the labels they use to refer to themselves reflect more than membership in an ethnic or cultural group; they imply the values, attitudes, preferences, and behaviors of that group.

In her study of Mexican American adolescents in one high school, Matute-Bianchi (1986), for example, found that they fell into five different identity subgroups: Mexicanos, Mexican-oriented, Mexican American, Chicano, and Cholo. Matute-Bianchi described the first three groups as compliant and school oriented, and the latter two groups as uncooperative and oppositional. These groups differed considerably in their dress, language, social orientation, school participation, and relative social status. Mexican American students, for example, tended to be the most acculturated to U.S. society and were likely to hold in low esteem students who identified with Chicano or Cholo groups. According to Matute-Bianchi, "Among these students, maintaining an identity as Mexicano as distinct from Mexican-American or Chicano or Cholo appears to be much more significant in their lives at school" (p. 253). The majority of the Chicano and Cholo students saw their identities in conflict with that of the school and the larger Anglo culture and felt that to pursue academic success meant to deny one's own identity. Matute-Bianchi suggests that these conditions, which make the negotiation of ethnicity particularly problematic for Mexican American students, help to explain the pattern of school failure that is so prevalent for this population. Furthermore, Matute-Bianchi compares the multiple identities among the Mexican American students to the more unified identity profile presented by Japanese American students, who, except for physical differences, tend to align closely with the dominant culture, subscribe to the established values, and achieve accordingly.

Ramirez and Soriano (1981) asked Chicano university students what contributed to their success or failure. The respondents described both internal and external factors. University graduates listed desire and motivation to succeed as internal reasons and financial and social support as external reasons. Nongraduates listed predominately external factors such as financial need and lack of counseling and tutoring.

The differences noted among Hispanic American adolescents are similar to those identified by Fordham (1988) for African Americans and by Deyhle (1986) for Native Americans (see chapters 4 and 5 of this book). The conscious decision not to participate actively in schooling by attending classes and doing homework because it would mean "acting White" certainly provides a rationale for poor achievement, but it fails to shed light on the tendency of Hispanic American youngsters to rate their self-worth lower than do their peers from other ethnic groups. African American students, who present very similar divisions and attitudes, are found consistently to score higher on self-worth measures than their Hispanic American and White peers (e.g., Widaman et al., 1992). According to social comparison theory, minority youth are inclined to make in-group comparisons rather than compare themselves to the entire society of their age-mates. Although that notion is plausible, the degree to which it applies to any minority group is unclear, and it does not appear to explain the self-ratings of Hispanic American students to a significant degree. For this group, other factors (Iadicola, 1981) such as recent immigrant status, language difficulties, or a cultural tendency to understate or minimize one's personal attributes may be more important.

Peer Relations

Few studies have been conducted on the peer relationships of Hispanic American youth. One such investigation, by Lopez, La Greca, and Fetter (1994), shows that, as with White youth, the most popular fourth-, fifth-, and sixth-grade Hispanic American youngsters also had the highest academic, self-esteem, and friendship support ratings. Hispanic American and White females differed little on these measures, but Hispanic American males differed from White males, with higher rates of self-reported depression and lower rates of self-esteem. This finding is interesting in light of the emphasis in Hispanic culture on machismo and the tendency for boys to be socialized in informal male groups. Other research on depression among Hispanic American youth found that in contrast to the suicidal behavior of females, which was closely associated with reactions to family issues, no single distinct factor was related to suicide in Hispanic American males (Ward, 1994).

If Hispanic American males are indeed particularly disposed to depression and low self-esteem, the inclination to seek mood elevation and greater self-regard in peer social situations is understandable. Research indicates higher use of drugs (i.e., toxic inhalants) among Mexican American adolescents who displayed problems in school conduct and school performance and whose peer group associates were also drug users (Menon, Barrett, & Simpson, 1990). Schwartz (1989) proposes that, in some instances, children seek the individual and cultural status they lack in the school environment through membership in gangs or social groups. Children with similar concerns band together and establish alternative values that confer prestige on their activities. Not all groups of young minority males should be pejoratively labeled *gangs*. However, for many minority young people, cultural background and social conditions lead to group participation that may result in authentic gang membership. As Schwartz (1989) points out, the major functions of some gangs for their members are self-glorification, social and psychological support, and opportunities to have fun with people who are similar. Fewer gang members come from families that nurture skills and knowledge to supplement the school's academic offerings. If schools are to counteract the effects of gang membership, gang-affiliated youth must be made to feel that they are legitimate members of the school community who are expected to perform at acceptable scholastic levels and to participate in school activities. Hispanic gang members need encouragement to interact with Hispanic nongang members around tasks that recognize and reinforce their common cultural background (Schwartz, 1989). More emphasis should be placed on integration into the school social system, an experience that will engender ethnic pride and make youngsters aware of alternatives to gang life.

The Media Image

Television and other media are common sources of information—and misinformation—about various cultural groups. Stereotyping a group of people on the basis of what is seen or heard without knowing the individuals only reinforces prejudice toward that group. What is seen in television movies and sitcoms is taken to be the truth about the people represented by the characters. The scripts for these programs are usually written by members of the majority culture. Because the writers are not members of the group portrayed, they are less likely to represent it accurately or to reflect on the wide variety that exists within any cultural group. Hispanics, for example, have often been portrayed negatively, as ignorant and lazy. They have been cast in the roles of gang members and drug users (e.g., in *West Side Story*).

Such portrayals give others, especially future teachers, distorted pictures of Hispanic Americans. Rarely are the various elements of the Hispanic population cast as honest professionals or conscientious white-collar workers. More recent changes may be due in part to the increased power that Hispanic Americans are gaining in civic and political life as well as the economic power associated with improved employment opportunities and increased purchasing capability. With increased power come changes. Hispanic Americans advocate for more accurate portrayals of their people and lives.

The Role of Music

As immigrants and refugees came to this country, their music came, too. Originally, the music they played was based on these "old" songs, but as they assimilated into American society, the music changed. Because "ethnic" music was not generally accepted, Hispanic American musicians did not obtain popular success. With the increased focus on their cultural identity and the growth of their economic power, Hispanic Americans are reestablishing ties to their cultural roots. "Old" songs are being updated, and "new" songs are acquiring a cultural flavor that reflects the breadth of Hispanic culture (e.g., "La Bamba"). Song writers and composers with Hispanic backgrounds (e.g., Gloria Estefan, Julio Iglesias) are finding the success that eluded their predecessors. Research shows that children have difficulties with self-esteem and self-concept when their culture is constantly regarded as inferior. Thus, Hispanic Americans benefit by hearing music that reflects their own culture. They are able to emulate the visible role models that Hispanic artists provide and to observe the appreciation around those artists.

A Social Skill Profile of Hispanic Americans

Cognitive Style and Social Behavior

According to Saracho (1991), people have various cognitive styles, which range along a continuum from "field-dependent" to "field-independent." These styles denote the distinctive ways in which individuals perceive, think, understand, remember, judge, and solve problems. Each person responds to different situations within his or her particular cognitive style. Field-dependent individuals are described by Saracho and Spodek (1981) as those who experience their environment globally, are strongly interested in people, and have a sensitivity to others that helps them to acquire social skills. On the other hand, field-independent individuals tend to view their environment analytically, are socially detached, and appear cold and distant.

According to Ramirez (1989; cited in Saracho, 1991), children from minority groups are "less competitive, less sensitive to spatial incursions by others, less comfortable in trial and error situations, and less interested in the fine details of concepts, materials, or nonsocial tasks" (p. 23). These children would be considered field dependent. Unfortunately, many researchers have oversimplified, misunderstood, and misconstrued the relationship between socialization practices and the cognitive styles of Hispanic American children (Saracho, 1991). It is assumed that children's environment influences their thinking, learning, and language in particular ways. Traditional, sedentary, and agricultural cultures characterize the antecedents of field-dependent traits, whereas the socialization practices in modern, mobile, urban industrialized societies stress individuality and repressive performance, leading to the development of field-independent traits. Some studies suggest that the average Hispanic American is more field dependent than the average Anglo American (Saracho, 1991). This distinction has been attributed to the traditional child-rearing practices of Hispanic families, which emphasize social integrative values with the result that children tend to be more socially oriented. Middle-class Anglo families focus on assertiveness, autonomy, and a more individualistic sense of self-identity.

The assumption that all Hispanic American children have a field-dependent, prosocial orientation has not been supported by all researchers (Saracho, 1991). Through a series of studies, Saracho found that some Mexican American children made more analytic inferences while reading, a behavior that is indicative of field independence. Attempting to generalize about social orientation and cognitive style in Hispanic American children is impossible, especially at early ages, and cognitive styles are relative, not absolute.

The findings from Saracho's (1991) study challenged the assumption about Mexican American children's being field dependent and the relationship of field dependence to social competence. The cognitive styles of the children ranged from field dependent to field independent, with the field-independent children being more popular than their field-dependent peers. Dependent children were observed more often to reject other dependent children, whereas independent children selected other independent children as playmates. Physical, block, and manipulative play activities were selected by the independent children more often than by the dependent children. Independent children participated in social play areas more than did dependent children.

Saracho (1991) found field-independent children better able to solve social problems, and classroom teachers evaluated independent children as more socially competent than dependent children. Independent children also received higher scores on sociometric nominations, engaged in more social play, and initiated their own play activities more often. Furthermore, both dependent and independent children selected the independent children more often as playmates. Although the academic superiority of the independent children may have influenced teacher and peer selections, the findings are in conflict with the assumption that dependent children are more socially competent; they also call into question the notion that Mexican American children are primarily field dependent in cognitive style.

A related issue pertains to the relative effects of instrument and examiner on the measurement of the cognitive styles and capabilities of Hispanic American children. Selecting test instruments without bias toward someone has proven to be a nearly impossible task (Bauermeister, Berrios, Jimenez, Acevedo, & Gordon, 1990). Test developers try to reduce the bias of each test, but guarantees are never given. For the child whose native language is not English, this presents an additional problem (Aguilar-Gaxiola, 1994; Aguilar-Gaxiola & Gray, 1994). Researchers are continuously developing better instruments, some written in different languages or having been normed on culturally diverse populations (Bauermeister et al., 1990). Earlier research demonstrated that students tested by examiners of the same culture received scores higher than students tested by examiners of a different culture. Fuchs and Fuchs (1989) checked the effects of familiarity on the scores of African American, Hispanic, and Caucasian students and found evidence of significant differences. Minority students (African and Hispanic American) scored significantly and dramatically higher with familiar examiners, whereas Caucasian students performed similarly in familiar and unfamiliar examiner conditions. These results suggest not only that factors such as the instrument used (Bauermeister et al., 1990) and the cultural background of the examiner affect student scores but that the examiner's familiarity with the students can play a part as well (Fuchs & Fuchs, 1989).

Behaviors

Interpersonal Behaviors

LaGreca (1983) described interpersonal behaviors as classifiable into seven major areas: smiling, greeting others, joining current peer activities, extending invitations to others, conversing, sharing and cooperating, and complimenting others. Some studies with elementary-aged students revealed that teacher social skill ratings for Mexican Americans on average were equal to or higher than those for European Americans (Carlson & Stephens, 1986; Casas, Furlong, Solberg, & Carranza, 1990). Mexican American students are often described as being cooperative, quiet, and obedient. Hispanic American females, especially, were viewed by teachers as passive and docile (Moore, 1988).

Reciprocity is regarded as an important principle in social skill training programs; it requires not only that a child emit behaviors that are rewarding but also that others reinforce the child for emitting these behaviors. The paired nature of these behaviors determines whether the initial behavior will persist. If a child emits a behavior and is not reinforced or is punished, she or he may choose alternative behaviors, some of which may be socially inappropriate. Kafer (1982) suggests that teachers need to determine the reason or purpose behind inappropriate behavior before beginning social skill training. The teacher who knows why an inappropriate behavior is occurring will not be tempted to believe that the behavior is due only to a deficiency.

Carlson and Stephens (1986) noted social skill difficulties that were linguistically based. These difficulties were seen in Mexican American students' failure to initiate verbal behavior and to respond appropriately on cue. The authors identified a set of 13 behavioral deficiencies that pertained to various verbal acts such as initiating positive statements and compliments, discussing feelings, and offering opinions. Along the same lines, Moore (1988) observed more language-based leadership skills among Anglo students than among Mexican American students. In this study, teachers observed Anglo and Mexican American students during a cooperative group game and rated Anglo students as evidencing significantly more leadership behaviors (in terms of verbal interruptions and speaking time) than their Hispanic peers.

Task-Related Behaviors

A major concern regarding Hispanic American students involves poor academic achievement and low high school graduation rates. Several authorities note that Hispanic Americans lag behind the national averages, as well as those of other minority groups, in graduation and school achievement (Bernal et al., 1991; Casas et al., 1990; Matute-Bianchi, 1986; Moll, 1988; Moore, 1988). In examining factors associated with school failure for Mexican American youth, Casas et al. found that in contrast to their low-achieving Anglo peers, low-achieving Mexican Americans demonstrated a more positive attitude toward academic achievement and appeared to desire an education. Mexican American students also differed from their peers in considering that pregnancy was not a good reason for dropping out of school but that more legitimate reasons included falling behind in school, being needed to help out with the family, or hanging out with friends. Considering the significantly lower achievement scores and greater indications of life stressors among Mexican American students, Casas et al. point to a need for intensive academic assistance to address low achievement and social skill instruction to improve the ability to cope with problems of daily living.

In some cases, it is the teacher who plays the key role in the success or failure of Hispanic American students. Moll (1988) looked at the characteristics of teachers whose Latino students attained high rates of academic success. The findings showed several significant factors that influenced these students. First and second were the intellectual level of the curriculum and the importance of the curriculum content. Did the teacher challenge the students with a rigorous curriculum? How much time was the teacher willing to devote to creating, clarifying, expanding, and monitoring student understanding? Students are more attentive to lessons that have meaning and force them to "stretch." The next two factors were the diversity of instruction and the use of the students' experience. As Moll points out, by using and allowing others to use different modes of instruction, teachers can give all students the opportunity to interact with the content in unique ways.

Self-Related Behaviors

Compared to their Anglo peers, Hispanic American youth evidence more daily stress and depression (Aguilar-Gaxiola & Gray, 1994; Casas et al., 1990; Hoernicke, Kallam, & Tablada, 1994; Inclan & Herron, 1989; Ramirez, 1989). Casas et al. indicate that Mexican American students reported having more numerous and more serious stressors, which included being new in classes, having friends move away, feeling peer pressure, lacking privacy at home, fearing for their physical safety, and worrying about changes in family composition. They also reported greater fears of dying, with one-quarter having experienced the death of a parent within the past year. Hoernicke et al. identify additional stressors related to "problems in cultural identity, conflicting demands from parents and peer groups, problems in maintaining their primary language, inadequate knowledge of English, economically depressed and stressful home situations, and racial and ethnic intolerance on the part of peers" (p. 118).

The higher level of stress and the greater incidence of emotional problems such as phobias and depression (Inclan & Herron, 1989) undoubtedly lead to disturbances in relationships with other children and to substance abuse. According to Ramirez (1989), Mexican Americans are 14 times as likely as their Anglo counterparts to abuse inhalants. Additionally, the use of alcohol, stimulants, tranquilizers, and heroin is significantly higher in small Mexican American communities than in the nation as a whole.

The previously noted interpersonal, task-related, and self-related problems are accentuated during adolescence; the result may be economic and social incompetence. For a significant minority of Hispanic American youth, the negative influences of poverty, inadequate schooling, urban living conditions, and psychological alienation contribute to a focus on aggression and violence. Hispanic youth account for approximately 33 percent of the 120,636 current gang members in the United States (Soriano, 1993). Homicide rates for Hispanic youth are estimated to be three or four times higher than those for their nonminority age-mates (Hammond & Yung, 1993). Other young people who fall prey to academic underachievement, substance abuse, and premature parenting are also at risk for marginality in this society (Menon, Barrett, & Simpson, 1990; Sciarra, Ponterotto, Bruase, & Alexander, 1994). Programs designed to strengthen the ability to cope with daily stressors; to encourage the development of positive, productive relationships; and to reduce the attractiveness of antisocial gang behavior are critical for many Hispanic American children and youth.

Social Skill Interventions

To access educational, social, and employment environments in the most effective ways, the Hispanic American youngster needs to learn the necessary social skills. Using information gained from studies of ethnic minorities, educators are able to adapt academic and social skill instruction so that immigrants, refugees, or their descendants can participate fully and not be subjugated or marginalized in this society. In order for critical learning to occur, educators must be aware of the distinctions that characterize Hispanic American children. This awareness allows teachers to personalize social skill instruction according to their students' cultural identities.

Cultural Scripts

A cultural script is a pattern of social interaction that is characteristic of a particular cultural group. In Hispanic cultures, various Spanish terms are used to describe social interactions and particular behavioral styles. *Simpatia*, which refers to a permanent personal quality, indicates that an individual is perceived as likable, attractive, fun to be with, and easygoing (Triandis, Marin, Lisansky, & Betancourt, 1984). Other common terms are used to designate group as well as gender-specific behavioral characteristics (Paniagua, 1994; Ramirez, 1989). *Machismo*, for example, is used to describe physical strength, sexual attractiveness, masculinity, aggressiveness, and an ability to consume excessive amounts of alcohol without getting drunk. Men with machismo are expected to get *respecto,* or respect, from others. Children are expected to give respect to authority figures such as parents and elders. For women there is the term *marianismo,* which designates them as submissive, obedient, dependent, timid, docile, sentimental, gentle, and virginal until marriage. Women are expected to assume traditional domestic duties and, at the same time, to be spiritually superior to men and to endure all the suffering occasioned by men. The emphasis on the family relationship, which is the source of emotional and financial support, is referred to as *familismo*. *Personalismo* is associated with being people oriented and expecting physical closeness and contact in personal interactions. *Individualisimo* implies the uniqueness of the individual and the fact that this leads to cooperation rather than competition—that is, "everyone has something to offer" (Paniagua, 1994, p. 42). *Fatalismo* is used to describe a sense of vulnerability, a perception that one cannot control or prevent adversity.

The importance of the cultural script decreases as the group is assimilated into the majority. Second-generation Hispanic Americans will not necessarily follow the same script as their parents because increasing time spent in the new country lessens the ties to the home country, and children often adapt to new customs more quickly than adults (Ramirez, 1989). Recent immigrants and refugees may also differ in their scripts. Immigrants seeking a new and better life, with a desire to establish themselves permanently, revere and relish their new country's language and culture. On the other hand, refugees seeking temporary shelter may be slow in assuming behaviors and mannerisms of their adopted culture. With the variety of reasons underlying their immigration to this country, the Hispanic groups differ in their rates of assimilation. If people do not plan to return to their native country, they are more willing to accept the new country's ways; and if they do aspire to return, they will continue to perpetuate their former ways. Teachers and others hoping to meet the needs of children from different cultural backgrounds must implement various strategies and techniques that will help the children assimilate into this nation without compromising their cultural integrity.

Interventions with Hispanic American populations have focused largely on language differences and the related difficulties that affect academic and social competence. Some of these strategies have implications for direct and indirect social learning. In addition to teaching social skills directly, teachers and other professionals need to be aware of social conditions within the school that may have negative impact on the social development and overall school success of language minority students. The following section, which focuses on language and the related implications for social skill teaching, also highlights factors important to the three major Hispanic American subgroups and suggests applications for direct instruction and peer-based interventions.

The Importance of Language

Language is a critical consideration in the academic and social learning of Hispanic youth. Language among Hispanic American students varies greatly. Many may be monolingual Spanish speakers, others may be bilingual in Spanish and English, and yet others may know mostly English and perhaps only rudimentary Spanish (Hoernicke, Kallam, & Tablada, 1994). Bilingual education or instruction in English as a second language (ESL) is considered by many to be the first step in educating Hispanic American students (Fradd & Correa, 1989). Fradd and Correa document at least one court ruling stating that failure to address the special needs of linguistically diverse students contributed to their high dropout rate; the schools were ordered to provide educational programs for those students. The Hispanic immigrant population has grown dramatically over recent years, and with nearly 40 percent of this group being of school age or younger, increasing attention is being given to effective ways to teach non-English-speaking learners (Fradd & Correa, 1989; Lacey, 1995). Procedures for teaching linguistically different students vary. Ravetta and Brunn (1995) suggest that these approaches typically follow either a "submersion" model, where students spend all their time in classes with native English speakers and receive no additional organized instruction in language, or a pull-out model, where students receive ESL instruction for a designated period in the school day. Although schools appear to have had more success with non-English-speaking students at the elementary than at the secondary level, problems in language use and school performance are noted at both levels (Lacey, 1995; Ravetta & Brunn, 1995). Where younger children are concerned, Ravetta and Brunn refer to research indicating that the time needed to acquire conversational or surface language facility is much less than the time needed to acquire the second language skills essential for academic competence. They advocate a more natural approach to learning language, arguing that language is acquired best when it is used to transmit messages during periods of lower anxiety, not when the focus is solely on language learning.

The importance of language learning to social development is evident in the role of language in social interaction. Social relationships are predicated on social communication skills or pragmatics. That is, the ability to transmit and receive messages skillfully determines to some degree whether one is accepted and valued by others (Cartledge & Kleefeld, 1989). Language facility aids in social interaction, and there also is some indication that language may be learned most effectively within a social context. Ravetta and Brunn (1995) present a case study of a 7-year-old Spanish-speaking girl who was submerged into an English-speaking elementary class without additional English instruction. The child interacted with her bilingual classmates in cooperative learning, social, and reading activities that permitted her to speak Spanish at will. The researchers observed that the child's peers switched between English and Spanish according to the child's apparent level of understanding. Ravetta and Brunn concluded that these conditions, where English was acquired slowly and naturally, not only facilitated the child's ability to communicate but helped her develop friendly relationships and an understanding of what was occurring in the class.

At the secondary level, Lacey (1995) also argues for greater integration of Spanish-speaking students into mainstream programs to enhance their academic and social growth. Many non-English-speaking students are tracked into ESL classes for all 4 years of high school. This practice results in a second-rate, segregated education and limits their opportunities to learn English and interact with their mainstream peers. Lacey followed the 4-year high school progress of 70 students enrolled in an ESL program. Of the original 70 students, only 20 graduated from high school and only 2 were mainstreamed into regular classes by the senior year. The negative academic impact can be seen in the group's high dropout rate and poor academic achievement. The average grade achievement level for the remaining seniors was 7.8, with a range of 4.4 to 10.8. Students in ESL took only general education courses, with no opportunity to move to more advanced courses. These conditions also threatened the students' personal and social development. Lacey reported that the teachers expressed negative opinions about the students—for example, that the Mexican American students were simply trying to take advantage of the United States and that they did not value education. Additionally, they labeled the students as lazy, infantile, hedonistic, and likely to experience premature parenting. The ESL students also expressed frustration. They wanted to be in learning situations where they would be forced to use English. They wanted to take courses according to their personal interests, not at the discretion of the counselor, and they felt that regular courses could have helped them overcome their fears of speaking and interacting with the English-speaking population. Despite these students' expressed desire for greater integration, peer-based social factors presented substantial impediments for them. Students in ESL were at risk of being ridiculed and ostracized by both their Spanish-speaking and their English-speaking classmates. Many students were reluctant to leave the ESL classes for fear of being accused by their fellow ESL students of trying to "act White." ESL students often were ridiculed by English-speaking Hispanic American or Chicano students for speaking Spanish; ESL students in turn criticized Chicano students for being ashamed of their background. Poor treatment by mainstream teachers and peers often led ESL students to return to ESL programs.

The teacher attitudes and actions noted by Lacey (1995) are by no means universal. Necochea and Cline (1995), for example, report that many of the teachers in their training program expressed genuine concern for their linguistically different students and actively sought ways to educate them. There is agreement, however, that too many language minority students are placed in mainstream classes with teachers who are not prepared to teach them. Although recommended procedures would vary somewhat between elementary and secondary levels, following are some general guidelines for school programs to maximize the academic and social development of language minority students:

1. Provide support for learning English, but integrate students into mainstream programs as soon and as extensively as possible.

2. Structure mainstream classes so that language minority students are not isolated; include additional students with similar backgrounds.

3. Provide mainstream teachers with inservice training on multi-cultural education and teaching language minority students.

4. Incorporate students' linguistic and cultural backgrounds into instruction to engender pride on the part of Hispanic-background students and respect on the part of non-Hispanic students.

5. Prepare mainstream students to be supportive of non-English-speaking classmates.

6. Provide a supportive classroom climate for non-English-speaking students to try out their English skills.

7. Provide direct instruction to non-English-speaking students to develop critical skills relative to verbal assertion and dealing with ridicule.

8. Structure classroom environments to foster positive peer interactions across language, social, and racial groups.

9. Model accepting and helping attitudes toward language minority students.

Literacy and Social Learning

Reading instruction and other literacy activities provide a means for incorporating the learner's language and cultural background into learning that leads to academic and social growth. According to Maldonado-Colon (1993), traditional approaches to reading that fail to integrate the learner's cultural background risk causing the learner to lose interest because of obscure concepts and fail to make meaningful connections between the instructional materials and the learner's own life. Maldonado-Colon recommends a teaching approach she labels "strategic application of cultural resources." Teachers are to select reading material reflecting "issues that are meaningful and relevant to these students—issues that will tap their funds of personal experiential knowledge, issues that will enable them to perceive through their dialogue different perspectives and instances of actualization" (p. 2). Maldonado-Colon cites as examples two books by Tomie de Paola, *The Legend of the Bluebonnet* (1983) and *The Legend of the Indian Paintbrush* (1988), which deal with aspects of giving. In the first story, a little girl gives up her most treasured possession to secure the welfare of her tribe; in the second, a boy discovers how to share a talent with his group. Discussions of both books center on the ways in which the characters give to others, the effects of these actions, and the emotions they might have evoked. Students are helped to personalize these experiences, considering ways in which they may have given in the past or may want to give in the future. The same theme might be pursued in Spanish with a book such as *La Moneda de Oro* (Ada, 1991), the story of an old woman who goes about doing good through giving and sharing. A young man, who initially follows the old woman for selfish gain, instead acquires similar altruistic behaviors. Maldonado-Colon (1993) further recommends the use of semantic maps and diagrams to help students clearly identify concepts, make proper associations, and relate them to their own lives. She points out that through such graphic displays students "not only capture visually a series of apparently unrelated concepts, but display a set of collected or aggregated information which lends itself rather well for further reflective thinking and critical dialogue" (p. 4).

To illustrate, Maldonado-Colon (1993) uses a Venn diagram to help students integrate knowledge gained from stories and make personal applications. Three overlapping circles are drawn. On one side of the left circle, the key action of the principal character of the first book is noted (e.g., "Female gives in order to improve conditions"). In the right circle, similar information is written for the main character of the second book (e.g., "Male gives in order to please others"). In the space where the two circles overlap, the common traits of both main characters are noted (e.g., "strong," "children," and so forth). In the third circle, designated as "me," the learner is asked to note what he or she shares with the book characters. According to Maldonado-Colon, this procedure helps students to reflect on their lives as well as to organize their thinking and their words.

Fletcher and Cardona-Morales (1990) likewise point out the importance of semantic mapping in literacy learning for minority language children. They recommend, as part of this activity, having children write down on their own as many words they can think of that relate to the key concept. The words are then shared with the group and used to make a map of the students' interpretations. The teacher can deliberately program social skill understanding into this process; for example, by having the students generate a list of the many ways they have given or could engage in giving. The group could extend the map by identifying emotions and possible outcomes associated with each type of giving. Helping students find commonalities among readings as well as in their own lives, Maldonado-Colon (1993) contends, provides for "coherent whole, rather than fragmented learnings" (p. 5). In addition to reading, she recommends that students expand on these learnings through other literacy activities such as writing in interactive journals, recording personal experiences, and writing original stories.

Related strategies involve building on the students' oral history tradition and using a storytelling format in which students are encouraged to join in and supply possibilities for subsequent actions. For example, the teacher might pause and ask, "What do you think [the main character] will do to solve this problem?" (Maldonado-Colon, 1991). Students may be encouraged to generate several possible endings and then select the best ones for particular contexts. The language experience approach is considered an especially useful way to structure activities of this nature for second-language students (Fletcher & Cardona-Morales, 1990; Maldonado-Colon, 1991). Together, students and teacher generate thoughts that are recorded on the chalkboard. The teacher guides the students through a discussion that helps them to clarify their thinking and organize material into a logical, meaningful sequence. To continue with the theme of giving, for instance, students could be guided through simple scenarios where failing to give or share resulted in undesired consequences such as isolation and general unhappiness, whereas generosity and genuine altruism produced more positive peer interactions.

A further adaptation would be for students to receive story starters presenting conflict situations. In small groups students would collaborate to generate story endings that were logical and that also incorporated prosocial solutions. In large groups, students would present and critique their endings. Oral language, concept development, and social learning would be further enhanced if students were invited to role-play both the original story and the stories with their constructed endings, pointing out the most productive outcomes and the specific actions that produced them.

Written language experiences are an obvious extension and integral component of the reading process. Fletcher and Cardona-Morales (1990) advocate systematic instruction in written expressive language, with content and ideas emphasized over mechanics. One recom-mended form is the dialogue journal, a vehicle for personal commu-nication between student and teacher. The student makes regular entries in a personal journal; the teacher reads the entries and responds as appropriate. Dialogue journals are considered particularly valu-able for second-language or reluctant learners because they stress communication rather than the mechanics of writing, students tend to be motivated to write in them, and they "provide a means for teachers to become more aware of each student's interests and con-cerns" (Fletcher & Cardona-Morales, 1990, p. 168). The latter point is particularly relevant for social skill instruction. Students might use these journals to log especially problematic social situations. They might share certain situations with the teacher, note their progress with a particular skill, and request special advice or assis-tance from the classroom teacher or the social skill trainer. A further benefit of dialogue journals is that they provide opportunities to personalize instruction without bringing students' specific problems to the attention of the entire group.

The attractiveness of dialogue journals might be enhanced through the medium of electronic mail (e-mail). Most schools are sufficiently equipped that students have ready access to computers. With their personal e-mail codes, students have private mailboxes through which they may communicate with teachers, counselors, and others. The novelty of e-mail communication is likely to motivate students to engage in these instructional dialogues. Maldonado-Colon (1993) asserts that participatory language-based activities rep-resent the best pedagogy and the most empowering experiences for language minority learners. The higher-level cognitive and writing activities are especially beneficial for older students.

Instruction through Literature

In addition to helping students become more literate, books by and about Hispanic Americans can be useful in helping young people form healthy identities and deal with real-life personal and social issues. Barton (1995) exposed fourth-grade Hispanic American stu-dents with varying levels of English proficiency to multicultural picture books. With assistance from adult tutors, the students read the books and identified cultural features in the stories. At the end of a 6-month period, the students attributed an average of 6.9 cultural influences to themselves, compared to an average of 2.9 prior to the intervention. According to Barton, these multicultural readings aided in the learners' cultural identity formation and helped them see commonalities between themselves and others they previously considered different. The importance of culturally based literature for the development of positive self-identity and self-esteem is noted by Walter Dean Myers (1989; cited in de Cortes, 1992):

> Through reading the literature that reflects their own cultural experiences, through learning of their history, and through seeing themselves in the literature for children, then perhaps minority youngsters too can begin to see a future for themselves in a society that every day continues to demand more intellectual output than they are currently prepared for. (p. 123)

Beginning in early childhood, children need experiences with literature that reflects their race, culture, heritage, and daily living situations. De Cortes (1992) presents an annotated bibliography of fiction and nonfiction books for children and adolescents that focus on the Hispanic and Hispanic American experience. In compiling this bibliography, de Cortes relates, she had difficulty locating sufficient numbers of appropriate books. She points out that many of the titles are published by small publishing houses and do not appear in the index of *Children's Books in Print 1990–91*. Additionally, she reports a dearth of materials for young adults, with more nonfiction than fiction works about Hispanics for children and youth. To explain the latter shortfall, de Cortes suggests that authors outside the culture find it easier to write factual literature that tends to be less subject to criticism. Most of the books listed by de Cortes pertain to Mexican Americans, with a representative number about Puerto Ricans. Particularly scarce are books on the Cuban American experience. People working with this subgroup may need to tap literary resources within Cuban American communities to obtain similarly relevant materials. As vehicles for transmitting the culture, many of the books for young children (preschool to grade 3) are bilingual, written in Spanish and English, and have religious, spiritual, and family themes. An example of a bilingual story with a religious theme is *A Chicano Christmas Story/Un Cuento Navideno Chicano* (Manuel & Cruz, 1980). This is a story of a poor young immigrant child who learns about the Santa Claus tradition in the U.S. He experiences the generosity of others and comes to understand the meaning and significance of giving. Information about more traditional Mexican Christmas practices can be found in books like *The Farolitos of Christmas* (Anaya, 1987) and *Rosita's Christmas Wish* (Bruni, 1985). Both books depict in story form long-standing traditions. Another bilingual offering that is more informative regarding Mexican American culture and family life is *Family Pictures/Cuadros de Familia* (Garza & Rohmer, 1990). In this beautifully illustrated book by one of the country's finest Mexican American artists, the author relates aspects of her childhood in a Mexican American town in Texas. Aspects of Puerto Rican culture and family life are shared in *Yaqua Days* (Martel, 1987), the story of a young boy from New York who visits the place in Puerto Rico where his father grew up.

The difficulties of being different and being an immigrant are portrayed in some of the books written for young children. In *The Adventures of Connie and Diego/Las Aventuras de Connie y Diego* (Garcia, 1987), a sister and brother born in a fictitious land tire of being taunted because of their skin color and run away. During their adventures they learn to appreciate differences and to accept themselves. *I Speak English for My Mom* (Stanek, 1989) details the difficulties of an immigrant, female-headed family in which the young daughter is required to translate everything for her mother. The strong mother-daughter relationship is further strengthened when the girl helps her mother to learn English and become more self-sufficient. Lessons about self-determination and empowerment can be drawn from two fictionalized biographies of females who achieve against the odds to become scientists: a Puerto Rican American woman (*Scientist from Puerto Rico, Maria Cordero Hardy;* Verheyden-Hilliard, 1985a) and a Mexican American woman (*Scientist with Determination, Elma Gonzalez;* Verheyden-Hilliard, 1985b).

The books identified by de Cortes (1992) for the intermediate level (grades 4 through 6) deal largely with the experiences and difficulties of immigration, particularly for Mexican Americans. One such story, *Lupita Mañana* (Beatty, 1981), tells of the hardships that caused two adolescents to immigrate to the United States and the difficulties they experience trying to survive without the benefit of education or knowledge of the language. A somewhat different immigrant portrait is *Hector Lives in the United States Now: The Story of a Mexican-American Child* (Hewett, 1990), which concerns a 10-year-old boy who lives a typical lifestyle in California as a result of changes in immigration laws.

Felita (Mohr, 1989) is about the taunting and discrimination a girl experiences when her family moves out of the Puerto Rican American community. Stories of this nature may be particularly useful in helping students identify constructive ways to respond to peer taunting prompted by differences. As noted previously, linguistically different youth are likely to shy away from valuable and challenging opportunities for fear of the reactions of peers and others. For these youngsters, positive, affirming stories such as *Class President* (Hurwitz, 1990) can be very appealing and encouraging. In this story, a child of Puerto Rican heritage is low in self-confidence but exhibits admirable leadership skills, leading his non-Hispanic classmates to elect him class president.

Some of the books identified by de Cortes (1992) contain stories from the overlooked Hispanic American history. An example is *Vilma Martinez* (Codye, 1990), an inspirational account of a Mexican American woman who became a lawyer and successfully challenged laws that discriminated against her people. Other examples of books about noted personalities include *Our Tejano Heroes: Outstanding Mexican-Americans in Texas* (Munson, 1989), *Cesar Chavez and La Causa* (Roberts, 1986a), and *Henry Cisneros: Mexican American Mayor* (Roberts, 1986b).

Issues pertaining to the stresses of the Hispanic American immigrant experience continue to be prominent in the literature selections for junior high youth (grades 7 to 9), but at this level, in addition to Mexican Americans (*Across the Great River;* Beltran Hernandez, 1989), the works feature South Americans (*The South Americans;* Gullison, 1991) and Dominican Americans (*The Dominican Americans;* Dwyer, 1991). The latter two books not only detail specific immigrant experiences but also note the group's achievements in architecture, sports, social work, and fashion. *New Kids on the Block: Oral Histories of Immigrant Teens* (Bode, 1989) depicts the immigrant experience through interviews of teens from various

Hispanic countries. The narrators relate their unique experiences, such as living as illegal immigrants and adjusting to a more permissive, crime-ridden society.

Two books for this age group are particularly noteworthy for their attention to typical social experiences of Hispanic teens: *El Bronx Remembered: A Novella and Stories* (Mohr, 1986a) and *Baseball in April: And Other Stories* (Soto, 1990). Both books are collections of short stories about everyday events, but as de Cortes (1992) states, "The importance of these stories to Hispanic youth lies in their ability to transform simple everyday events steeped in a familiar culture into meaningful, memorable literary works" (p. 148). Although the concerns and conflicts expressed in the stories are universal, their portrayal of Hispanic culture may help young readers apply them to their own lives. One of the few books on Cuban Americans is *Luisa's American Dream* (Mills, 1981). Although the main character, Luisa, is a typical teenager in many ways, the story shows how the pressures of adolescence are compounded by minority group membership, low socioeconomic status, and language difference. Luisa struggles with her pursuit of a romantic interest and the shame she feels over her family background.

Although the selections are limited, at the high school level (grades 10 through 12) more attention is given to self-identity and to social and political issues. For example, *Bless Me, Ultima: A Novel* (Anaya, 1972), considered a classic of Chicano literature, describes a year in which a faith healer, who is the object of much controversy, lives in the home of a Hispanic American youth. During this period the youth deals with issues related to self-discovery, compassion, family conflict, and community conflict. The themes of interpersonal conflict and antisocial behavior run through three major works identified by de Cortes (1992): *In Nueva York* (Mohr, 1988), *Famous All Over Town* (Santiago, 1983), and *Living up the Street: Narrative Recollections* (Soto, 1985). In *Famous All Over Town*, for example, the author depicts gang and conflict situations typical among youngsters in the barrios of Los Angeles. The main character is a 14-year-old youth who lives with his sister after the separation of their parents. According to de Cortes, the author of this highly praised book presents the events "authentically, without heavy-handedness or sensationalism" (p. 154).

Key Issues for Different Populations

Hispanic Americans are united by language and influence of Spanish culture, but they differ greatly in historical background, race, and certain aspects of cultural tradition. Because of these differences in their backgrounds and their circumstances in the United States, as Banks (1991) notes, students will present different issues to be addressed in the classroom. These issues have implications as well for the social development of young people in the various groups. According to Banks, the major concerns for Mexican Americans are immigrant status, stereotyping, and social protest. Next to Native Americans, Mexican Americans are the second oldest group of residents of this country, but they often see themselves as a conquered people. Because of their surnames, they are often stereotyped as foreigners. For example, long-term residents are often asked their country of origin or the pronunciation of their names.

For primary-aged children, Banks (1991) presents a scenario that might be useful in social skills instruction. It involves a young Mexican American child from the Southwest whose family had lived in the United States for at least a century. The father, an engineer, was transferred to a position in the Midwest. In school in the new community, the son's teacher had trouble pronouncing the boy's name and understanding that he was a citizen of this country. For social skill instruction, the teacher could ask students how they feel when they encounter such misunderstandings and could explore with students assertive ways of responding (e.g., "I'm from this country; my family has lived in _____ for _____ years. My ancestors came from _____. Where did yours come from? Would you like to learn something about the state of _____ [child's previous state]? Would you like to learn some Spanish words?"). The important social skill in this situation involves responding in a friendly but assertive way. Instruction should focus on steering a path between aggressive and passive reactions. Students should understand that questions of this nature often arise from ignorance and are not always meant to be offensive. For non-Hispanic children, this discussion would be a good opportunity to learn about their country's diversity and to imagine how it would feel to be treated as if one did not belong in one's own land.

Newer Mexican American residents often experience ridicule and embarrassment, both from non-Hispanic Americans and from Hispanic American or Chicano residents with longer tenure (e.g., Lacey, 1995). Recent immigrant students are the most vulnerable to social and academic failure. Direct intervention is needed to help these students deal constructively with ostracism from peers and to help their more acculturated peers to be more understanding and compassionate in their interactions. Some of the literature noted previously might be useful in helping non-Hispanic youngsters understand the immigrant experience. These stories also might provide recent immigrants valuable models for handling negative reactions related to their status in U.S. society. Beyond simply learning to withstand the taunts of others, these students might learn creative responses such as using humor and enticing others to learn about and share in their rich cultural heritage. If linguistically different students are to persevere in their efforts to achieve and be successful in this country, they must retain their pride in their identity. Banks (1991) suggests several learning activities centered on Mexican Americans that would enlighten non-Hispanics while contributing to greater self-knowledge and self-regard for both Chicanos and recent immigrants. In addition to direct instruction, support systems can ensure that linguistically different students are not isolated in classes without other students of similar backgrounds. At the same time, it is important to create groups that are heterogeneous (in terms of race, culture, gender, and ability) for cooperative learning and tutoring experiences.

For Puerto Ricans, Banks (1991) notes the salient issues of cultural conflict, racism, and colonialism. Though U.S. society is sharply divided along racial lines, it is quite common for Puerto Rican families to include members who span a continuum of colors or races. Upon coming to the mainland, they may find their very family members categorized into racial groups and contact among them minimized. Our adaptation from Banks (1991) reflects such a situation:

Two friends or cousins may have been quite close in
Puerto Rico. One looked Caucasian, and one *de color*.
When they started attending school in the mainland,
they gradually spent less and less time with each other.

The white youth stopped visiting his dark friend and felt that he should socialize only with whites.

Students might be taken through a valuing exercise noting the most important attributes of good friends (e.g., loyalty, honesty, sense of humor, shared interests, etc.). The least important characteristics might be appearance, race, clothes, and money. The discussion could explore why friendships with people who place too much importance on superficial features might be less rewarding.

Puerto Ricans are a unique group in several ways. First of all, because they are U.S. citizens, they are not truly immigrants, although they may be treated as such. Moreover, people of Puerto Rican background who live on the mainland are in the unique position of experiencing rejection from Puerto Ricans still living on the island. *Nuyorican*, a term applied to Puerto Ricans living in New York, initially was used pejoratively by Puerto Rican intellectuals who felt that the former could not legitimately identify themselves as Puerto Ricans because they were not fluent in Spanish. Acosta-Belen (1993) points out that rejection by island Puerto Ricans only compounds the marginalization many Puerto Rican Americans experience in this country. The literature of Nuyoricans (see Acosta-Belen, 1993) addresses their feelings of being caught between several worlds: the island of Puerto Rico, the New York Puerto Rican culture, and the larger U.S. culture. The pain of a child treated as a Nuyorican is conveyed in a children's book entitled *Going Home* (Mohr, 1986b). De Cortes (1992) describes this book as the story of a young girl's excitement over spending the summer in Puerto Rico, away from the domination of her parents. Instead, she finds that she and her brothers are taunted as "gringos" and "Nuyoricans." The book also deals with the emotions associated with growing independence, new friendship, and extended family. Literary works such as those noted here may be useful in addressing feelings aroused by rejection or taunting from island Puerto Ricans.

Direct Instruction

As discussed in chapter 2 of this book, direct instruction involves a prescribed, structured format to help students acquire a specific academic or social skill. The instruction is directed by the teacher, with allowance for some input from the students about the focus of the lesson or the direction in which the lesson should move. Once learners have basic mastery of the skill, they are given opportunities to personalize the learning and apply their creativity in adapting it to their own unique interests. In other words, the previously scripted language is transformed into a variety of different scripts directed by the learners. The use of direct instruction in social skills holds special advantages for Hispanic students, who are less inclined to use language and open-ended approaches to explore issues surrounding social behavior and feelings. By recognizing the importance of students' backgrounds, teachers can organize and present information in ways to reflect the students' heritage and personal experiences. A study by Carlson and Stephens (1986) with Mexican American children, noted previously in this chapter, revealed language-based social skill problems relative to verbal initiations and responses. Specifically, the researchers identified the following skill deficiencies that distinguished the Mexican American children from their Anglo peers:

Failure to initiate verbal behavior

> Makes positive statements about the qualities and accomplishments of others
>
> Compliments others
>
> Apologizes for hurting or infringing on others
>
> Describes one's feelings or moods verbally
>
> Initiates and assists in conducting a group activity

Failure to respond appropriately on cue

> Answers when asked about wrongdoing
>
> Makes relevant remarks in class discussions
>
> Participates in class discussions
>
> Shares relevant items in class discussions
>
> Discusses contrary opinions in class discussions
>
> Provides reasons for opinions expressed
>
> Initiates and assists in conducting a group activity
>
> Participates in role playing (p. 197)

Carlson and Stephens (1986) also noted that Mexican American students had fewer problems dealing with conflict than their Anglo counterparts, a finding that perhaps reflected a cultural orientation toward passivity. This trait, coupled with a tendency toward "fatalism," may not serve students well when they deal with negative social conditions in school. This is particularly true for recent immigrants. As noted in studies by Hayes (1989/1990) and Lacey (1995), language minority students often experience peer ridicule and teacher insensitivity, which lead them to shy away from more challenging and rewarding school experiences. This suggests a need for direct instruction in effective coping strategies such as the following strategies for coping with conflict, outlined by Stephens (1992):

To respond to teasing or name-calling by ignoring, changing the subject, or using some other constructive means.

To respond to physical assault by leaving the situation, calling for help, or using some other constructive means.

To walk away from peer when angry to avoid hitting.

To refuse the request of another politely.

To express anger with nonaggressive words rather than physical action or aggressive words.

To handle constructively criticism or punishment perceived as undeserved. (p. 17)

A related set of skills that could be emphasized in direct instruction are useful for dealing with stress. As noted previously, Hispanic American students disproportionately report stress in their daily lives, and they experience higher levels of depression than their Anglo peers. Goldstein (1988) lists a set of skills for dealing with stress and provides instructional strategies that address these specific concerns:

Making a complaint

Answering a complaint

Sportsmanship after the game

Dealing with embarrassment

Dealing with being left out

Standing up for a friend

Responding to persuasion

Responding to failure

Dealing with contradictory messages

Dealing with an accusation

Getting ready for a difficult conversation

Dealing with group pressure (p. 304)

Instruction on managing conflict and stress would focus on helping students think positively about themselves while trying to identify constructive ways to ignore or react to the misguided and unkind actions of others (Malgady, Rogler, & Costantino, 1990). At the same time, students would come to understand the counterproductive effects of typical reactions such as leaving school, avoiding mainstream classes, or responding with counteraggression. Teachers also should aim to create classroom environments and plan instruction designed to help other students develop more accepting, friendly behaviors.

Stress-inoculation training as described by Meichenbaum (1977) or Novaco (1975) would be appropriate for the conditions just mentioned. In Meichenbaum's model, the learner is helped to understand the nature of the stressor and to prepare for it, to make self-statements that help him or her handle the stress, to recognize the emotional reactions that accompany the stressful situation, and to deliver self-reinforcement. A student dealing with ridicule in a mainstream classroom, for example, may be helped to prepare useful self-statements before entering the classroom (e.g., "They want to see me get upset," "I know I can avoid reacting emotionally," "I know I can do the work in this class"). The student is prompted to use the self-statements while in the class and to note in writing specific physical or emotional responses to classmates' taunting. After class, the student evaluates and, when appropriate, compliments him- or herself. The student might be guided through a few role-plays before being required to follow these steps in real-life situations.

For many Hispanic American adolescents, limited academic success and poor social conditions make antisocial options, often as embodied in gang cultures, especially attractive. Direct instruction in prosocial skills and alternatives to aggression are recommended for these youngsters (Darrah, 1986; Schwartz, 1989). Goldstein (1988) presents a 10-course program designed to teach critical social skills to adolescents inclined toward antisocial cultures. Within this curriculum he identifies a set of behaviors useful in helping students choose more productive ways to act. Goldstein (1988, p. 304) lists the following as skill alternatives to aggressive actions:

Asking permission

Sharing something

Helping others

Negotiating

Using self-control

Standing up for your rights

Responding to teasing

Avoiding trouble with others

Keeping out of fights

A number of curriculum programs (e.g., Cartledge & Kleefeld, 1991, 1994; Goldstein, 1988; Stephens, 1992) would be useful in teaching these and other skills. Other social skill curriculum programs feature cognitive-behavioral methods (Matson & Ollendick, 1988), developmental models (Schneider, Rubin, & Ledingham, 1985), behavioral models (Michelson, Sugai, Wood, & Kazdin, 1983; Strain, Guralnick, & Walker, 1986), and a variety of other approaches (Dowrick, 1986). To suggest that a single approach is suitable for all children would not be realistic. Social skill trainers need to adapt the approach to the specific backgrounds and interests of the learners. That is, as emphasized in chapter 4, on African American students, students should be encouraged to use their own words and communication styles following initial presentations. Soriano (1993) addresses the importance of communication styles and preferences for minority individuals, particularly those involved in gang cultures. He asserts that

lower class Chicanos and Hispanics tend to employ non-verbal communication along with Spanish . . . and . . .

[have] a preference for one-way communication, from an authority figure to the individual in question. . . . In general, effective communication requires that gang intervention workers and researchers not only understand the dominant language and the linguistic preferences and nuances of a particular cultural subgroup, but also pay particular attention to nonverbal behaviors and cues. (p. 445)

Peer-Based Approaches

Cooperative Learning

American education historically has focused on competition among students within classes or across schools. Students are taught to do their best in an attempt to outperform those less capable than themselves. The bell-curve mentality forces students into one category, excluding others. Maintaining one's place on the curve is incompatible with cooperation. If one is to be the best, then someone else must be less than the best. Cooperative learning is the opposite of competition: It seeks to allow all students a chance to excel by helping others to be the best that they can be (Cartledge & Milburn, 1995; Trueba & Delgado-Gaitan, 1985). Students promote and bolster their peers, assume responsibility for their own and their peers' learning, acquire and use group-related social skills such as decision making and trust building, and assess the group's intellectual and social growth (Vaughn & Lancelotta, 1986, 1990). In cooperative activities, each student has an equal chance to move forward, and shared responsibility and work form the basis for successful interpersonal interactions.

Cooperative learning may have special advantages for language minority students. Cooperative groups allow for a less stressful classroom atmosphere and more informal learning conditions, which often facilitate second language acquisition (Ravetta & Brunn, 1995). Although heterogeneous groupings are preferred, it is best not to isolate a language minority student in a group but rather to include at least one other student who is bilingual. However, it is crucial to make sure that each student (especially students less proficient in English) participates actively in the group. Under cooperative conditions, the language minority student may be tempted to participate as a "silent" member, permitting others to complete the tasks and assume all communication responsibilities. As noted in chapter 2, students need direct instruction in the techniques of cooperative learning, and the teacher might use this instruction as a means to address the special needs of Hispanic American learners. One suggestion is to review the steps for cooperative learning in both English and Spanish. For instance, a Spanish-speaking student may be asked to describe one or more of the instructional steps in English for the group, while a monolingual English-speaking student gives the same direction in Spanish (e.g., "Let's get started"/ "Vamos a comenzar" or "I need help"/ "Yo necesito ayudar"). Group members are expected to give one another corrective language feedback as warranted. That is, the Spanish-speaking student would provide corrective feedback on the directions given in Spanish by the English-speaking students and vice versa. Such procedures are intended to add to the comfort of language minority students in such settings as well as to enhance the pride of Hispanic American students who may not fully appreciate their own cultural heritage. An additional benefit may be that non-Hispanic students will better appreciate the difficulties experienced by linguistically different students and will grow in their respect for the language and cultural background of their language minority peers.

The success of cooperative learning depends in great part on the selection of appropriate tasks or assignments. Tasks that are too difficult will force less capable students to rely on others for continuous assistance; tasks that are too easy will eliminate the need for students to seek assistance from their peers. Considering that the academic achievement of Hispanic youths (particularly recent immigrants) tends to lag considerably behind that of their majority peers (Casas et al., 1990; Lacey, 1995), teachers must exercise caution not to set these students up for additional peer ridicule due to gross underachievement. Review materials and games are suggested because they control for the level of difficulty while allowing students to concentrate on the newly learned cooperative steps. Materials might be individualized so that each student responds mainly to items at his or her own level. For example, for a cooperative group practicing the reading of sight words, the teacher might identify an individual set of 15 to 20 words for each student. In each set the student would have 10 words that have been mastered, 5 words on the instructional level, and 5 unknown words. Groups would be structured so that every student had at least one other peer on the same level who might assist with unknown words. Such a configuration would allow meaningful practice for all students but would avoid singling out low-achieving students as the only ones to need help (Trueba & Delgado-Gaitan, 1985).

Similar modifications could be employed in other subject areas such as math, writing, and so forth. The Jigsaw Method (Aronson, 1978) may be particularly appropriate for these subjects. Jigsawing is a cooperative learning procedure in which each student becomes the expert on one portion of the material and is required to teach it to other members of the group. The teacher—for instance, in social studies—divides a topic into parts (e.g., "Five Major Community Helpers" or "Five Steps for Becoming Registered to Vote"). Each student or student pair is given one part, directions on how to research that part, and specifications for the type of information they are to obtain. Members from different teams who are studying the same parts meet, discuss their information, and then return to their groups to teach the information to their group-mates. Language minority students may need to work with partners instead of individually, but if pairs are used, the teacher should make sure that all students participate actively.

Jigsawing is an effective option for all children, especially young children. Many tasks or activities can be taught in cooperative groups when each child is responsible only for one step in the process. Groups of two or three can be used initially. Young children can be paired and allowed to perform simple games such as "blower and popper with bubbles, hider and seeker in the sand with hidden toys, filler and dumper with buckets and assorted materials" (Fad, Ross, & Boston, 1995, p. 31). Various activities can illustrate cooperation for groups of two or three. Acting out stories (e.g., "The Three Bears," "The Three Little Pigs," "The Three Little Kittens Who Lost Their Mittens"), planting a garden, or building a sand castle can introduce a child to other children in less structured situations and can encourage nonverbal communication (Fad et al., p. 32). The child who does not speak English or is not fluent may recognize enough commonalities in these informal activities to participate in some capacity. Young children may not feel that verbal communication is a requirement for cooperative play.

Cooperative learning groups need to be organized so more competent students are encouraged to prompt and model the desired behaviors on an ongoing basis for their less skilled peers. The models should be individuals whom the other students respect and will want to imitate. To facilitate smooth interaction, teachers assign roles to each group member—for example, recorder of peer performance, demonstrator of a certain task, initiator of positive statements, or any other role deemed necessary. Assigned specific roles, the students can observe how each group member functions and affects the collective outcome. Roles can be changed periodically to allow each member to sample the variety of choices and gain proficiency in all roles. Shifting roles may also be useful when the students must mediate disagreements between themselves or deal with lackadaisical performance of group members. Assigning roles can be an effective way to help students practice and monitor desired social skills such as making positive or encouraging statements to peers.

Peer Tutoring and Social Learning

Peer tutoring is a potentially effective means for addressing the social and academic needs of many Hispanic American students. Through direct instruction (e.g., Cooke, Heron, & Heward, 1983; Heward & Orlansky, 1992), students learn to serve as same-age or cross-age tutors for their peers. It is important to specify clearly the skills to be taught and learned, such as sight words, math facts, or social studies concepts. Students serving as tutors on a given day meet in a "tutor huddle" to practice the target items. They follow simple scripts in presenting the items to their peers—for example, asking the learner to identify the item, telling the learner to respond again if the answer is incorrect, giving the answer if it is incorrect on the second try, and telling the learner to repeat the answer after the tutor. Correct responses are followed by positive statements such as "Good job." After all target items are presented, the students practice the new material briefly with a game, which is followed by a simple assessment.

Cochran, Feng, Cartledge, and Hamilton (1993) used these procedures successfully in a cross-age tutoring study with fifth-grade tutors and second-grade tutees. Although the study involved African American males with behavior disorders, the procedures are equally appropriate for other students, including Hispanic American students who also have a history of limited school success. Tutoring, which was used extensively in the one-room schoolhouse of the past, has found its way back into the classroom because of its potential benefits for all participants. Students engaged in tutoring have gained in academic performance as well as in social skills. Teachers, who are being asked to complete more and more tasks during the limited school day, find that tutoring keeps students more actively involved in their education, promotes increased student interaction, and frees time for more one-on-one and group instruction.

Students serving as both tutors and tutees have demonstrated improved performance in various academic tasks when tutoring was the primary instructional strategy. Tutoring by nature requires interaction between two or more students. These tutoring interactions provide an opportunity for developing social skills. Establishing rules for tutoring structures the interactions so that the academic tasks that are their focus can be accomplished without problems or negative results. The rules can ensure that everyone stays on task and gets along in the process. This structure lets students know what is expected of them and, it is hoped, lets them meet and work with their fellow students at the same time. The role of tutor need not be restricted to high-performing students; even those who are usually seen as less capable can serve as tutors (e.g., Giesecke, Cartledge, & Gardner, 1993). All students benefit from the tutoring interactions: the tutees as they learn new information or skills and the tutors as they make academic gains and display altruism and positive behavior toward other students (Cochran et al., 1993; Giesecke et al., 1993).

Teachers have found that tutoring can be implemented with little effort. After the initial instruction of tutors, the teacher needs to monitor the tutoring pairs periodically, to update the subject(s) used in tutoring, and perhaps to revamp the pairs for compatibility in personality or skill. All students should have the opportunity to participate as both tutor and tutee. As a tutor the student assumes the role of teacher aide, with responsibility for instructing other students, keeping the lesson moving, and providing feedback. As a tutee the student is given a chance to receive instruction from another source and to discuss subjects and concerns without the pressure of teacher restrictions and judgments. Both roles give students some control over their academic learning and social interactions. Often, students lack the opportunity to discuss and work with all of their classmates and may only know a select group of students in their school. Tutoring, whether peer or cross-age, encourages these interactions and may actually initiate new friendships or associations (Vaughn & Lancelotta, 1990). Tutoring activities give teachers the flexibility to schedule a variety of grouping options during the school day. Flexible grouping allows for the individualization that some students require; Hispanic American students needing special instructional programming can be easily accommodated within a tutoring program.

Summary

Hispanic populations in this country are united by language and by some similarities in background. Although they differ in terms of racial composition, country of origin, and specific traditions, their commonalities include strong family involvement and extendedness, a collectivistic orientation, and gender-specific roles. Historically representing some of this country's longest-term residents, Hispanic Americans range from those whose families have been in the United States for centuries to the most recent immigrants. Within the next decade, they will become the largest minority group in the United States. Although the major issues for Hispanic Americans vary, depending partly on country of origin, principal concerns center on language difference and poverty level immigrant status. Unlike other groups discussed in this book, white Hispanic Americans who have been in this country for two or more generations are able to assimilate within the dominant society and avoid the stressors that accompany membership in a minority group. In contrast, Hispanic Americans of other races will continue to be recognized as minorities, a situation that may be complicated by their Spanish surnames.

Teachers often characterize Hispanic American students as cooperative, quiet, well behaved, and passive, particularly at the elementary level. These students' typical social skill needs tend to involve the language-based skills of being verbally assertive and responding on cue. They can also benefit from learning effective ways to cope with daily stressors and, especially during adolescence, learning to identify alternatives to aggression and antisocial actions.

Learning a new language and new ways of doing things presents significant problems for many of these young people. Schools need to become less stressful, friendlier places. Creating informal, low-anxiety environments might encourage more natural and effective learning of language and social skills. Along with direct instruction in specific social skills, peer-based strategies such as cooperative learning and peer tutoring hold much promise for this purpose. Instruction needs to be responsive to the cultural backgrounds of Hispanic American students, engendering pride on their part and respect on the part of non-Hispanics. Teachers are advised to draw on literature and specific situations that reflect the experience of students from Hispanic cultures. The students should be involved as much as possible in the development of this instruction.

References

Acosta-Belen, E. (1993). Beyond island boundaries: Ethnicity, gender, and cultural revitalization in Nuyorican literature. In T. Perry & J.W. Fraser (Eds.), *Freedom's plow: Teaching in the multicultural classroom.* New York: Routledge.

Ada, A.F. (1991). *La moneda de oro.* Madrid: Editorial Everest.

Aguilar-Gaxiola, S.A. (1994, August). *A Spanish language expert system for computer-aided diagnosis of depression.* Paper presented at the annual convention of the American Psychological Association, Los Angeles.

Aguilar-Gaxiola, S.A., & Gray, T. (1994, August). *Diagnostic concordance between computerized and paper-and-pencil Spanish versions of the mood disorders section of the SCID-P in Hispanics.* Paper presented at the annual convention of the American Psychological Association, Los Angeles.

Anaya, R.A. (1972). *Bless me, Ultima: A novel.* Berkeley, CA: TSQ Publications.

Anaya, R.A. (1987). *The Farolitos of Christmas.* Santa Fe: New Mexico Magazine.

Aronson, E. (1978). *The Jigsaw classroom.* Beverly Hills, CA: Sage.

Banks, J.A. (1991). *Teaching strategies for ethnic studies* (5th ed.). Boston: Allyn & Bacon.

Barton, J. (1995, April). *Self-confidence in literacy learners: Can cultural interactions help?* Paper presented at the annual meeting of the American Educational Research Association, San Francisco.

Bauermeister, J.J., Berrios, V., Jimenez, A.L., Acevedo, L., & Gordon, M. (1990). Some issues and instruments for the assessment of attention-deficit hyperactivity disorder in Puerto Rican children. *Journal of Clinical Child Psychology, 19*(1), 9–16.

Beatty, P. (1981). *Lupita Mañana.* New York: Morrow.

Beltran Hernandez, I. (1989). *Across the great river.* Houston: Arte Publico.

Bernal, M.E., Saenz, D.S., & Knight, G.P. (1991). Ethnic identity and adaptation of Mexican American youths in school settings. *Hispanic Journal of Behavioral Sciences, 13,* 135–154.

Bode, J. (1989). *New kids on the block: Oral histories of immigrant teens.* New York: Franklin Watts.

Bruni, M.A.S. (1985). *Rosita's Christmas wish.* San Antonio: TexArt.

Carlson, P.E., & Stephens, T.M. (1986). Cultural bias and identification of behaviorally disordered and learning disabled students. *Behavioral Disorders, 3*(11), 191–199.

Cartledge, G., & Kleefeld, J. (1989). Teaching social communication skills to elementary school students with handicaps. *Teaching Exceptional Children, 22*(1), 14–17.

Cartledge, G., & Kleefeld, J. (1991). *Taking part: Introducing social skills to children.* Circle Pines, MN: American Guidance Service.

Cartledge, G., & Kleefeld, J. (1994). *Working together: Building children's social skills through folk literature.* Circle Pines, MN: American Guidance Service.

Cartledge, G., & Milburn, J.F. (1995). *Teaching social skills to children and youth: Innovative approaches* (3rd ed.). Boston: Allyn & Bacon.

Casas, J.M., Furlong, M.J., Solberg, V.S., & Carranza, O. (1990). An examination of individual factors associated with the academic success and failure of Mexican-American and Anglo students. In A. Barona & E.E. Garcia (Eds.), *Children at risk: Poverty, minority status, and other issues in educational equity.* Washington, DC: National Association of School Psychologists.

Castex, G.M. (1994). Providing services to Hispanic/Latino populations: Profiles in diversity. *Social Work, 39*(3), 288–296.

Cochran, L.L., Feng, H., Cartledge, G., & Hamilton, S. (1993). The effects of cross-age tutoring on the academic achievement, social behaviors, and self-perceptions of low-achieving African-American males with behavioral disorders. *Behavioral Disorders, 18,* 292–302.

Codye, C. (1990). *Vilma Martinez.* Milwaukee: Raintree.

Cooke, N.L., Heron, T.E., & Heward, W.L. (1983). *Peer tutoring: Implementing classwide programs in the primary grades.* Columbus: Special Press.

Darrah, P.E. (1986). The effects of interpersonal skills training on academic, behavioral, and personality characteristics of low-income high school students. *Dissertation Abstracts International, 47*(3), 853–A. (University Microfilms No. 24–53913)

de Cortes, O.G. (1992). United States: Hispanic Americans. In L. Miller-Lachmann (Ed.), *Our family, our friends, our world.* New Providence, NJ: Bowker.

de Paola, T. (1983). *The legend of the bluebonnet.* New York: Putnam.

de Paola, T. (1988). *The legend of the Indian paintbrush.* New York: G.P. Putnam's Sons.

Delgado-Gaitan, C., & Trueba, H. (1991). *Crossing cultural borders: Education for immigrant families in America.* London: Falmer.

DeRosier, M.E., & Kupersmidt, J.B. (1991). Costa Rican children's perceptions of their social networks. *Developmental Psychology, 27*(4), 656–662.

Deyhle, D. (1986). Break dancing and breaking out: Anglos, Utes, and Navajos in a border reservation high school. *Anthropology & Education Quarterly, 17,* 111–127.

Dowrick, P.W. (1986). *Social survival for children: A trainer's resource book.* New York: Brunner/Mazel.

Dwyer, C. (1991). *The Dominican Americans.* New York: Chelsea House.

Fad, K.S., Ross, M., & Boston, J. (1995). We're better together: Using cooperative learning to teach social skills to young children. *Teaching Exceptional Children, 27*(4), 28–34.

Fletcher, T.V., & Cardona-Morales, C. (1990). Implementing effective instructional interventions for minority students. In A. Barona & E.E. Garcia (Eds.), *Children at risk: Poverty, minority status, and other issues in educational equity.* Washington, DC: National Association of School Psychologists.

Fordham, S. (1988). Racelessness as a factor in black students' school success: Pragmatic strategy or pyrrhic victory? *Harvard Educational Review, 58,* 54–84.

Fradd, S.H., & Correa, V.I. (1989). Hispanic students at risk: Do we abdicate or advocate? *Exceptional Children, 56,* 105–110.

Fu, V.R. (1979). A longitudinal study of the self-concepts of Euro-American, Afro-American, and Mexican-American preadolescent girls. *Child Study Journal, 9,* 279–288.

Fu, V.R., Hinkle, D.E., & Korslund, M.K. (1983). A developmental study of ethnic self-concept among preadolescent girls. *The Journal of Genetic Psychology, 142,* 67–73.

Fuchs, D., & Fuchs, L.S. (1989). Effects of examiner familiarity on Black, Caucasian, and Hispanic children: A meta-analysis. *Exceptional Children, 55*(4), 303–308.

Garcia, M. (1987). *The adventures of Connie and Diego/Las aventuras de Connie y Diego.* San Francisco: Children's Book Press.

Garza, C.L., & Rohmer, H. (1990). *Family pictures/Cuadros de familia.* San Francisco: Children's Book Press.

Giesecke, D., Cartledge, G., & Gardner, R. (1993). Low-achieving students as cross-age tutors. *Preventing School Failure, 37,* 34–43.

Goldstein, A.P. (1988). *The Prepare Curriculum: Teaching prosocial competencies.* Champaign, IL: Research Press.

Graf, M.H. (1986). The use of kinetic family drawing with Hispanic mothers in the school setting. *School Psychology International, 7,* 217–223.

Gullison, A. (1991). *The South Americans.* New York: Chelsea House.

Hammond, W.R., & Yung, B.R. (1993). Psychology's role in the public health response to assaultive violence among young African-American men. *American Psychologist, 48,* 142–154.

Harrison, A.O., Wilson, M.N., Pine, C.J., Chan, S.Q., & Buriel, R. (1990). Family ecologies of ethnic minority children. *Child Development, 61,* 347–362.

Hayes, K.G. (1989/1990). Que se porten bien: Social competency of Mexican-American teenagers in special education. *Dissertation Abstracts International, 50*(9), 2811–A. (University Microfilms No. 27–57572)

Heward, W., & Orlansky, M. (1992). *Exceptional children* (4th ed.). New York: Merrill.

Hewett, J. (1990). *Hector lives in the United States now: The story of a Mexican-American child.* Baltimore: HarperCollins.

Hidalgo, N.M. (1993, April). *Profile of a Puerto Rican family's support for school achievement.* Paper presented at the annual meeting of the American Educational Research Association, Atlanta.

Hoernicke, P.A., Kallam, M., & Tablada, T. (1994). Behavioral disorders in Hispanic-American cultures. In R.L. Peterson & S. Ishii-Jordan (Eds.), *Multicultural issues in the education of students with behavioral disorders.* Cambridge, MA: Brookline.

Hurwitz, J. (1990). *Class president.* New York: Morrow.

Iadicola, P. (1981). Schooling and social control: Symbolic violence and Hispanic students' attitudes toward their own ethnic group. *Hispanic Journal of Behavioral Sciences, 3*(4), 361–383.

Inclan, J.E., & Herron, D.G. (1989). Puerto Rican adolescents. In J.T. Gibbs, L.N. Huang, & Associates (Eds.), *Children of color.* San Francisco: Jossey-Bass.

Kafer, N.F. (1982). Interpersonal strategies of unpopular children: Some implications for social skills training. *Psychology in the Schools, 19*(2), 255–259.

Lacey, B.N. (1995, April). *Tracked through high school: A four-year study of Hispanic immigrants.* Paper presented the annual meeting of the American Educational Research Association, San Francisco.

LaGreca, A.M. (1983). Teaching interpersonal skills: A model for instruction in the schools. *School Psychology International, 4,* 109–112.

Lopez, N.N., La Greca, A.M., & Fetter, M.D. (1994, August). *Peer relations and support as factors in adjustment—Role of ethnicity.* Paper presented at the annual convention of the American Psychological Association, Los Angeles.

Maldonado-Colon, E. (1991). Development of second language learners' linguistic and cognitive abilities. *The Journal of Educational Issues of Language Minority Students, 9,* 37–47.

Maldonado-Colon, E. (1993). Cultural integration of children's literature. In J.V. Tinajero & A.F. Ada (Eds.), *The power of two languages: Literacy and biliteracy for Spanish-speaking students.* New York: Macmillan/McGraw-Hill.

Malgady, R.G., Rogler, L.H., & Costantino, G. (1990). Culturally sensitive psychotherapy for Puerto Rican children and adolescents: A program of treatment outcome research. *Journal of Consulting and Clinical Psychology, 58*(6), 704–712.

Manuel, M., & Cruz, R. (1980). *A Chicano Christmas story/Un cuento Navideno Chicano.* South Pasadena, CA: Bilingual Educational Services.

Martel, C. (1987). *Yaqua days.* New York: Dutton/Dial.

Martinez, E.A. (1988). Child behavior in Mexican American/Chicano families: Maternal teaching and child-rearing practices. *Family Relations, 37*, 275–280.

Matson, J.L., & Ollendick, T.H. (1988). *Enhancing children's social skills: Assessment and training.* New York: Pergamon.

Matute-Bianchi, M.E. (1986). Ethnic identities and patterns of school success and failure among Mexican-descent and Japanese-American students in a California high school: An ethnographic analysis. *American Journal of Education, 95*, 233–255.

Meichenbaum, D. (1977). *Cognitive-behavior modification: An integrative approach.* New York: Plenum.

Menon, R., Barrett, M.E., & Simpson, D.D. (1990). School, peer group, and inhalant use among Mexican American adolescents. *Hispanic Journal of Behavioral Sciences, 12*(4), 408–421.

Michelson, L., Sugai, D.P., Wood, R.P., & Kazdin, A.E. (1983). *Social skills assessment and training with children: An empirically based handbook.* New York: Plenum.

Mills, C. (1981). *Luisa's American dream.* New York: Four Winds Press.

Mohr, N. (1986a). *El Bronx remembered: A novella and stories.* Houston: Arte Publico.

Mohr, N. (1986b). *Going home.* New York: Bantam.

Mohr, N. (1988). *In Nueva York.* Houston: Arte Publico.

Mohr, N. (1989). *Felita.* New York: Dutton/Dial.

Moll, L.C. (1988). Some key issues in teaching Latino students. *Language Arts, 65*(5), 465–471.

Moore, H. (1988). Effects of gender, ethnicity, and school equity on students' leadership behaviors in a group game. *Elementary School Journal, 5*, 514–526.

Munson, S. (1989). *Our Tejano heroes: Outstanding Mexican-Americans in Texas.* Austin: Eakin.

Myers, W.D. (1989). The reluctant reader. *Interracial Books for Children Bulletin, 19*(34), 14–15.

Necochea, J., & Cline, Z. (1995, April). *The role of monolingual English speaking teachers in education of language minority students.* Paper presented at the annual meeting of the American Educational Research Association, San Francisco.

Novaco, R. (1975). *Anger control: The development and evaluation of an experimental treatment.* Lexington, MA: Lexington Books.

Paniagua, F.A. (1994). *Assessing and treating culturally diverse clients.* Thousand Oaks, CA: Sage.

Quintana, S.M., Villanueva, J., & Castaneda-English, P. (1994, August). *Ethnic socialization and ethnic identity for Mexican-American adolescents.* Paper presented at the annual meeting of the American Psychological Association, Los Angeles.

Ramirez, A., & Soriano, F. (1981). Causal attributions of success and failure among Chicano university students. *Hispanic Journal of Behavioral Sciences, 3*(4), 397–407.

Ramirez, O. (1989). Mexican American children and adolescents. In J.T. Gibbs, L.N. Huang, Associates (Eds.), *Children of color.* San Francisco: Jossey-Bass.

Ravetta, M.K., & Brunn, M. (1995, April). *Language learning, literacy and cultural background: Second language acquisition in a mainstreamed classroom.* Paper presented at the annual meeting of the American Educational Research Association, San Francisco.

Roberts, N. (1986a). *Cesar Chavez and La Causa.* Chicago: Children's Press.

Roberts, N. (1986b). *Henry Cisneros: Mexican American Mayor.* Chicago: Children's Press.

Rotheram-Borus, M.J. (1990). Adolescents' reference-group choices, self-esteem, and adjustment. *Journal of Personality and Social Psychology, 59*(5), 1075–1081.

Rotheram-Borus, M.J., & Phinney, J.S. (1990). Patterns of social expectations among Black and Mexican-American children. *Child Development, 61,* 542–556.

Santiago, D. (1983). *Famous all over town.* New York: Simon and Schuster.

Saracho, O.N. (1991). Cognitive style and social behavior in young Mexican American children. *International Journal of Early Childhood, 23*(2), 2–138.

Saracho, O.N., & Spodek, B. (1981). Teachers' cognitive styles: Educational implications. *Educational Forum, 45,* 153–159.

Schneider, B.H., Rubin, K.H., & Ledingham, J.E. (Eds.) . (1985). *Children's peer relations: Issues in assessment and intervention.* New York: Springer-Verlag.

Schwartz, A.J. (1989). Middle-class educational values among Latino gang members in East Los Angeles County high schools. *Urban Education, 24*(3), 323–342.

Sciarra, D.T., Ponterotto, J.G., Bruase, R.S., & Alexander, C.M. (1994, August). *Teenage motherhood among low-income, urban Hispanics: Familial and cultural considerations of mother-daughter dyads.* Paper presented at the annual meeting of the American Psychological Association, Los Angeles.

Soriano, F. (1993). Cultural sensitivity and gang intervention. In A.P. Goldstein & C.R. Huff (Eds.), *The gang intervention handbook.* Champaign, IL: Research Press.

Soto, G. (1985). *Living up the street: Narrative recollections.* San Francisco: Strawberry Hill Press.

Soto, G. (1990). *Baseball in April: And other stories.* Orlando, FL: Harcourt Brace Jovanovich.

Stanek, M. (1989). *I speak English for my mom.* Niles, IL: Albert Whitman.

Stephens, T.M. (1992). *Social skills in the classroom.* Odessa, FL: Psychological Assessment Services.

Strain, P.S., Guralnick, M.J., & Walker, H.M. (Eds.). (1986). *Children's social behavior: Development, assessment, and modification.* London, England: Academic.

Suarez-Orozco, M.M. (1987). Becoming somebody: Central American immigrants in U.S. inner-city schools. *Anthropology & Education Quarterly, 18,* 287–299.

Triandis, H.C., Marin, G., Lisansky, J., & Betancourt, H. (1984). Simpatia as a cultural script of Hispanics. *Journal of Personality and Social Psychology, 47*(6), 1363–1375.

Trueba, H.T., & Delgado-Gaitan, C. (1985). Socialization of Mexican children for cooperation and competition: Sharing and coping. *Journal of Educational Equity and Leadership, 5*(3), 189–204.

Valdez, J.N. (1994, August). *Ethnic identity, sex roles, and sexual attitudes.* Paper presented at the annual meeting of the American Psychological Association, Los Angeles.

Vaughn, S., & Lancelotta, G.X. (1986, March). *An interpersonal problem solving approach to teaching social skills to socially rejected students.* Paper presented at the meeting of the Association for Children with Learning Disabilities, New York.

Vaughn, S., & Lancelotta, G.X. (1990). Teaching interpersonal social skills to poorly accepted students: Peer-pairing versus non-peer-pairing. *Journal of School Psychology, 28,* 181–188.

Verheyden-Hilliard, M.E. (1985a). *Scientist from Puerto Rico, Maria Cordero Hardy.* Bethesda, MD: The Equity Institute.

Verheyden-Hilliard, M.E. (1985b). *Scientist with determination, Elma Gonzalez.* Bethesda, MD: The Equity Institute.

Ward, A.J. (1994, August). *Gender differences in prediction of suicidal behavior in Hispanic adolescents.* Paper presented at the annual meeting of the American Psychological Association, Los Angeles.

Widaman, K.F., MacMillan, D.L., Hemsley, R.E., Little, T.D., & Balow, I.H. (1992). Differences in adolescents' self-concept as a function of academic level, ethnicity, and gender. *American Journal on Mental Retardation, 96,* 387–404.

CHAPTER 7

Social Skills and the Culture of Gender

CAROLYN TALBERT JOHNSON, GWENDOLYN
CARTLEDGE, AND JOANNE FELLOWS MILBURN

No one doubts that there are differences between males and females, but the number of differences, their specific nature, and the reasons for their existence are all topics of controversy and ongoing study on the part of scholars in many disciplines. There are also political overtones in gender studies, which have been particularly salient since the beginning of the feminist movement in the sixties and seventies. Some writers on gender are said to minimize differences—for example, Maccoby and Jacklin (1974), who offered a definitive review of research on gender differences. Others with a feminist orientation—for example, Gilligan (1992)—are said to emphasize the differences toward the goal of calling attention to and redressing inequities in the status of women in our society. This chapter first will identify those differences in social behaviors between boys and girls in the United States on which there is some general agreement among researchers, then will present some implications for social skills teaching.

Two-Culture Theories

One rationale for presenting a discussion of gender differences in the context of multicultural social skill education arises from the proposition that boys and girls in our society grow up in different cultures and are socialized to behave differently. Maccoby (1990), in a description of early childhood play behavior, presents data to support this notion. From age 3 or even younger through the elementary grades and beyond, children consistently sort themselves into same-gender groups. When given spontaneous choice, they chose same-sex playmates. Maccoby stresses the situational aspects of social behavior in this context, in that girls behave passively when paired with boys but not when playing with other girls. In looking at reasons for the pattern of segregation, she suggests that girls may be wary of boys' rougher play style and their orientation toward competition and dominance. In particular, girls appear to be ineffective in attempting to influence boys. Maccoby suggests that the segregated play groups "constitute powerful socialization environments in which children acquire distinctive interaction skills that are adapted to same-sex partners" and that children's differing ways of acting toward their own and the other sex persist into adulthood, where gender segregation still exists in the workplace and in leisure activities.

A contrary view of the two-cultures hypothesis is presented by Thorne (1993). In an extensive series of observations in elementary school settings, she found much separation of boys and girls, both as structured by the schools and as chosen by the children. She points out, however, that male and female siblings are together in the family and in other environments outside the school and that much research is skewed toward the "most visible and dominant youth," ignoring those who do not fit the stereotypes. Thorne argues that rather than stressing differences and "oppositeness," adults need to understand that gender relations do vary by situation and context and are capable of changing. She suggests, for example, that teachers should be alert to the need to avoid stereotypes, to minimize opportunities for gender segregation (e.g., by not letting children choose their own seating), to promote cooperative relations between boys and girls by setting up heterogeneous work groups, and to confront situations in which stereotypes related to power and status appear to be operating.

Psychosocial Variables

Considerable data exist to suggest that males and females are more similar than they are different and that the only behavior exclusive to one sex is that of childbearing (Best & Williams, 1993). Nevertheless, Best and Williams have found in their research that beliefs in stereotypes related to male and female characteristics are well established in children in the United States by age 8. With the help of researchers in 24 other countries, they found that children throughout the world began acquiring stereotypes before age 5 and that the stereotypes seemed to be "universal models," modified by specific cultural influences. Explanations for the acquisition of sex-role stereotypes include social learning theory, based on the assumption that boys and girls are treated differentially by significant adults, and developmental-cognitive theory, which assumes that children develop gender identity over a series of stages tied to development of cognitive understanding of male-female differences. Another explanation for the acquisition of stereotypes is found in social role theory, which suggests that different expectations are established for behaviors associated with roles defined as male and female.

Certain attributes or behaviors take on different connotations depending on the sex of the individual to whom the trait is ascribed. Aggression, for example, is often seen favorably in males but discouraged in females. In a study with elementary-aged children, Villimez, Eisenberg, and Carroll (1986) found that size and bulk related positively to teachers' ratings of competence for boys but that heaviness related negatively to their ratings of competence for girls. Deaux and Major (1987) assert that gender-linked social behaviors have multiple determinants, that they are flexible, and that behaviors based on stereotypes can change depending on the situation and expectations for behavior.

Gender Identity

Much of the literature on gender identity suggests that females are distinguished from males by a collectivistic or relational orientation (Mellor, 1989; Mizrahi & Deaux, 1994; Stein, Newcomb, & Bentler, 1992). As noted in previous chapters, in a collectivistic orientation the emphasis is on being connected to the group, and individuals have their group's well-being as a major goal. In contrast, in an individualistic orientation, considered to be more characteristic of males, the interests and pursuits of the individual are the primary focus. In terms of the relational dimension, women are considered more likely than men to view group membership as central to their self-concept and to believe that members of their gender share common attributes as well as a common fate (Mizrahi & Deaux, 1994).

Stein et al. (1992) use the terms *agency (agentic)* and *communion (communal)* to differentiate males and females. Agency, associated with males, is defined as concern for oneself and one's own goals as manifested in self-assertion and self-protectiveness. Other related descriptors include individualistic, objective, and distant. Communion, on the other hand, viewed as a female trait, is concern for oneself in relation to others. Using the same framework, other researchers distinguish male and female identity according to self-definition (e.g., Gilligan, 1992; Mellor, 1989): Males are assumed to use self-definitions that separate them from others, whereas females focus on attachment to others. These theorists propose that females assume more responsibility for maintaining ongoing, caring relationships; that they have greater commitment toward intimacy-oriented relationships; and that they evidence more relational maturity with both male and female peers.

Self-Esteem

The literature on self-esteem and gender consistently points to higher levels of self-esteem among males than among females (Cate & Sugawara, 1986; Jones, Perera, & Tiongson, 1994; Stein et al., 1992; Widaman, MacMillan, Hemsley, Little, & Balow, 1992). Males are found to report higher levels of self-esteem in the areas of general academics, math, sports, and physical appearance. Females are likely to express the greatest confidence in their social competence. In a longitudinal study, Stein et al. found that different traits predicted heightened self-esteem for female and male adolescents. Traits considered masculine, such as having positive plans for the future, were more important to the self-esteem of males; females placed more emphasis on current warm and supportive relationships. However, the masculine traits of planning and realistic goal setting also appeared to be important to present (rather than future) levels of self-esteem for these females. That is, female students displaying the highest levels of current self-esteem evidenced more traits associated with males. Supporting data are reported in another study, where women in the workforce were found to exhibit higher levels of self-esteem than those not working (Stein, Newcomb, & Bentler, 1990). Stein et al. (1992) propose the need to promote both female communality and male independence and autonomy among females to help them achieve desired levels of self-confidence. An example might be found in a study conducted by Shmurak (1995) of a group of high school girls who defined their success in terms of friends, academics, and sports and intended to pursue nontraditional careers. Shmurak described them as "a remarkably self-confident and high-aspiring group of young women" (p. 10).

Cate and Sugawara (1986) also found that traits of masculinity related significantly with self-esteem for females, as measured by the Personal Attributes Questionnaire (PAQ ; Spence, Helmreich, & Stapp, 1975). Although females rated themselves as more socially competent than their male peers, further analysis showed masculine traits to be significant contributors to their social self-confidence, suggesting that "females may feel competent only when they are high on masculinity" (p. 152). Widaman et al. (1992) found that females had higher self-concept levels than males for honesty and same-sex relationships, but males reported higher levels for physical appearance and opposite-sex relationships. Even though intimacy and communality may be valued more highly by females, the masculine indicators of independence and autonomy may be essential ingredients for adequate levels of security leading to feelings of social competence. From another perspective, it may be appropriate to propose that women who are comfortable with their feminine state and are purposeful and confident about the future may have achieved a clear sense of identity, which Newman and Newman (1995) report is associated with higher levels of self-esteem, moral reasoning, and inner-directed behavior.

Peer Relations

As suggested earlier, by the time children reach age 5 or 6, gender and stereotypical behaviors are well developed, and this socialization process continues as they enter school (Bernard, 1981; Gollnick & Chinn, 1994). In a 4-year study of peer interactions in elementary school, Best (1989) found that boys and girls separated themselves from teachers at different ages. During the second grade, boys began to develop peer solidarity, which influenced their gender development in a manner compatible with society's expectations for males. Girls did not establish peer solidarity until the fourth grade. The importance of the peer group for the boys was reflected in their segregation in informal settings such as the lunchroom and the playground; it was also visible in the emphasis on hierarchical order within the group.

Play

Play behavior is one way in which gender is reflected in social behavior (Crombie, 1988; Maccoby, 1990). As noted earlier, children tend to behave differently when playing with same-sex partners and when playing with partners of the opposite sex. Gender segregation is widespread, found in all cultural settings, and difficult to change. Gender-specific patterns also can be seen in group size, sites of play, nature of peer relationships, and socializing factors. Girls tend to prefer smaller, more exclusive groups with more intimate friendships, whereas boys emphasize large-group play, often in team sports with many male playmates. Boys are more likely to play in public places, with play oriented toward mutual interests in activities; the play of girls typically occurs near home under adult supervision. Additional examples of play differences are given by Tannen (1990), who observes that boys tend to play in hierarchically structured large groups with leaders who tell others what to do and how to do it. Boys achieve high status by giving orders and making them stick. Boys can also achieve status by telling stories and jokes and by sidetracking or challenging the stories and jokes of others. Boys' games usually have winners and losers and elaborate rule systems that are frequently the subjects of arguments. Finally, boys are frequently heard to boast of their skill and argue about who is best at what. Because intimacy is key for girls, many of their activities focus on everyone's taking a turn (e.g., jump rope and hopscotch) and do not have winners or losers (e.g., playing school or house). Girls tend not to boast or consider themselves better than others. Girls don't usually give orders; they express their concerns through suggestions, which are generally accepted. Boys are likely to use phrases such as "Gimme that!" and "Get outta here!" whereas girls are likely to say, "How about doing that?" and "Let's do this." Girls don't challenge one another directly, and frequently they simply sit together and talk. The key issue for girls is being liked.

Crombie (1988) posits that through sex-segregated play, children acquire different values, skills, and goals. The goals and skills of girls are more likely to be consistent with those of adults, but boys appear to be more highly influenced by male peers. The play social behavior observed by Maccoby (1990) helps illustrate this point. She notes that the speech of boys is largely egoistic, used to establish and protect individual turf, often including threats and accompanied by physical force. Girls, on the other hand, engage in more socially binding conversation and use conflict-mitigating strategies in efforts to bring about agreement to restore or maintain group functioning.

Altruism

The female role is universally associated with caring and nurturing acts. Eagly and Crowley (1986) state that "women are expected to care for the personal and emotional needs of others, to deliver routine forms of personal service and more generally to facilitate the progress of others toward their goals" (p. 284). The research on helping behavior, however, shows that males are more likely than females to give help (Eagly & Crowley, 1986; Maccoby, 1990). In a meta-analysis of empirical data on helping behavior, Eagly and Crowley explain this finding according to male and female gender roles and the conditions governing the research studies examined. They describe the male helping role as being within the heroic domain, which "encompasses nonroutine and risky acts of rescuing others as well as behaviors that are courteous and protective of subordinates" (p. 285). Male helping commonly occurs with strangers as well as within close relationships, whereas female helping is most likely to occur within close relationships. Furthermore, women are likely to be more cautious about helping strangers because of fear of personal harm. According to Eagly and Crowley, much of the pertinent research has been conducted within the context of the male helping role—that is, based on brief encounters with strangers rather than long-term, close relationships. It may be that men and women give help equally but that their responses differ according to the conditions under which help is needed. Men may be more responsive under emergency, short-term conditions, whereas women are most giving on an extended basis within close relationships.

Empathy

Empathy is another class of behavior considered more predominant among females. Women generally are seen as more caring and more emotionally responsive to the needs and emotions of others. In a review of the related literature, however, Eisenberg and Lennon (1983) found only small or insignificant differences in the gender research on empathy. Aside from females' displaying more reflexive crying upon hearing the crying of a newborn infant, the greatest gender difference in favor of females was found on self-report instruments where the assessment of empathic behaviors was explicit. The authors speculated that the demonstrated differences were due to females' responding in ways they believed consistent with their gender-specific role. Although data in this area slightly favor females as more empathic, it appears that more gender-neutral research needs to be conducted before conclusions can be drawn.

Aggression

Despite suggestions by some authors (e.g., Best & Williams, 1993) that the real differences between males and females are few, many discussions of gender point out essential biological and social differences, some of which seem to be universal. Kenrick and Trost (1993) outline some differences that appear to exist in all cultures and even across species. These include a tendency for males to be more aggressive, to be more dominant, and to be more polygamous in sexual relationships. They point out that "males commit more murders and are more involved in producing weapons in every culture ever studied"; that despite the presence of some well-known women leaders, men generally have more positions of social dominance in almost every country in the world; and that women are "less inclined toward having multiple sexual partners" and seek older partners who have more resources and social status. Because these differences are so pervasive worldwide in humans and even in other mammals, Kenrick and Trost attribute them to evolutionary processes interacting with the social environment rather than to cultural influences alone.

As more empirical attention is given to gender differences in aggression, authorities begin to question some of these long-held assumptions. Much of the existing research shows males to be more physically aggressive than females (e.g., Eagly & Steffen, 1986; Harris, 1994; Maccoby, 1990; Tremblay, 1991), and because of its greater impact, researchers and other professionals have focused more on male than on female aggression (Tremblay, 1991). Although males are typically perceived as more aggressive, frequency may be less of an issue in gender differences concerning aggression than are social role, age, the type of aggression, and mediating factors. Eagly and Steffen posit that aggression might be viewed as role behavior, regulated by prevailing social norms, and that aggressiveness is encouraged or discouraged in males and females according to the respective roles they occupy. Eagly and Steffen argue that the typical male role includes considerable emphasis on aggression as well as on related behaviors such as competitiveness and assertion. Occupations and pursuits such as the military, sports, and business management further socialize males in aggressive, competitive behaviors. On the other hand, aggression is deemphasized in the typical female role. Indeed, one great debate in the nineties concerns whether women should be required or encouraged to enter the military and assume combat duties. Women are expected to be caring and nurturing. Assertiveness increasingly has been encouraged, but it is distinguished from aggression: Female assertiveness implies no intent to inflict injury or harm. Traditional female occupations emphasize helping or giving.

Gender differences in aggression appear to vary with age. In a meta-analysis of behavioral studies of aggression among adults, Eagly and Steffen (1986) found the gender differences in aggression to be less significant among adults than among children. Research with children shows boys to be more physically aggressive than girls (Crick & Grotpeter, 1995) and male gender to be a consistent predictor of aggression and conduct disorders (Offord, Boyle, & Racine, 1991). Male aggression is a relatively stable construct, predictive of negative outcomes such as delinquency and criminal activities in adolescence and adulthood. In addition to occurring at lower levels, aggression in females appears to have fewer negative outcomes (Serbin, Moskowitz, Schwartzman, & Ledingham, 1991).

Crick and Grotpeter (1995) argue convincingly, however, that even among children, the gap between male and female aggression is narrowed considerably if the type of aggression is figured into the analysis. Because females tend to be communal or relationship oriented, Crick and Grotpeter identified a construct of aggression labeled "relational aggression" and defined it as "behaviors that are intended to significantly damage another child's friendships or feelings of inclusion by the peer group" (p. 711). Following are some sample items used by Crick and Grotpeter to assess this form of aggression:

> When mad, gets even by keeping the person from being in their group of friends

> Tells friends they will stop liking them unless friends do what they say

> When mad at a person, ignores them or stops talking to them

> Tries to keep certain people from being in their group during activity or play time (p. 713)

In this study, elementary school children evaluated their peers for relational aggression, overt aggression (verbal and physical), and peer acceptance. Aggression was found with almost equal frequency among boys (27 percent) and girls (21 percent), with relational aggression associated primarily with girls and overt aggression mainly with boys. Very few of the children were described as exhibiting both forms of aggression. Erdley (1995) found a relationship between self-reported aggression and peer-assessed aggressive behavior for boys but not for girls, possibly suggesting that the girls' aggressive behavior may not be viewed as such by peers and that the girls may be using relational aggression.

Other somewhat related studies also point out the importance of relationships to female aggression. Harris (1994) had male and female college students indicate how they would respond to four different provocative scenarios. Although males showed a greater general tendency to use verbal and physical aggression, females responded more aggressively specifically to a scenario depicting a dating relationship. Bosworth and Hammer (1995) found that female middle school students reported considerably more aggression toward friends and family (88 percent) than did males (64 percent), whereas males directed more aggression toward school and teachers (16 percent) and in outside situations (e.g., jobs and sports, 20 percent) than did females (5 and 4 percent, respectively).

Gender-differentiated aggression also appears to be influenced by mediating factors such as thought processes, the targets of aggression, and expectations of reinforcement. Erdley (1995) found, for both boys and girls, that thoughts such as attributing hostile intent in an ambiguous situation were related to self-reported aggression. Some other studies, however, suggest that guilt and fear may serve to inhibit aggression in females (Eagly & Steffen, 1986; Harris, 1994). College students' responses to questionnaires provided Eagly and Steffen with some evidence of empathy as a mitigating factor among women. Female students expressed more anxiety and guilt over hurting someone through an aggressive act and more fear of harm to themselves through retaliation. These studies revealed other possible mediators—namely, that males are more likely to target other males than females for aggression and that males have greater expectations for social reinforcement of male-on-male aggression.

The failure of school and mental health professionals to address female aggression has important major implications. Crick and Grotpeter (1995) found relational aggression in females to relate significantly to social-psychological adjustment variables: Females with a high degree of relational aggression were more disliked than other children and reported more loneliness and depression, as well as less peer acceptance. Other researchers also argue for more attention to female aggression (Tremblay, 1991) and behavior problems (Caseau, Luckasson, & Kroth, 1994). It is pointed out that relatively few girls (compared to conduct-disordered boys) receive treatment. Yet female conduct disorders are predictive of mental health and adjustment problems later in life. Caseau et al. found that girls are more likely to be treated in private facilities than to be identified for intervention by school personnel, perhaps because girls more commonly have internalizing than externalizing problems. Particularly noteworthy, however, is the fact that girls with conduct disorders are more likely to become single teen mothers who are likely to be incompetent parents and to produce children with similar disorders. According to Tremblay (1991), "We forget that the less intense, less disruptive, conduct-disordered girls quickly become mothers who start a new generation of highly disruptive conduct-disordered boys" (p. 76).

Cross-Sex Relationships

Girls seem to have more intimate and exclusive friendships than boys do, although the overall pattern of sex differences in friendships is more complex (Berndt, 1982). The literature indicates that females value caring, responsibility, and interrelationship, whereas males value assertiveness and logic; these characteristics frequently are carried into adulthood. Douvan and Adelson (1966) argued that girls have more intimate friendships than boys during adolescence because, in the socialization of girls, great importance is attached to interpersonal relationships. In contrast, boys are oriented toward assertiveness and achievement rather than toward warmth and empathy. Intimacy among boys also may be discouraged because of fears that it will lead to homosexuality.

An additional body of research reports some difference between males and females in the development, need, and expression of intimacy. Buhrmester and Furman (1987) found that development of intimacy in preadolescence and early adolescence was important for females but that for males no change in need for, or display of, intimacy emerged over these years. Females appeared to be more sensitive and more sympathetic in terms of helping friends (Berndt, 1982; Blyth, Hill, & Thiel, 1982; Sharabany, Gershoni, & Hofman, 1981) than their male counterparts. Girls also initiated intimate relationships with boys before boys did with girls (Sharabany et al., 1981). Generally, girls' friendships were focused on meeting their emotional needs, whereas boys' friendships tended to retain the shared activity level of middle childhood (Berndt, 1982).

There is evidence that teachers, instead of encouraging mixed-gender groups, often discourage male-female interaction through practices such as assigning chores according to gender— for example, girls put things in order while boys move furniture. Some teachers separate boys and girls when assigning seats or areas to hang up clothes and when forming study and work groups and committees. Lockheed and Harris (1984) report a particularly sexist management approach: "In classrooms, assignment to mixed-sex seating adjacencies or groups often is used as a punishment designed to reduce student interaction instead of as a learning technique designed to foster cooperative interaction" (p. 276). Roberts (1986) explains why some educators follow such practices:

> The physical separation of boys and girls can be interpreted
> in a variety of ways. At one level, teachers continue this
> practice because of their belief that a certain degree of

mischief and teasing will be avoided. Also, some teachers feel that girls need this kind of protection and insulation from supposedly aggressive boys who might take advantage of and dominate the girls. Another explanation of teacher and school policy that separates the sexes is the fear that boys and girls will become involved in sexual games together. For many teachers this very terrifying possibility is avoided by turning girls and boys into "natural" rivals, and by accentuating stereotypical behavior differences. This process helps to prevent girls and boys from developing open, healthy friendships with one another. (pp. 156–157)

Bakken and Romig (1992) suggest that educational programs emphasizing and providing motivation for development of some intimacy or affection in same-sex relationships might teach males to have a different relationship style based less on hierarchy and more on interaction and intimacy. In terms of addressing leadership within relationships, programs encouraging assertiveness would be helpful to females. Both genders could be encouraged to value intimacy and taught ways to give and request closeness in relationships. Programs could also benefit adolescents by helping them learn to balance leadership and intimacy needs in relationships so that neither is sacrificed for the other.

Communication

Communication is another area in which gender issues are relevant. For instance, girls are considered to be more polite, to suggest more often than command, and to allow males to dominate the conversation. Maccoby (1988) describes differences in communication for boys and girls:

Boys in all-boy groups, compared with girls in all-girl groups, more often interrupt one another, more often use commands, threats, and boasts of authority, more often refuse to comply with another child's demand, more often give information, heckle a speaker, tell jokes or suspenseful stories, "top" someone else's story, or call another child names. Girls in all-girls groups, on the other hand, more often express agreement with what another speaker has just said, pause to give another girl a chance to speak, and acknowledge what another speaker has said when starting a speaking turn. It is clear that speech serves more egoistic functions among boys and more socially binding functions among girls. (p. 758)

Likewise, anthropologists Maltz and Borker (1982) conclude from research on children's play that boys and girls have very different ways of talking to their friends. They observe that, although some of the play activities of girls and boys are similar, their favorite games are different, and their ways of using language in games are separated by a world of difference. Tannen (1990) proposes that the worlds of play, as described earlier in this chapter, shed light on the worldviews of women and men in relationships. Status is important to men, and the way to acquire and maintain status is to give orders and get others to follow them. In direct contrast to this is the female community, in which the chief commodity is intimacy. Girls monitor their friendships for subtle shifts in alliance, and they seek to be friends with popular girls. Popularity is a kind of status, but it is founded on connection. Girls' friendships must necessarily be limited in number because they entail intimacy rather than large-group activities.

Children unquestionably are influenced by their parents' styles, just as adults are influenced by what they learned as children. According to Tannen (1990), the literature documents the facts that fathers issue more commands to their children than mothers do and that they issue more commands to their sons than to their daughters. This pattern appears to be a key element in the socialization process of girls and boys.

Tannen (1990) further states that boys and girls both want to get their own ways, but they tend to pursue this goal differently. Women and men talk in the ways they learned as children within their same-gender friendships. For girls, talk is the glue that holds relationships together. Male relationships are held together primarily by activities: doing things together or talking about activities such as sports or politics. The forums in which men are most inclined to talk are those in which they feel the need to impress, in situations where their status is in question.

It is important to consider the genders' communication styles in the context of race and ethnicity. Grossman (1995a) postulates that gender differences in communication style are most likely to be seen in Hispanic American and Asian Pacific American females reared in families espousing traditional values. Females from these ethnic groups who grow up in less traditional families and females from certain other ethnic backgrounds do not behave in these gender-stereotypical ways. African American females, for example, do not generally behave passively or allow males to dominate mixed-gender groups.

Grossman (1995a) further contends that both culture and race help to explain some characteristics of communication styles. Culturally, African Americans do not expect the genders to behave differently in communication, nor do parents model such differences to the extent that European Americans do. Lewis (1975; cited by Grossman) illustrates this point:

> The Black child, to be sure, distinguishes between males and females, but unlike the white child he is not inculcated with standards which polarize behavioral expectations according to sex. . . . . Many of the behaviors which whites see as appropriate to one sex or the other, blacks view as equally appropriate to both sexes or equally inappropriate to both sexes; and the sex differences that do exist are more in the nature of contrasts than of mutually exclusive traits. (p. 212)

Child-Rearing and Family Issues

Although rules associated with one's sex role may vary by race, ethnicity, social class, religion, and even by geographical region, primary socialization and learning in this realm typically occur within the family through intimate relationships with parents, other adult relatives, siblings, and playmates. Cushner, McClelland, and Safford (1992) describe a three-part process of sex role learning:

1. The child learns to *distinguish* between men and women, and between boys and girls, and to know what kinds of behavior are characteristic of each.

2. The child learns to *express* appropriate sex role preferences for himself or herself.

3. The child learns to *behave* in accordance with sex role standards.

Differences in socialization practices for boys and girls are many and obvious, beginning at birth and continuing throughout child-hood. Cushner et al. (1992), for example, cite Howe (1974) in the following statement:

> We throw boy babies up in the air and roughhouse with them. We coo over girl babies and handle them delicately. We choose sex related colors and toys for our children from their earliest days. We encourage the energy and physical activity of our sons, just as we expect girls to be quieter and more docile. We love both our sons and daughters with equal fervor, we protest, and yet we are disappointed when there is no male child to carry on the family name. (p. 195)

Similarly, Kramer (1988) reviews research showing not only that infant boys are handled more roughly than their sisters but that infant girls receive more verbal attention. Also, young boys are given more freedom to explore than young girls. Rubin, Provenzano, and Luria (1974) compared 30 newborns of the same length, weight, and Apgar scores (i.e., rating of the infant's color, muscle tone, reflexes, irritabil-ity, and heart and respiratory rates) and found that parents described girls and boys differently. Girls were more likely to be described as little, beautiful, pretty, and cute, whereas boys were described as big, strong, and hardy.

Kramer (1988) notes several important features of sex-based socialization during the developing years. Girls are generally kept closer to the supervising parents and receive more help on tasks than boys, who are encouraged to "fight it out for yourself." Boys are socialized early to emit "manly" behaviors. Parents and families also use toys as an agent of gender socialization. Children are encouraged to play with "sex-appropriate" toys. Appropriate male toys include planes, work tools, boats, chemistry sets, and cars, whereas females receive dolls, doll houses, sewing equipment, kitchen toys, and clean-ing toys. Currently, however, there is a reversal of roles regarding toys.

One is more likely to see both boys and girls playing with "cross-sex" toys than with traditional gender-specific toys. Nonetheless, if girls play exclusively with toys that are considered masculine (e.g., guns, airplanes, boats), they are viewed as tomboys. The same is true of boys who play with toys exclusively for females (e.g., dolls, sewing kits, etc.): They are viewed as being too "girlish." Boys are likely to be punished if they emit behaviors perceived as girlish.

Evidence of the internalization of gender roles is provided by Hartley (1974) as cited by Cushner et al. (1992). Hartley asked a representative group of boys (aged 8 and 10) to describe what boys and girls must know and be able to do. They received the following responses from the boys:

> [They] have to be able to fight in case a bully comes along; they have to be athletic; they have to be able to run fast; they must be able to play rough games; they need to know how to play many games—curb ball, baseball, basketball, football; they need to be smart; they need to be able to take care of themselves; they should know what girls don't know—how to climb, how to make a fire, how to carry things; they should have more ability than girls. . . . They are expected to be noisy; to get dirty; to mess up the house; to be naughty; to be "outside" more than girls are; not to be cry-babies; not to be "softies"; not be "behind" like girls are; and to get into trouble more than girls do. (p. 197)

School Experiences

Academic Performance Variables

The empirical literature shows that girls start out ahead of boys in a variety of attributes—notably verbal ability, eye-hand coordination, and mathematical ability—typically earning better grades and presenting far fewer disciplinary problems. However, by the seventh grade, girls begin to fall behind boys in achievement on standardized tests, and this decline continues and even accelerates during high school (Cushner et al., 1992; Grossman, 1995a). A recent study conducted at the University of Chicago found that "boys dominated girls by a 7 to 1 ratio on the highest levels in math and science tests" ("Study Finds Boys," 1995, p. 3A). Combining test results from thousands of students nationwide, this study was considered the strongest such investigation to date. In contrast to the findings for minorities (i.e., Hispanic and African Americans), who had logged dramatic improvements over the previous 20 years, the study showed that the gap between the sexes was not closing.

Rather than to genetic inferiority, this poorer performance by females in math and science is more likely attributable to issues unrelated to ability such as self-perception and differential schooling (Horgan, 1995; Oakes, 1990). Gender differences in academic programming are noted and undoubtedly contribute to differences in achievement. Oakes (1990) contends that a major difference between genders in math and science achievement is the result of courses taken. Teachers encourage males more. Males have more experience with science than females throughout most of their schooling, and regardless of ability, girls are less likely than boys to choose advanced math classes. Girls with high mathematical ability are less likely than boys to be identified, and when they are identified they are less likely than boys to participate in accelerated math classes (Cushner et al., 1992). Sadker and Sadker (1994b) note that girls are more likely to be invisible members of classes.

It is not unusual to find computer labs generally dominated by males. According to Campbell (1984), boys receive much more encouragement than girls to work with computers from childhood on. One need only examine a few currently popular video games to determine to which sex they were meant to appeal. As a result of differential socialization, genders bring to school different skills, interests, and confidence levels relative to mathematics, science, and computer science learning.

Horgan (1995) stresses the importance of psychological factors such as self-concept. He observes that boys are less likely to be bogged down by their failures but that girls tend to be less confident and find failure debilitating. In contrast to girls, boys evidence more persistence and less frustration with subjects in math and science. Horgan also proposes that grades are more important to girls than they are to boys and that girls need good grades to feel valued.

Although most of the attention to gender differences in achievement has focused on the poorer performance of females in science and math, it is equally important to emphasize that school presents problems for many boys as well as for girls. The University of Chicago study also found that boys "overwhelm the bottom ranks in reading and writing" ("Study Finds Boys," 1995, p. 3A). In this study, girls typically outperformed boys in reading comprehension, perceptual speed, word association memory, and writing. Boys were at a distinct disadvantage in the area of writing. Other sources (e.g., Cushner et al., 1992; Grossman, 1995a, 1995b) point out that more boys fail grades, drop out of school, get assigned to special education classes, and become disciplinary problems. Boys are expected to dislike school and misbehave and often feel like outsiders in a school environment that expects them to sit quietly, be docile and polite, and please the teacher. Boys are often less concerned than girls about grades and performance goals.

Teacher Behaviors

Teachers appear to have different standards for males and females. In the classroom, boys receive more attention than girls. There is evidence that males receive more extensive and specific feedback on performance as well as more positive comments and praise from teachers. Boys are called upon far more often than girls, even when girls have their hands raised. The expectation is that girls will perform well in school with few behavior problems (Horgan, 1995).

Research on teacher-student interaction patterns tells us that teachers talk differently to female and male students. Sadker and Sadker (1994b) report a 3-year study conducted in more than 100 elementary and secondary classrooms in four states and the District of Columbia that yielded the following findings:

Teachers interact more frequently with male students.

White male students were asked questions more frequently.

Boys typically get to answer more questions and talk more due to their assertiveness in grabbing teacher attention.

Boys are eight times more likely than girls to call out the answers to questions.

However, when boys call out the answers to questions, teachers are likely to accept their responses.

When girls call out the answers to questions, teachers often remind them to raise their hands.

When teachers initiate interaction with a male student, they are likely to keep calling on male students for several more interactions. The same behavior is emitted with female students; however, it is not as strong.

Regardless of the gender or race of the educator, the same patterns of boys being given the opportunity to answer more questions persist. (p. 422)

Without doubt teachers want to teach all students in an equitable manner and may not realize that they are showing favoritism in the process. A key issue is that teachers must become aware of gender-related inequities. As Sadker and Sadker (1994a) point out:

When girls do not see themselves in the pages of text-books, when teachers do not point out or confront the omissions, our daughters learn that to be female is to be an absent partner in the development of our nation. And when teachers add their stereotypes to the curriculum bias in books, the message becomes even more damaging. (p. 8)

Media Influences

The media, especially television, represent another socializing agent in the lives of young children. Both programming and commercials project ideas associated with gender roles. However, commercials tend to reflect traditional expectations of children's behavior. Gender stereotypes portrayed in the mass media do not accurately reflect the nation in which we live (Gollnick & Chinn, 1994). The stereotypical situation with a father working full-time, a stay-at-home mother, and one or more school-age children at home was typical in 1950 of 70 percent of all U.S. households. Today, however, only 4 percent of all households fit that stereotype (Hodgkinson, 1986). About 30 percent of the families in this country are headed by females, and one of every four American children lives in a single-parent family.

The prevailing images of females on television are those of shallow, nondirected individuals whose lives fail to reflect those of most women in U.S. society. Television often shows girls with few skills, academic interests, or abilities, somehow miraculously catapulting themselves into professional careers. For girls, looks are presented as more important than brains. Adult working women are portrayed on television, but both they and adolescent females are predominantly rich or at least middle class. Strong, intelligent working-class women are usually invisible. Gollnick and Chinn (1994) observe that the heroines of television are not social workers, teachers, or secretaries.

The print media also stereotype women and men. Most newspapers have women's pages that include articles on fashion, food, and social events—pages specifically written for what are believed to be the interests of women alone. Magazines directed at predominantly male or female audiences serve to perpetuate stereotypes (Gollnick & Chinn, 1994).

A Social Skill Profile

The literature related to gender differences suggests the existence of gender-specific strengths and deficiencies in social behaviors, whether biological or cultural in origin, that have implications for social skill instruction. In comparison to males, females appear to be more concerned with social relationships, more oriented toward a few close intimate relationships, more prone to avoid open conflict and express aggression in subtle exclusionary rather than physical ways, and more likely to use language to resolve conflicts. Females are expected to be caring, altruistic, helpful, empathetic, and conforming, attending more to others' needs than to their own. For girls, self-esteem appears linked more to social competence than to academic accomplishment. Girls become passive and feel ineffective in mixed-group situations, allow males to dominate, and are less persistent and less able to tolerate academic failure. Because many gender-related social behaviors appear to be situational and context dependent, a particular goal for girls is that of learning to behave assertively in a wider variety of situations, especially those involving male participation.

Males in our society tend to be valued more highly than females. They are more overtly aggressive, independent, logical, adventurous, self-confident, and ambitious, and are not particularly emotional

(Cushner et al., 1992). Although males are expected to emit short-term helping behaviors of a heroic nature (e.g., rescuing a drowning person), they are less likely than females to exhibit altruistic nurturing and caring in long-term relationships, and they may be less empathetic and less oriented toward feelings and emotions. Males are oriented toward competition, dominance, power and status, and independence and autonomy; they like to give orders, and they expect others to follow. Males are more socialized toward assertiveness and achievement. They are persistent and less frustrated by failure. Overt physical aggression or implied aggression in the form of threat is more tolerated in males and can be especially destructive. Males could benefit by broadening their social behavior repertoires with more alternatives to aggression in conflict situations. It would be helpful to both genders to develop male-female interaction skills based on empathy, respect, and caring rather than on dominance and power, especially as male-female behaviors become expressed sexuality.

Also implied in research on gender-specific social behaviors is the need for adult socializing agents—parents, teachers, and other significant persons—to create environments for children in which social behaviors are not narrowly defined in terms of gender appropriateness and in which children are taught those behaviors (whether considered "male" or "female") that improve their ability to interact with individuals of both sexes. The following section addresses some specific methods for teaching these social behaviors.

Teaching Social Behaviors

Gender-Related Learning

Instruction can be implemented so that learning will be equitable and affirming for both males and females. The American Association of University Women Educational Foundation (1992) prepared a report consisting of recommendations for rectifying gender inequalities in our educational system. They include the following:

1. Strengthened reinforcement of Title IX (act which specifically prohibits many forms of sex discrimination in education) is essential. School districts would be required

to evaluate and monitor on a regular basis to the Office for Civil Rights in the U.S. Department of Education.

2. Teachers, administrators, and counselors must be prepared and encouraged to bring gender equity and awareness to every aspect of schooling. State certification and standards for teachers and administrators should require course work on gender issues, including new research on women, bias in classroom-interaction patterns, and the ways in which schools can develop and implement gender-fair multicultural curricula.

3. The formal school curriculum must include the experiences of women and men from all walks of life. Girls and boys must see women and girls reflected and valued in the materials they study. Federal and state funding must be used to support research, development, and follow-up study of gender-fair multicultural curricular models.

4. Girls must be educated and encouraged to understand that mathematics and the sciences are important and relevant to their lives. Girls must be actively supported in pursuing education and employment in these areas. Existing equity guidelines should be effectively implemented in all programs supported by local, state, and federal governments. Specific attention must be directed toward including women on planning committees and focusing on girls and women in the goals, instructional strategies, teacher training, and research components of these programs.

5. Continued attention to gender equity in vocational education programs must be a high priority at every level of educational governance and administration. Linkages must be developed with the private sector to help ensure that girls with training in nontraditional areas find appropriate employment.

6. Testing and assessment must serve as stepping stones, not stop signs; new tests and testing techniques must accurately reflect the abilities of both girls and boys.

Test scores should not be the only factor considered in admissions or the awarding of scholarships.

7. Girls and women must play a central role in educational reform. The experiences, strengths, and needs of girls from every race and social class must be considered in order to provide excellence and equity for all our nation's students. National, state, and local governing bodies should ensure that women of diverse backgrounds are equitably represented on committees and commissions on educational reform.

8. A critical goal of education reform must be to enable students to deal effectively with the realities of their lives, particularly in areas such as sexuality and health. Strong policies against sexual harassment must be developed. All school personnel must take responsibility for enforcing these policies. (pp. 145–154, *discontinuous pages*)

The educator is a key variable in the learning environment for males and females. Grossman (1995a) suggests several ways for teachers to ensure equitable treatment:

1. Pay equal attention to boys and girls who volunteer answers or ask questions

2. Provide the same amount and kind of assistance to students, regardless of their gender

3. Praise male and female students equally for high achievement and creativity

4. Attribute the cause of students' poor performance accurately

5. Allow flexibility in the roles students assume as they engage in activities that reflect societal gender stereotypes

6. Encourage students to conform to the same standards of behavior, including issues such as cooperative versus competitive behavior, assertive versus passive behavior, risk-taking, politeness, emotional expressiveness, conformity, and docility (pp. 223–224)

In addition, it is important to recognize all students' unique learning styles and adapt instructional techniques accordingly. Small as well as major improvements need to be acknowledged because that feedback contributes to the development of self-esteem and self-confidence. Teachers need to devise classroom management systems applicable to all students, with the central concern of treating all students equitably.

In their 1986 study, *Women's Ways of Knowing*, Belenky, Clinchy, Goldberger, and Tarule point out that for many girls and women, successful learning takes place in an atmosphere that enables students to enter empathetically into the subject under study, an approach the authors term "connected knowing." They suggest that an acceptance of each individual's personal experiences and perspectives facilitates students' learning. They argue for classrooms that emphasize collaboration and provide space for exploring diversity of opinion.

Cooperative Learning

Where learning styles are concerned, there is evidence that females are less likely than males to take risks and react positively to difficult and challenging situations. They tend to be oriented toward group rather than individual goals. Males, on the other hand, are more competitive, are risk takers who seek challenging situations, and are less self-critical of their own behavior and more likely to cheat. Females emit more conforming behaviors, whereas males are more likely to maintain their own ideas and opinions regardless of what others think (Grossman, 1995a).

As for other cultural groups discussed in this book, cooperative learning procedures appear to have advantages for both females and males and may be effective in promoting more positive and supportive relations between the sexes. Thorne (1993) suggests that teachers can engage their students, even first graders, in thinking critically about collaborative ways to transcend social divisions and inequalities.

Belenky et al. (1986), in a study with third-, fifth-, and seventh-grade students, found that the effects of gender varied as a function of grade level. Third-grade girls were more cooperative than their male peers, but by fifth grade the gender difference had disappeared. Belenky et al. warn that the need to evaluate, rank, and judge students can undermine collaborative approaches. The cooperative learning procedures and resources described in chapter 2 are appropriate for creating cooperative environments relative to gender issues.

Direct Instruction

Skills training approaches as outlined elsewhere in this book, especially in chapter 2, are valuable for developing some critical gender-based social skills. Some of the most salient skills pertain to aggression and opposite-sex relationships.

Aggression/Assertion—Female

Some points made by Crombie (1988) are instructive for gender-based interventions. She suggests that it is probably easier to teach social skills to girls during middle childhood than to boys because girls are more developmentally advanced and more motivated to assume gender-related roles. Moreover, girls tend to place more emphasis on relational issues and engage in less complicated play, thereby minimizing the complexity of group social skills that need to be developed.

Because close same-sex friendships are especially important to females, Crombie (1988) suggests pairing girls who lack reciprocal relationships with other girls. This technique, referred to as "peer pairing," offers promise in helping youngsters who may be deficient in the skills needed to establish and foster good peer relationships. Once reciprocal relationships are established, girls should be helped to enter other girls' group play activities. As Crombie notes, girls are more likely to experience difficulty with group entry behavior; this skill can be systematically taught (see curriculum programs such as Cartledge & Kleefeld, 1991, 1994; Stephens, 1992). These lessons might be same-sex until youngsters show sufficient skill to participate in mixed-sex instructional sessions dealing with entry into mixed-group activities.

A related and especially significant skill domain for females is assertiveness within mixed-sex environments. As noted earlier, girls are likely to become more reticent and defer inappropriately to males when engaged in mixed-group activities. Girls who may be assertive under homogeneous conditions may become quite passive and ineffective when males are included. Assertiveness training needs to involve coeducational groups and focus on specific behaviors such as entering a group conversation, expressing one's opinion, expressing a contrary opinion, maintaining one's opinion if one remains convinced of its validity, and yielding to others on the basis of the strength and wisdom of others' positions, not on their gender or group status. Trainers need to monitor their roles and actions carefully during such instruction, guarding against showing preference for males during instruction, taking pains to encourage female contributions, and making certain all students are affirmed for their assertiveness (refraining from passive or aggressive responses).

Empathy/Aggression—Male

Learning to be more empathetic is considered a realistic antidote to aggressive behaviors. Goldstein (1988) explains, "The more we tune in to the other person, experience her emotional and/or cognitive world, and take her perspective, the less likely or able we are to inflict harm or injury on the other" (p. 405). In his review of established approaches for empathy training, Goldstein distinguishes between training in "empathy communication" and a "more complex, multiphasic process, in which communication is merely one component" (p. 404). In empathy communication models, the learner is trained in communication skills pertaining to the feelings and messages experienced and related by others. The learner also is helped to transmit empathy in the form of understanding, respect, interest, and genuine concern for the other. For example, nonverbal behaviors may include more intense facial expressions, physical closeness, and touching to communicate empathy.

Goldstein (1988) presents several exercises taken from an empathy communication program developed by Egan (1976). In one of the first exercises, the learner is helped to understand the feelings being experienced by a speaker. The learner is to read a statement and then describe in writing the speaker's feelings. The statement is read again, and the learner reflects on the accuracy of the initial interpretation. The learner also is expected to construct responses that label and rationalize the speaker's affect. For example, "You feel (label for feelings) because (experiences or behaviors causing feelings)." Following is a portion of one of the exercises.

> This is a hell of a mess! Everybody here's ready to talk but nobody is ready to listen. Are we all so self-centered that we can't take time to listen to one another?
>
> a. Your immediate response: "You feel _____ ."
>
> b. Your response on reflection: "You feel _____."
> (Goldstein, 1988, p. 416)

In a subsequent exercise, the learner is given the feeling words and required to provide only a statement about the content (e.g., "You feel angry because _____").

This and several other training programs, according to Goldstein (1988), are inadequate alone. He suggests that such a program fails to provide for the complete "meaning of empathy, teaches form but not complete substance, provides the skeleton without the flesh, and yields a too-often mechanical caricature of the prosocial attitude" (p. 439). Instead, Goldstein proposes a six-step empathy training program, summarized as follows:

1. *Readiness Training.* The learner needs to be trained in a set of skills that will enable him or her to derive maximum benefit from the instruction. Two types of skills are to be developed. First are cognitive skills such as imagination or observation skills, which help one to understand more accurately the meanings conveyed by others or to predict the overt behaviors of others. The second set of skills are affective in nature and pertain to reducing anxiety that might interfere with empathy.

2. *Perceptual Training.* At this stage, emphasis is placed on distinguishing overt behaviors, such as what was done or said, from inferences and interpretations of others' feelings or motivations.

3. *Affective Reverberation Training.* This step incorporates a varied set of "somatopsychic methods" such as meditation, dance therapy, sensory awareness training, and bioenergetics, intended to help the individual experience more fully the affect of the other.

4. *Cognitive Analysis Training.* The learner receives discrimination training in order to label accurately the affect displayed by the other.

5. *Communication Training.* Here the focus is on empathy communication, conveying an understanding of the feelings and content being conveyed by the other.

6. *Transfer and Maintenance Training.* Specific procedures such as homework exercises, overlearning, and manipulation of reinforcement contingencies are recommended to help the learner display empathy under real-life conditions.

Goldstein (1988) offers this sequence as "not *the* set . . . as far as training goes, but rather that *sets* of optimal techniques be utilized prescriptively with different types of trainees and trainers" (p. 447). Although not validated empirically, these and many other established procedures or programs show promise for helping children and youth identify and become responsive to the affect of others. A number of programs teach about emotions in the self and others (e.g., Camp & Bash, 1981; Cartledge & Kleefeld, 1991, 1994; Dinkmeyer, 1982; Feshbach, Feshbach, Fauvre, & Ballard-Campbell, 1983). Special attention needs to be given to teaching empathy communication to males, in both single-sex and cross-sex groups. To make caring behaviors a reality, trainers and others must foster and reinforce these behaviors in real-life conditions. Cartledge and Milburn (1995), for example, list the following strategies for promoting empathetic behaviors in children and youth:

1. Establish on-going procedures such as silent cheers (thumbs up signs) or applause where each child's success (which may be as small as recognizing a sight word) is recognized by the class.

2. Make certain each child has frequent opportunities to give and receive group affirmation.

3. Make certain children know you are aware of and value the caring kind acts they express toward others.

4. Encourage students to call or send notes to a fellow student who experienced some misfortune such as death of a relative, an accident, or illness.

5. Provide opportunities for students to tutor a peer in the classroom or in another classroom.

6. Structure community projects that promote caring behaviors such as contributing toys to orphaned or impoverished children or visiting older people in nursing homes.

7. Emphasize the feelings associated with conflict situations. Help children understand how their actions may have hurt others.

8. From films shown in class discuss acts of caring or how characters might have been more empathic.

9. Discuss disasters in the news such as hurricanes, earthquakes, famines, and wars. Note how the victims of these events might be feeling and what you might do to assist them.

10. Encourage students to keep logs of caring acts they performed for the last week. Arrange for that child's actions to be recognized by the entire class and display each log on the "caring" bulletin board. (p. 102)

According to Crombie (1988), group entry and group participation are major issues for boys as well as girls, as is learning to develop and maintain dyadic relationships. Because male social activities typically involve large groups, learning how to enter and effectively participate in group activities is an important aspect of male socialization. Crombie notes that boys need to learn to deal with their own tendencies to dominate others as well as the dominance efforts of other males. She further suggests that boys need to distinguish mock-fighting from true fighting, exercise self-control, and depersonalize attack during competitive activities. Instruction in these skills is especially important to counter the overt aggression commonly found among skill-deficient males. Because young males are generally more receptive to peer-based than to adult instruction and reinforcement, conducting initial instruction within same-sex groups is recommended. Peer-based instruction (e.g., the peer mediation approach discussed in chapter 4) may also be suitable for this purpose.

Gang Prevention and Intervention

As noted previously, boys tend to be more overtly aggressive and peer oriented than girls. Boys are likely to socialize in large groups, often away from adult supervision, in situations where they deemphasize compliance with adult wishes and social rules. Much of this peer orientation is considered developmental and normal—that is, "boys need other boys" (Goldstein & Glick, 1994, p. xi). Furthermore, adolescent loneliness may be a sign of maladjustment (Huff, 1993). Under certain circumstances, however, this natural tendency toward male groupings may take on unhealthy forms, especially when young people organize into gangs that engage in violent and destructive behavior. Youth gangs are largely a male phenomenon. Although since the sixties the number of female gang members and their involvement in violent activities have increased, they represent only about 5 percent of all gang members (Huff, 1993; Stephens, 1993).

Huff (1993) provides some demographics concerning youth gangs. The typical age of youth gang members is between 14 and 24 but may range from 10 to 30 years of age. Most of these young people come from female-headed households, and the gang tends to serve as an extended family, providing for "belonging, nurturance, and acceptance" (p. 6). Other perceived benefits of gang affiliation include support during grieving for fellow gang members, male bonding, and protection from rival gangs. Gangs represent various racial and ethnic groups, including European Americans (e.g., skinheads) as well as African, Hispanic, and Asian Americans. The latter three groups have received the most attention. Goldstein and Glick (1994) note factors contributing to gang affiliation and violent behavior, with poverty being the most prominent. With few resources, these young men find that the reputation earned through fighting and other gang activities is the principal way to attain status. Drug trade is another major influence. Fighting today tends to be more over drug selling and economics than over neighborhood ownership.

Although only 20 percent of gang members are under the age of 18, it is crucial that school-based prevention efforts begin early, in the intermediate if not the primary grades. Stephens (1993) suggests that if school personnel are to be proactive in countering gang membership and violence, they must be savvy about gang behavior. That is, they must educate themselves about the codes gang members use in dress, oral language, and graffiti. Concerning graffiti, for example, Stephens recommends that school officials follow the three R's: read, record, and remove. That is, graffiti is first read and translated for the messages being conveyed. It may be photographed for record-keeping purposes before being removed from school premises. The messages may be communicating some criminal or destructive actions that need to be brought to the attention of other authorities.

Stephens (1993) describes a gang prevention curriculum entitled Mission SOAR (Set Objectives, Achieve Results) developed by the Los Angeles Unified School District. This curriculum focuses on building self-esteem, setting and achieving goals, developing communication skills, and developing awareness of gangs and skills for dealing with peer pressure. The instructional strategies include lectures, cooperative learning, role-playing, games, and written activities. Though mission SOAR was developed for third- and fourth-grade students, according to Stephens, it can be modified for younger children down to kindergarten and for older youth through adulthood. It also provides for some Spanish translations. Much of the curriculum is geared toward improving self-esteem. This emphasis is based on the notion that poor self-image and limited self-confidence make students vulnerable to self-destructive behaviors such as substance abuse, premature parenting, and gang membership. Stephens (1993) quotes the program manual: "Mission SOAR develops or rebuilds self-esteem by guiding students to become responsible for themselves and to avoid negative people, destructive activities, and harmful substances" (p. 137). Specific lessons within the category of self-esteem address leadership, positive self-image, self-motivation, positive attitude and positive thinking, strategies for overcoming negativity, self-confidence, responsibility for self, acceptance and trust of self and others, and respect for self and others.

Goldstein and Glick (1987, 1994) propose an intervention program for gang-oriented youth called Aggression Replacement Training, which involves training in interpersonal skills, anger control, and moral reasoning. The curriculum for interpersonal skills training consists of 50 social skills that relate to basic competencies such as starting a conversation or using persuasion, dealing with feelings in self and others, developing coping skills, responding without aggressing, and planning constructively. Each skill is analyzed into specific performance steps, and suggestions for modeling and role-plays are given. Teaching procedures for this curriculum are similar to those outlined in chapter 2 of this book.

Anger control strategies draw heavily on the cognitive approaches also referred to in chapter 2. Essentially, learners are helped to develop self-statements and other internal actions that help them gain control over their emotions and think rationally and respond in constructive ways. For example, some suggested anger reducers are breathing deeply, counting backward, and evoking pleasant imagery (Goldstein & Glick, 1994). Anger control training helps learners recognize events that might trigger anger in themselves and also to identify their own behaviors that elicit angry reactions from others. Learners also are encouraged to think about the possible effects of their behaviors and to evaluate their actions. Goldstein and Glick provide a "Hassle Log," a check sheet for learners to use in recording the conditions surrounding anger-producing events. Each learner notes when the event occurred, what happened, who was involved, how the learner responded, and how the learner would evaluate his or her reactions and feelings. This log is used throughout training to help learners more accurately perceive their behavior and understand how problem situations might be handled in the future. Another purpose of recording these events is to provide role-playing situations in future sessions.

The third component, moral reasoning training, helps learners develop a moral framework for guiding their behavior, for distinguishing right from wrong. The empirical literature offers some evidence of a relationship between moral reasoning and prosocial behavior in adolescents (Eisenberg, Miller, Shell, McNalley, & Shea, 1991; Goldstein, 1988). The potential impact of moral reasoning is determined, at least in part, by the behavior being taught as well as by the moral developmental level of the learner. Nevertheless, Goldstein contends that training in moral reasoning, combined with interpersonal skill and anger control training, holds promise as a means of intervention for delinquency-prone youth. Moral reasoning training is based on group discussions of moral dilemmas designed to help learners improve their moral reasoning skills and to use them under real-life conditions. Goldstein (1988) stresses that trainers must refrain from imposing their views on learners but rather must focus on helping adolescents "develop the effective problem-solving skills needed to arrive at their own solutions to moral conflicts they may be faced with in life" (p. 303). Trainers are encouraged to become familiar with the stages of moral development, as identified by Kohlberg (1964) and described in this curriculum. Guidelines are given for assessing stages of moral development and conducting discussions. Trainers select moral dilemmas from the curriculum, then systematically guide learners through a discussion of the moral development stages represented by members of the group. The discussion is ended following a debate of the highest stage presented or when major differences have been addressed. Specific instructions are given for selecting trainees, choosing dilemmas, and guiding discussions. An example of a dilemma is given in Table 8.

As part of this training Goldstein (1988) suggests that role-playing portions of the dilemma may help the learners gain insight into the situation, especially if they take the roles of characters whose positions they previously failed to understand. Learners also might be encouraged to take dilemmas with them to solicit input from others in their environments, to be discussed at subsequent sessions.

Other important resources for countering antisocial or gang-related behavior among young people, particularly males, are involved parents and prosocial mentors or role models. Stephens (1993) stresses the need to educate parents about the signs of gang membership and related behaviors. The SOAR curriculum includes the Gang Banger Test for Parents, with items such as the following: "My child constantly wears his hair in braids or ponytails," "My child constantly talks in slang terms (cuzz, book, homie, O.G., etc.)," and "My child's friends are always older than he is" (p. 243). Parents are

---

Table 8
Joe's Problem Situation

Joe is a member of a gang of teenagers who live near an old school. The school is run-down and dirty. One night, the gang decides to have a rock-throwing contest to see who can break out the most windows in the school. Since the school is next to the railroad tracks, there is little chance that the boys will get caught. The rest of the gang doesn't know it, but Joe's father is the principal of the old school. Joe's father will be the one who will get into trouble for not making sure the school has better protection. But Joe and his father don't get along too well—Joe feels that his father is too bossy. The gang asks Joe to join in the rock throwing.

What should Joe say or do?

1. Should Joe join in the rock throwing at the windows?

   yes, should join/no, shouldn't join/can't decide

2. What about the fact that the gang will think Joe's chicken if he doesn't join them in breaking windows? Then should Joe join in the rock throwing?

   yes, should join/no, shouldn't join/can't decide

3. The school can probably get insurance money to pay for new windows. Does that make it all right to break the windows?

   yes, should join/no, shouldn't join/can't decide

4. What if the school is new and clean, and the students enjoy being there? Then should Joe join in the rock throwing?

   yes, should join/no, shouldn't join/can't decide

5. What if Joe's father will lose his job if the windows are broken? Then should Joe join in the rock throwing?

   yes, should join/no, shouldn't join/can't decide

6. What if Joe and his father get along great? Then should Joe join in the rock throwing?

   yes, should join/no, shouldn't join/can't decide

7. How important is it to go along with what your friends are doing?

   very important/important/not important

8. In general, how important is it not to vandalize buildings or property?

   very important/important/not important

Note. From *Small-Group Sociomoral Discussions: Problem Situations for Use with Antisocial Adolescents* by J.C. Gibbs, 1988, unpublished manuscript, The Ohio State University, Columbus. Copyright 1988 by the author. Adapted by permission.

advised of ways to supervise their children more effectively and are encouraged to come to school to monitor hallways, playgrounds, and restrooms.

As noted previously, many at-risk youngsters are in female-headed households and do not have access to positive male role models in either the home or community. Positive role models may be a key factor in deterring gang membership and delinquent behavior (Stephens, 1993). Goldstein (1988) discusses at length ways to recruit and engage supportive models. He points out that the best potential models are those who have fairly regular contact with the youth, are emotionally stable, are respected by the youth, can relate to the youth's personal experiences, are of the same racial or ethnic background, and are able to provide emotional support and guidance. Supportive models may be peers, relatives, school personnel, ministers, or other members of the community. On the basis of a review of the empirical literature, Goldstein observes that among youngsters subjected to socially oppressive conditions, the most resilient and successful were those who had recruited supportive models. In his Prepare Curriculum, Goldstein (1988) gives guidelines for teaching youth explicitly how to recruit and maintain supportive models. Learners are taught how to identify potential models, how to determine what they want to accomplish in interactions with those models, how to initiate and conduct conversations, and how to evaluate their interactions. Skills from the interpersonal skill training component of Goldstein's curriculum are used for this purpose.

In addition to teaching youth how to recruit supportive models, school personnel and other interested persons might create conditions to increase the availability of support. Young people might be encouraged to form relationships with models in differing roles (e.g., peers, school personnel, community figures, relatives). Some schools train young people in the schools to serve as peer counselors. These peer counselors should reflect the diversity of the school population and should include males who have successfully resisted the pressures of gangs and antisocial behaviors. Once these youths are convinced of the benefits of prosocial actions and are thoroughly trained in ways to listen and help their peers engage in socially appropriate problem solving, they can be valuable allies in prevention efforts. Men from the community employed in professional, semiprofessional, and skilled occupations are another potential resource (e.g., Petri,

Mungin, & Emerson, 1992). A particularly effective procedure is to invite men into the schools during the school day to serve as tutors and informal counselors for low-achieving, vulnerable youth. College students can also serve in this capacity (e.g., Stephens & Mand, 1995), as can retirees, who tend to be highly reliable. Some school programs provide financial compensation for these mentors, thereby increasing the likelihood of consistent participation.

Opposite Sex Relationships

For young people moving into adolescence, a critical area of growth and learning pertains to heterosexual relationships. Both males and females give increasing attention to the opposite sex and are keenly interested in ways to engage and make themselves more attractive to their opposite-sex peers. Despite this natural attraction, relationships between males and females often are not only painful but abusive and destructive. To promote healthier relationships and interactions between females and males, it is important to look at their respective roles in these relationships. The subservient, passive roles typically assumed by females contribute to their subjugation by males and their preoccupation with pleasing men. Fine (1993), who studied the issue of sexuality and pregnancy among low-income high school students, warns of the potential consequences of this orientation:

> Growing evidence suggests that women who lack a sense
> of social or sexual entitlement, who hold traditional
> notions of what it means to be female—self-sacrificing
> and relatively passive—and who undervalue themselves,
> are disproportionately likely to find themselves with an
> unwanted pregnancy and to maintain it through to mother-
> hood. While many young women who drop out, pregnant
> or not, are not at all traditional in these ways, but are quite
> feisty and are fueled with a sense of entitlement, it may
> also be the case that young women who do internalize
> such notions of "femininity" are disproportionately at risk
> for pregnancy and dropping out. (pp. 96–97)

As a remedy, Fine (1993) argues for a curriculum of empowerment consisting of sex education, access to in-school clinics, and nontraditional vocational training for females. Although sex education programs have been in the schools to varying degrees for at least a decade, Fine observes that many such programs emphasize anatomy rather than dealing with more pressing issues of contraception and interpersonal relationships. According to Fine, research indicates that students receiving sex education at school are more likely to use contraceptives and possibly to delay heterosexual activity. Fine also reports that female adolescents empowered through vocational training programs are likely to alter their views and rethink previously favorable or laissez-faire attitudes toward early pregnancy.

With the issue of sexual harassment becoming more prominent, researchers have begun to track this phenomenon into the schools among young adolescents. Shakeshaft, Barber, Hergenrother, Johnson, Mandel, and Sawyer (1995), for example, found that both boys and girls were harassed in middle and high schools. Both unattractive and exceptionally attractive girls were harassed for the way they looked; boys were harassed if their behaviors were seen as unmasculine. Girls were typically taunted as sluts, whores, and bitches; boys as faggots and queers. Although students employed various strategies to deal with this verbal abuse, ranging from ignoring to fighting back, they generally agreed that the taunting was painful and that school personnel should take steps to stop it. According to the students in this study, teachers often observed the harassment but were either too busy or too indifferent to take any action. Furthermore, these negative, misogynous themes are reinforced in popular culture (e.g., in television sitcoms and popular music).

Although typically listed as a component of the sex education curriculum, skills pertaining to male-female relationships seldom are explicitly taught in public schools. Appropriate dating behaviors, social communication skills, and ways to establish and maintain relationships are important understandings for young people. For example, boys and girls of dating age should know how to ask for and accept or refuse a date, as well as understand a range of dating behaviors. These include appropriate behaviors under various circumstances (e.g., manners at a restaurant or deciding who pays for what), refusing an inappropriate request, and what constitutes date rape.

Barth, Middleton, and Wagman (1989) describe a social skill curriculum designed to teach skills related to preventing pregnancy. Scripted role-plays are used to help young people act out dialogue for resisting requests for unwanted or unprotected sex. The emphasis is on resisting the request while preserving the relationship. The authors point out that young people often are caught between these two concerns and frequently act from fear rather than from desire. Role-play participants act out scripts that portray effective and ineffective behaviors. Other group members observe; they note the key responses, critique the enactments, and make suggestions for improvement. Barth et al. give guidelines for approaching such potentially sensitive matters, and they signal the need to obtain parental permission. Additionally, they stress the importance of establishing rapport among group members as well as between students and teacher before such instruction is undertaken. They also point out that scripted role-plays (rather than open-ended scenarios) have the advantage of reducing awkwardness but that students might be engaged in writing their own scripts with more familiar scenarios.

In addition to structured presentations, instruction in the area of male-female relationships lends itself to informal coeducational discussions and the use of some inductive strategies. For example, in discussing attributes desired in an opposite-sex partner, young people often focus on superficial characteristics such as looks, money, possessions (e.g., cars or clothes), and popularity. In describing their good friends, these same youngsters will focus on more substantive character traits, such as trustworthiness, honesty, intelligence, commonality of interests, and loyalty. A suggested strategy is to have students generate two lists: one of attributes desired in an opposite-sex partner and the other of attributes desired in a good friend. Students can then be helped to recognize that they are likely to use higher standards in selecting a friend than in choosing someone who may potentially be an intimate partner for life. Such activities are intended to help students begin thinking critically about extremely important interpersonal and sexual decisions that will affect their entire lives.

Curriculum and Literature

Appropriate Materials and Curriculum

Researchers and other authorities are increasingly aware of the gender bias prevalent in instructional materials that leads to discrimination and reinforcement of nonproductive attitudes. Examples of this bias are curricula in which males and females are presented in stereotypical roles, in which women are not identified as major contributors to society, or in which women and minorities are simply underrepresented. Along with invisibility, stereotyping, and imbalance, Sadker and Sadker (1994a) identified three other forms of bias in instructional materials, referred to as unreality, fragmentation and isolation, and linguistic bias. With unreality, unpleasant or negative circumstances—such as exploitation, oppression, or sexism on the part of leaders, states, or the nation—are ignored or glossed over. Fragmentation and isolation occur when information on subjugated groups is presented in separate sections of a book or curriculum rather than being integrated into the whole, and members of these groups are shown interacting mainly among themselves as opposed to being part of mainstream society. Linguistic bias is at work when terms are used exclusively to apply to one group in a somewhat pejorative way. For example, Native Americans are frequently referred to as "roaming," "wandering," or "roving" across the land, terms that might describe the actions of buffalo or wolves. The authors recommend monitoring for these biases.

Teachers need to incorporate into their curricula literature that is representative of the whole society, which includes women and minority groups. Horgan (1995) suggests the following criteria for gender-fair materials:

1. They must acknowledge and affirm *variation*—that is, that females are not all the same.

2. They must be *inclusive*—that is, they need to be about both females and males, as well as about people from different ethnic groups.

3. They must be *accurate*.

4. They must be *affirmative*—that is, they must stress the dignity and worth of all people.

5. They must be *representative*—that is, they must present a balanced perspective.

6. They must be *integrated*—that is, they must weave together the experiences and the lives of both females and males.

Horgan (1995) contends not only that materials about females are scarce in the classroom but that little attention is given to feelings, interpersonal relationships, and emotional development.

Rudman (1995) points out that many publishers of children's readers purposely include more male-oriented topics than topics typically associated with females, arguing that because boys are more likely than girls to need remedial reading, it is more important to appeal to masculine interests. The publishers reason that girls are more likely to read male-associated materials than the reverse. Rudman concedes that this argument has some merit in that some boys have been taught to shun materials that emphasize females or relationships. However, she counters by asserting that boys as well as girls can and do appreciate materials including well-constructed stories with "heroes, male and female, who are well balanced in their action and inventiveness" (p. 181).

We have seen some improvements in curricula relative to gender and minority issues, especially in terms of numeric representation. Reviews of elementary readers and arithmetic and science textbooks, for example, show males and females represented in equal numbers (Purcell & Stewart, 1990; Sadker, Sadker, & Klein, 1991). Girls are shown in a wide range of activities; however, they still tend to be portrayed as more helpless than boys. Unfortunately, history texts continue to minimize women's contributions (Sadker et al., 1991). In a study of the five most widely used primary and intermediate basal readers, King (1989) found that female minority representation in stories ranged from 7 to 15 percent. The most frequently represented minority characters were African American; Asian American females appeared the least often (only twice). Despite the need for further qualitative improvement, the noted changes are encouraging, underscoring the importance of a more representative and empowering portrayal of all members of this society. According to Rudman (1995), "Publishers have now recognized that sexist bias harms everyone, male and female. Many publishers of children's texts issue guidelines to authors and artists to assist them in using nonsexist, nonracist language and images" (p. 181).

Instruction through Literature

Children's literature has a major effect on the development of sex-role identity (Kramer, 1988). The importance of literature for social and personal development is also noted by Stier and Clark (1991), who assert that as youngsters move into adolescence, they are confronted with issues like these:

> Who am I? How can I lead a moral life? How should I act toward others? Families and peers may help them find answers, but another potential source of guidance is in the school setting, with literature as a constant. (p. 756)

Reflecting on traditional children's stories, especially the classic fairy tales such as such as "Cinderella," "Little Red Riding Hood," "Snow White," and "Sleeping Beauty," one is struck by the stereo-typical female heroine who is weak, fearful, and victimized, and who needs to be rescued by a handsome young man. In most children's literature, the male is usually seen as the stronger one who must protect females and save them from great danger, whereas females in these same stories are seen as helpless, waiting to be saved. The ultimate reward for being good, kind, compliant, and beautiful is marrying the prince and being subservient to him "happily ever after." These stories not only stress female deference and inferiority to males but also strongly suggest that the primary focus and mission for females is male acceptance and favor.

Alternative collections of folk and fairy tales provide a female image more consistent with contemporary society. Rudman (1995) cites several examples of such works. One is a set of tales compiled by Rosemary Minard (1975) and entitled *Womenfolk and Fairy Tales*. Stories from various lands, such as Africa, Ireland, Scandinavia, Japan, and China, are retold; they present women as assertive, clever, and admirable without denigrating males. Rudman also notes collections and books by Jane Yolen, including *The Hundredth Dove* (1977) and *The Girl Who Cried Flowers and Other Tales* (1974). According to Rudman, Yolen's intent is "to stretch the imagination and communicate a sense of universality. She usually manages within the context of the fairy tale to create characters who are active, intense, thoughtful, and complete, whether they are males or females" (p. 184).

Rudman (1995) also notes the lighthearted but didactic stories created by Richard Gardner (1974) under the title *Dr. Gardner's Fairy Tales for Today's Children*. Written with humor, these stories are designed to instruct by providing present-day, realistic outcomes for traditional stories. "Cinderelma," for example, gets to the ball through her own efforts, separates from the prince after discovering they are not compatible, establishes her own business, and marries someone of shared interests.

The lessons of folk and fairy tales can be powerful ones, and as Rudman (1995) suggests, teachers need to be aware of the messages they communicate. The stories might be analyzed according to gender, with students noting who initiates the actions and determining whether various characters have positive or negative traits. Students might be asked how well the traits might correspond with present-day expectations and how the story might be reconstructed to be more contemporary and socially acceptable.

Increasing numbers of nonsexist books counter some of the images contained in previous tales and present females in more active and unique roles. One example for young children is *Flossie and the Fox*, by Patricia McKissack (1986). In contrast to the tale of Little Red Riding Hood, who had to be rescued from the fox by the hunter, this engaging and light-hearted story centers on a young girl who uses her intelligence to outwit the fox on her way to deliver a basket of eggs to a nearby farm. Another example is *Mufaro's Beautiful Daughters* (Steptoe, 1987), an African-based narrative incorporating a folktale theme. Two very attractive sisters strive for the favor of the king. The two sisters differ in personality: One mean-spirited and cunning, the other generous and loving. The latter is the successful one. In addition to validating virtuous behavior, this story appeals to the self-esteem of racially different females, endorsing models of beauty other than the typical European standard.

Some of the more recent books are designed to affirm females by suggesting that they might aspire to the same positions as males. *Amazing Grace*, by Mary Hoffman (1991), serves this function with respect to both gender and race. Grace is a young black girl with a vivid imagination who loves drama and play acting. When roles are being considered for the school play *Peter Pan*, Grace expresses a desire to play the leading part. Classmates attempt to discourage her because Peter Pan is neither female nor black. Grace, encouraged by her family and inspired to believe she can be anything she wants to be, eventually achieves the desired role.

Much of the award-winning children's literature is generally sensitive to issues of gender and ethnic diversity and often presents females with active, adventurous lives who display intelligence, courage, and skill (Gollnick & Chinn, 1994). The stories have appeal for girls and boys alike. A choice for young children is *The Girl Who Loved Wild Horses,* by Paul Goble (1978). This Caldecott Medal picture book tells the heartwarming story of a Native American girl who understands horses in a special way. She takes care of her people's horses and spends time with them daily. One day a storm drives the girl and her horses far from her people to a place where wild horses roam. The leader of the wild horses, a magnificent stallion, invites her to live with them. Living free with the wild horses, the girl is filled with true happiness. Though she returns briefly to the people she loves many times, the girl chooses to live with the wild horses forever. A similar example for slightly older children is *Julie of the Wolves* (George, 1972), noted in chapter 5 on Native Americans. The survival of the young heroine in an Alaskan wilderness, with a focus on intelligence, fearlessness, and love, makes the story a good vehicle for learning about gender equity.

According to Rudman (1995), contemporary books with such strong-willed, self-directed females are the exception rather than the rule. She points out that the loneliness and unhappiness that often trouble these "supergirls" render their lives less than enviable. *Harriet the Spy,* by Louise Fitzhugh (1964), depicts such a situation. Rudman does acknowledge the existence of several books portraying nontraditional, nonconforming, and feisty females who are not unhappy or rejected. Among them are *A Year in the Life of Rosie Bernard,* by Barbara Brenner (1971) and *Christina Katerina and the Box,* by Patricia Lee Gauch (1971).

Rudman (1995) points out that some of the classics provide desirable role models and should have universal appeal. For example, *Little Women,* by Louisa May Alcott (1868) features active, unusual characters, and "most of the values transmitted by this book concern people's relationships to each other as respected individuals. There is also much emphasis on the responsibility of each human being to care about every other person" (p. 185). These concerns are not gender specific, and Rudman advises that the reading of this book should not be limited to girls. Threaded throughout are the themes of intimacy and connectedness, which are central features of the feminine identity. Intimacy in terms of family, same-sex, and opposite-sex relationships is prominent also in the Newbery Award–winning book *After the Rain* (Mazer, 1987). This book, as well as other well-written works, would provide an excellent resource for helping young people discover ways to establish, maintain, and improve the relationships in their lives.

Histories and biographies are another valuable kind of literature profiling powerful, independent female role models. For example, biographies of outstanding women such as Eleanor Roosevelt or Harriet Tubman show women who lived under different conditions but who both assumed nontraditional roles and exercised courage to act and give aid and comfort to others. Biographies of other prominent women, such as Amelia Earhart, Emily Dickinson, Ida Wells-Barnett, Fannie Lou Hamer, Maria Tallchief, Margaret Sanger, Sojourner Truth, and Edna St. Vincent Millay, show women in different eras, from different races, and of different social stations who, in their own ways, defy conventions to help themselves and others. For example, Margaret Sanger, as Rudman (1995) relates, was a pioneer in birth control. Although she was widely criticized for her views, her efforts had far-reaching and long-lasting effects. It is important to bring out that many of these and other such women are noteworthy due to unconventional actions based on deeply held principles rather than on self-serving eccentricities.

Boys as well as girls should be encouraged to read and enjoy literature that is free of stereotypical images and that promotes adaptive behaviors and roles critical for modern society. Most books for children and young adults have male protagonists, with females occupying subservient or helping roles. This common portrayal directly or indirectly reinforces the perception of the relative status of men and women in real life. Most of the books mentioned here should be among the assigned readings for both genders. Males must learn to see females as multidimensional beings who are equally capable of a wide range of endeavors that require intelligence, courage, strength, leadership, risk taking, and caring. Furthermore, all individuals deserve respect and admiration for their unique achievements. Special talents and goals need to be cultivated and affirmed, not denigrated because of gender. For example, a female with leadership abilities who aspires to be a major political figure needs to be seen as a viable future candidate rather than an aberration.

By the same token, boys are often locked into stereotypical roles that restrict their opportunities to explore activities and interests often considered part of the female domain. For example, boys who desire to dance ballet, teach young children, or become nurses are often discouraged from these "unmasculine" pursuits. Books such as *A Special Gift* (Simon, 1978) and *My Ballet Class* (Isadora, 1980) are useful in addressing such issues in that they present dance as a legitimate option for boys. Stier and Clark (1991) review some Newbery Award books that address issues of special concern to adolescent boys. Two stories by Gary Paulsen, *Hatchet* (1987) and *Dogsong* (1985) present the "prototypical male-initiation-rite" in which the protagonist sets out to conquer nature but emerges with a clearer sense of self (Stier & Clark, 1991, p. 762). In *The Whipping Boy* (Fleischman, 1986), a young man grows in empathy, learning to be less selfish and more caring of others. *Scorpions* (Myers, 1988) is a realistic portrayal of inner-city life and the involvement of the main character in a youth gang. The young man and his friend encounter not only the power of firearms and aggression in addressing problems but their destructive effects as well. It is hoped that in reading and discussing this book, readers will recognize the pitfalls of using violence in attempting to achieve goals.

One neglected theme in children's literature appears to be fatherhood. In a random sample of 100 picture books, Stewig (1988) observed that fathers appeared in only 40 books, with few depicted in professional activities. In young adult fiction, Unsworth (1988) found that father figures were becoming more numerous but was disturbed by the prevalence of abusive and troubled fathers. Rudman (1995) identifies several books with attractive father figures. For young children, she recommends *The Sick Day* (MacLachlan, 1979), *Ramona and Her Father* (Cleary, 1975), *Daddy Is a Monster . . . Sometimes* (Steptoe, 1980), *June Mountain Secret* (Kidd, 1991), and *The Long Red Scarf* (Hilton, 1990). In the last book, the grandfather grudgingly learns to knit a scarf for himself and finds that he enjoys knitting. Rudman comments that the father figures in these books are "models of nurturing adult males, not because they are perfect fathers but because they exhibit characteristics that counteract stereotypes" (p. 191).

Along with books that show fathers as nurturers, young people should identify and read books that highlight other prosocial behaviors, such as making and keeping friends. Rudman (1995) describes a book entitled *Magical Hands* (Barker, 1989), which is about the friendship between four working-class, middle-aged men. The men show their caring and friendship for one another by helping to make each one's special birthday wishes come true.

Trainers need not shy away from typical male-oriented books such as those with sport or adventure themes. Often these books provide good examples of prosocial and caring behaviors that need to be stressed and analyzed. As noted in chapter 4, books such as the biographies of Jackie Robinson and Arthur Ashe or the male-oriented books of Walter Dean Myers (e.g., *Hoops*) can be used to teach extremely important social skill lessons. Many biographies of popular personalities provide opportunities for valuable social learning. For example, the inner strength that Jackie Robinson displayed during the first years of his baseball career testifies to the beneficial effects of prosocial alternatives to aggression. The close, caring relationship of Brian Piccolo and Gale Sayers in *I Am Third* (Sayers, 1970), subsequently depicted in the film *Brian's Song*, is a touching account of the development and maintenance of a good, caring friendship between two football players. The biography of Bill Bradley (Jaspersohn, 1992) profiles not only an athlete and scholar but a political leader who displays a genuine concern and interest for others in society. The basketball player John Lucas (1994) offers a moving account of overcoming drug and alcohol addiction in his autobiography *Winning a Day at a Time*. Cal Ripken, Jr., baseball player for the Baltimore Orioles, is the subject of a few biographies written for children (e.g., Rambeck, 1993; Thornley, 1992) that highlight several positive features of his life. Another player with a great reputation as a role model for youngsters is Dave Stewart, pitcher for the Oakland A's. Unfortunately, a biography of Stewart is not yet available, but written material on his life might be found in a reference book entitled *Official Celebrity Register 1994–95 Sports Stars* (Steele, 1994).

Summary

The research on gender differences is the subject of much debate; nevertheless, there is general agreement about some distinctions. For one thing, males tend to rate themselves higher than females on self-esteem measures. There are differences in interpersonal styles, with females preferring intimacy and males emphasizing large-group activities with a hierarchical structure and designated leaders. Communication is more often used for egoistic purposes by males, whereas females are inclined to use speech as a means for social binding. Aggression is common to both sexes but generally is manifested differently: Males are likely to be verbally and physically abusive, whereas females tend to resort to exclusionary practices.

Issues of gender difference can be problematic for both genders, with negative implications for both childhood and adult competence. The lower self-esteem often found among females may manifest itself in poor self-confidence and low aspirations, as well as in various social skill deficits. The resulting sense of impotence contributes to an unhealthy dependency that interferes with a female's ability to become a self-actualizing adult, as evidenced in circumstances such as premature pregnancy, parenting difficulties, underachievement, underemployment, persistent poverty, and general dissatisfaction with life. Although encouraged by the larger society, the overt aggression and dominant behaviors characteristic of males often increase the risk of various violent and destructive outcomes for themselves and others. A major concern is the need to eliminate sexual harassment and peer aggression.

In terms of social learning, these issues can be addressed through direct and indirect means. Males and females can be taught directly how to deal with conflict and to handle problem situations constructively. Special attention and appropriate curriculum programs are needed for addressing gang-related behaviors and male-female relationships. School personnel need to examine more deliberately the way in which we socialize the sexes, taking pains to create cooperative environments and offer nonsexist curricula and literature in order to foster respect and adaptive behaviors between the sexes for the betterment of all. The American Association of University Women Educational Foundation (1992) summarizes these needs:

> Across the whole spectrum of the K–12 curriculum there
> is currently more emphasis on the development of
> assertive than affiliative skills, more reward for solo
> behavior than collaborative behavior, more reward for
> speaking than for listening. The curriculum can be

strengthened by consciously focusing on the development of reflective, caring, collaborative skills as well as those skills emphasizing individual performance and achievement. (p. 116)

References

Alcott, L.M. (1968). *Little women.* Boston: Little, Brown.

American Association of University Women Educational Foundation. (1992). *How schools short-change girls: A study of major findings on girls and education.* Washington, DC: Author.

Bakken, L., & Romig, C. (1992). Interpersonal needs in middle adolescents: Companionship, leadership and intimacy. *Journal of Adolescence, 15,* 301–316.

Barker, M. (1989). *Magical hands.* Saxonville, MA: Picture Book Studio.

Barth, R.P., Middleton, K., & Wagman, E. (1989). A skill building approach to preventing teenage pregnancy. *Theory into Practice, 28,* 183–190.

Belenky, M.F., Clinchy, B.M., Goldberger, N.R., & Tarule, J.M. (1986). *Women's ways of knowing.* New York: Basic.

Bernard, J. (1981). *The female world.* New York: Free Press.

Berndt, T.J. (1982). The features and effects of friendship in early adolescence. *Child Development, 53,* 1447–1460.

Best, D.L., & Williams, J.E. (1993). A cross-cultural viewpoint. In A.E. Beall & R.J. Sternberg (Eds.), *The psychology of gender.* New York: Guilford.

Best, R. (1989). *We've all got scars: What boys and girls learn in elementary school.* Bloomington: Indiana University Press.

Blyth, D., Hill, J., & Thiel, K. (1982). Early adolescents' significant others: Grade and gender differences in perceived relationships with familial and non-familial adults and young people. *Journal of Youth and Adolescence, 11,* 425–450.

Bosworth, K., & Hammer, R. (1995, April). *Urban middle school student responses to anger situations.* Paper presented at the annual meeting of the American Educational Research Association, San Francisco.

Brenner, B. (1971). *A year in the life of Rosie Bernard.* New York: Harper.

Buhrmester, D., & Furman, W. (1987). The development of companion-ship and intimacy. *Child Development, 58,* 1101–1113.

Camp, B.W., & Bash, M.A.S. (1981). *Think aloud: Increasing social and cognitive skills--A problem-solving program for children.* Champaign, IL: Research Press.

Campbell, P.B. (1984). The computer revolution: Guess who's left out? *Interracial Books for Children, 15,* 3–6.

Cartledge, G., & Kleefeld, J. (1991). *Taking part: Introducing social skills to children.* Circle Pines, MN: American Guidance Service.

Cartledge, G., & Kleefeld, J. (1994). *Working together: Building children's social skills through folk literature.* Circle Pines, MN: American Guidance Service.

Cartledge, G., & Milburn, J.F. (1995). *Teaching social skills to children and youth: Innovative approaches* (3rd ed.). Boston: Allyn & Bacon.

Caseau, D.L., Luckasson, R., & Kroth, R.L. (1994). Special education services for girls with serious emotional disturbance: A case of gender bias? *Behavioral Disorders, 20,* 51–60.

Cate, R., & Sugawara, A.I. (1986). Sex role orientation and dimensions of self-esteem among middle adolescents. *Sex Roles, 15,* 145–158.

Cleary, B. (1975). *Ramona and her father.* New York: William Morrow.

Crick, N.R., & Grotpeter, J.K. (1995). Relational aggression, gender, and social-psychological adjustment. *Child Development, 66,* 710–722.

Crombie, G. (1988). Gender differences: Implications for social skills assessment and training. *Journal of Clinical Child Psychology, 17,* 116–120.

Cushner, K., McClelland, A., & Safford, P. (1992). *Human diversity in education: An integrative approach.* New York: McGraw-Hill.

Deaux, K., & Major, B. (1987). Putting gender into context: An interactive model of gender-related behavior. *Psychological Review, 94,* 369–389.

Dinkmeyer, D. (1982). *Developing understanding of self and others (DUSO Program).* Circle Pines, MN: American Guidance Service.

Douvan, E., & Adelson, J. (1966). *The adolescent experience.* New York: Wiley.

Eagly, A.H., & Crowley, M. (1986). Gender and helping behavior: A meta-analytic review of the social psychological literature. *Psychological Bulletin, 100,* 283–308.

Eagly, A.H., & Steffen, V.J. (1986). Gender and aggressive behavior: A meta-analytic review of the social psychological literature. *Psychological Bulletin, 100,* 309–330.

Egan, G. (1976). *Interpersonal living: A skills/contract approach to human-relations training in groups.* Pacific Grove, CA: Brooks/Cole.

Eisenberg, N., & Lennon, R. (1983). Sex differences in empathy and related capacities. *Psychological Bulletin, 94,* 100–131.

Eisenberg, N., Miller, P.A., Shell, R., McNalley, S., & Shea, C. (1991). Prosocial development in adolescence: A longitudinal study. *Developmental Psychology, 27,* 849–857.

Erdley, C.A. (1995, April). *The relation of social-cognitive processes, aggressive behavior, and peer acceptance for boys and girls.* Paper presented at the annual meeting of the American Educational Research Association, San Francisco.

Feshbach, N.D., Feshbach, S., Fauvre, M., & Ballard-Campbell, M. (1983). *Learning to care.* Glenview, IL: Scott, Foresman.

Fine, M. (1993). Sexuality, schooling, and adolescent females: The missing discourse of desire. In M. Fine & L. Weis (Eds.), *Beyond silenced voices: Class, race, and gender in U.S. schools.* Albany: SUNY Press.

Fitzhugh, L. (1964). *Harriet the spy.* New York: Harper.

Fleischman, S. (1986). *The whipping boy.* New York: Greenwillow.

Gardner, R. (1974). *Dr. Gardner's fairy tales for today's children.* New York: Prentice-Hall.

Gauch, P.L. (1971). *Christina Katerina and the box.* New York: Coward, McCann & Geohegan.

George, J.C. (1972). *Julie of the wolves.* New York: Harper and Row.

Gilligan, C. (1992). *In a different voice: Psychological theory and women's development.* Cambridge, MA: Harvard University Press.

Goble, P. (1978). *The girl who loved wild horses.* New York: Macmillan.

Goldstein, A.P. (1988). *The Prepare Curriculum: Teaching prosocial competencies.* Champaign, IL: Research Press.

Goldstein, A.P., & Glick, B. (1987). *Aggression Replacement Training: A comprehensive intervention for aggressive youth.* Champaign, IL: Research Press.

Goldstein, A.P., & Glick, B. (1994). *The prosocial gang: Implementing Aggression Replacement Training.* Thousand Oaks, CA: Sage.

Gollnick, D.M., & Chinn, P.C. (1994). *Multicultural education in a pluralistic society* (4th ed.). New York: Merrill.

Grossman, H. (1995a). *Classroom behavior management in a diverse society* (2nd ed.). Mountain View, CA: Mayfield.

Grossman, H. (1995b). *Teaching in a diverse society.* Boston: Allyn & Bacon.

Harris, M.B. (1994). Gender of subject and target as mediators of aggression. *Journal of Applied Social Psychology, 24,* 453–471.

Hartley, R.E. (1974). Sex role pressures and the socialization of the male child. In J. Stacey, S. Bereaud, & J. Danields (Eds.), *And Jill came tumbling after: Sexism in American education.* New York: Dell.

Hilton, N. (1990). *The long red scarf.* Minneapolis: Carolrhoda.

Hodgkinson, H. (1986). *The schools we need for the kids we've got.* Paper presented at the annual meeting of the American Association of Colleges for Teacher Education, Washington, DC.

Hoffman, M. (1991). *Amazing Grace.* New York: Dial.

Horgan, D.D. (1995). *Achieving gender equity: Strategies for the classroom.* Boston: Allyn & Bacon.

Howe, F. (1974). Sexual stereotypes start early. In L.O. Johnson (Ed.), *Nonsexist curriculum materials for elementary schools.* Old Westbury, NY: Feminist Press.

Huff, C.R. (1993). Introduction. In A.P. Goldstein & C.R. Huff (Eds.), *The gang intervention handbook.* Champaign, IL: Research Press.

Isadora, R. (1980). *My ballet class.* New York: Greenwillow.

Jaspersohn, W. (1992). *Senator, a profile of Bill Bradley in the U.S. Senate.* San Diego: Harcourt Brace Jovanovich.

Jones, J.E., Perera, G.M., & Tiongson, A. (1994, August). *Gender differences in ethnic identity development among adolescents.* Paper presented at the annual meeting of the American Psychological Association, Los Angeles.

Kenrick, D.T., & Trost, M.R. (1993). In A.E. Beall & R.J. Sternberg (Eds.), *The psychology of gender.* New York: Guilford.

Kidd, N. (1991). *June mountain secret.* New York: Harper.

King, Y.M. (1989, March). *Equity in basal readers.* Paper presented at the annual meeting of the American Educational Research Association, San Francisco.

Kohlberg, L. (1964). Development of moral character and moral ideology. In M.L. Hoffman & L.W. Hoffman (Eds.), *Review of child development research* (Vol. 1). New York: Russell Sage Foundation.

Kramer, S. (1988). Sex role stereotyping: How it happens and how to avoid it. In A. O'Brien Carelli (Ed.), *Sex equity in education.* Springfield, IL: Charles C. Thomas.

Lewis, D. (1975). The Black family: Socialization and sex roles. *Phylon, 36,* 221–237.

Lockheed, M.E., & Harris, A.M. (1984). Cross-sex collaborative learning in elementary classrooms. *American Educational Research Journal, 21*(2), 275–294.

Lucas, J.H. (1994). *Winning a day at a time.* Center City, MN: Hazelden.

Maccoby, E.E. (1988). Gender as a social category. *Developmental Psychology, 24*(6), 755–765.

Maccoby, E.E. (1990). Gender and relationships. *American Psychologist, 45,* 513–520.

Maccoby, E.E., & Jacklin, C. (1974). *The psychology of sex differences.* Stanford, CA: Stanford University Press.

MacLachlan, P. (1979). *The sick day.* New York: Pantheon.

Maltz, D.N., & Borker, R.A. (1982). A cultural approach to male-female miscommunication. In J.J. Gumperz (Ed.), *Language and social identity.* New York: Cambridge University Press.

Mazer, N.F. (1987). *After the rain.* New York: Morrow.

McKissack, P.C. (1986). *Flossie and the fox.* New York: Dial.

Mellor, S. (1989). Gender differences in identity formation as a function of self-other relationships. *Journal of Youth and Adolescence, 18,* 361–375.

Minard, R. (1975). *Womenfolk and fairy tales.* Boston: Houghton Mifflin.

Mizrahi, K., & Deaux, K. (1994, August). *Conceptualizing gender identity.* Paper presented at the annual meeting of the American Psychological Association, Los Angeles.

Myers, W.D. (1988). *Scorpions.* New York: Harper and Row.

Newman, B.M., & Newman, P.R. (1995). *Development through life: A psychosocial approach* (6th ed.). Pacific Grove, CA: Brooks/Cole.

Oakes, J. (1990). Opportunities, achievement, and choice: Women and minority students in science and mathematics. In C.B. Cazden

(Ed.), *Review of research in education*. Washington, DC: American Educational Research Association.

Offord, D.R., Boyle, M.H., & Racine, Y.A. (1991). The epidemiology of antisocial behavior in childhood and adolescence. In D.J. Pepler & K.H. Rubin (Eds.), *The development and treatment of childhood aggression*. Hillsdale, NJ: Erlbaum.

Paulsen, G. (1985). *Dogsong*. New York: Bradbury.

Paulsen, G. (1987). *Hatchet*. New York: Bradbury.

Petri, A.E., Mungin, C., & Emerson, B. (1992, April). *More precious than gold: African-American male mentors*. Paper presented at the 70th annual convention of the Council for Exceptional Children, Baltimore.

Purcell, P., & Stewart, L. (1990). Dick and Jane in 1989. *Sex Roles, 22,* 177–185.

Rambeck, R. (1993). *Cal Ripken, Jr*. Mankato, MN: Child's World.

Roberts, L.R. (1986). *Gender differences in patterns of achievement and adjustment during early adolescence*. (ERIC Document Reproduction Service No. ED 288 134)

Rubin, J.Z., Provenzano, F.J., & Luria, Z. (1974). The eye of the beholder: Parents' views on sex of newborns. *American Journal of Orthopsychiatry, 44*(4), 512–519.

Rudman, M.K. (1995). *Children's literature: An issues approach* (3rd ed.). White Plains, NY: Longman.

Sadker, M., & Sadker, D. (1990). *Sex equity handbook for schools* (2nd ed.). New York: Longman.

Sadker, M., & Sadker, D. (1994a). *Failing at fairness: How America's schools cheat girls*. New York: Macmillan.

Sadker, M., & Sadker, D. (1994b). *Teachers, schools, and society* (3rd ed.). New York: McGraw-Hill.

Sadker, M., Sadker, D., & Klein, S. (1991). The issue of gender in elementary and secondary education. In G. Grant (Ed.), *Review of research in education*. Washington, DC: American Educational Research Association.

Sayers, G. (1970). *I am third*. New York: Viking.

Serbin, L.A., Moskowitz, D.S., Schwartzman, A.E., & Ledingham, J.E. (1991). Aggressive, withdrawn, and aggressive/withdrawn children in adolescence: Into the next generation. In D.J. Pepler & K.H. Rubin

(Eds.), *The development and treatment of childhood aggression.* Hillsdale, NJ: Erlbaum.

Shakeshaft, C., Barber, E., Hergenrother, M.A., Johnson, Y., Mandel, L., & Sawyer, J. (1995, April). *Peer harassment and the culture of caring in schools.* Paper presented at the annual meeting of the American Educational Research Association, San Francisco.

Sharabany, R., Gershoni, R., & Hofman, J. (1981). Girlfriend, boyfriend: Age and sex differences in intimate friendship. *Developmental Psychology, 17,* 800–808.

Shmurak, C.B. (1995, April). *Attitudes and aspirations of female adolescents: A longitudinal study-in-progress.* Paper presented at the annual meeting of the American Educational Research Association, San Francisco.

Simon, M.A. (1978). *A special gift.* San Diego: Harcourt Brace Jovanovich.

Spence, J.T., Helmreich, R.L., & Stapp, J. (1975). Ratings of self and peers on sex role attributes and their relation to self-esteem and concepts of masculinity and femininity. *Journal of Personality and Social Psychology, 32,* 29–39.

Steele, S. (1994). *Official celebrity register 1994–1995 sports stars.* Los Angeles: General Publication Group.

Stein, J.A., Newcomb, M.D., & Bentler, P.M. (1990). The relative influence of vocational behavior and family involvement on self-esteem: Longitudinal analyses of young adult women and men. *Journal of Vocational Behavior, 36,* 320–338.

Stein, J.A., Newcomb, M.D., & Bentler, P.M. (1992). The effect of agency and communality on self-esteem: Gender differences in longitudinal data. *Sex Roles, 26,* 465–483.

Stephens, R.D. (1993). School-based interventions: Safety and security. In A.P. Goldstein & C.R. Huff (Eds.), *The gang intervention handbook.* Champaign, IL: Research Press.

Stephens, T.M. (1992). *Social skills in the classroom.* Odessa, FL: Psychological Assessment Resources.

Stephens, T.M., & Mand, C. (1995). *Drug-free middle schools: Adventure-based initiatives* (Grant supported by the United States Department of Education—841848). Unpublished manuscript.

Steptoe, J. (1980). *Daddy is a monster . . . sometimes.* New York: Harper.

Steptoe, J. (1987). *Mufaro's beautiful daughters.* New York: Lothrop, Lee & Shepard.

Stewig, J.W. (1988). Fathers: A presence in picture books? *Journal of Youth Services in Libraries, 1,* 391–395.

Stier, E., & Clark, R. (1991). Adolescence: A literary passage. *Adolescence, 26,* 757–767.

Study finds boys tops in science, math, poor readers. (1995, July 7). *The Columbus Dispatch,* p. 3A.

Tannen, D. (1990). *You just don't understand: Women and men in conversation.* New York: Ballantine.

Thorne, B. (1993). *Gender play: Girls and boys in school.* New Brunswick, NJ: Rutgers University Press.

Thornley, S. (1992). *Cal Ripken, Jr., Oriole iron man.* Minneapolis: Learner.

Tremblay, R.E. (1991). Aggression, prosocial behavior, and gender: Three magic words but no magic wand. In D.J. Pepler & K.H. Rubin (Eds.), *The development and treatment of childhood aggression.* Hillsdale, NJ: Erlbaum.

Unsworth, R. (1988). Welcome home, I think: The changing role of fathers in recent young adult fiction. *School Library Journal, 34,* 48–49.

Villimez, C., Eisenberg, N., & Carroll, J.L. (1986). Sex differences in the relation of children's height and weight to academic performance and others' attributions of competence. *Sex Roles, 15,* 667–681.

Widaman, K.F., MacMillan, D.L., Hemsley, R.E., Little, T.D., & Balow, I.H. (1992). Differences in adolescents' self-concept as a function of academic level, ethnicity, and gender. *American Journal on Mental Retardation, 96,* 387–404.

Yolen, J. (1974). *The girl who cried flowers and other tales.* New York: Harper.

Yolen, J. (1977). *The hundredth dove.* New York: Schocken.

Name Index

Perera, G.M., 300
Perry, D.G., 154
Perry, T.B., 66, 114
Peters, M.F., 142, 144, 145
Peterson, R.L., 108
Petri, A.E., 192, 332–333
Philips, S.V., 15
Phinney, J.S., 28, 29, 30, 32, 252
Piccolo, Brian, 343
Pinciotti, P., 20
Pine, C.J., 142, 144, 249
Pipe, P., 49
Pitton, D., 211, 212, 214, 215
Pitts, P., 226
Polgar, S., 215
Ponterotto, J.G., 262
Powless, D.L., 52, 212, 216
Prothrow-Stith, D., 159, 160, 162,
    173, 180
Provenzano, F.J., 312
Purcell, P., 337

Quintana, S.M., 252
Quintero, G.A., 218

Racine, Y.A., 305
Rambeck, R., 343
Ramirez, A., 253
Ramirez, O., 249, 251, 257, 261,
    262, 263
Rampersad, A., 186
Randolph, A. Phillip, 185
Rapkin, B.D., 63
Ravetta, M.K., 264, 265, 282
Reeder, E., 73
Reese, L.E., 31
Reglin, G.L., 102
Reid, R., 76, 77
Rhode, G., 72, 75
Richter, L.L., 177
Rickey, Branch, 185–186
Rie, E.D., 51

Ripkin, Cal, Jr., 343
Rist, R.C., 147
Ritter, D.R., 5
Roberts, L.R., 308–309
Roberts, N., 273
Robinson, J.A., 25, 26
Robinson, Jackie, 185–186, 343
Rogers, M., 176
Rogler, L.H., 251, 280
Rohmer, H., 272
Rolf, J.E., 218
Romig, C., 309
Roosevelt, Eleanor, 341
Rosando, L., 213
Rose, S.D., 56
Rose-Krasnor, L., 159
Ross, M., 284
Rotatori, A.F., 52
Rotheram-Borus, M.J., 252
Rouse, R., 145
Rowe, W., 233, 235, 236
Rubin, K.H., 103, 159, 281
Rubin, J.Z., 312
Rudman, M.K., 337, 338, 339, 340,
    341, 342
Rumbaut, R.G., 105
Rutherford, R.B., 73
Ryujin, D.H., 139

Sadker, D., 314, 315–316, 336, 337
Sadker, M., 314, 315–316, 336, 337
Saenz, D.S., 30, 32, 208, 251, 260
Safford, P., 311, 312, 313, 314, 315,
    317–318
St. Vincent Millay, Edna, 341
Salend, S.J., 73
Sanger, Margaret, 341
Santiago, D., 274
Santogrossi, D.A., 47
Sapon-Shevin, M., 20, 70
Saracho, O.N., 213, 256, 257, 258
Sawyer, J., 334

Subject Index

About the Authors

Gwendolyn Cartledge (PhD, The Ohio State University) is a professor in special education at The Ohio State University in the College of Education, where her primary responsibility is the preparation of teachers of students with learning and behavioral disabilities. Her professional interests center on behavior disorders, social skill development, and cultural diversity. Included among her many publications in this area are a coauthored book with JoAnne Fellows Milburn, *Teaching Social Skills to Children and Youth* (Allyn & Bacon, 1995), and two social skill curriculum programs, coauthored with James Kleefeld, *Taking Part* (American Guidance Service, 1991) and *Working Together* (American Guidance Service, 1994).

JoAnne Fellows Milburn (MSW, UCLA; PhD, The Ohio State University) has worked with children and families in clinical and school settings, served on the faculty of the College of Social Work at The Ohio State University, and directed a multiservice children's mental health facility for a number of years. She currently works in child advocacy and child abuse prevention.

Hua Feng (PhD, The Ohio State University) is an associate professor in the Department of Special Education, National Chang-Hua University of Education in Taiwan. Her primary responsibility is the preparation of teachers of students with mild disabilities, and her research and professional interests center on teaching strategies and social skills training for students with disabilities.

Myra B. Middleton (PhD, The Ohio State University) is an Area Director of Exceptional Children for the Orange County Public Schools in Orange County, Florida. Her professional interests include social skills development for students with behavioral disorders, collaborative work with parents from diverse populations, and methods of effective school discipline for students with disabilities.

Jeanette W. Lee (PhD, The Ohio State University) is an associate professor at West Virginia State College in the Department of Education. Her primary role is instructing prospective teachers of children with exceptionalities. She has been a classroom teacher of children with learning disabilities, behavior disorders, and mental impairments. Her major research interests include interventions for academic and affective growth, and empowering parenting skills.

Lessie L. Cochran (PhD, The Ohio State University) is an assistant professor in special education at Pennsylvania State University, Department of Educational Psychology and School Psychology and Special Education. Her professional and research interests include early intervention for young children with disabilities and diversity in education. She has received several awards and honors for her research and teaching skills.

Carolyn Talbert Johnson (PhD, The Ohio State University) is an assistant professor in the Department of Teacher Education at the University of Dayton, Ohio. Her research interests include preparing teachers for changing roles in restructured schools, multicultural education, theories of learning, and behavior management.